NBER
Macroeconomics Annual 2000

Editors
Ben S. Bernanke and
Kenneth Rogoff

THE MIT PRESS
Cambridge, Massachusetts
London, England

NBER/*Macroeconomics Annual*, Number 15, 2000
ISSN: 0889-3365
ISBN: Hardcover 0-262-02503-5
Paperback 0-262-52314-0
Published annually by The MIT Press, Cambridge, Massachusetts 02142

An electronic, full-text version of NBER/*Macroeconomics Annual* is available from MIT Press Journals when purchasing a subscription.

Subscription Rates
Hardcover/Print and Electronic: $60.00
Paperback/Print and Electronic: $30.00
Outside the U.S. and Canada add $10.00 for postage and handling. Canadians add 7% GST.

Subscription and address changes should be addressed to:
MIT Press Journals, Five Cambridge Center, Cambridge, MA 02142-1407, phone 617-253-2889; fax 617-577-1545; email journals-orders@mit.edu. Claims will be honored free of charge if made within three months of the publication date of the issue. Claims may be submitted to journals-claims@mit.edu. Prices are subject to change without notice.

In the United Kingdom, continental Europe, and the Middle East and Africa, send back volume orders and business correspondence to:
The MIT Press, Ltd., Fitzroy House, 11 Chenies Street, London WC1E 7ET England, phone 44-020-7306-0603, fax 44-020-7306-0604, email info@hup-MITpress.co.uk

In the United States and for all other countries, send single copy and back volume orders to:
The MIT Press, Five Cambridge Center, Cambridge, MA 02142, toll-free book orders 800-356-0343, fax 617-625-6660, email mitpress-orders@mit.edu

Copyright Information
Permission to photocopy articles for internal or personal use, or the internal or personal use of specific clients, is granted by the copyright owner for users registered with the Copyright Clearance Center (CCC) Transactional Reporting Service, provided that the fee of $10.00 per copy is paid directly to CCC, 222 Rosewood Drive, Danvers, MA 01923. The fee code for users of the Transactional Reporting Service is: 0889-3365/00 $10.00. For those organizations that have been granted a photocopy license with CCC, a separate system of payment has been arranged.

© 2001 by the National Bureau of Economic Research and the Massachusetts Institute of Technology.

NBER BOARD OF DIRECTORS BY AFFILIATION

OFFICERS

Carl F. Christ, *Chairman*
Kathleen B. Cooper, *Vice Chairman*
Martin Feldstein, *President and Chief Executive Officer*
Robert Mednick, *Treasurer*

Susan Colligan, *Corporate Secretary*
Kelly Horak, *Controller and Assistant Corporate Secretary*
Gerardine Johnson, *Assistant Corporate Secretary*

DIRECTORS AT LARGE

Peter C. Aldrich
Elizabeth E. Bailey
John H. Biggs
Andrew Brimmer
Carl F. Christ
Don R. Conlan
Kathleen B. Cooper
George C. Eads

Martin Feldstein
Stephen Friedman
George Hatsopoulos
Karen N. Horn
Judy C. Lewent
John Lipsky
Michael H. Moskow
Alicia H. Munnell

Rudolph A. Oswald
Robert T. Parry
Peter G. Peterson
Richard N. Rosett
Kathleen P. Utgoff
Marina v.N. Whitman
Martin B. Zimmerman

DIRECTORS BY UNIVERSITY APPOINTMENT

George Akerlof, *California, Berkeley*
Jagdish Bhagwati, *Columbia*
William C. Brainard, *Yale*
Glen G. Cain, *Wisconsin*
Franklin Fisher, *Massachusetts Institute of Technology*
Saul H. Hymans, *Michigan*
Marjorie B. McElroy, *Duke*

Joel Mokyr, *Northwestern*
Andrew Postlewaite, *Pennsylvania*
Nathan Rosenberg, *Stanford*
Michael Rothschild, *Princeton*
Craig Swan, *Minnesota*
David B. Yoffie, *Harvard*
Arnold Zellner, *Chicago*

DIRECTORS BY APPOINTMENT OF OTHER ORGANIZATIONS

Mark Drabenstott, *American Agricultural Economics Association*
Gail D. Fosler, *The Conference Board*
A. Ronald Gallant, *American Statistical Association*
Robert S. Hamada, *American Finance Association*
Robert Mednick, *American Institute of Certified Public Accountants*
Angelo Melino, *Canadian Economics Association*

Richard D. Rippe, *National Association for Business Economics*
John J. Siegfried, *American Economic Association*
David A. Smith, *American Federation of Labor and Congress of Industrial Organizations*
Josh S. Weston, *Committee for Economic Development*
Gavin Wright, *Economic History Association*

DIRECTORS EMERITI

Moses Abramovitz
Thomas D. Flynn
Lawrence R. Klein

Franklin A. Lindsay
Paul W. McCracken

Bert Seidman
Eli Shapiro

Since this volume is a record of conference proceedings, it has been exempted from the rules governing critical review of manuscripts by the Board of Directors of the National Bureau (resolution adopted 8 June 1948, as revised 21 November 1949 and 20 April 1968).

Contents

Editorial: *Ben S. Bernanke and Kenneth Rogoff*   1

Abstracts   5

HOW LARGE ARE HUMAN-CAPITAL EXTERNALITIES? EVIDENCE FROM COMPULSORY-SCHOOLING LAWS   9
Daron Acemoglu and Joshua Angrist
COMMENTS: Mark Bils   59
              Cecilia Elena Rouse   68
DISCUSSION   72

THE POLITICAL BUSINESS CYCLE AFTER 25 YEARS   75
Allan Drazen
COMMENTS: Alberto Alesina   117
              Carl E. Walsh   124
DISCUSSION   135

RETHINKING MULTIPLE EQUILIBRIA IN MACROECONOMIC MODELING   139
Stephen Morris and Hyun Song Shin
COMMENTS: Andrew Atkeson   162
              Hélène Rey   171
DISCUSSION   179

RE-EXAMINING THE CONTRIBUTIONS OF MONEY AND BANKING SHOCKS TO THE U.S. GREAT DEPRESSION   183
Harold L. Cole and Lee E. Ohanian

COMMENTS: Michael Bordo, Christopher Erceg, and
Charles Evans   227
Mark Gertler   237
DISCUSSION   258

TRADE POLICY AND ECONOMIC GROWTH: A SKEPTIC'S GUIDE TO THE
CROSS-NATIONAL EVIDENCE   261
Francisco Rodríguez and Dani Rodrik
COMMENTS: Chang-Tai Hsieh   325
Charles I. Jones   330
DISCUSSION   337

THE SIX MAJOR PUZZLES IN INTERNATIONAL MACROECONOMICS:
IS THERE A COMMON CAUSE?   339
Maurice Obstfeld and Kenneth Rogoff
COMMENTS: Olivier Jeanne   390
Charles Engel   403
DISCUSSION   411

Editorial, NBER Macroeconomics Annual 2000

If there is a common theme to the papers in this year's issue of the *NBER Macroeconomics Annual*, it is that each takes a fresh if sometimes controversial perspective on an important issue in macroeconomics.

Daron Acemoglu and Joshua Angrist challenge the conventional presumption that there are large social externalities associated with higher educational attainment, a claim often used to justify maintaining and increasing public expenditures on education. In data for U.S. states, there is indeed a high correlation between wages and average schooling levels; indeed, an individual with a given level of education will earn more in a high-education state than in a low-education state, a finding that is suggestive of externalities. However, causation could run in either direction; for example, high-paying industries and more able workers might choose to locate in areas with greater amenities, including a higher general level of education. To disentangle the various effects in samples of male workers drawn from the 1960–1980 Censuses, the authors apply an instrumental-variables technique that exploits historical state-to-state variation in child labor laws and school attendance laws. Variations across states in such laws in the past affect today's average education levels but are unlikely to be correlated with factors such as the tastes of people currently employed in a state, permitting identification of the effects of changes in education on wages. The authors' empirical results contrast sharply with those of many earlier studies, some of which have found the external benefits of education to be as much as twice the private benefits. Instead, Acemoglu and Angrist find that the external returns to investments in primary and secondary education are less than one percent per year of schooling, and are insignificantly different from zero.

Francisco Rodríguez and Dani Rodrik also challenge a common tenet of the empirical literature, in this case the view that free and open trade promotes economic growth. After systematically critiquing the main studies that have been used to support the hypothesized link between trade and growth, they conclude that, contrary to popular perception, the evidence that the policy-induced trade restrictions are harmful to growth in fact is quite thin. In particular, they argue that many measures of restrictiveness used in the literature either reflect aspects of countries other than trade policy, are not robustly related to economic growth, or both. In understanding the authors' claim, it is important to recognize that they distinguish between *policy-induced* openness, and openness due to natural factors such as access to water, size, etc. Further, they do not assert that trade restrictions are helpful to growth, only that the relationship of trade policy to growth is not firmly established (and may well depend on the particular circumstances of the country). Since this position is clearly a contrarian one, the paper provoked considerable discussion at the conference. The authors' careful analysis and critique will no doubt continue to provoke debate for some time to come.

In recent years, macroeconomists have attempted to explain an increasing number of phenomena by models that allow multiple equilibria. In models exhibiting multiple equilibria, a bank run or an attack on a fixed exchange rate may be interpreted as the result of a self-fulfilling change in investor sentiment, rather than of a change in fundamentals. In their contribution, Stephen Morris and Hyun Song Shin question this general approach to economic modeling, arguing that the existence of multiple equilibria in standard models may well be an artifact of unrealistic assumptions about the information available to market participants. Specifically, they show that the assumption of "common knowledge," while often convenient for modeling purposes, can mislead us by effectively requiring us to assume that agents have a greater capacity for coordinated action than is actually the case. They illustrate their point in a simple Diamond–Dybvig-style model of bank runs, generalized to allow agents to have some degree of private information. They show that under their (arguably more realistic) specification of the distribution of information, the model's equilibrium is often (though not always) unique. Morris and Shin's paper, which applies some ideas they have developed in earlier, more theoretical articles, should prove quite useful to more policy-oriented economists. An interesting general issue, raised by discussant Andrew Atkeson and others, is the degree to which Morris and Shin's assumption of differential information remains reasonable when publicly observable prices effectively aggregate information in the market.

The relationship between electoral cycles and business cycles, or *political business cycles,* elicited much interest in both the mid-1970s and the mid-1980s; Alberto Alesina's paper on this topic in the 1988 *Macroeconomics Annual* has been widely cited. The theory of political business cycles has lately again become a lively research area. In his paper, Allan Drazen provides a fresh perspective on both the new literature and the old. Drazen is particularly critical of a conventional premise of this literature, that politicians induce business cycles through manipulation of monetary policy; he argues that the evidence that politicians do this, either from partisan or purely opportunistic motives, is quite thin. Instead, he argues, political influences are more likely exerted through the government budget. Although he raises some criticisms of traditional models featuring a "political budget cycle," Drazen suggests that the empirical evidence can best be explained by a model that combines opportunistic fiscal policy with accommodative monetary policy.

The worldwide Great Depression of the 1930s, which in some sense gave birth to modern macroeconomics, has long proven an enigma. What set off the Depression, how did it spread across the world, and why was the fall in output so persistent? Recent years have seen a new wave of research on the Depression, which in the view of many has significantly deepened our understanding of that economic collapse. Key elements of this evolving "consensus" include misguided monetary policies in the United States; dissemination of the deflationary forces around the world through the workings of the international gold standard; wage and price rigidities that converted monetary contraction into a protracted real downturn; and the collapse of financial intermediation, as banks and other financial institutions failed. In the face of this apparent consensus, the contribution by Hal Cole and Lee Ohanian has to be considered quite radical, or quite refreshing, depending on one's perspective. Cole and Ohanian point out that the "consensus" story is based on qualitative but not quantitative reasoning; in particular, it has not been evaluated in a quantitative general-equilibrium model. Although Cole and Ohanian do not present a comprehensive model of the Depression, they do use small models to illustrate some of the issues. They also make a number of historical comparisons, in particular between the downturns of 1920–1921 and 1929–1933. The authors' main conclusion is that sticky nominal wages and shocks to the banking system can account for at most a small part of the collapse of output in the United States during the 1930s, implying that one must turn elsewhere for an explanation of the Depression. The wide-ranging discussion at the conference covered areas ranging from the reliability of 1930s data to debates about how best to model phenomena like the purported collapse of financial intermediation. The sources of the Great Depression clearly remain an exciting and active area of research.

Finally, in a paper entitled "The Six Major Puzzles in International Macroeconomics: Is There a Common Cause?" Maurice Obstfeld and Kenneth Rogoff argue that allowing for plausible-sized costs of international trade in *good markets* can help us make substantial progress in explaining, in quantitative terms, many apparent empirical paradoxes observed in international *financial markets*. Among the "puzzles" that may be reduced or resolved by allowing for trade costs, according to the authors, are the Feldstein–Horioka puzzle, the consumption-correlations puzzle, the home-bias-in-equity-portfolios puzzle, the home-bias-in-trade puzzle, the purchasing-power-parity puzzle, and a class of findings they term "the exchange-rate disconnect puzzles." The Feldstein–Horioka puzzle, that rates of national saving and investment are highly correlated across countries, has proved particularly recalcitrant to explanation. Obstfeld and Rogoff show that, in a simple model with trade costs, real interest rates change nonlinearly with changes in the current-account deficit or surplus, in a manner that can plausibly account for the Feldstein–Horioka phenomenon. An issue raised at the conference was whether costs of trade alone can account for all the puzzling observations, or whether allowing financial-market frictions will also prove necessary. Clearly, more research will be needed. At the very least, however, the paper's suggestion that a single factor may help to resolve such a range of apparently disparate puzzles is intriguing.

The editors would like to take this opportunity to thank Martin Feldstein and the National Bureau of Economic Research for continued support of this conference and publication. The NBER's conference department handled the logistics in its usual flawless manner.

Thanks are also due to the National Science Foundation for financial support, and to Refet Gurkaynak for his dedicated editorial assistance.

Ben S. Bernanke and Kenneth Rogoff

Abstracts

How Large Are Human Capital Externalities? Evidence from Compulsory Schooling Laws
DARON ACEMOGLU AND JOSHUA ANGRIST

Many economists and policymakers believe that education creates positive externalities. Indeed, average schooling in U.S. states is highly correlated with state wage levels, even after controlling for the direct effect of schooling on individual wages. We use variation in child labor laws and compulsory attendance laws over time and across states to investigate whether this relationship is causal. Our results show external returns to education around 1% and not significantly different from zero.

The Political Business Cycle after 25 Years
ALLAN DRAZEN

Research on the political business cycle since the mid-1970s is surveyed and assessed. We argue that models based on monetary surprises as the driving force are unconvincing explanations of either opportunistic or partisan cycles. Research should concentrate on fiscal policy as the driving force, with monetary effects being the result of accommodation of fiscal impulses. We present a model political business-cycle model (which we term the AFPM model) that combines active fiscal policy and passive monetary policy and that addresses a number of objections to earlier models.

Rethinking Multiple Equilibria in Macroeconomic Modeling
STEPHEN MORRIS AND HYUN SONG SHIN

Are beliefs as indeterminate as suggested by models with multiple equilibria? Multiplicity of equilibria arises largely as the unintended consequence of two modeling assumptions—the fundamentals are assumed to be common knowledge, and economic agents know others' actions in equilibrium. Both are questionable. When others' actions are not known with certainty (as when actions rely on noisy signals), self-fulfilling beliefs lead to a unique outcome determined by the fundamentals and the knowledge that others are rational. This paper illustrates this approach in the context of a model of bank runs and other similar applications. Such an approach places comparative statics and policy analyses on a firmer footing. It also suggests that public information has a disproportionately larger influence on the outcome than private information.

Re-Examining the Contributions of Money and Banking Shocks to the U.S. Great Depression
HAROLD L. COLE AND LEE E. OHANIAN

This paper quantitatively evaluates the hypothesis that deflation can account for much of the Great Depression (1929–1933). We examine two popular explanations of the Depression: (1) the *high-wage* story, according to which deflation, combined with imperfectly flexible wages, raised real wages and reduced employment and output; (2) the *bank-failure* story, according to which deflationary money shocks contributed to bank failures and to a reduction in the efficiency of financial intermediation, which in turn reduced lending and output. We evaluate these stories using general-equilibrium business-cycle models, and find that wage shocks and banking shocks account for a small fraction of the Great Depression. We also find that some other predictions of the theories are at variance with the data.

Trade Policy and Economic Growth: A Skeptic's Guide to the Cross-National Evidence
FRANCISCO RODRIGUEZ AND DANI RODRIK

Do countries with lower policy-induced barriers to international trade grow faster, once other relevant country characteristics are controlled for? There exists a large empirical literature providing an affirmative answer to this question. We argue that methodological problems with the empirical strategies employed in this literature leave the results open to diverse interpretations. In many cases, the indicators of openness used by researchers are poor measures of trade barriers or are highly correlated with other sources of bad economic performance. In other cases, the methods used to ascertain the link between trade policy and growth have serious shortcomings. Papers that we review include those by Dollar (1992), Ben-David (1993), Sachs and Warner (1995), Edwards (1998), and Frankel and Romer (1999). We find little evidence that open trade policies—in the sense of lower tariff and nontariff barriers to trade—are significantly associated with economic growth.

The Six Major Puzzles in International Macroeconomics: Is There a Common Cause?
MAURICE OBSTFELD AND KENNETH ROGOFF

The central claim in this paper is that by explicitly introducing costs of international trade (narrowly, transport costs, but more broadly, tariffs, nontariff barriers, and other trade costs), one can go far toward explaining a great number of the main empirical puzzles that international macroeconomists have struggled with over twenty-five years. Our approach elucidates J. McCallum's home-bias-in-trade puzzle, the Feldstein–Horioka saving-investment puzzle, the French–Poterba equity-home-bias puzzle, and the Backus–Kehoe–Kydland consumption-correlations puzzle. That one simple alteration to an otherwise canonical international macroeconomic model can help substantially to explain such a broad range of empirical puzzles, including some that previously seemed intractable, suggests a rich area for future research. We also address a variety of international pricing puzzles, including the purchasing-power-parity puzzle emphasized by Rogoff, and what we term the *exchange-rate disconnect puzzle*. The latter category of riddles includes the Meese–Rogoff exchange-rate forecasting puzzle and the Baxter–Stockman neutrality-of-exchange-rate-regime puzzle. Here, although many elements need to be added to our extremely simple model, trade costs still play an essential role.

Daron Acemoglu and Joshua Angrist
MASSACHUSETTS INSTITUTE OF TECHNOLOGY

How Large Are Human-Capital Externalities? Evidence from Compulsory Schooling Laws

1. Introduction

The effect of human capital on aggregate income is of central importance to both policymakers and economists. A tradition going back to Schultz (1967) and Nelson and Phelps (1966) views the human capital of the workforce as a crucial factor facilitating the adoption of new and more productive technologies (see Foster and Rosenzweig, 1996, for evidence). Similarly, many recent endogenous growth models emphasize the link between human capital and growth. For example, in Lucas's (1988) model, worker productivity depends on the aggregate skill level, whereas Romer (1990) suggests that societies with more skilled workers generate more ideas and grow faster. More generally, many economists believe that cross-country income disparities are due in large part to differences in human capital (e.g., Mankiw, Romer, and Weil, 1992). Figure 1 plots the logarithm of output per worker relative to the United States for 103 countries against average years of schooling in 1985. Consistent with this view, the figure shows a strong correlation between output per worker and schooling. In fact, the bivariate regression line plotted in Figure 1 has an R^2 of 65%.[1]

We thank Alexis Leon, Chris Mazingo, and Xuanhui Ng for excellent research assistance, and our discussants Mark Bils and Cecelia Rouse for their comments. Thanks also go to Paul Beaudry, Bill Evans, Bob Hall, Larry Katz, Enrico Moretti, Jim Poterba, Robert Shimer, and seminar participants at the Canadian Institute for Advanced Research, the 2000 NBER Macroeconomics Annual Conference, the 1999 NBER Summer Institute, University College London, Cornell University, the University of Maryland, and the University of Toronto for helpful discussions and comments. Special thanks to Stefanie Schmidt for advice on compulsory-schooling data.

1. Data on output per worker are from Summers and Heston (1991), with the correction due to Hall and Jones (1999). Education data are from Barro and Lee (1993). See Krueger

Figure 1 LOG OUTPUT PER WORKER AND YEARS OF SCHOOLING ACROSS COUNTRIES

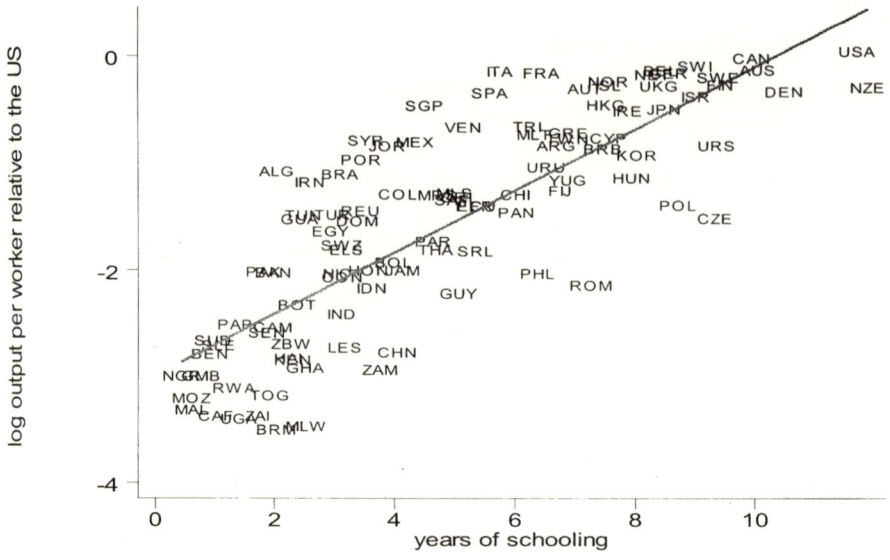

The line shows the fitted OLS relationship. The slope coefficient is 0.29, and the standard error is 0.02.

A simple calculation suggests that for education to raise income as steeply as suggested by Figure 1, there must be large human-capital externalities. To see this, note that the *private return to schooling*, i.e., the increase in individual earnings resulting from an additional year of schooling, is about 6–10% (e.g., Card, 1999). If the *social return to schooling*, i.e., the increase in total earnings resulting from a one-year increase in average schooling, is of roughly the same magnitude, then differences in schooling can explain little of the cross-country variation in income. More specifically, the difference in average schooling between the top and bottom deciles of the world education distribution in 1985 is less than 8 years. With social returns to schooling around 10%, we would expect the top-decile countries to produce about twice as much per worker as the bottom-decile countries. In fact, the output-per-worker gap is approximately 15. Put differently, a causal interpretation of Figure 1 requires

---

and Lindahl (1999) for a detailed analysis of the cross-country relationship between education and income.

human-capital externalities on the order of 25–30%, approximately three times as large as the private returns to schooling.[2]

Human-capital externalities are important for education policy as well as for cross-country income differences. Current education policies are often justified on the basis of at least modest externalities. Nevertheless, there is little empirical work estimating human-capital externalities. Moreover, even as a theoretical matter, it is not clear whether social returns should exceed private returns. Despite the emphasis on human-capital externalities in recent growth models, education may also play a signaling role (e.g., Spence, 1973; Lang and Kropp, 1986). If schooling has signaling value, social returns to education can be less than private returns. In the extreme case where schooling does not increase human capital but is only a signal, aggregate income is unchanged when all workers increase their schooling by one year, so social returns are zero. Social returns may also be less than private returns if some other factor of production is inelastically supplied.

Rauch (1993) is the first attempt to estimate human-capital externalities. His results suggest there are externalities on the order of 3–5%, though he also reports some considerably larger estimates. Rauch's estimates are driven by differences in average schooling across cities. But higher incomes might cause more schooling instead of vice versa. Cities with greater average schooling may also have higher wages for a variety of other reasons. This highlights the fact that a major challenge in estimating the effects of education on income is identification. To solve this problem, we use instrumental variables to estimate the effect of the average schooling level in an individual's state. An ideal instrument for average schooling would affect the schooling of the majority of workers in a given area. Differences in compulsory attendance laws and child labor laws in U.S. states between 1920 and 1960 provide such variation.

State compulsory attendance laws and child labor laws, which we refer to together as *compulsory schooling laws* (CSLs), generate an attractive natural experiment for the estimation of human-capital externalities (or *external returns*) for a number of reasons. First, while these laws were determined by social forces operating in states at the time of passage, the CSLs that affected an individual in childhood are not affected by future wages. Childhood CSLs are therefore exogenous to adult

---

2. The slope of the line in Figure 1, 0.29, corresponds to social returns of 34% ($e^{0.29} - 1 \simeq 0.34$). The difference between top- and bottom-decile countries implies social returns on the order of 40%. To rationalize Figure 1, we therefore need human-capital externalities of 25–30% on top of the 6–10% private returns.

wages. Second, although in principle CSLs may be correlated with omitted factors that also affect schooling and future wages, we provide evidence suggesting this is not a problem. Omitted variables related to family background or tastes would likely induce correlation between CSLs and college attendance as well as secondary and middle schooling. The results below show that CSLs affected schooling exclusively in middle-school and high-school grades, suggesting that omitted factors do not bias estimates using CSLs as instruments. A third consideration is that changing CSLs were part of the 1910–1940 high-school movement that Goldin (1998) has argued was responsible for much of the human-capital accumulation in the United States in the twentieth century.

The baseline results in the paper use samples of white men aged 40–49 from the 1960–1980 Censuses, though some results use 1950 and 1990 data and samples of men aged 30–39. We focus on the 1960–1980 Censuses because the Census schooling variable changed in 1990. Also, we show below that it is important to control for private returns correctly by instrumenting for individual schooling when estimating external returns. The 1960–1980 Censuses include information on quarter of birth, which can be used as an instrument for individual schooling as in Angrist and Krueger (1991). We start with men in their 40s because they are on a relatively flat part of the age–earnings profile. This makes it easier to control for the effect of individual education on earnings, and facilitates the use of quarter-of-birth instruments for individual schooling. Finally, blacks are excluded because blacks in these cohorts experienced marked changes in school quality (see, e.g., Welch, 1973; Margo, 1990; or Card and Krueger, 1992a).

Ordinary least-squares (OLS) estimates using data from the 1960–1980 Censuses show a large positive relationship between average schooling and individual wages. A one-year increase in average schooling is associated with about a 7% increase in average wages, over and above the roughly equal private returns. In contrast with the OLS estimates, instrumental variables (IV) estimates of external returns for men aged 40–49 in 1960–1980 are typically around 1–2%, and significantly lower than the corresponding OLS estimates. Adding data from the 1950 Census and/or data for men aged 30–39 yields slightly smaller and more precise estimates.[3] We therefore conclude there is little evidence for large external returns, though the results are consistent with modest external returns of 1–3%. The confidence intervals typically exclude human capital externalities greater than 5–6% and therefore rule out magnitudes in the

---

3. Adding data from the 1990 Census results in somewhat larger estimates of external returns, but this finding seems to be generated by problems with the schooling variable in the 1990 Census.

range of the OLS estimates. They also rule out magnitudes necessary to rationalize the steep relationship between schooling and output per worker observed in Figure 1. This implies that differences in average education are unlikely to be a major source of cross-country income differences.

A shortcoming of the approach used here is that it identifies local human-capital externalities only. We miss externalities that arise if, for example, more-skilled workers generate ideas used in other parts of the country. It should be noted, however, that most theories of externalties suggest an important local component (see, e.g., Glaeser et al., 1992, and Jaffe, Trajtenberg, and Henderson, 1993). Another limitation of estimation based on CSLs is that CSL variation mainly affects secondary education. A recent paper by Moretti (1999) explores the relationship between increasing numbers of college graduates and income in U.S. cities. Moretti finds sizable human-capital externalities. These results might be driven by greater externalities from college education, though they might also reflect differences in empirical strategy. In any case, externalities from high school are probably at least as important as externalities from college education; the bulk of twentieth-century U.S. human-capital accumulation is accounted for by changes in secondary schooling, as are most of the differences in schooling between high- and low-education countries.

The next section lays out two simple economic models that show how human-capital externalities can arise. These models are used to develop an estimation framework and to highlight the econometric issues involved in identifying the external returns to education. Section 3 discusses the data and reports OLS estimates from regressions on individual and average schooling. Section 4 describes the CSL instruments, Section 5 reports the IV estimates, and Section 6 concludes.

2. Theories of Human-Capital Externalities

Many different interactions can lead to human-capital externalities. Here, we discuss two possibilities, and derive a simple theoretical relationship to be estimated.

2.1. THEORIES OF NONPECUNIARY EXTERNALITIES

In *The Economy of Cities*, Jane Jacobs (1970) argued that cities are an engine of economic growth because they facilitate the exchange of ideas, especially between entrepreneurs and managers (see also Bairoch, 1988). This notion also provides part of the motivation for Lucas's (1988) argument that human capital has important external returns. We refer to externality theories in this mold as *nonpecuniary* because the external effects work not through prices, but rather through the exchange of ideas, imitation, or learning by doing.

To discuss these ideas more formally, suppose that the output (or marginal product) of a worker, i, is

$$y_i = Ah_i^\nu,$$

where h_i is the human capital (schooling) of the worker, and A is aggregate productivity. So individual earnings are $W_i = Ah_i^\nu$.

The notion that the exchange of ideas among workers raises productivity can be captured by allowing A to depend on aggregate human capital. In particular, suppose that

$$A = BH^\delta \equiv B(E[h_i^\rho])^{\delta/\rho}, \tag{1}$$

where H is a measure of aggregate human capital, E is the expectation operator, B is a constant, and ρ determines how the human capital of different workers are aggregated into this measure. In Lucas's model, $\rho = 1$, so what matters is average human capital in a society or city. Another possibility, discussed by Murphy, Shleifer, and Vishny (1991), is that the skills of the most talented individuals create externalities, in which case we have $\rho \to \infty$. Finally, Benabou (1996) proposes an equation similar to (1) with $\rho < 0$, so that inequality in the distribution of human capital depresses aggregate productivity. Acemoglu (1997b) derives a similar relationship with $\rho < 0$ from imperfect job matching.

For any value of ρ, the parameter δ measures the importance and sign of external effects in the production process. Individual earnings can be written as $W_i = Ah_i^\nu = BH^\delta h_i^\nu$. Therefore, taking logs, we have

$$\ln W_i = \ln B + \delta \ln H + \nu \ln h_i. \tag{2}$$

If external effects are stronger within a geographical area, as seems likely in a world where human interaction and the exchange of ideas are the main forces behind the externalities, then equation (2) should be estimated using measures of H at the local level.

2.2. THEORIES OF PECUNIARY EXTERNALITIES

Marshall (1961) argued that increasing the geographic concentration of specialized inputs increases productivity, since the matching between factor inputs and industries is improved. A similar story is developed in

Acemoglu (1997a), where firms find it profitable to invest in new technologies only when there is a sufficient supply of trained workers to replace employees who quit. We refer to this sort of effect as a pecuniary externality, since greater human capital encourages more investment by firms and raises other workers' wages via this channel. Here, we outline a related theory of pecuniary human-capital externalities based on Acemoglu (1996).

Consider an economy lasting two periods, with production only in the second period, and a continuum of workers normalized to 1. For now, take human capital, h_i, as given. There is also a continuum of risk-neutral firms. In period 1, firms make an irreversible investment decision, k, at cost Rk. Workers and firms come together in the second period. The labor market is not competitive; instead, firms and workers are matched randomly, and each firm meets a worker. The only decision workers and firms make after matching is whether to produce together or not to produce at all (since there are no further periods). If firm f and worker i produce together, their output is

$$k_f^\alpha h_i^\nu, \tag{3}$$

where $\alpha < 1$, $\nu \leq 1 - \alpha$. Since it is costly for the worker–firm pair to separate and find new partners in this economy, employment relationships generate quasi-rents. Wages will therefore be determined by rent sharing. Here, we simply assume that the worker receives a share β of the output, while the firm receives the remaining share, $1 - \beta$.

An equilibrium in this economy is a set of physical capital investments for firms. Firm f maximizes the expected profit function

$$(1 - \beta)k_f^\alpha E[h_i^\nu] - Rk_f \tag{4}$$

with respect to k_f. Since firms do not know which worker they will be matched with, their expected profit is an average of profits from different skill levels. The function (4) is strictly concave, so all firms choose the same level of capital investment, $k_f = k$, given by

$$k = \left(\frac{(1 - \beta)\alpha H}{R}\right)^{1/(1-\alpha)}, \tag{5}$$

where

$$H \equiv E[h_i^\nu]$$

is now the measure of aggregate human capital. Substituting (5) into (3), and using the fact that wages are equal to a fraction β of output, the wage income of individual i is given by $W_i = \beta\big((1-\beta)\alpha H/R\big)^{\alpha/(1-\alpha)} h_i^\nu$. Taking logs, this is

$$\ln W_i = c + \frac{\alpha}{1-\alpha} \ln H + \nu \ln h_i, \qquad (6)$$

where c is a constant and $\alpha/(1-\alpha)$ and ν are positive coefficients.[4]

Human-capital externalities arise here because firms choose their physical capital in anticipation of the average human capital of the workers they will employ in the future. Since physical and human capital are complements in this setup, a more educated labor force leads to greater investment in physical capital and to higher wages. In the absence of the need for search and matching, firms would immediately hire workers with skills appropriate to their investments, and there would be no human-capital externalities.[5]

Nonpecuniary and pecuniary theories of human-capital externalities lead to similar empirical relationships, since equation (6) is identical to equation (2), with $c = \ln B$ and $\delta = \alpha/(1-\alpha)$. A similar relationship also arises if more-educated workers produce higher-quality intermediate goods, and monopolistically competitive upstream and downstream producers locate in the same area. Thus, an empirical strategy based on relationships of this sort cannot distinguish between the types of externalities we have discussed. Nevertheless, lack of evidence of a role for H in individual wage determination weighs against all of these mechanisms, at the least at the local level.

2.3 ESTIMATING THE EXTERNAL RETURNS TO EDUCATION

The models discussed above are closed by a mechanism explaining individual education decisions. Suppose that an individual's human capital is given by

---

4. As in Acemoglu (1996), human-capital externalities are additive in logs, so the marginal product of a more skilled worker increases when the average workforce skill level increases. Acemoglu (1998, 1999) discusses models in which log wage *differences* between skilled and unskilled workers increase with average skill levels.
5. In a frictionless world, firms maximize profits conditional on realized worker–firm matches instead of conditional on the expected match, and pay the full marginal product of the worker. In this case, firm j matched to worker i chooses capital $k_j = (\alpha h_i^\nu/r)^{1/(1-\alpha)}$, and worker i's wages is $\ln W_i = c' + [\nu\alpha/(1-\alpha)] \ln h_i$.

$h_i = \exp(\eta_i s_i),$

where s_i is worker i's schooling. Workers have unobserved ability $\eta_i = \theta_i \eta(s_i)$, which depends on an individual characteristic, θ_i, and also potentially on schooling. This dependence captures potential decreasing returns to individual schooling, as in Lang (1993).

Suppose also that a worker's consumption, C_i, is equal to his labor income, and that schooling is chosen by workers so as to maximize

$$\ln C_i - \frac{1}{2} \psi_i s_i^2. \tag{7}$$

The parameter ψ_i is the cost of education for individual i and can be interpreted as a personal discount rate, along the lines of Card (1995).

Individual schooling decisions will then be determined by maximizing (7), taking (6) as given. In both models, this yields equilibrium schooling levels satisfying

$$\nu \theta_i [\eta(s_i) + s_i \eta'(s_i)] = \psi_i s_i, \tag{8a}$$

or

$$\eta'(s_i)(\epsilon_\eta^{-1} + 1) = \frac{\psi_i}{\nu \theta_i}, \tag{8b}$$

where ϵ_η is the elasticity of the function η. The population average return to optimally chosen schooling levels is $E[\nu \theta_i \{\eta_i(s_i) + s_i\, \eta'_i(s_i)\}]$. But the average return for particular subpopulations interacts with discount rates in a manner noted by Lang (1993) and Card (1995). For example, if $\eta'(s_i) < 0$, those with high ψ_i get less schooling, and a marginal year of schooling is worth more to such people than the population average return.

Equations (2) and (6) provide the theoretical basis for our empirical work. Since H is unobserved, however, we approximate $\ln H$ by the state average schooling $\bar{S}$.[6] Estimation can therefore be based on the following equation for individual i residing in state j:

6. In the pecuniary externality model, and in the nonpecuniary externalities model with $\rho = 1$, this approximation is natural. Specifically, we have $\ln H = \ln E[\exp(\nu \eta_i s_i)] \approx c_0 + c_1 E[\eta_i s_i] \approx c_2 + c_3 E[s_i]$. The first step approximates the mean of the log with the log of the mean. The second step takes $E[\eta_i]$ and the covariance between η_i and s_i to be constant, unaffected by changes in average education. When $\rho \neq 1$ in the nonpecuniary externalities model, the variance of education will also matter. With $\rho < 1$, greater variance reduces H, and with $\rho > 1$, greater variance increases H.

$$\ln W_{ijt} \approx \gamma_0 + \gamma_1 \bar{S}_{jt} + \gamma_2 \eta_i s_i + u_{jt} \tag{9}$$

where $\bar{S}_{jt} = E_{jt}(s_i)$ is the average schooling in state j at time t, and u_{jt} captures other factors that affect wages in that state at time t. An important implication of equation (9) is that if $\bar{S}_{jt}$ is correlated with average ability among workers in area j, then OLS will not estimate γ_1. One reason for such correlation is the endogenous nature of educational choices. Another is selective migration.

2.4 EFFECTS OF MIGRATION

Suppose that individuals choose to live in one of two states, indexed by $j = 1$ and 2, paying rent (user cost of housing) r_j in state j. Suppose also that i receives additional utility, ζ_i, from living in state 1 instead of state 2, where ζ_i is an independent draw from the continuous distribution function $G(\zeta)$. This taste shock introduces some degree of heterogeneity in worker preferences regarding residential location.

We normalize the total housing stock of each state to 1, so that total population is fixed at 1 in each state. Individuals have to live and work in the same state. Rents will adjust to clear the housing market. The consumption of individual i when he lives in state j is the difference between his labor income and his rent, that is, $C_{ij} = W_{ij} - r_j$, where W_{ij} is his earnings when he lives and works in state j.

To facilitate the discussion, assume that a random factor, v_j, also affects wages in each state, so the earnings of individual i in state j are given by

$$W_{ij} = BH_j^\delta h_i^\nu + v_j$$

(in the model of pecuniary externalities, $\delta = \alpha/(1-\alpha)$ and $B = \beta[(1-\beta)\alpha/R]^{\alpha/(1-\alpha)}$. An individual with human capital h will be indifferent between living in state 1 and state 2 if he has $\zeta_i = \zeta(h, \Delta v, \Delta r)$, where

$$BH_1^\delta h^\nu + \zeta(h, \Delta v, \Delta r) + \Delta v - \Delta r = BH_2^\delta h^\nu, \tag{10}$$

with $\Delta r = r_1 - r_2$ and $\Delta v = v_1 - v_2$. This implies that among people with human capital h, those with ζ greater than $\zeta(h, \Delta v, \Delta r)$ would prefer to live in state 1 when the rent differential is Δr. Denoting the distribution of human capital by $F(\cdot)$, and exploiting the fact that ζ_i's are independent across individuals, housing markets clear when

$$\int G(\zeta(h, \Delta v, \Delta r)) \, dF(h) = \frac{1}{2}, \tag{11}$$

i.e., when half of the population prefers state 1. Intuitively, G ($\zeta(h, \Delta v, \Delta r)$) is the fraction with human capital h who prefer to live in state 2, and the integral sums over all levels of education. Equation (11) determines the equilibrium rent differential between the two states.

One implication of this simple framework is that an increase in H_1 encourages some (though not all) skilled workers to live in state 1. This is because increasing H_1 raises the wages of skilled workers by more than the wages of unskilled workers [recall that equations (2) and (6) are additive in logs]. Positive state-specific shocks to wages (i.e., $\Delta v > 0$) therefore attract more high-education workers to a state and raise average human capital via migration. This differential impact by schooling group generates positive correlation between average education and wages across states, potentially biasing OLS estimates of external returns.

It is also interesting to note that because rents tend to be higher in the state with greater average education, observed wage differences exaggerate differences in living standards. Nevertheless, for our purposes, it is differences in wages without cost-of-living adjustments that are relevant. Firms pay (unadjusted) wages and, in equilibrium, receive the same return to physical capital in both states.[7] Thus, human-capital externalities are required if firms in the state with greater average education and higher wages are to be able to produce more and break even.

3. Econometric Framework

This section discusses instrumental-variables (IV) strategies to estimate equation (9), the causal relationship of interest.[8] In practice, of course, there are many factors beside schooling that determine wages. An error term is therefore added to the estimating equation. Also, we adopt notation that reflects the fact that different individuals are observed in different years in our data. The resulting equation is

$$Y_{ijt} = X_i'\mu + \delta_j + \delta_t + \gamma_1 \bar{S}_{jt} + \gamma_{2i} s_i + u_{jt} + \epsilon_i, \tag{12}$$

where Y_{ijt} is the log weekly wage, u_{jt} is a state–year error component, and ϵ_i is an individual error term. The vector X_i includes state-of-birth and year-of-birth dummies, and δ_j and δ_t are state-of-residence and Census-

---

7. Firms producing nontraded goods may care only about local prices. But firms producing traded goods face the same prices and have to receive the same rate of return to physical capital. These firms must therefore have a more productive work force in high-wage states. Hence, as long as there are some firms producing traded goods in every state, average productivity has to be higher in states where wages are higher.
8. Brock and Durlauf (1999) survey non-IV approaches to estimating models with social effects.

year effects. The random coefficient on individual schooling is $\gamma_{2i} \equiv \gamma_2 \eta_i$, while the coefficient on average schooling, γ_1, is taken to be fixed.

The most important identification problem raised by equation (12) is omitted-variables bias from correlation between average schooling and other state–year effects embodied in the error component u_{jt}. The theoretical discussion suggests at least two reasons for omitted-variables bias. First, economic growth may increase wages in a state, while also raising the demand for (or supply) of schooling. For example, state university systems often expand during cyclical upturns, and higher wealth levels typically increase investments in schooling. Alternatively, labor productivity and tastes for schooling in a state may change at the same time. These scenarios correspond to correlation between u_{jt} and the average cost of, or returns to, schooling in the theoretical model. To solve this problem, we construct instruments for $\bar{S}_{jt}$ using CSLs effective in individuals' states of birth at the time they were 14. These instruments are called state-of-birth CSLs (SOB CSLs). Since roughly two-thirds of the people in our sample live in their states of birth, the SOB CSLs are correlated with average schooling in states of residence. SOB CSLs generate variation in average schooling levels but are unlikely to be correlated with contemporaneous state-specific shocks, since they are derived from laws passed roughly 30 years before education and wages were recorded.[9]

In addition to generating exogenous variation in average education, the SOB-CSL instruments provide an attractive starting point because they are attached to individuals as opposed to states. We can therefore compare IV estimates of the individual returns to schooling using SOB CSLs with other IV estimates using individual characteristics (such as quarter of birth). Human-capital externalities should cause IV estimates of individual returns using SOB CSLs to diverge from these other estimates.[10]

A drawback of the SOB-CSL strategy is that it does not necessarily eliminate bias from state-specific wage shocks if there is substantial interstate migration in response. To see this, suppose that wages increase in, say, New York, and workers from out of state are attracted to New York. The model outlined above suggests more-educated workers may respond more to the pull of higher wages. Since more-educated workers are, on average, from states with more restrictive SOB CSLs, selective

---

9. The endogenous variable is state average schooling for all residents, while the estimation sample is limited to certain age groups. The CSLs these men were exposed to are nevertheless highly correlated with overall average schooling in a state because this sample contributes to the overall average, and because the CSLs of neighboring cohorts are correlated with the CSLs of the estimation cohort.

10. A second reason we focus initially on the SOB-CSL instruments is that these instruments can be used without controlling for state of residence, a potentially endogenous variable due to migration.

migration by the more educated can cause these instruments to be correlated with state-specific shocks.

To solve this problem, we create an alternative set of instruments based on state of residence (SOR CSLs). These instruments assign CSLs to each individual according to the laws in effect in their current state of residence 30 years before the year they are observed (i.e., approximately the time they were 14). SOR CSLs are uncorrelated with contemporary state-specific shocks, since they are (by construction) invariant to the population mix in a particular state. In practice, SOB CSLs and SOR CSLs lead to similar estimates of human-capital externalities, suggesting that differences in migration patterns by state of birth are not important.

While omitted state–year effects are the primary motivation for these two IV strategies, the fact that one regressor, $\bar{S}_j$, is the average of another regressor, s_i, also complicates the interpretation of OLS estimates. To see this, consider an "atheoretical" regression of Y_{ij} on both s_i and $\bar{S}_j$, which for purposes of illustration is assumed to have constant coefficients and a cross-section dimension only:

$$Y_{ij} = \mu^* + \pi_0 s_i + \pi_1 \bar{S}_j + \xi_i, \quad \text{where} \quad E[\xi_i S_i] = E[\xi_i \bar{S}_j] \equiv 0. \tag{13}$$

Now, let ρ_0 denote the coefficient from a bivariate regression of Y_{ij} on s_i only, and let ρ_1 denote the coefficient from a bivariate regression of Y_{ij} on $\bar{S}_j$ only. Note that ρ_1 is the two-stage least squares (2SLS) estimate of the coefficient on s_i in a bivariate regression of Y_{ij} on s_i using a full set of state dummies as instruments. Appendix A.1 shows that

$$\pi_0 = \rho_1 + \phi(\rho_0 - \rho_1), \\ \pi_1 = \phi(\rho_1 - \rho_0), \tag{14}$$

where $\phi = 1/(1 - R^2) > 1$, and R^2 is from a regression of s_i on state dummies. Thus, if *for any reason* OLS estimates of the bivariate regression differ from 2SLS estimates using state-dummy instruments, the coefficient on average schooling in (13) will be nonzero. For example, if grouping (averaging across all individuals within a state) corrects for attenuation bias due to measurement error in s_i, we have $\rho_1 > \rho_0$ and the appearance of positive external returns even when $\gamma_1 = 0$ in (12). In contrast, if grouping eliminates correlation between s_i and unobserved earnings potential, we have $\rho_1 < \rho_0$ and the appearance of negative external returns.[11]

---

11. The coefficient on average schooling in an equation with individual schooling can be interpreted as the Hausman (1978) test statistic for the equality of OLS estimates and

The interpretation of OLS estimates is complicated even further when returns to education vary across individuals, as in our random-coefficients specification, (12). Nevertheless, an IV strategy that treats both s_i and $\bar{S}_j$ as endogenous can generate consistent estimates of external returns. The key to the success of this approach is finding the right instrument for individual schooling. Appendix A.2 shows that if the instrument for individual schooling generates the same average return as would be generated using CSLs as instruments for individual schooling, the resulting IV estimates of social returns are consistent. Quarter-of-birth instruments, as in the work of Angrist and Krueger (1991), are therefore appropriate for individual schooling in our context because CSL and quarter-of-birth instruments both estimate individual returns for people whose schooling was affected by compulsory schooling laws. (In fact, we show below that, like quarter-of-birth instruments, CSLs changed the distribution of schooling primarily in the 8–12 range.)

4. Data and OLS Estimates

4.1 DATA SOURCES

The analysis begins with data for U.S.-born white males aged 40–49 from the 1960–1980 Censuses. These samples were chosen because they include data on quarter of birth and are limited to groups on the flattest part of the age–earnings profiles. This reduces bias from age or experience effects when using quarter-of-birth dummies as instruments. Following the results using 1960–1980 data, we look at samples including data from the 1950 and 1990 Censuses. Because these censuses do not have quarter of birth, estimates using the extended sample must treat individual schooling as exogenous. A second problem with the 1990 data is that the schooling variable is categorical. The last set of results in the paper are for men aged 30–39. Men younger than 30 are excluded because many in this group have yet to finish school.[12]

The schooling variable for individuals in the 1950–1980 data is the

---

2SLS estimates of private returns to schooling using state dummies as instruments. Borjas (1992) discusses a similar problem affecting the estimation of ethnic-background effects.

12. Data are from the following IPUMS files (documented in Ruggles and Sobek, 1997): the 1% sample for 1960, Form 1 and Form 2 state samples for 1970 (giving a 2% sample), and the 5% PUMS-A sample for 1980. The 1950 sample includes all sample-line individuals in the relevant age–sex–race group, and the 1990 data are from the IPUMS self-weighting 1% file. All regressions are weighted to population proportions. For additional information, see Appendix B.

highest grade completed, capped at 17 years to impose a uniform topcode across censuses. Average schooling in a state and year is measured as the average of the capped highest grade completed for the full sample of workers aged 16–64 (i.e., not limited to white men). The averages are weighted by individuals' weeks worked the previous year. For 1990 data, we assigned average years of schooling to categorical values using the imputation for white men in Park (1994). Average schooling in 1990 is the average capped value of this imputed-years-of-schooling variable.[13]

The relevant labor market for the estimation of equation (12) is taken to be a state. Previous work on external returns in the United States has used cities, while macroeconomic studies of education and growth use countries (see, e.g., Mankiw, Romer, and Weil, 1992; Barro and Sala-i-Martin, 1995; Benhabib and Spiegel, 1994; Bils and Klenow, 1998; Topel, 1999; or Krueger and Lindahl, 1999). We work with states because all three PUMS samples record state of residence, while the 1960 and part of the 1970 PUMS fail to identify cities or metropolitan areas. Since our instruments are derived from individuals' states of birth and not their cities of birth, little is lost from this aggregation.

Table 1 gives descriptive statistics for men aged 40–49 in all five censuses. The average age is constant across censuses, while average schooling increased by slightly less than a year between 1950 and 1960, and by slightly more than a year between 1960 and 1970, 1970 and 1980, and 1980 and 1990. The mean of state average schooling, shown in the row below individual schooling, refers to the entire working-age population. The standard deviation of average schooling summarizes the extent of variation in average schooling across states. The next two rows record the lowest and highest average schooling. For example, in 1980 the lowest average education was 11.8 years, in Kentucky, while Washington, DC had the highest average education at 13.1. The last eight rows of Table 1 report the fraction in each census affected by child labor and compulsory attendance laws (coded as SOB CSLs). We discuss these variables in detail in Section 5 below.

4.2 OLS ESTIMATES

OLS estimates of private returns are similar to those reported elsewhere, and do not change much with controls for average schooling. For example, the estimates show a marked increase in schooling coefficients between 1980 and 1990. This can be seen in Table 2, which reports OLS estimates for men aged 40–49 from models with and without $\bar{S}_{jt}$, using

---

13. Only 1% samples are used for the calculation of averages. Alternative weighting schemes for measures of average schooling (e.g., unweighted) generated similar results.

Table 1 DESCRIPTIVE STATISTICS

Variables	QOB Samples				
	1950	1960	1970	1980	1990
Covariates					
Age	44.16	44.55	44.74	44.66	44.10
	(2.87)	(2.88)	(2.90)	(2.94)	(2.84)
Individual education	9.67	10.52	11.59	12.62	13.70
	(3.40)	(3.22)	(3.18)	(2.98)	(2.49)
Regressors					
State average education	9.94	10.65	11.52	12.46	13.10
	(0.72)	(0.54)	(0.41)	(0.30)	(0.23)
Lowest state average education	7.87 [MS]	9.24 [MS]	10.45 [SC]	11.81 [KY]	12.62 [AR]
Highest state average education	11.18 [UT]	11.80 [UT]	12.38 [UT]	13.07 [DC]	13.74 [DC]
Dependent Variable					
Log weekly wage	4.06	4.64	5.17	5.90	6.44
	(0.77)	(0.63)	(0.65)	(0.72)	(0.73)
Instruments					
Percent child labor 6	0.45	0.23	0.19	0.05	0.03
Percent child labor 7	0.45	0.36	0.24	0.24	0.16
Percent child labor 8	0.10	0.36	0.50	0.41	0.37
Percent child labor 9+	0.01	0.05	0.07	0.31	0.44
Percent compulsory attendance 8	0.57	0.35	0.24	0.11	0.11
Percent compulsory attendance 9	0.40	0.53	0.44	0.44	0.44
Percent compulsory attendance 10	0.02	0.06	0.08	0.09	0.06
Percent compulsory attendance 11+	0.01	0.07	0.24	0.37	0.39
N	16659	72344	161029	376479	103184

Notes: Standard deviations are in parentheses. Bracketed entries in the "Lowest state average education" and "highest state average education" rows are abbreviations indicating the state with the lowest and highest average schooling. All other entries are means. The data are from the Census IPUMS for 1960 through 1980, with the sample restricted to white males aged 40–49 in the Census year.

Table 2 OLS ESTIMATES OF PRIVATE AND EXTERNAL RETURNS TO SCHOOLING

	1960–1980 (1)	1950–1980 (2)	1950–1990 (3)	1950 (4)	1960 (5)	1970 (6)	1980 (7)	1990 (8)
(a) Private Returns								
Private return to schooling	0.073 (0.0003)	0.068 (0.0003)	0.075 (0.0003)	0.055 (0.002)	0.069 (0.001)	0.076 (0.001)	0.075 (0.001)	0.102 (0.001)
State of residence main effects?	Yes	Yes	Yes	No	No	No	No	No
(b) Private and External Returns								
Private return to schooling	0.073 (0.000)	0.068 (0.000)	0.074 (0.000)	0.055 (0.002)	0.068 (0.001)	0.075 (0.001)	0.074 (0.000)	0.102 (0.001)
External return to schooling	0.073 (0.016)	0.061 (0.004)	0.072 (0.003)	0.136 (0.017)	0.136 (0.016)	0.128 (0.021)	0.160 (0.027)	0.168 (0.047)
State of residence main effects?	Yes	Yes	Yes	No	No	No	No	No
N	609,852	626,511	729,695	16,659	72,344	161,029	376,479	103,184

Notes: Standard errors corrected for state–year clustering are shown in parentheses. The data are from the Census IPUMS for 1950 through 1990, with the sample restricted to white males aged 40–49 in the Census year. All regressions contain Census-year, year-of-birth, and state-of-birth main effects.

pooled samples, and separately by census year. The pooled regressions include state-of-residence effects, year effects, year-of-birth effects, and state-of-birth effects. All standard errors reported in the paper are corrected for state–year clustering using the formula in Moulton (1986). Corrected standard errors are typically twice as large as uncorrected standard errors because of the group structure of some of the instruments and regressors.

OLS estimates of external returns for 1960–1980 imply that a one-year increase in state average schooling is associated with a 0.073 increase in the wages of all workers in that state. Using data from 1950–1980 generates an estimate of 0.061, whereas the 1950–1990 sample leads to an estimated external return of 0.072. These are similar to Moretti's (1999) estimates of external returns using within-city variation, which range from 0.08 to 0.13.[14] These OLS estimates of external returns are large, but substantially smaller than the external returns required to rationalize the relationship in Figure 1.

Interestingly, the external returns estimates from using single censuses are considerably larger than the estimates that control for state effects. This suggests that at least part of the relationship between average schooling and wages is due to omitted state characteristics. The remainder of the paper presents evidence on whether the association between state average schooling and wages reflects human-capital externalities.

5. Compulsory Schooling Laws and Schooling

5.1 CONSTRUCTION OF CSL VARIABLES

The CSL instruments were coded from information on five types of restrictions related to school attendance and work permits that were in force at the time census respondents were aged 14. These restrictions specify the maximum age for school enrollment (enroll_age), the minimum dropout age (drop_age), the minimum schooling required before dropping out (req_sch), the minimum age for a work permit (work_age), and the minimum schooling required for a work permit (work_sch). Information was collected for 3–6-year intervals from 1914 to 1965, with missing years interpolated by extending older data. For example, data for cohorts aged 14 in 1924–1928 come from a source for 1924. Sources for the CSLs are documented in Appendix B.

The five CSLs vary considerably over time and across states. This can be seen in Table 3, which reports the mean and standard deviation for

---

14. Rauch (1993) reports cross-section estimates around 0.05 using data from the 1980 Census. These estimates are not directly comparable with ours because Rauch's model includes occupation dummies and average experience.

Table 3 DESCRIPTION OF CHILD LABOR AND COMPULSORY SCHOOLING LAWS

Year at Age 14 (Census Year)	Earliest Dropout Age (1)	Latest Enrollment Age (2)	Minimum Schooling for Dropout (3)	Earliest Work Age (4)	Required Schooling for Work Permit (5)
1914 (50)	15.31 (1.20)	7.49 (0.52)	1.90 (3.40)	11.00 (5.75)	1.70 (2.56)
1917 (50)	15.55 (0.89)	7.63 (0.49)	1.93 (2.74)	13.43 (1.98)	2.98 (2.66)
1921 (50)	15.69 (0.99)	7.42 (0.51)	4.28 (3.63)	13.94 (1.71)	4.19 (2.97)
1924 (60)	15.88 (0.97)	7.29 (0.57)	5.64 (3.64)	14.11 (1.33)	4.91 (3.04)
1929 (60)	15.97 (0.93)	7.30 (0.58)	5.66 (3.62)	14.16 (1.33)	5.31 (3.01)
1935 (70)	15.96 (0.94)	7.24 (0.55)	7.24 (3.73)	14.14 (0.76)	6.02 (2.67)
1939 (70)	16.16 (1.05)	7.16 (0.51)	7.29 (3.74)	14.15 (0.77)	6.01 (2.70)
1946 (80)	16.31 (0.63)	7.09 (0.53)	7.91 (4.00)	14.77 (1.16)	4.67 (3.37)
1950 (80)	16.27 (0.60)	7.08 (0.53)	7.94 (4.49)	15.03 (1.14)	3.51 (3.47)
1954 (80)	16.30 (0.63)	7.05 (0.52)	7.79 (4.65)	15.02 (1.20)	4.06 (3.67)
1959 (90)	16.25 (0.60)	7.05 (0.53)	7.40 (4.79)	15.19 (1.19)	3.49 (3.56)
1964 (90)	16.20 (0.60)	7.05 (0.54)	7.44 (4.79)	15.17 (1.22)	3.51 (3.57)

Notes: Standard deviations are in parentheses. All other entries are means. The data are from the Census IPUMS for 1950 through 1990, with the sample restricted to white men aged 40–49 in the Census year. See Appendix B for sources and method.

each CSL component in the years for which we have CSL data. Statistics in the table are averages using micro data; that is, they weight state requirements using the sample distribution of states for each cohort. The data show that compulsory attendance requirements have generally been growing more restrictive, with the maximum enrollment age falling and the minimum dropout age rising. The minimum age for work has also increased. The cross-section variability in age requirements for dropout and work permits has also fallen over time.

Margo and Finegan (1996) show that in the 1900s child labor laws were at least as important as attendance restrictions for educational attainment, and the evidence in Schmidt (1996) suggests the same for 1920–1935.[15] This is probably because the main reason for leaving school was to work. We therefore combine the five CSL components into two variables, one summarizing compulsory attendance laws and one summarizing child labor laws. Compulsory attendance laws are summarized as the minimum years required before leaving school, taking account of age requirements. This is the larger of schooling required before dropping out and the difference between the minimum dropout age and the maximum enrollment age:

$$CA = \max\{req\_sch; drop\_age - enroll\_age\}.$$

Similarly, child labor laws are summarized as the minimum years in school required before work was permitted. This is the larger of schooling required before receiving a work permit and the difference between the minimum work age and the maximum enrollment age:

$$CL = \max\{work\_sch; work\_age - enroll\_age\}.$$

These variables collapse the CSLs into two measures that are highly related to educational attainment both conceptually and empirically.

Over 95 percent in the sample of men aged 40–49 have CL in the 6–9 range, while CA is concentrated in the 8–12 range, with almost no one in the 11 category. The distribution of CL and CA can therefore be captured using four dummies for each variable. For CL, the dummies are:

CL6   for $CL \leq 6$,
CL7   for $CL = 7$,
CL8   for $CL = 8$,
CL9   for $CL \geq 9$.

Similarly, for CA, the dummies are:

---

15. Edwards (1978), Ehrenberg and Marcus (1982), Lang and Kropp (1986), and Angrist and Krueger (1991) also present evidence that compulsory schooling laws affected schooling.

CA8   for CA ≤ 8,
CA9   for CA = 9,
CA10   for CA = 10,
CA11   for CA ≥ 11.

Table 1 shows the fraction of individuals in our sample in each group when CL and CA are assigned according to the laws that were in effect in individuals' state of birth at the time they were 14 (i.e., SOB CSLs). The distribution of SOR CSLs is similar. In the empirical work, the omitted categories are the least restrictive groups for CL and CA, viz. CL6 and CA8.

5.2 CSL EFFECTS ON INDIVIDUAL SCHOOLING

There is a large and statistically significant relationship between individual schooling and the CSL dummies. Results for men aged 40–49 with SOB CSLs are shown in Tables 4 and 5. Results using SOR CSLs and/or men aged 30–39 are similar, and are omitted to save space.

Table 4 reports estimates from regressions of individual schooling on CL7–CL9 and CA9–CA11, along with controls for Census-year effects, year-of-birth effects, and state-of-birth effects. For example, the entry in column 1 shows that in the 1950–1980 sample, men born in states with a child labor law that required 9 years in school before allowing work ended up with 0.26 more years of school completed than those born in states that required 6 or fewer years. The results are similar in models that do not include state-of-residence effects.

The right half of Table 4 shows that adding 1950 Census data to the sample leads to CSL effects similar to or slightly smaller than those estimated in the 1960–1980 data alone. Incorporating both 1950 and 1990 data leads to larger effects. Also, the relationship between CSLs and schooling is larger and more precisely estimated in samples that pool three or more censuses than in a sample using 1980 data only. For example, column 4 shows that with 1980 data alone, the effect of CL9, though still statistically significant, falls to 0.17.

Overall, the estimates reflect a pattern consistent with the notion that more restrictive laws caused higher educational attainment. This pattern can be seen in Figures 2 and 3, which plot differences in the probability that educational attainment equals or exceeds the grade level on the X-axis (i.e., one minus the CDF). The differences are between men exposed to different CSLs in the 1960–1980 sample, with men exposed to the least restrictive CSLs as the reference group.

Figure 2 shows that men exposed to more restrictive child labor laws

Table 4 THE EFFECT OF STATE-OF-BIRTH COMPULSORY SCHOOLING LAWS ON INDIVIDUAL SCHOOLING

	Including State-of-Residence Controls				Without State-of-Residence Controls			
	1960–1980 (1)	1950–1980 (2)	1950–1990 (3)	1980 (4)	1960–1980 (5)	1950–1980 (6)	1950–1990 (7)	1980 (8)
(a) Child Labor Laws								
CL7	0.095 (0.030)	0.117 (0.024)	0.173 (0.021)	0.050 (0.041)	0.105 (0.077)	0.115 (0.051)	0.175 (0.043)	0.062 (0.041)
CL8	0.124 (0.034)	0.130 (0.032)	0.213 (0.026)	0.132 (0.034)	0.120 (0.093)	0.119 (0.075)	0.202 (0.059)	0.143 (0.034)
CL9	0.259 (0.039)	0.220 (0.038)	0.398 (0.028)	0.167 (0.041)	0.269 (0.098)	0.225 (0.084)	0.410 (0.059)	0.182 (0.041)
(b) Compulsory Attendance Laws								
CA8	0.117 (0.027)	0.083 (0.025)	0.189 (0.020)	−0.011 (0.034)	0.103 (0.072)	0.068 (0.057)	0.171 (0.043)	−0.009 (0.034)
CA9	0.095 (0.034)	0.059 (0.036)	0.113 (0.020)	0.100 (0.044)	0.106 (0.085)	0.074 (0.077)	0.133 (0.063)	0.104 (0.045)
CA10	0.167 (0.038)	0.144 (0.036)	0.260 (0.028)	0.115 (0.037)	0.184 (0.103)	0.165 (0.085)	0.290 (0.063)	0.119 (0.038)
N	609,852	626,511	729,695	376,479	609,852	626,511	729,695	376,479

Notes: Standard errors corrected for state–year clustering are shown in parentheses. The data are from the Census IPUMS for 1950 through 1990, with the sample restricted to white males aged 40–49 in the Census year. All regressions contain Census-year, year-of-birth, and state-of-birth main effects. Compulsory schooling laws were assigned according to the laws in effect in the individual's state of birth when he was 14.

Table 5 — THE EFFECT OF STATE-OF-BIRTH COMPULSORY SCHOOLING LAWS ON DISCRETE LEVELS OF SCHOOLING

	Results for 1960–1980					Results for 1950–1980				
	Completed 8 Years or Higher (1)	Completed 10 Years or Higher (2)	Completed 12 Years or Higher (3)	Completed 14 Years or Higher (4)	Completed 16 Years or Higher (5)	Completed 8 Years or Higher (6)	Completed 10 Years or Higher (7)	Completed 12 Years or Higher (8)	Completed 14 Years or Higher (9)	Completed 16 Years or Higher (10)
Dependent-variable mean	0.908	0.747	0.617	0.249	0.167	0.884	0.695	0.562	0.226	0.151
(a) Child Labor Laws										
CL7	0.019 (0.004)	0.019 (0.005)	0.014 (0.005)	−0.005 (0.006)	−0.005 (0.004)	0.031 (0.004)	0.014 (0.004)	0.009 (0.003)	−0.004 (0.004)	−0.004 (0.003)
CL8	0.032 (0.005)	0.023 (0.005)	0.018 (0.005)	−0.014 (0.007)	−0.014 (0.046)	0.033 (0.005)	0.019 (0.005)	0.016 (0.005)	−0.009 (0.006)	−0.010 (0.003)
CL9	0.061 (0.005)	0.045 (0.006)	0.035 (0.006)	−0.019 (0.007)	−0.018 (0.052)	0.065 (0.005)	0.034 (0.006)	0.024 (0.006)	−0.021 (0.007)	−0.007 (0.004)
(b) Compulsory Attendance Laws										
CA8	0.036 (0.004)	0.014 (0.004)	0.010 (0.004)	−0.009 (0.005)	−0.011 (0.004)	0.032 (0.004)	0.010 (0.004)	0.006 (0.004)	−0.010 (0.005)	−0.010 (0.003)
CA9	0.020 (0.004)	0.023 (0.005)	0.025 (0.005)	−0.011 (0.006)	−0.008 (0.005)	0.016 (0.005)	0.022 (0.005)	0.022 (0.005)	−0.011 (0.006)	−0.009 (0.005)
CA10	0.030 (0.005)	0.034 (0.006)	0.037 (0.006)	−0.013 (0.007)	−0.009 (0.005)	0.022 (0.005)	0.032 (0.006)	0.032 (0.005)	−0.010 (0.007)	−0.005 (0.005)

Notes: Standard errors corrected for state-year clustering are shown in parentheses. All entries are OLS estimates from a regression of a dummy for having completed the indicated year of schooling on child-labor-law or compulsory-attendance-law dummies. All regressions also contain Census-year, year-of-birth, state-of-birth, and state-of-residence main effects. The data are from the Census IPUMS for 1950 through 1980, with the sample restricted to white males aged 40–49 in the Census year. Compulsory schooling laws were assigned according to the laws in effect in the individual's state of birth when he was 14. The sample size for the 1960–1980 columns is 609,852; the sample size for the 1950–1980 columns is 626,511.

Figure 2 CDF DIFFERENCE BY SEVERITY OF CHILD LABOR LAWS

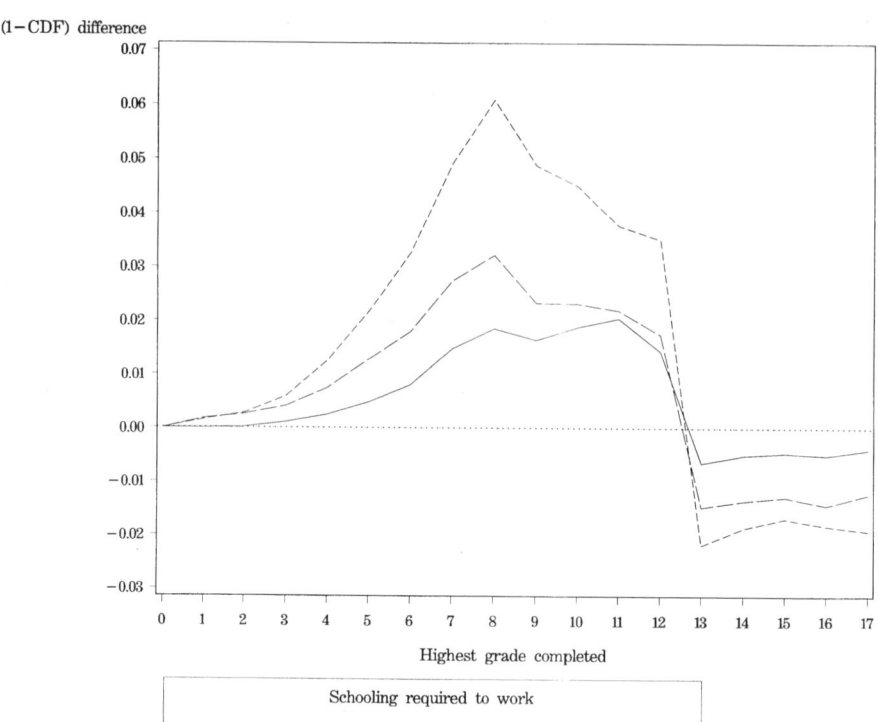

The figure shows the difference in the probability of schooling greater than or equal to the grade level on the X-axis. The reference group is 6 or fewer years of required schooling.

were 1–6 percentage points more likely to complete grades 8–12. For example, the top curve in Figure 2 shows that a person growing up in a state with the most restrictive child labor laws was about 6 percentage points more likely to have completed 8th grade than a person growing up with the least restrictive child labor laws. These differences decline at lower grades, and drop off sharply after grade 12. Figure 3 shows a similar pattern for compulsory attendance laws. These figures are encouraging in that they suggest that CSLs primarily shift the distribution of schooling in middle- and high-school grades. This is consistent with the notion that CSLs caused schooling changes, and not vice versa. Also, correlation between CSLs and omitted factors related to macroeconomic conditions, tastes for schooling, or family background would likely result in an association between more restrictive CSLs and

Figure 3 CDF DIFFERENCE BY SEVERITY OF COMPULSORY ATTENDANCE LAWS

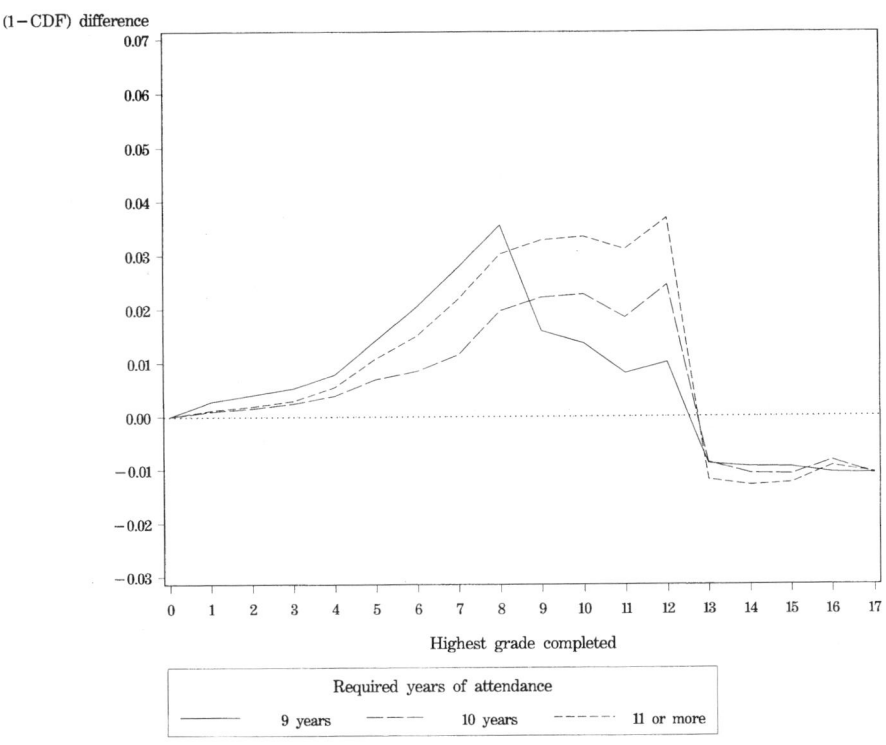

The figure shows the difference in the probability of schooling at greater than or equal to the grade level on the X-axis. The reference group is 8 or fewer years of required schooling.

the proportion of the population attending college.[16] Therefore, Figures 2 and 3 suggest that CSLs are not correlated with omitted factors that affected schooling across the board.

Table 5 quantifies the CDF differences plotted in the figures for 1960–1980 and shows analogous results for the 1950–1980 sample. The table reports CSL coefficients in regressions of dummy variables for whether an individual completed the level of schooling indicated in the column heading. All of the positive estimates for grades 8–12 are statistically significant. The negative estimates at schooling levels above 12 are smaller and

16. Up to 12th grade, the CSLs increase schooling above required levels. For example, CL9 makes high-school graduation more likely. This may reflect "lumpiness" of schooling decisions, peer effects, or the fact that our coding is imperfect. Lang and Kropp (1986) note that educational sorting might also lead people not affected directly by CSLs to change their schooling when CSLs change.

Table 6 2SLS ESTIMATES OF PRIVATE RETURNS TO SCHOOLING

	QOB Instruments			SOB-CL Instruments		CSL Instruments		SOB-CA Instruments	
	1960–1980 (1)	1980 (2)	1960–1970 (3)	1960–1980 (4)	1950–1990 (5)	1960–1980 (6)	1950–1990 (6)	1960–1980 (7)	1950–1990 (8)	1950–1990 (9)
Including state-of-residence main effects	0.073 (0.012)	0.090 (0.016)	0.063 (0.017)	0.076 (0.034)	0.103 (0.038)	0.113 (0.018)	0.092 (0.044)	0.099 (0.052)	0.081 (0.023)
No state-of-residence main effects	0.073 (0.012)	0.088 (0.016)	0.063 (0.017)	0.080 (0.064)	0.112 (0.060)	0.126 (0.027)	0.101 (0.088)	0.094 (0.086)	0.100 (0.040)
N	609,852	376,479	233,373	609,852	626,511	729,695	609,852	626,511	729,695

Notes: Standard errors corrected for state–year clustering are in parentheses. All entries are two-stage least-squares estimates of private returns to schooling, using the excluded instruments indicated above and discussed in the text. The data are from the Census IPUMS for 1950 through 1990, with the sample restricted to white males aged 40–49 in the Census year. QOB refers to the set of 30 dummies interacting quarter of birth and year of birth. SOB-CL refers to a set of dummies indicating state- and year-specific child labor laws assigned according to the laws in effect in the individual's state of birth when he was 14. SOB-CA refers to a set of dummies indicating state- and year-specific compulsory attendance laws assigned according to the laws in effect in the individual's state of birth when he was 14. All models contain Census-year, year-of-birth, and state-of-birth main effects.

less likely to be significant. The estimates also suggest that child labor laws shifted the distribution of schooling at younger grades more than compulsory attendance laws did. This too is consistent with a causal interpretation of the relationship between CSLs and schooling, since child labor laws refer to lower schooling levels than compulsory attendance laws. Interestingly, we replicate Margo and Finegan's (1996) finding for the 1900s that child labor laws were more important for educational attainment than compulsory attendance laws.

For the most part, the CDF differences in the figures and in Table 5 are ordered by increasing severity, as would be expected if these differences reflect increasingly restrictive laws. For example, using 1960–1980 data, the difference at grade 9 for men with CL9 $=1$ exceeds the difference for men with CL8 $= 1$. This in turn exceeds the difference for men with CL7 $= 1$. Adding 1950 data leaves this pattern unchanged.[17]

5.3 PRIVATE RETURNS TO EDUCATION

The CSL instruments are an important determinant of individual schooling, so in principle they can be used as instruments for individual schooling in wage equations. On the other hand, if there are external returns to schooling, IV estimates of private returns using CSL instruments will be biased by correlation between the instruments and state average schooling. In fact, one simple test for external returns is to compare estimates using quarter-of-birth instruments, which are uncorrelated with average education, to estimates using CSL instruments.

Table 6 reports two-stage least-squares (2SLS) estimates of the private returns to schooling using three different sets of instruments. Using 30 quarter-of-birth dummies (i.e., 3 quarter-of-birth dummies separately for each year of birth), the private return to schooling is estimated to be 0.073 (with a standard error of 0.012). This is less than the Angrist and Krueger (1991) estimate from a similar specification using 1980 data only. Columns 2 and 3 show that the discrepancy is explained by the fact that 1960 and 1970 data generate smaller quarter-of-birth estimates than the 1980 sample.[18]

17. A final noteworthy feature of the figures is their similarity to CDF differences induced by quarter of birth (as reported in Angrist and Imbens, 1995). Like CSLs, quarter of birth changes the distribution of schooling primarily in the 8–12 grade range. This supports our claim that CSL instruments and quarter-of-birth instruments are likely to generate similar estimates of the private return to schooling, since, as explained in Appendix A.2, IV estimates implicitly weight individual causal effects using CDF differences.
18. Bound, Jaeger, and Baker (1995) note that with many instruments, 2SLS estimates may be biased towards OLS estimates, and argue that this is a problem for some of the specifications reported by Angrist and Krueger (1991). However, reanalyses of

Estimates of private returns using CSL instruments in the 1960–1980 sample exceed those using quarter-of-birth instruments, though the differences are not large or statistically significant. The 2SLS estimate of private returns using CL6–CL8 as instruments, reported in column 4, is 0.076 (s.e. = 0.034). Using CA8–CA10 generates an estimate of 0.092 (s.e.=0.044), shown in column 7. Models estimated using CSL instruments without state-of-residence effects produce similar results. This last point is worth noting, since state of residence is a potentially endogenous variable.

The fact that quarter-of-birth and CSL instruments generate similar schooling coefficients in the 1960–1980 data already suggests that external returns are modest in this period. As noted above, significant external returns would likely lead to estimates of private returns that are biased upwards when using CSL instruments, since CSLs are correlated with average schooling. 2SLS estimates using quarter-of-birth instruments are not subject to this bias.

Estimates that include data from 1950 and 1990 use only CSL instruments, and not quarter of birth. Adding 1950 data to the basic sample leads to somewhat larger estimates with CL instruments. Adding 1990 data as well leads to even larger estimates using CL instruments, and to a substantial increase in precision with both sets of instruments. On the other hand, the estimates using CA instruments are remarkably insensitive to the inclusion of 1950 and 1990 data.

Finally, it is noteworthy that the IV estimates using quarter of birth are very close to the OLS estimates for the same period; compare, for example, the estimates of 0.073 in column 1 of Table 5 and column 1 of Table 2. Thus, estimates of external returns that treat individual schooling as exogenous and endogenous should give similar results, at least for the 1960–1980 sample.

6. External Returns to Education

6.1 RESULTS FOR 1960–1980

Table 7 reports estimates of external returns to education using data for 1960–1980. The bottom panel of Table 7 shows the first-stage relationship between SOB-CSL dummies and *average* schooling in 1960–1980

---

these data by, among others, Chamberlain and Imbens (1996), Staiger and Stock (1997), and Angrist and Krueger (1995) suggest that using 3 quarter-of-birth dummies interacted with 10 year-of-birth dummies as instruments produces approximately unbiased estimates.

data. These first-stage equations include year, year-of-birth, state-of-birth, and state-of-residence dummies. CSL effects are identified in these models because cohorts born in different years in the same state were exposed to different laws. The effect of SOB-CSL dummies on average schooling is similar to, though typically somewhat smaller than, the corresponding effect on individual schooling reported in Table 4. A moderately weaker relationship is not surprising, since the average schooling variables refer to a broader group than our sample of white men in their 40s.

The IV estimates reported in the top half of the table are from models that treat both s_i and $\bar{S}_{jt}$ as endogenous. Using quarter of birth and child labor laws as instruments generates a private return of 0.074 (s.e. = 0.012) and an external return of 0.003 (with s.e. = 0.040). This is considerably smaller, though less precise, than the corresponding OLS estimate of external returns. The 90% confidence interval for external returns, [−0.065, 0.066], excludes the OLS estimate of 0.073 (see Table 2). Using compulsory attendance laws as instruments generates somewhat higher external returns. These are not significantly different from the corresponding OLS estimates, but still considerably lower at 0.017 (s.e. = 0.043).

Using both sets of CSL dummies as instruments generates a more precisely estimated external return of 0.004 (s.e. = 0.035). The 90% confidence interval for this estimate is [−0.053, 0.061], which again excludes the OLS estimate. Finally, column 4 reports results using both CL and CA dummies, and a full set of interactions between them, as instruments. This is useful because child labor and compulsory attendance laws may work together to encourage students to stay in school longer. The results in this case are slightly more precise than estimates that do not use the interaction terms as instruments, showing external returns of 0.005 with standard error of 0.033.

Earlier we argued that it is important to use the "right" private return to adjust for individual schooling when estimating external returns. On the other hand, the IV estimates of private returns in columns 1–4 of Table 7 are remarkably close to the OLS estimates of private returns reported in Table 2. This suggests that estimates of external returns from models that treat individual schooling as exogenous may not be biased. Columns 5–8 in Table 7 report estimates from models that treat individual schooling as exogenous and drop the quarter-of-birth instruments. The resulting estimates of external returns again offer little evidence of external returns, and are virtually indistinguishable from those in columns 1–4, though slightly more precise. Since treating individual schooling as exogenous has little effect on the estimates, the results presented

Table 7 2SLS ESTIMATES OF PRIVATE AND EXTERNAL RETURNS TO SCHOOLING–STATE-OF-BIRTH INSTRUMENTS, 1960–1980 AND MEN AGED 40–49

	Individual Schooling Endogenous				Individual Schooling Exogenous			
	(1)	(2)	(3)	(4)	(5)	(6)	(7)	(8)
Instrument set	QOB & CL	QOB & CA	QOB, CA & CL	QOB, CA & CL, interactions	CL	CA	CL & CA	QOB, CA & CL, interactions
Second-Stage Estimates								
Private return to schooling	0.074 (0.012)	0.074 (0.012)	0.075 (0.012)	0.060 (0.013)	0.073 (0.0003)	0.073 (0.0003)	0.073 (0.0003)	0.073 (0.0003)
External return to schooling	0.003 (0.040)	0.017 (0.043)	0.004 (0.035)	0.005 (0.033)	0.002 (0.038)	0.018 (0.042)	0.006 (0.033)	−0.011 (0.030)

First-Stage Estimates for State–Year Average Schooling

	(1)	(2)	(3)	(4)
CL7	0.080 (0.028)	0.062 (0.025)	0.084 (0.028)	0.062 (0.025)
CL8	0.107 (0.035)	0.068 (0.031)	0.107 (0.035)	0.068 (0.031)
CL9	0.227 (0.036)	0.184 (0.034)	0.226 (0.035)	0.183 (0.034)
CA9	0.128 (0.026)	0.102 (0.023)	0.128 (0.026)	0.104 (0.030)
CA10	0.122 (0.030)	0.104 (0.029)	0.122 (0.030)	0.104 (0.029)
CA11	0.144 (0.038)	0.094 (0.036)	0.143 (0.038)	0.094 (0.036)

Notes: Standard errors corrected for state–year clustering are reported in parentheses. All entries are two-stage least-squares estimates of returns to schooling, using the excluded instruments indicated above and discussed in the text. QOB refers to a set of dummies interacting quarter of birth and year of birth. CL refers to a set of dummies indicating state- and year-specific child labor laws. CA refers to a set of dummies indicating state- and year-specific compulsory attendance laws. These are assigned according to the laws in effect in the individual's state of birth when he was 14. The data are from the Census IPUMS for 1960 through 1980, with the sample restricted to white males aged 40–49 in the Census year. All regressions contain Census-year, year-of-birth, state-of-birth, and state-of-residence main effects. The sample size for all columns is 609,852.

in the rest of the paper are from models where individual schooling is not instrumented.

Overall, the results in Table 7 suggest that the association between state average schooling and wages found in Table 2 is unlikely to be due to human-capital externalities alone. Furthermore, they indicate a total social return of around 8–9% (7% private return plus 1–2% external return). This is clearly too small to rationalize the steep relationship between average schooling and output per worker found in Figure 1.

6.2 ADDITIONAL ESTIMATES USING 1960–1980 DATA

Estimates of external returns using child labor laws as instruments (CL7–CL9) change little when the basic specification is modified. The first column of Table 8 shows the results of allowing the private return to schooling to vary by census year. Time-varying returns may be important, since the literature on wage inequality suggests the private returns to schooling have been changing (see, e.g., Katz and Murphy, 1992). Imposing a constant private return across years may lead to misleading estimates of external returns. In practice, allowing private returns to vary by year generates an estimated external return of 0.007 (s.e. = 0.036) with CL instruments, close to the baseline estimate in Table 7. Allowing private returns to vary by state as well as year generates a negative external return of −0.024 (s.e. = 0.039), reported in column 2. The corresponding estimates using compulsory attendance instruments, reported in the bottom panel of Table 8, are 0.021 and −0.018.

Many of the studies in Card's (1999) survey of research on the returns to schooling report IV estimates that exceed OLS estimates. To illustrate the consequences of a higher private return for estimates of external returns, Table 8 also shows estimated external returns from models imposing a private return of 0.08 or 0.09 (i.e., using $Y_{ijt} - 0.08s_i$ or $Y_{ijt} - 0.09s_i$ as the dependent variable). Not surprisingly, the estimated external returns in this case are even smaller than the baseline estimates in Table 7. With private returns of 9%, for example, the external return is estimated to be −0.018 (s.e. = 0.039) with SOB-CL instruments, and 0.010 (s.e. = 0.043) with SOB-CA instruments.

Columns 5–7 of Table 8 show external return estimates using SOR CSLs as instruments for state average schooling instead of SOB CSLs. These estimates are of interest in that, as noted in Section 3, they are less subject to bias from endogenous migration. Column 5 reports estimates corresponding to those in Table 7, while columns 6 and 7 are for models allowing private returns to vary by year and by state and year. The CL estimates are larger using SOR CSLs, while the CA estimates are smaller. The differences are not large enough, however, to suggest significant bias due to migration when using SOB-CSL instruments.[19]

6.3 ADDING 1950 AND 1990 DATA

Individual schooling must be treated as exogenous in analyses using 1950 and 1990 data since there is no quarter-of-birth information in these data sets. In principle, this may lead to biased estimates, though in practice the estimates of external returns for 1960–1980 are not sensitive to the exogeneity assumption. A second and potentially more serious problem is that schooling is a categorical variable in the 1990 Census, different from the earlier highest-grade-completed measure. We must therefore use an imputed years-of-schooling measure for 1990.

Table 9 reports estimates of external returns in the extended samples (still for men aged 40–49). Using child labor laws as instruments generates small positive or zero estimates of external returns with 1950–1980 data. These estimates are more precise than those using 1960–1980 data only. In column 1, for example, the estimated external return is 0.009 with a standard error of 0.025. As before, using compulsory attendance laws as instruments leads to somewhat larger estimates. But these estimates are less precise than those using CL instruments, and the first-stage relationships are not uniformly consistent with a causal interpretation of the correlation between these CSLs and schooling. For example, in column 1, CA9 has a larger coefficient than either CA10 or CA11.

In contrast with the results using 1950–1980 data, adding data from the 1990 Census leads to statistically significant positive estimates of external returns when child labor laws are used as instruments. Column 2 shows an external return of 0.048 with a standard error of 0.02. Allowing separate private returns by census year leads to an even larger external return of 0.074 with the CL instruments. In contrast, CA instruments do not generate significant estimates of external returns in the 1950–1990 sample. Results using SOR CSLs in the expanded samples are reported in Table 10. These show small and insignificant external returns in the 1950–1980 sample, but—as in Table 9—some of the estimates using CL instruments in the 1950–1990 sample are positive and significant.

The relatively large and significant external return estimates using CL instruments in 1950–1990 data may signal a change in the external value

---

19. Another possible source of bias in the estimates in Tables 7 and 8 is changing school quality. But school quality is associated with higher average wages, so omission of these variables cannot be responsible for the apparent lack of an external return to education. In fact, controlling for the school quality variables used by Card and Krueger (1992b) leads to more negative estimates, though also less precise, than reported in Table 7.

Table 8 2SLS ESTIMATES OF EXTERNAL RETURNS TO SCHOOLING: ADDITIONAL RESULTS FOR MEN AGED 40–49

	With State-of-Birth Instruments				With State-of-Residence Instruments		
	Private Returns Separate by Census (1)	Private Returns Separate by Census and State (2)	Private Returns =0.08 (3)	Private Returns =0.09 (4)	Baseline Estimates (5)	Private Returns Separate by Census (6)	Private Returns Separate by Census and State (7)

(a) Results Using Child Labor Laws as Instruments

External return to schooling	0.007 (0.039)	−0.024 (0.039)	−0.006 (0.038)	−0.018 (0.039)	0.048 (0.033)	0.051 (0.034)	0.015 (0.033)

First Stage for State–Year Average Schooling

CL7	0.083 (0.028)	0.080 (0.026)	0.084 (0.028)	0.084 (0.029)	0.124 (0.046)	0.123 (0.046)	0.120 (0.043)
CL8	0.104 (0.034)	0.100 (0.031)	0.107 (0.035)	0.107 (0.035)	0.158 (0.053)	0.157 (0.052)	0.154 (0.049)
CL9	0.223 (0.035)	0.210 (0.032)	0.227 (0.036)	0.227 (0.035)	0.402 (0.063)	0.399 (0.062)	0.390 (0.058)

(b) Results Using Compulsory Attendance Laws as Instruments

External return to schooling	0.021 (0.043)	−0.018 (0.043)	0.011 (0.042)	0.010 (0.043)	0.009 (0.053)	0.007 (0.054)	−0.031 (0.054)

First Stage for State–Year Average Schooling

CA9	0.125 (0.026)	0.118 (0.023)	0.128 (0.026)	0.128 (0.026)	0.164 (0.038)	0.162 (0.038)	0.155 (0.035)
CA10	0.120 (0.030)	0.112 (0.027)	0.122 (0.030)	0.122 (0.030)	0.161 (0.059)	0.159 (0.058)	0.151 (0.055)
CA11	0.141 (0.037)	0.134 (0.034)	0.143 (0.038)	0.143 (0.038)	0.207 (0.055)	0.205 (0.054)	0.199 (0.051)

(c) OLS Estimates

External return to schooling	0.079 (0.016)	0.044 (0.016)	0.069 (0.017)	0.063 (0.017)	0.073 (0.016)	0.079 (0.016)	0.044 (0.016)

Notes: Standard errors corrected for state–year clustering are reported in parentheses. All entries are estimates of returns to schooling, using dummies for child labor laws or compulsory attendance laws as excluded instruments. The data are from the Census IPUMS. The sample is restricted to white males aged 40–49 in the Census year. All regressions contain individual-education, Census-year, year-of-birth, state-of-birth, and state-of-residence main effects. The first four columns use state-of-birth child labor laws or compulsory attendance laws as instruments, which are assigned according to the laws in effect in the individual's state of birth when he was 14. The last four columns use state-of-residence child labor laws or compulsory attendance laws as instruments, which are assigned according to the laws in effect in the individual's state of residence 30 years ago. The sample size for all columns is 609,852.

Table 9 2SLS ESTIMATES: ADDITIONAL SAMPLES WITH STATE-OF-BIRTH INSTRUMENTS FOR MEN AGED 40–49

	Baseline Results		Separate Private Returns			
			By Census		By Census and State	
	50–80 (1)	50–90 (2)	50–80 (3)	50–90 (4)	50–80 (5)	50–90 (6)
(a) Results Using Child Labor Laws as Instruments						
External return	0.009 (0.025)	0.048 (0.019)	0.023 (0.025)	0.074 (0.019)	−0.034 (0.025)	0.041 (0.021)
First Stage for State–Year Average Schooling						
CL7	0.173 (0.024)	0.165 (0.019)	0.170 (0.023)	0.162 (0.019)	0.158 (0.020)	0.145 (0.016)
CL8	0.126 (0.036)	0.144 (0.027)	0.123 (0.035)	0.139 (0.027)	0.113 (0.031)	0.121 (0.022)
CL9	0.278 (0.039)	0.333 (0.026)	0.275 (0.039)	0.327 (0.026)	0.250 (0.034)	0.280 (0.022)
(b) Results Using Compulsory Attendance Laws as Instruments						
External return	0.040 (0.038)	0.0006 (0.027)	0.053 (0.039)	0.038 (0.027)	0.017 (0.038)	−0.008 (0.029)
First Stage for State–Year Average Schooling						
CA9	0.133 (0.028)	0.172 (0.019)	0.130 (0.027)	0.168 (0.019)	0.118 (0.023)	0.143 (0.015)
CA10	0.106 (0.037)	0.167 (0.028)	0.105 (0.036)	0.164 (0.027)	0.096 (0.031)	0.139 (0.022)
CA11	0.096 (0.042)	0.182 (0.029)	0.095 (0.041)	0.178 (0.028)	0.087 (0.036)	0.154 (0.023)
(c) OLS Estimates						
External return	0.061 (0.009)	0.072 (0.006)	0.076 (0.009)	0.094 (0.007)	0.039 (0.008)	0.057 (0.004)
N	626,510	729,695	626,510	729,695	626,510	729,695

Notes: Standard errors corrected for state–year clustering are reported in parentheses. Estimates of external returns to schooling use dummies for child labor and compulsory attendance laws as excluded instruments. Individual schooling is treated as exogenous. The sample is restricted to white males aged 40–49 in the Census year. All regressions contain individual-schooling, Census-year, year-of-birth, state-of-birth, and state-of-residence main effects. Compulsory schooling laws are assigned according to the laws in effect in the individual's state of birth when he was 14.

TABLE 10 2SLS ESTIMATES: ADDITIONAL SAMPLES WITH STATE-OF-RESIDENCE INSTRUMENTS FOR MEN AGED 40–49

	Baseline Results		Separate Private Returns by Census		Separate Private Returns by Census and State	
	50–80 (1)	50–90 (2)	50–80 (3)	50–90 (4)	50–80 (5)	50–90 (6)
(a) Results Using Child Labor Laws as Instruments						
External return	0.016 (0.028)	0.044 (0.022)	0.024 (0.028)	0.054 (0.022)	−0.007 (0.026)	0.016 (0.023)
First Stage for State–Year Average Schooling						
CL7	0.215 (0.035)	0.185 (0.031)	0.213 (0.035)	0.183 (0.031)	0.202 (0.031)	0.174 (0.027)
CL8	0.142 (0.054)	0.128 (0.045)	0.142 (0.054)	0.127 (0.044)	0.134 (0.049)	0.116 (0.039)
CL9	0.430 (0.068)	0.452 (0.048)	0.426 (0.067)	0.449 (0.047)	0.401 (0.061)	0.409 (0.043)
(b) Results Using Compulsory Attendance Laws as Instruments						
External return	0.007 (0.045)	−0.0004 (0.032)	0.014 (0.046)	0.020 (0.031)	−0.017 (0.043)	−0.029 (0.033)
First Stage for State–Year Schooling						
CA9	0.192 (0.043)	0.247 (0.030)	0.190 (0.042)	0.244 (0.030)	0.177 (0.038)	0.218 (0.026)
CA10	0.147 (0.075)	0.198 (0.056)	0.145 (0.074)	0.195 (0.056)	0.137 (0.067)	0.171 (0.049)
CA11	0.145 (0.063)	0.254 (0.046)	0.143 (0.063)	0.251 (0.045)	0.136 (0.057)	0.229 (0.040)
(c) OLS Estimates						
External return	0.061 (0.010)	0.072 (0.008)	0.076 (0.010)	0.094 (0.007)	0.038 (0.009)	0.057 (0.007)
N	626,511	729,625	626,511	729,625	626,511	729,625

Notes: Standard errors corrected for state–year clustering are reported in parentheses. Estimates of external returns to schooling use dummies for child labor and compulsory attendance laws as excluded instruments. Individual schooling is treated as exogenous. The sample is restricted to white males aged 40–49 in the Census year. All regressions contain individual-schooling, Census-year, year-of-birth, state-of-birth, and state-of-residence main effects. Compulsory schooling laws are assigned according to the laws in effect in the individual's state of residence 30 years ago.

of human capital. But this result could also reflect the switch to a categorical schooling variable in 1990. The econometric discussion in Section 3 highlights the possibility of spurious external-return estimates when the effect of individual schooling is poorly controlled. Measurement error in the 1990 schooling variable could generate a problem of this type.[20]

To check whether measurement problems could be responsible for the 1950–1990 results, we assigned mean values from the 1980 Census to a categorical schooling variable available in the 1960, 1970, and 1980 Censuses. This variable is similar to the categorical 1990 variable. We then reestimated external returns in 1960–1980, treating the imputed individual schooling variable as exogenous.[21] This leads to markedly larger estimates of external returns. For example, using CL instruments to estimate external returns with imputed schooling data generates an external return of 0.024 instead of the estimate of 0.003 reported in Table 7. Similarly, using CA instruments generates an external return of 0.034 instead of 0.017 with the better-measured schooling variable. This suggests that the higher external returns estimated with 1990 data are due to changes in the education variable in 1990.

6.4 RESULTS FOR MEN AGED 30–39

The last set of results is for men in their 30s. Since this group has a steep age–earnings profile, quarter of birth is confounded with age effects (Angrist and Krueger, 1991). Individual schooling is therefore treated as exogenous in this younger sample. With individual schooling exogenous, 1950 Census data can be included. 1990 data are omitted, however, because of the problems discussed above.

Columns 1–3 of Table 11 reports results for men aged 30–39 in 1950–1980, while results for a larger sample pooling men aged 30–49 appear in columns 4–6. The top panel shows results using CL instruments, while the bottom panel is for CA instruments (coded as SOB CSLs). The first-stage relationships are also reported in the table. They show significant effects of CSLs on the average schooling of men aged 30–39, very similar to those for men aged 40–49 reported in the bottom panel of Table 7. The baseline estimate using CL instruments in the younger sample, reported in column 1, is close to 0, with a standard error of 0.023. CA instruments

---

20. Note, however, that the measurement error in the 1990 schooling variable is not classical. Kane, Rouse, and Staiger (1999) discuss the implications of nonclassical measurement error for IV estimates. A detailed description of the schooling variables used here appears in Appendix B.
21. This exercise uses the IPUMS variable EDUCREC, which provides a uniform categorical schooling measure for the 1940–1990 Censuses.

Table 11 2SLS ESTIMATES OF EXTERNAL RETURNS TO SCHOOLING, 1950–1980

	Aged 30–39			Aged 30–49		
	Baseline Results (1)	Separate Private Returns by Census (2)	Separate Private Returns by Census and State (3)	Baseline Results (4)	Separate Private Returns by Census (5)	Separate Private Returns by Census and State (6)
(a) Results Using Child Labor Laws as Instruments						
External return	0.002 (0.023)	0.028 (0.022)	−0.018 (0.022)	0.011 (0.020)	0.030 (0.020)	−0.007 (0.023)
First Stage for State–Year Average Schooling						
CL7	0.070 (0.030)	0.069 (0.029)	0.067 (0.024)	0.128 (0.023)	0.125 (0.022)	0.116 (0.019)
CL8	0.137 (0.037)	0.133 (0.037)	0.123 (0.030)	0.136 (0.032)	0.132 (0.032)	0.121 (0.040)
CL9	0.284 (0.037)	0.278 (0.037)	0.254 (0.031)	0.285 (0.030)	0.279 (0.030)	0.252 (0.024)
(b) Results Using Compulsory Attendance Laws as Instruments						
External return	−0.006 (0.028)	0.017 (0.027)	−0.030 (0.026)	0.022 (0.027)	0.041 (0.027)	−0.006 (0.030)
First Stage for State–Year Schooling						
CA9	0.202 (0.027)	0.198 (0.027)	0.180 (0.022)	0.162 (0.025)	0.158 (0.024)	0.142 (0.027)
CA10	0.156 (0.032)	0.153 (0.032)	0.137 (0.026)	0.127 (0.029)	0.125 (0.028)	0.111 (0.020)
CA11	0.230 (0.039)	0.225 (0.039)	0.205 (0.032)	0.161 (0.035)	0.157 (0.034)	0.142 (0.040)
(c) OLS Estimates						
External return	0.081 (0.009)	0.095 (0.009)	0.054 (0.009)	0.071 (0.009)	0.087 (0.009)	0.048 (0.009)
N	812,864	812,864	812,864	1,439,375	1,439,375	1,439,375

Notes: The table reports results for men aged 30–39 and a pooled sample of men aged 30–49. Standard errors corrected for state–year clustering are reported in parentheses. Estimates of external returns to schooling use dummies for child labor and compulsory attendance laws as excluded instruments. Individual schooling is treated as exogenous. All regressions contain individual-schooling, Census-year, year-of-birth, state-of-birth, and state-of-residence main effects as well as a quartic function of potential experience. Compulsory schooling laws are assigned according to the laws in effect in the individual's state of birth when he was 14.

generate a less precisely estimated external return of −0.006. Estimates that allow private returns to vary by year are larger, but those from models allowing private return to vary by state and year are negative. Pooling age groups leads to similar estimates. Overall, the results for men aged 30–39 are consistent with the results for men in their 40s, showing no evidence of significant external returns. Once again, the estimated confidence intervals exclude returns above 5–6% percent.

7. Concluding Remarks

The returns to education are important for both economic policy and economic theory. A large literature in labor economics reports estimates of private returns to education on the order of 6–10%. However, private returns may be only part of the story. With positive external returns to education, private returns underestimate the economic value of schooling. On the other hand, if education plays a major signaling role, the total economic value of schooling may be less than suggested by private returns.

This paper exploits potentially exogenous variation in average schooling caused by changes in compulsory schooling laws in U.S. states. Census data from 1960–1980 generate statistically insignificant external-return estimates around 1% (mostly ranging from −1% to 3%). Adding data from 1950 leads to somewhat more precise estimates, without changing the basic pattern. Regressions using data from the 1990 Census, in contrast, generate statistically significant estimates of external returns of 4% or more with one set of instruments. This may reflect the increased importance of human capital after 1980. Further investigation, however, suggests that the larger estimates in samples with 1990 data are likely due to changes in the schooling variable in the 1990 Census.

On balance, the analysis here offers little evidence for sizable external returns to education, at least over the range of variation induced by changing CSLs. Moreover, while some of the estimates are positive, they are nowhere near large enough to rationalize the cross-country association between average education and average income documented in Figure 1 or even the cross-state (OLS) association documented in Table 2.

Some final caveats are in order. First, the standard errors associated with the estimates reported here lead to confidence intervals that include external returns of, say, 1–3%. External returns of this magnitude are sufficient to justify significant public subsidies for education. Second, our strategy identifies local effects, missing external returns that raise wages nationwide. Finally, our estimates are driven by changes in secondary schooling and not changes in higher education. Weak external returns to secondary school do not rule out the possibility of external returns to schooling at higher levels.

Appendix A. Mathematical Details

A.1 DERIVATION OF EQUATION (14)

Rewrite equation (13) as follows:

$$Y_{ij} = \mu^* + \pi_0 \tau_i + (\pi_0 + \pi_1)\bar{S}_j + \xi_i,$$

where $\tau_i \equiv s_i - \bar{S}_j$. Since τ_i and $\bar{S}_j$ are uncorrelated by construction, we have

$$\rho_1 = \pi_0 + \pi_1,$$

$$\pi_0 = \frac{C(\tau_i, Y_{ij})}{V(\tau_i)}.$$

Simplifying the second line,

$$\pi_0 = \frac{C((s_i - \bar{S}_j), Y_{ij})}{V(s_i) - V(\bar{S}_j)}$$

$$= \left(\frac{C(s_i, Y_{ij})}{V(s_i)}\right)\left(\frac{V(s_i)}{V(s_i) - V(\bar{S}_j)}\right) - \left(\frac{C(\bar{S}_j, Y_{ij})}{V(\bar{S}_j)}\right)\left(\frac{V(\bar{S}_j)}{V(s_i) - V(\bar{S}_j)}\right)$$

$$= \rho_0 \phi + \rho_1(1 - \phi) = \rho_1 + \phi(\rho_0 - \rho_1),$$

where $\phi \equiv V(s_i)/[V(s_i) - V(\bar{S}_j)]$. Solving for π_1, we have

$$\pi_1 = \rho_1 - \pi_0 = \phi(\rho_1 - \rho_0).$$

A.2 HOW TO INSTRUMENT FOR INDIVIDUAL SCHOOLING?

To discuss this issue more formally, consider a simplified version of the random-coefficient model (12), again with no covariates and no time dimension. Assume also that a single binary instrument is available to estimate γ_1, say z_i, a dummy for having been born in a state with restrictive CSLs. Finally, suppose we adjust for the effects of s_i by subtracting $\gamma_2^* s_i$, where γ_2^* is some average of γ_{2i}. In other words, subtract $\gamma_2^* s_i$ from both sides of (12) to obtain

$$Y_{ij} - \gamma_2^* s_i \equiv \tilde{Y}_{ij}$$
$$= \mu + \gamma_1 \bar{S}_j + [u_j + \epsilon_i + (\gamma_{2i} - \gamma_2^*)s_i]. \tag{15}$$

What value of γ_2^* allows us to use z_i as an instrument for $\bar{S}_j$ in (15) to obtain a consistent estimate of γ_1? The instrumental variables estimand in this case, γ_1^{IV}, is given by the Wald formula:

$$\gamma_1^{IV} = \frac{E[\tilde{Y}_{ij} \mid z_i = 1] - E[\tilde{Y}_{ij} \mid z_i = 0]}{E[\bar{S}_j \mid z_i = 1] - E[\bar{S}_j \mid z_i = 0]}$$

$$= \gamma_1 + \left(\frac{E[\gamma_{2i} s_i \mid z_i = 1] - E[\gamma_{2i} s_i \mid z_i = 0]}{E[s_i \mid z_i = 1] - E[s_i \mid z_i = 0]} - \gamma_2^* \right)$$

$$\left(\frac{E[s_i \mid z_i = 1] - E[s_i \mid z_i = 0]}{E[\bar{S}_j \mid z_i = 1] - E[\bar{S}_j \mid z_i = 0]} \right).$$

This shows that γ_1^{IV} estimates external returns to education consistently (i.e., equals γ_1) if the adjustment for individual schooling uses the coefficient

$$\gamma_2^* = \frac{E[\gamma_{2i} s_i \mid z_i = 1] - E[\gamma_{2i} s_i \mid z_i = 0]}{E[s_i \mid z_i = 1] - E[s_i \mid z_i = 0]}$$
$$= \frac{E[Y_{ij} - \gamma_1 \bar{S}_j \mid z_i = 1] - E[Y_{ij} - \gamma_1 \bar{S}_j \mid z_i = 0]}{E[s_i \mid z_i = 1] - E[s_i \mid z_i = 0]}. \tag{16}$$

In other words, the adjustment for effects of s_i should use the (population) IV estimate of *private returns* generated by z_i, once we subtract the effect of human-capital externalities.

Of course, we cannot use z_i to estimate both private and external returns, even though (16) appears to require this. But instruments based on quarter of birth can be used to estimate γ_2^*. Let q_i denote a single instrument derived from quarter of birth, say a dummy for first-quarter births. Since q_i is orthogonal to $\bar{S}_j$, we have

$$\gamma_q^* = \frac{E[Y_{ij} \mid q_i = 1] - E[Y_{ij} \mid q_i = 0]}{E[s_i \mid z_i = 1] - E[s_i \mid z_i = 0]} = \frac{E[\gamma_{2i} s_i \mid q_i = 1] - E[\gamma_{2i} s_i \mid q_i = 0]}{E[s_i \mid q_i = 1] - E[s_i \mid q_i = 0]}.$$

If $\gamma_q^* = \gamma_2^*$, the quarter-of-birth instrument provides an appropriate adjustment for private returns in (15).[22]

To see why γ_q^* should be close to γ_2^*, let $w_i(s_i) \equiv \gamma_{2i} s_i$, and note that $w_i'(s_i)$ is the causal effect of schooling on i's (log) wages with $\bar{S}_j$ fixed [see equation (12)]. Also, let s_{1i} denote the schooling i would get if $z_i = 1$, and let s_{0i} denote the schooling i would get if $z_i = 0$.[23] Angrist, Graddy, and Imbens (1995) show that

$$\gamma_2^* = \frac{\int E[w_i'(\sigma) \mid s_{1i} \geq \sigma > s_{0i}] P[s_{1i} \geq \sigma > s_{0i}] \, d\sigma}{\int P[s_{1i} \geq \sigma > s_{0i}] \, d\sigma}, \tag{17}$$

which is an average derivative with weighting function $P[s_{1i} \geq \sigma > s_{0i}] = P[s_i \leq \sigma \mid z_i = 0] - P[s_i \leq \sigma \mid z_i = 1]$. In other words, IV estimation using z_i produces an average of the derivative $w_i'(\sigma)$, with weight given to each value σ in proportion to the instrument-induced change in the cumulative distribution function (CDF) of schooling at that point. Similarly, γ_q^* is a CDF-weighted average with s_{1i} and s_{0i} defined to correspond to the values of q_i.

CSL instruments and quarter-of-birth instruments both estimate individual returns for people whose schooling is affected by compulsory schooling laws—i.e., individuals who would have otherwise dropped out of school. So the weighting functions $P[s_i \leq \sigma \mid z_i = 0] - P[s_i \leq \sigma \mid z_i = 1]$ and $P[s_i \leq \sigma \mid q_i = 0] - P[s_i \leq \sigma \mid q_i = 1]$ should be similar. In fact, Figure 2 shows that, like quarter-of-birth instruments, CSLs changed the distribution of schooling primarily in the 8–12 range. This suggests that γ_q^* and γ_2^* capture similar features of the causal relationship between individual schooling and earnings.

Appendix B. Data Sources and Methods

B.1 MICRO DATA

The paper uses data from the 1950, 1960, 1970, 1980, and 1990 PUMS files. Census data were taken from the IPUMS system (Ruggles and Sobek, 1997). The files used are as follows:

22. In practice, we have more than one CSL instrument, so it may be possible to use CSLs to instrument s_i and $\bar{S}_{jt}$ simultaneously. Note, however, that because of the group structure of $\bar{S}_{jt}$ and the CSL instruments, the projection of s_i on the CSL instruments is almost identical to the projection of $\bar{S}_{jt}$ on the CSL instruments. This is not a problem with quarter-of-birth instruments, since they are independent of $\bar{S}_{jt}$.
23. These potential schooling choices can be described in terms of the theoretical framework. Suppose, for example, that $\eta(s_i) = \bar{\eta}$ and the CSL instrument changes discount rates from ψ_{0i} or ψ_{1i} as in Card (1995). Using (8), individual schooling choices would be $s_{0i} = \nu \theta_i \bar{\eta} / \psi_{0i}$ and $s_{1i} = \nu \theta_i \bar{\eta} / \psi_{1i}$.

1950 General (1/330 sample)
1960 General (1% sample)
1970 Form 1 State (1% sample)
1970 Form 2 State (1% sample)
1980 5% State (A Sample)
1990 1% unweighted (a 1% random self-weighted sample created by IPUMS)

Our initial extract included all U.S.-born white men aged 21–58. The 1950 sample is limited to *sample-line* individuals (i.e., those with long-form responses). Our sample excludes men born or living in Alaska or Hawaii. Estimates were weighted by the IPUMS weighting variable SLWT, adjusted in the case of 1970 to reflect the fact that we use two files for that year (i.e., divided by 2). The weights are virtually constant within years, but vary slightly to reflect minor adjustments by IPUMS to improve estimation of population totals.

The schooling variable was calculated as follows: For 1950–1980, the variable is HIGRADED (General), the IPUMS recode of highest grade enrolled and grade completed into highest grade completed. For the 1990 Census, which has only categorical schooling, we assigned group means for white men from Park (1994, Table 5), who uses a one-time overlap questionnaire from the February 1990 CPS to construct averages for essentially the same Census categories. This generates a years of schooling variable roughly comparable across censuses (GRADCOMP). Finally, we censored GRADCOMP at 17, since this is the highest grade completed in the 1950 census. We call this variable GRADCAP.

The dependent variable is log weekly wage, calculated by dividing annual wages by weeks worked, where wages refer to wage and salary income only. Wage topcodes vary across censuses. We imposed a uniform topcode as follows. Wage data for every year for the full extract of white men aged 21–58 were censored at the 98th percentile for that year. The censoring value is the 98th percentile times 1.5. Weeks worked are grouped in the 1960 and 1970 Censuses. We assigned means to 1960 categorical values using 1950 averages, and we assigned means to 1970 categorical values using 1980 averages.

The analyses in the paper, including first-stage relationships, are limited to men with positive weekly wages. Analyses using 1960–1980 data are limited to men born 1910–1919 in the 1960 Census, 1920–1929 in the 1970 Census, and 1930–1939 in the 1980 Census. Since year-of-birth variables are not available in the 1950 and 1990 Censuses, analyses using those data sets are limited to men aged 40–49.

B.2 CALCULATION OF AVERAGE SCHOOLING

Average schooling is the mean of GRADCAP by state and census year for all U.S.-born persons aged 16–64. For 1970, we used only the Form 2 State sample (a 1% file), and for 1980 we used a 1% random subsample, drawn from the 5% State (A Sample) using the IPUMS SUBSAMP variable. The SLWT weighting variable was adjusted to reflect the fact that this leaves a 1% sample for each year. The averages use data excluding Alaska and Hawaii (residence or birthplace). Average schooling was calculated for individuals with positive weeks worked and weighted by the product of SLWT and weeks worked. Categorical weeks worked variables were imputed as described above.

B.3 MATCH TO CSLs AND STATE AVERAGE SCHOOLING

The CSLs in force in each year from 1914 to 1972 were measured using the five variables described in Section 4 of this appendix. For each individual in the microdata extract, we calculated the approximate year the person was age 14 using age on census day (not year of birth, which is not available in 1950 and 1990). The CSLs in force in that year in the person's state of birth were then assigned to that person. State average schooling was matched to individual state of residence and census year.

B.4 CSL VARIABLES

Data on CSLs were collected and organized by Ms. Xuanhui Ng, in consultation with us.

B.4.1 Sources The sources are collected in Table 12, in which

enroll_age is the maximum age by which a child has to enroll at school,
drop_age is the minimum age a child is allowed to drop out of school,
req_sch is the minimum years of schooling a child has to obtain before dropping out,
work_age is the minimum age at which a child can get a work permit,
work_sch is the minimum years of schooling a child needs for obtaining a work permit.

Source abbreviations are given with the references (Section B.5).

B.4.2 Methods Data were drawn from the sources listed in Table 12. In some cases sources were ambiguous or there were conflicts between sources for the same year. For resolution, we looked for patterns across years that seemed to make sense, and tried to minimize the number of

Table 12 SOURCES OF CSL DATA

Year	enroll_age	drop_age	req_sch	work_age	work_sch
1914	Commissioner	Schmidt Commissioner	Schmidt	Schmidt	Schmidt
1917	Biennial	Biennial	Biennial	Biennial	Biennial
1921	Chart1–1921	Chart1–1921	Chart1–1921	Chart2–1921	Chart2–1921
1924	Chart1–1924	Chart1–1924	Chart1–1924	Chart2–1924	Chart2–1924
1929	M	#197	M	#197	#197
1935	Deffenbaugh	Deffenbaugh; Schmidt	Deffenbaugh; Schmidt	Deffenbaugh; Schmidt	Deffenbaugh; Schmidt
1939	Umbeck	Umbeck	M	M	M
1946	SCLS-1946	SCLS-1946	SCLS-1946	SCLS-1946	SCLS-1946
1950	SCLS-1949	SCLS-1949	SCLS-1949	SCLS-1949	SCLS-1949
1954	Keesecker-1950	Keesecker-1950	Keesecker-1950	Keesecker-1950	Keesecker-1950
1959	Keesecker-1955	Keesecker-1955	Keesecker-1955	M	Keesecker-1955
	SCLS-1960	SCLS-1960	SCLS-1960	SLCS-1960	SLCS-1960
	Umbeck	Umbeck	Umbeck		Umbeck
1965	SLCS-1965	SLCS-1965	SLCS-1965	SCLS-1965	SLCS-1965
	Steinhilber	Steinhilber	Steinhilber	LLS	Steinhilber

source changes. In the table, M denotes missing, i.e., we found no source or reliable information for that variable in that year. Missing data were imputed by bringing older data forward. Intersource years were imputed and the data set expanded by bringing older data forward to make a complete set of five CSL laws for each year from 1914 to 1965.

The imputed data set contains either numerical entries or NR, indicating we found laws that appeared to impose no restriction (e.g., 6 years schooling required for a work permit, so work_sch = 6, but a work permit available at any age, so work_age = NR). The algorithm for calculating required years of schooling for dropout and the required years of schooling for a work permit handles NR codes as follows:

If req_sch = NR, then req_sch = 0;
If enroll_age = NR or drop_age = NR, then CA = max(0, req_sch);
If enroll_age ≠ NR and drop_age ≠ NR then CA = max(drop_age-enroll_age, req_sch).
If work_age = NR, then work_age = 0;
If work_sch = NR, then work_sch = 0;
If enroll_age = NR then CL = max(0, work_sch);
If enroll_age ≠ NR then CL = max(work_age-enroll_age, work_sch).

We coded a general literacy requirement without a grade or age requirements as NR. We coded a grade requirement of "elementary school" as 6, even though this was distinct from sixth grade in some sources (our dummies would group these requirements anyway).

B.5 REFERENCES FOR TABLE 12

[Deffenbaugh] Deffenbaugh, W. S., and W. W. Keesecker. *Compulsory School Attendance Laws and Their Administration.* U.S. Department of Interior, Office of Education, Bulletin 1935, No. 4. Washington: U.S. GPO (1935).

[Keesecker-1950] Keesecker, W. W., and A. C. Allen. *Compulsory School Attendance and Minimum Educational Requirements in the United States, 1950.* Federal Security Agency, Office of Education, Circular No. 278 (September 1950).

[Keesecker-1955] ——, and ——. *Compulsory School Attendance and Minimum Educational Requirements in the United States.* U.S. Department of Health, Education and Welfare, Office of Education, Circular No. 440. Washington: U.S. Department of Health, Education and Welfare (March 1955).

[Schmidt] Schmidt, S. R., School quality, compulsory education laws, and the growth of American high school attendance, 1915–35. MIT. PhD Dissertation (1996).

[Steinhilber] Steinhilber, A. W., and Sokolowski, C. J. *State Law on Compulsory Attendance.* U.S. Department of Health, Education and Welfare, Office of Education, Circular 793. Washington: U.S. GPO (1966).

[Umbeck] Umbeck, N. *State Legislation on School Attendance and Related Matters—School Census and Child Labor.* U.S. Department of Health, Education and Welfare, Office of Education, Circular No. 615. Washington: U.S. GPO (January 1960).

[Biennial] U.S. Department of the Interior, Bureau of Education. *Biennial Survey of Education 1916–18.* Bulletin 1919, No. 90 (1921).

[Commissioner] U.S. Department of the Interior, Office of Education. *Report of the Commissioner of Education for the Year Ended June 30, 1917,* Vol. 2. Washington: U.S. GPO, p. 69.

[LLS] U.S. Department of Labor, Bureau of Labor Standards. *Summary of State Child Labor Laws.* Labor Law Series No. 3-A. Washington: U.S. Department of Labor (September 1966).

[SCLS-1946] U.S. Department of Labor, Division of Labor Standards. *State Child-Labor Standards: A State-by-State Summary of Laws Affecting the Employment of Minors under 18 Years of Age.* Child Labor Series No. 2. Washington: U.S. GPO (July 1946).

[SCLS-1949] ———. *State Child-Labor Standards: A State-by-State Summary of Laws Affecting the Employment of Minors under 18 Years of Age.* Bulletin 114. Washington: U.S. GPO (September 1949).

[SCLS-1960] ———. *State Child-Labor Standards: A State-by-State Summary of Laws Affecting the Employment of Minors Under 18 Years of Age.* Bulletin 158 (Revised 1960). Washington: U.S. GPO (May 1960).

[SCLS-1965] ———. *State Child-Labor Standards: A State-by-State Summary of Laws Affecting the Employment of Minors Under 18 Years of Age.* Bulletin 158 (Revised 1965). Washington: U.S. GPO (September 1965).

[Chart1-1921] U.S. Department of Labor, Children's Bureau. *State Child-Labor Standards, January 1, 1921.* Chart Series No. 1. Washington: U.S. GPO.

[Chart1-1924] ———. *State Child-Labor Standards, January 1, 1924.* Chart Series No. 1. Washington: U.S. GPO.

[Chart2-1921] ———. *State Compulsory School Attendance Standards Affecting the Employment of Minors, January 1, 1921.* Chart Series No. 2. Washington: U.S. GPO.

[Chart2-1924] ———. *State Compulsory School Attendance Standards Affecting the Employment of Minors, January 1, 1924.* Chart Series No. 2. Washington: U.S. GPO.

[#197] ———. *Child Labor Facts and Figures.* Bulletin 197. Washington: U.S. GPO (October 1929).

REFERENCES

Acemoglu, D. (1996). A microfoundation for social increasing returns in human capital accumulation. *Quarterly Journal of Economics* 111(3):779–804.

———. (1997a). Training and innovation in an imperfect labor market. *Review of Economic Studies* 64:445–464.

———. (1997b). Matching, heterogeneity and the evolution of income distribution. *Journal of Economic Growth* 2:61–92.

———. (1998). Why do new technologies complement skills? Directed technical change and wage inequality. *Quarterly Journal of Economics* 113(4):1055–1089.

———. (1999). Changes in unemployment and wage inequality: An alternative theory and some evidence. *American Economic Review* 89:1259–1278.

Angrist, J., K. Graddy, and G. Imbens. (1995). Nonparametric demand analysis with an application to the demand for fish. Cambridge, MA: National Bureau of Economic Research. NBER Technical Working Paper 178, April. *Review of Economic Studies*, forthcoming.

———, and G. W. Imbens. (1995). Two-stage least squares estimates of average causal effects in models with variable treatment intensity. *Journal of the American Statistical Association* 90(430):431–442.

———, and A. B. Krueger. (1991). Does compuslory school attendance affect schooling and earnings?" *Quarterly Journal of Economics* 106:979–1014.

———, and ———. (1995). Split-sample instrumental variables estimates of the return to schooling. *Journal of Business and Economic Statistics* 13:225–235.

Bairoch, P. (1988). *Cities and Economic Development: From the Dawn of History to the Present*, translated by Christopher Braider. Chicago: University of Chicago Press.

Barro, R. J., and J.-W. Lee. (1993). International comparisons of educational attainment. *Journal of Monetary Economics* 32:363–394.

———, and X. Sala-i-Martin. (1995). *Economic Growth*. New York: McGraw-Hill.

Benabou, R. (1996). Heterogeneity, stratification and growth: Macroeconomic implications of community structure and school finance. *American Economic Review* 86(3):584–609.

Benhabib, J., and M. M. Spiegel. (1994). The role of human capital in economic development: Evidence from aggregate cross-country data. *Journal of Monetary Economics* 34:143–173.

Bils, M., and P. J. Klenow. (1998). Does schooling cause growth or the other way around? Cambridge, MA: National Bureau of Economic Research. NBER Working Paper 6393.

Borjas, G. (1992). Ethnic capital and intergenerational mobility. *Quarterly Journal of Economics* 107:123–150.

Bound, J., D. Jaeger, and R. Baker. (1995). Problems with instrumental variables estimation when the correlation between the instruments and the endogenous explanatory variable is weak. *Journal of the American Statistical Association* 90:443–450.

Brock, W., and S. Durlauf. (1999). Interactions-based models. Forthcoming in *The Handbook of Econometrics*, J. Heckman and E. Leamer (eds.). Amsterdam: Elsevier.

Card, D. E. (1995). Earnings, schooling and ability revisited. In *Research in Labor Economics*, S. W. Polachek (ed.). Greenwich, CT: JAI Press.

———. (1999). The causal effect of education on earnings. In *The Handbook of Labor Economics*, Vol. III, O. Ashenfelter and D. Card (eds.). Amsterdam: Elsevier.

———, and Alan Krueger. (1992a). School quality and black–white relative earnings: A direct assessment. *Quarterly Journal of Economics* 107:151–200.

———, and ———. (1992b). Does school quality matter? Returns to education and the characteristics of public schools in the United States. *Journal of Political Economy* 100:1–40.

Chamberlain, G., and G. W. Imbens. (1996). Hierarchical Bayes models with many instrumental variables. Cambridge, MA: National Bureau of Economic Research. Technical Paper 204, September.

Edwards, L. (1978). An empirical analysis of compulsory schooling legislation. *Journal of Law and Economics* 21:203–222.

Ehrenberg, R., and A. Marcus. (1982). Minimum wages and teenagers enrollment—employment outcomes. *Journal of Human Resources* 27:39–58.

Foster, A., and M. Rosenzweig. (1996). Technical change in human capital return and investments: Evidence from the Green Revolution. *American Economic Review* 86:931–953.

Glaeser, E. L., H. Kallal, J. Scheinkman, and A. Shleifer. (1992). Growth in Cities. *Journal of Political Economy* 100(6):1126–1152.

Goldin, C. (1998). America's graduation from high school: The evolution and spread of secondary schooling in the twentieth century. *Journal of Economic History* 58:345–74.

Hall, R., and C. I. Jones. (1999). Why do some countries produce so much more output per worker than others? *Quarterly Journal of Economics* 114:83–116.

Hausman, J. (1978). Specification tests in econometrics. *Econometrica* 46:1251–1271.

Jacobs, J. (1970). *The Economy of Cities*. New York: Vintage Books.

Jaffe, A. B., M. Trajtenberg, and R. Henderson. (1993). Geographic localization of knowledge spillovers as evidenced by patent citations. *Quarterly Journal of Economics* 108:577–598.

Kane, T., C. Rouse, and D. Staiger. (1999). Estimating returns to schooling when schooling is misreported. Cambridge, MA: National Bureau of Economic Research. NBER Working Paper 7235, July.

Katz, L. F., and K. M. Murphy. (1992). Changes in relative wages, 1963–1987: Supply and demand factors. *Quarterly Journal of Economics* 107(1):35–78.

Krueger, A., and M. Lindahl. (1999). Education for growth in Sweden and the world. Cambridge, MA: National Bureau of Economic Research. NBER Working Paper 7190, June.

Lang, K. (1993). Ability bias, discount rate bias and the return to education. Department of Economics, Boston University. Mimeo.

———, and D. Kropp. (1986). Human capital versus sorting: The effects of compulsory attendance laws. *Quarterly Journal of Economics* 101:609–624.

Lucas, R. (1988). On the mechanics of economic development. *Journal of Monetary Economics* 22:3–42.

Mankiw, N. G., D. Romer, and D. N. Weil. (1992). A contribution to the empirics of economic growth. *Quarterly Journal of Economics* 107:407–437.

Margo, R. A. (1990). *Race and Schooling in the South: 1880–1950*. Chicago: University of Chicago Press.

———, and T. A. Finegan. (1996). Compulsory schooling legislation and school attendance in turn-of-the-century America: A "natural experiment" approach. *Economics Letters* 53:103–110.

Marshall, A. (1961). *Principles of Economics*. London: MacMillan, for the Royal Economic Society.

Moretti, E. (1999). Estimating the external return to education: Evidence from repeated cross-sectional and longitudinal data. Department of Economics, University of California, Berkeley. Mimeo.
Moulton, B. R. (1986). Random group effects and the precision of regression estimates. *Journal of Econometrics* 32:385–397.
Murphy, K., A. Shleifer, and R. Vishny. (1991). The allocation of talent: The implications for growth. *Quartelry Journal of Economics* 106:503–530.
Nelson, R., and E. Phelps. (1966). Investment in humans, technological diffusion and economic growth. *American Economic Association Papers and Proceedings* 56:69–75.
Park, J. H. (1994). Estimation of sheepskin effects and returns to schooling using the old and new CPS measures of educational attainment. Working Paper 338. Princeton Industrial Relations Section, December.
Rauch, J. E. (1993). Productivity gains from geographic concentration of human capital: Evidence from the cities. *Journal of Urban Economics* 34:380–400.
Romer, P. M. (1990). Endogenous technological change. *Journal of Political Economy* 98:S71–S102.
Ruggles, S., and M. Sobek. (1997). *Integrated Public Use Microdata Series Version 2.0, Volume 1: User's Guide*. Historical Census Projects, University of Minnesota, Department of History.
Schultz, T. (1967). *The Economic Value Education*. New York: Columbia University Press.
Schmidt, S. (1996). School quality, compulsory education laws, and the growth of American high school attendance, 1915–1935. PhD Dissertation. MIT.
Spence, M. (1973). Job market signalling. *Quarterly Journal of Economics* 87:355–374.
Staiger, D., and J. H. Stock. (1997). Instrumental variables regression with weak instruments. *Econometrica* 65(3):557–586.
Summers, L., and A. Heston. (1991). The Penn World Table (Mark 5): An expanded set of international comparisons, 1950–1988. *Quarterly Journal of Economics* 106:327–368.
Topel, R. (1999). Labor markets and economic growth. In *The Handbook of Labor Economics*, Vol. III, O. Ashenfelter and D. Card (eds.). Amsterdam: Elsevier.
Welch, F. (1973). Black–white differences in returns to schooling. *American Economic Review* 63:893–907.

Comment

MARK BILS
University of Rochester

1. Introduction

Daron Acemoglu and Joshua Angrist attack the important and difficult problem of measuring external returns from an individual's schooling investment. As the authors discuss, much of the work that stresses human capital in growth relies on such externalities, as private returns to schooling are not nearly large enough to justify the claims of importance made for schooling. Education externalities also play a prominent role in the literatures on city formation and neighborhood effects, and, more generally, in discussions of income inequality. With the exception of leisure, education is no doubt the good most heavily subsidized by the government. Heckman and Klenow (1997) calculate that about 30% of the costs of an individual's schooling, at the margin, is absorbed by other persons' budgets through government subsidies. These policies are often rationalized on the basis of important external effects from increased schooling and school spending.

More exactly, Acemoglu and Angrist use an instrumental variables (IV) approach to examine the relationship

$$\ln w_i = \gamma_1 \bar{S} + \gamma_2 s_i, \qquad (1)$$

where w_i and s_i refer to the wage and schooling for person i, and $\bar{S}$ denotes average schooling for a broader group, whose schooling may have an external impact on person i.[1] For Acemoglu and Angrist, this group is persons living in the same U.S. state as person i.

I first discuss Acemoglu and Angrist's model interpretation of the parameter γ_1 in equation (1) as capturing externalities from human capital. I then discuss why an OLS estimate of γ_1 in equation (1) is problematic and briefly discuss the authors' IV approach. I then attempt to gauge the potential magnitude of γ_1 on the basis of growth accounting.

2. Interpreting the External Return to Schooling

Acemoglu and Angrist discuss two distinct rationales for a positive γ_1 in equation (1), that is, a positive effect of other persons' schooling on an individual's earnings. The first follows literature on cities (e.g., Rauch, 1993), growth (e.g., Lucas, 1988), and neighborhood effects (e.g., Borjas, 1995) by assuming that the human capital of others acts as a complementary input to your own labor through the exchange of ideas, making you more productive and increasing your wage. More novel, the authors consider a model of search that also leads to a causal increase in your earnings from operating in an economy with greater average human capital.

In the empirical work, the authors make equation (1) operational by measuring the broader group's human capital by schooling of other persons in the state of residence. Particularly for models based on externalities in production, it is not clear if the state of residence is the relevant economy. Ideas can probably be exchanged across state lines nearly as

---

[1]. This is a simplified depiction of Acemoglu and Angrist's more explicit equation (9).

easily as within. Suppose that the externality from human capital operates by increasing the adoption of technology because it effectively spreads the fixed costs of invention and innovation across a greater number of skilled workers who will make use of the technology. Provided the innovation can diffuse across states, the externality from human capital will not project on the level of schooling in a person's state of residence. This criticism is particularly relevant given that Acemoglu and Angrist's IV estimates do not suggest externalities at the state level.

Their model of search externalities from human capital can be briefly described as follows. A pool of workers and a pool of firms look to form matches. A worker brings his human capital h and a firm its physical capital k to a prospective match. If a match occurs, output equal to $k^\alpha h^\nu$ is produced. The key is that, regardless of how much capital the firm provides or how much human capital the worker possesses, this output is split with a fraction β going to the worker and a fraction $1 - \beta$ going to the firm. This environment yields three implications:

1. There is underinvestment in both physical and human capital.
2. Because human and physical capital are complementary in production, firms invest in greater physical capital if they anticipate matching with a pool of workers with greater human capital.
3. Directly related to the second result, a worker's wage is increasing in the human capital of other workers in their search pool, as well as their own. This last result clearly rationalizes relating a worker's wage to other workers' schooling, as in equation (1).

The critical assumption in this story of search externalities is that the pie is split independently of how much each side brings to the match. This will not be the case, for instance, if there is directed search as in Acemoglu and Shimer (1999). More precisely, if a worker by building human capital and a resumé can gain access to job opportunities, then, given that firms can choose what set of workers to consider, a worker should be able to achieve higher earnings commensurate with the marginal product of the acquired human capital. This seems like a good description of the labor market, as least in developed economies. Potential employers ask for resumes, conduct interviews, call references, etc. Furthermore, job listings often quote a salary range, with starting pay depending on the education, experience, and other relevant characteristics of the applicant.

Acemoglu and Angrist's description of match externalities brings to mind another arena in which matching is important. Consider marriages that form between two persons. For convenience, I will refer to the two persons as husband and wife. Suppose that the husband and wife share their household income independently of how much the husband produces and how much the wife produces—for simplicity, say equally. Then consumption for both husband and wife equal $(w_{husb} + w_{wife})/2 = [f(s_{husb}) + f(s_{wife})]/2$, where s_i is the schooling of member i, and $f(s_i)$ is the earnings for a member with that schooling. Suppose schooling is determined prior to forming marriages. If matches form independently of a person's earnings potential and if students, in choosing when to leave school, do not show altruism to their future (unknown) spouse, then this model generates an important externality to schooling. As in Acemoglu and Angrist's setting, persons underinvest in schooling because they only internalize half of the gain in future earnings. In contrast to their setting, this externality does not show up in a wage equation such as equation (1).

But at least one of the assumptions above, that marriages form independently of a person's schooling, appears at odds with the evidence. Based on 22,102 households that were respondents in the 1980 to 1994 Consumer Expenditure Surveys, I projected years of schooling for wives on the schooling of their husbands, and vice versa. The results, with standard errors in parentheses, are

$$s_{wife} = 0.58 s_{husb}, \qquad s_{husb} = 0.70 s_{wife}.$$
$$\quad (0.005) \qquad\qquad\quad (0.006)$$

So conditional on the husband having one more year of schooling, we should expect the household to have 1.58 more years; and conditional on the wife having one more year of schooling, we should expect the household to have 1.70 more years. Matching in marriage looks very directed. Thus individuals are able to obtain a total return on their schooling that is much of the total household gain. This should provide persons with incentive to obtain schooling, even if they are not concerned with providing for their future spouse. So even here, match externalities to schooling may not be very important.

3. The OLS Relationship

Estimating equation (1) by OLS, Acemoglu and Angrist find that one more year of schooling for a worker is associated with 7.3% higher earnings, with a standard error of less than 0.1%. (Here I focus on results for the sample period of 1960–1980.) But, more striking, one year of schooling of others in the worker's state, holding the worker's schooling constant, is also associated with 7.3% higher earnings, with a standard error of 1.6%. This estimate is comparable to, though slightly smaller than, estimates in Moretti (1999).

The authors are concerned that OLS estimates may provide an upward bias of the external effects of others schooling on a worker's earnings. I would like to expand on their discussion of this problem in Section 2.4 of their paper. They describe an economy with free migration. The externality from schooling drives up the price of the scarce resource, land, in areas with more schooling. The resulting higher cost of living in areas with more average schooling means that, even though there is an important productivity gain from living there, the market clears with no gains for additional workers to migrate to areas with more schooling. This is a standard view on the role of land pricing in allocating persons across locations in the presence of a productive or consumptive public good at a location (e.g., Roback, 1982).

For the present issue of measuring externalities from schooling, the concern is that any factor that results in higher productivity in location X will not only result in higher wages and higher costs of living at X, but will also attract workers with more schooling and greater unmeasured ability. The market equilibrium will tend to concentrate human capital on the most valuable land. As a result, the OLS relation showing higher earnings for those living in areas where others have more schooling need not reflect any structural external benefit of schooling. Instead, the results may show only that areas that are productive, with higher wages and higher living costs, attract workers with more schooling and greater unmeasured skills.

The notion that areas with higher levels of schooling also display higher housing prices is supported in the data. For 45 states I was able to relate the 1995 CPI for housing for the state's most populous city to average schooling level in the state. The housing cost is from the ACCRA Cost of Living Index; the state schooling levels were provided to me by Joshua Angrist. $\bar{S}$ denotes average schooling for all male workers in the state; $\bar{S}_{40-50}$ denotes average schooling for men aged 40 to 50. The relationship as estimated by OLS, with standard errors in parentheses, is

$$\ln(\text{housing CPI}) = 0.10\,\bar{S} \quad \text{or, alternatively,}$$
$$(0.003)$$
$$= 0.15\,\bar{S}_{40-50}.$$
$$(0.003)$$

Housing makes up about a third of the cost of living. So, allowing for the higher price of housing alone eats up about half of the wage gain, as measured by OLS, to moving to a state with more schooling.

There is also evidence that persons who live in states with more average schooling display above-average human capital, even if they themselves do not have above-average schooling. That is, more schooling in a state is correlated with higher unmeasured abilities. In 1979 the National Longitudinal Survey of Youth (NLSY) gave its respondents the Armed Forces Quantitative Test (AFQT). The AFQT scores are understood to reflect acquired knowledge as well as innate intelligence. For 5629 respondents I can project their AFQT on their own schooling as well as average schooling in their state or residence. The result is

$$\text{AFQT}_i = 5.82\ s_i + 4.34\ \bar{S}.$$
$$\qquad\qquad (0.18)\qquad (0.44)$$

So a person's test score projects nearly as much on the average schooling in one's state as on their own schooling.

This suggests that an OLS estimate of the key parameter γ_1 in equation (1) will be biased upward, as the projection of wages on $\bar{S}$ may reflect the higher unmeasured ability, as reflected in the AFQT score, rather than an externality. For workers in the NLSY data set, 4.34 extra points of AFQT score is associated with 2.0% higher earnings (with standard error of 0.2%), controlling for individual schooling. This would explain about one-third of the OLS estimate of γ_1.

Another interpretation is that growing up in a state with more average schooling is what actually causes AFQT to be higher in those states after controlling for an individual's level of schooling. Thus this again would point to an important externality from schooling, though occurring through learning as opposed to production or search as in Acemoglu and Angrist's interpretation.

4. Discussion of Acemoglu and Angrist's IV Results

Given concerns that an OLS estimate of the schooling externality is upward biased, Acemoglu and Angrist pursue an IV estimator based on state regulations that restrict young persons' ability to drop out of school or work before a certain age. They document that more stringent restrictions in a state are clearly associated with more years of high-school attendance. Looking at their Table 7, columns (4) and (8), upon instrumenting for schooling, they continue to find a private return to a year of schooling of about 7%. But now they find an external effect from state-wide schooling roughly equal to zero, with a standard error of about 3%.

I see their work as very valuable. As discussed above and in their introduction, an assumption of positive human-capital externalities plays an important role in economic theorizing as well as in public policies. Yet, empirically the question is very open. The presumptive positive externalities are supported by a small body of empirical work (e.g., Rauch, 1993; Moretti, 1999) in which causality is difficult to decipher. Secondly, I see their IV estimator as a natural attack on the problem. I believe it should move one's prior quite clearly toward a fairly small or no external effect of schooling, unless, as in my case, that result is already close to your prior.

At the same time, I would note a few limitations. First of all, the standard error associated with their IV point estimate is sizable at about 3%. Thus a 95% confidence interval would include an external return to schooling of 6%, which is smaller, but of the same order of magnitude as, the OLS estimate. A 90% confidence interval includes an external return to schooling of 3%.

Secondly, their experiment in raising years of schooling is very specific. The increased years in schooling generated by their instruments are associated with keeping boys in high school who would prefer to leave. It may be that external benefits from such enforced schooling are smaller than could be garnered by encouraging college attendance through tuition subsidies. On the other hand, the relevant sample in this paper are boys who were in high school in approximately the years 1930 to 1950. Choosing to drop out of high school during that period was much more common than it is today.

Finally, there may be important externalities from schooling not reflected in higher wage rates for others. My example above of the return to schooling benefiting a future spouse is a possible example. It is often argued that increased education makes citizens better voters, though I could never follow the reasoning. A cursory reading of Dickens's *Oliver Twist* suggests the external benefits in lower crime from keeping young men in a monitored setting such as a school or a prison. Related to this, Lochner (1999) calculates that the social benefits from reduced crime associated with men graduating from high school are at least $7000 (1996 dollars), and perhaps considerably more.

5. Limiting the Magnitude of Schooling Externality by Means of Growth Accounting

Given the difficulty in constructing arguably valid instruments to estimate the return to schooling, and especially the external return to schooling, it is worthwhile attacking the problem from other directions as well. I consider one direction based on examining the growth-accounting implications of schooling externalities. I will argue that externalities of the size estimated by OLS in the authors' Table 2 are implausibly large.

Given the rapid rise in schooling levels in the United States and worldwide, externalities of that magnitude would constitute an unreasonable fraction of measured growth in total factor productivity (TFP) in recent decades.

Annualized growth rates for TFP for the United States for 1950 to 1997, and for subperiods, are given in the first row of the following table:

	1950–1997	1950–1970	1970–1997
g_{TFP}	1.13%	1.78%	0.65%
Schooling	8.9→13.4	8.9→10.7	10.7→13.4
Adj. g_{TFP} ($\gamma_1 = 0.073$)	0.66%	1.34%	0.16%

The TFP numbers come from the U.S. Bureau of Labor Statistics. (They are available at Web site stats.bls.gov/mprhome.htm.) These growth rates in TFP already account for the increased schooling in the workforce and changes in workforce composition in terms of experience and gender, as discussed by Jorgenson (1995). The adjustment for increased schooling reflects a private return to schooling, as estimated in wage regressions of the Mincer (1974) type. But it does not consider an external return to schooling above the Mincerian return. TFP growth averages a little more than 1.1% per year for 1950 to 1997. As is well known, TFP growth has been much slower in the latter portion of the postwar period, averaging 0.65% per year for 1970 to 1997.

In the second row of the above table I report the growth rate in average years of schooling in the working-age population. (I calculate this for earlier years from historical statistics derived from the Current Population Surveys. 1997 values are available at the BLS Web site cited above.) Schooling attainment has grown rapidly, by about a year of attainment per decade. This growth has not subsided.

In the third and final row of the table, I adjust the Commerce Department's measure of TFP growth for an external return to schooling equal to 7.3% higher labor input for each additional year of schooling in the national workforce. The externality of 7.3% reflects the OLS estimate of γ_1 from the authors' Table 2. I use a labor share of two-thirds to convert the effect of the externality on effective labor input to an effect on GDP. For 1950 to 1997 this reduces residual TFP growth from 1.13% to 0.66% per year. More striking is the period from 1970 to 1997. Adjusting TFP for the externality from schooling reduces it nearly to zero, viz., to 0.16% per year. Another way to state this is that more than three-fourths of TFP growth for 1970 to 1997 is attributable to the external benefits of rising schooling. This strikes me as implausible. It leaves almost no room for a contribution of new approaches, new technologies, and new types of equipment to productivity growth over the past 30 years.[2]

Similar, and in fact stronger, statements apply if we look across a broader set of countries. Using the Mincerian approach to relate human capital to years of schooling and experience, as discussed in Bils and Klenow (2000), I calculated average annual TFP growth for 89 countries for the years 1960 to 1990. All specifications require that the private returns to schooling and experience be consistent with empirical estimates of Mincer equations across more than 50 countries. The specifications differ in whether the Mincerian return decreases in years of schooling. Depending on this choice, the growth rate of TFP, across the 89 countries, averages from 0.10% to 0.40% per year. Over the same 30 years, schooling attainment (based on Barro and Lee, 1996) grew by an average of 2.1 years, or 0.07 schooling years per year. Externalities from schooling consistent with the OLS estimate, $\gamma_1 = 0.073$, by themselves would yield a rate of growth in TFP of 0.34% per year. This falls very high in the range of total TFP growth of 0.10% to 0.40% per year, leaving no room for improvements in ideas and adoption of technologies as a source of worldwide growth from 1960 to 1990.

The upshot, I would argue, is that growth accounting suggests externalities from schooling that are no more than a fraction of the OLS estimate of γ_1. On the other hand, this type of exercise is certainly unable to rule out some smaller external effect of schooling.

I believe readers should take away from Acemoglu and Angrist's paper that external benefits as large as private returns are very unlikely. Furthermore, external benefits greater than about 40% of the private benefit (an external return of 3% on earnings for each extra year of aggregate schooling) are fairly unlikely. I would draw similar conclusions from these growth accounting exercises.

REFERENCES

Acemoglu, D., and R. Shimer. (1999). Efficient unemployment insurance. *Journal of Political Economy* 107:893–928.
Barro, R. J., and J.-W. Lee. (1996). International measures of schooling years and schooling quality. *American Economic Review (Papers and Proceedings)* 86(2):218–223.
Bils, M., and P. J. Klenow (2000). Does schooling cause growth? *American Economic Review*, forthcoming.

2. An important caveat here is that if there has been very considerable unmeasured growth in the economy (as suggested by the Boskin Commission, 1996), then the TFP growth rates in the table are also understated. This would allow more room for a contribution from technological growth.

Borjas, G. J. (1995). Ethnicity, neighborhoods, and human-capital externalities. *American Economic Review* 86(3):365–390.
Boskin Commission. (1996). Toward a more accurate measure of the cost of living. Final Report to the Senate Finance Committee from the Advisory Commission to Study the Consumer Price Index. Available at http://gopher.ssa.gov/history/reports/boskinrpt.html.
Heckman, J. J., and P. J. Klenow. (1997). Human capital policy. University of Chicago. Mimeo.
Jorgenson, D. W. (1995). *Productivity: Volume 1, Postwar U.S. Economic Growth.* Cambridge, MA: The MIT Press.
Lochner, L. (1999). Education, work, and crime: Theory and evidence. RCER Working Paper 465. University of Rochester.
Lucas, R. E. (1988). On the mechanics of economic development. *Journal of Monetary Economics* 22(1):3–42.
Mincer, J. (1974). *Schooling, Experience, and Earnings.* New York: Columbia University Press.
Moretti, E. (1999). Estimating the external return to education: Evidence from repeated cross-sectional and longitudinal data. University of California, Berkeley. Mimeo.
Rauch, J. E. (1993). Productivity gains from geographic concentration of human capital: Evidence from the cities. *Journal of Urban Economics* 34:380–400.
Roback, J. (1982). Wages, rents, and the quality of life. *Journal of Political Economy* 90(6):1257–1278.

Comment

CECILIA ELENA ROUSE
Princeton University

One of the few areas on which many economists agree is that market failures justify government intervention, particularly when it comes to education. For example, in *Capitalism and Freedom*, Milton Friedman (1982 ed., pp. 85–86; original 1962) writes, ". . . government intervention into education can be rationalized on . . . the existence of substantial 'neighborhood effects,' i.e., circumstances under which the action of one individual imposes significant costs on other individuals for which it is not feasible to make him compensate them, or yields significant gains to other individuals for which it is not feasible to make them compensate him—circumstances that make voluntary exchange impossible." Based on the belief, the subsidization (and provision in the case of K–12 education) of education is a major focus of government at all levels. Indeed, in 1997 direct expenditures on education by state and local governments accounted for over 7% of GDP.

And yet, because these neighborhood effects, or externalities, can be difficult to measure, we have precious little direct evidence that the social return to education does, indeed, differ from the private return. Previous authors have attempted to measure the social return to education by studying the effect of education on other outcomes such as crime and welfare dependence, but these studies are few and far between because of the difficulty of obtaining credible information on both education and the outcome of interest (which can vary considerably over a lifetime). In addition, it is difficult to design an analytic approach that credibly generates a consistent estimate of the causal effect of education on the outcome.

Another approach is to interpret the coefficient on an aggregate measure of schooling in a regression of individual wages on individual schooling and aggregate schooling as an estimate of the externalities to schooling. The interpretation is that, conditional on one's own schooling, if one earns more as the educational level of one's "neighbors" increases, it is because the others' education is generating positive externalities for the individual in question. This is the approach followed in this ambitious paper by Acemoglu and Angrist. Other papers using this approach have found large and statistically significant effects of aggregate schooling on one's own schooling, suggesting positive externalities to education.

However, this paper goes further than most of the previous literature. The authors attempt to address head-on the concern that aggregate schooling may be spuriously positively correlated with wages because economic growth may increase both wages and the supply of, or demand for, schooling, or because positive area-specific shocks may attract more "able" individuals to the geographic area under consideration (a U.S. state, in this paper). Therefore, they instrument for aggregate schooling, using (1) compulsory schooling laws in effect in the state in which the individual grew up during the time the individual was young and (2) compulsory schooling laws in effect in the state in which the individual currently resides during the time the individual was young. Identification comes from changes within states in compulsory schooling laws, the identifying assumption being that the legal changes are independent of (the residual of) the wages of the individual 30 years later.

As with most of Angrist's other work, this is a clever empirical strategy. A key question for identification is why and when states change their compulsory schooling laws. For example, are they changed in response to economic conditions? If so, do changes occur during times of economic prosperity or during economic downturns? I can imagine it going either way. On the one hand, during times of economic prosperity residents may be wealthier and, through an income effect, willing to increase the compulsory schooling age. On the other hand, perhaps residents are willing to increase the compulsory schooling age during times of economic downturns when the opportunity cost of attending school is lower. And yet it will matter to the interpretation of the authors' results which "story" is more plausible. If one believes that the laws are changed during economic upswings (which may lead to other changes that affect future wages, such as an improvement in school quality), then the authors' estimates, as small as they are, may actually overstate schooling externalities. Conversely, if the laws are changed during downturns (and there are other changes that occur during that time that affect future wages), then the authors' estimates may understate education externalities. Either way, it would be useful to know more about the political economy of the decision to change compulsory schooling laws.

I would also like to have a better understanding of how the instruments work. The figures that the authors provide are quite useful, but I do not understand why the instruments have a negative (but not always significant) effect on completion of postsecondary education (as measured by 14 and 16 years or more of schooling). While most of the estimates are not statistically significant, they are consistently negative. A typical (naive?) sorting model would suggest that on an increase in the schooling of individuals at the lower end of the distribution, others would complete more schooling in order to differentiate themselves. However, the authors find that those not likely affected by the laws get *less* schooling. One possible explanation is that when states strengthen compulsory schooling laws, increased expenditures for secondary schooling are required. If the states do not increase their total expenditures on all education (including postsecondary education), it is possible that funds are shifted from postsecondary schooling to secondary schooling to pay for the increased numbers of students. This hypothesis may have implications for future wages that complicate their identification strategy.

So, what do Acemoglu and Angrist find? When the authors estimate their equation by OLS, they estimate private returns to schooling of about 7%, a tad lower than what most researchers estimate today, but in the same ballpark. They also estimate external returns to schooling of roughly the same magnitude (once state-of-residence effects have been included). With IV, the private returns to schooling do not change much, but the coefficient on the external returns falls to 1–2%.

Why might these results differ from those found by others? One explanation is that the estimates of the external return to schooling in the other papers are biased upward by omitted variables. Another is that the authors' empirical strategy identifies the social return to secondary education. In contrast, previous papers may identify the social return to other levels of education. For example, in a recent paper Enrico Moretti (1999) identifies social returns to postsecondary education that are positive and statistically significant. One can reconcile the results by concluding that there are minimal social returns to secondary education but large social returns to post-secondary education. A third explanation is that the other papers use a different level of aggregation in order to identify the external return to schooling. For example, many of the previous papers use the average level of schooling in a metropolitan area; Acemoglu and Angrist use the state. And yet, perhaps the metropolitan area is conceptually more appropriate, since it is closer to the level at which workers can meet and exchange ideas regularly. Similarly, it is not clear whether, conceptually, it is the schooling of *all* workers in the state (or metropolitan area) that makes a difference, or the schooling of individuals who would interact with the individual in production, such as those in the same industry or occupation. Given the results from the previous literature and the presumption in the field that externalities in education are present, it is important to understand why Acemoglu and Angrist estimate such small external returns.

Finally, suppose these results represent the truth. What do they imply for economic theory and/or public policy? On the one hand, they may be extremely important. For, even though the estimates are imprecise, Acemoglu and Angrist's results imply that the bulk of the return to secondary education is a private return. And yet, as I mentioned at the beginning, most economists and policymakers justify public subsidies to, and perhaps even provision of, elementary and secondary education by potential positive externalities. As some evidence of the commitment, state and local direct expenditures on K–12 education outpace those on higher education by almost 4 : 1. Should this public commitment to K–12 (or at least secondary) education be reconsidered?

On the other hand, the results may not be so important for policy today. One reason is that the sample includes only white men aged 40–49 from 1950 to 1980. Today's policymaking regarding high-school dropouts is focused on low-income youths and African–American and Hispanic youth. These coefficients may not apply to them. Most importantly, the approach followed by the authors captures a relatively narrow form of externality. From a policy perspective there are many others that may be equally or more important, such as the effects on tax revenues, government transfers, and criminal activity. As a reminder, recall the earlier evaluation of the federal Job Corps program, a training program targeted at low-income youths. In this evaluation, the increased earnings of participants only accounted for about one-half of the total benefits of the program. The other one-half was accounted for by reduced criminal activity and reduced reliance on transfer programs. On net, as a result, there was a social benefit of the program once allowing for costs. This illustration is simply a reminder that when we consider externalities to schooling they come in many forms.

In all, I enjoyed the paper and commend the authors for attempting to tackle an extremely difficult and yet extremely important issue in economics.

REFERENCES

Friedman, M. (1982, originally 1962). *Capitalism and Freedom.* Chicago: The University of Chicago Press.
Moretti, E. (1999). Estimating the social return to education: Evidence from repeated cross-sectional and longitudinal data. Berkeley: University of California, Center for Labor Economics. Working Paper 22.

Discussion

In responding to Cecilia Rouse's comments, Daron Acemoglu said he was also puzzled by the finding that the instruments are negatively correlated with postsecondary educational attainment (that is, tougher compulsory K–12 attendance laws in a state are negatively correlated with subsequent college attendance). He agreed that investigating political-economy explanations for this correlation would be interesting, but was skeptical that these could imply significant biases in the estimates. Acemoglu also acknowledged the potential importance of directed search, as pointed out by discussant Mark Bils.

Joshua Angrist concurred with the discussants that the imprecision of the estimates unavoidably reduced the sharpness of their conclusions. He also agreed with Rouse that externalities might be stronger at the city than at the state level; but he noted that, as the instruments are available only at the state level, further disaggregation is simply not feasible. On the issue of potential selection bias, Angrist said one should remember that compulsory schooling laws were passed in the early twentieth century, at a time when many children left school to enter the labor market; at that time, school-leavers were not necessarily troublemakers who did badly in school and whose benefit from extra schooling might be smaller than average. Regarding policy implications, he noted that the absence of externalities does not necessarily justify cutting subsidies to education, as there are also distributional consequences.

Benjamin Friedman suggested that it might be possible to exploit data on geographical mobility by state to get sharper estimates. In particular, we might expect the externality to be smaller in states with higher labor mobility. Acemoglu agreed in principle, but worried about adding more endogenous variables to the analysis; he also thought the approach might make more sense at the city level. Andrew Atkeson noted the high rates of mobility, both within and across countries, of educated workers; he argued that with sufficient migration the method of the paper would be unable to detect an externality. Acemoglu pointed out that 65% of the people between ages 45 and 49 are still living in their states on birth, so that mobility is far from complete; still, he conceded that 30–35% rates of migration might be enough to arbitrage away the externalities created by local schooling laws.

John Leahy said that it is not obvious that mobility reduces the externality. He cited Michael Kremer's O-ring theory, which implies that the ability to move increases external returns. On the subject of the validity of the instruments, Leahy wondered whether CSLs might not be correlated with urbanization, which differs across states and is highly persistent over time. If so, their exogeneity with respect to wages thirty years later might be questioned.

Valerie Ramey warned that one should be careful in using this type of estimate in cross-country comparisons, as doing so implicitly assumes constant returns in the externality. She pointed out that the economic implications of moving from average education of 9 years to 12 years might be very different from moving from a population that cannot read to one that can. The authors agreed with this comment.

About the negative correlation of the instruments with college attendance, Olivier Blanchard mentioned the possibility that states view their education budgets as fixed, so that if more is spent on high school then the subsidy to postsecondary education falls; in principle, at least, this is testable. Gregory Mankiw noted that, if Blanchard is right and if it is also the case that externalities differ by level of education, then the paper's findings are suspect. Acemoglu agreed that if Blanchard's hypothesis is right and if the returns to college education are much higher than the returns to attending high school, this paper would be underestimating the externality; but he thought it unlikely that the overall bias would be large.

Mankiw also raised the issue of how one should frame the null hypothesis: Is it, for example, that the externality is large enough to justify current education policy? From that perspective, if one-third of education costs are borne by taxpayers and the external effect is roughly half the private effect, then on the basis of this paper we cannot reject the hypothesis that current policy is optimal. Ben Bernanke added that, since the wage measure is before tax, a marginal tax rate of about one-third already justifies the current level of subsidy. Mark Bils objected to Bernanke's conclusion on the ground that it ignores the fact that school subsidies themselves must be financed through distortionary taxation.

Allan Drazen
UNIVERSITY OF MARYLAND, HEBREW UNIVERSITY OF JERUSALEM,
AND NBER

The Political Business Cycle after 25 Years

1. Introduction

A quarter of a century has passed since the initial outburst of formal theoretical and empirical work on political business cycles, that is, on political determinants of macroeconomic cycles. On the empirical side, there was Kramer's (1971) influential study of economic determinants of U.S. congressional voting, followed by the work of Tufte (1975, 1978) and Fair (1978).[1] Nordhaus's (1975) pioneering formal model of the political business cycle (PBC) due to opportunistic pre-electoral manipulation was published exactly twenty-five years ago.[2] Soon after, Hibbs (1977) presented a model of partisan policymakers (that is, policymakers having different macroeconomic goals) in an environment similar to that of the Nordhaus, but where these partisan differences were the key driving force. Perhaps as influential in stimulating research was the 1972 Presidential election in the United States, in which incumbent Richard Nixon was justifiably viewed as engaging in significant pre-electoral manipulation.[3]

I wish to thank my discussants, Alberto Alesina, Carl Walsh, and conference participants and seminar participants at the Hebrew University of Jerusalem and the Bank of Israel for helpful comments, and Stefan Hubrich for extraordinarily able research assistance and many very useful discussions. This research was supported in part by the Maurice Falk Institute for Economic Research, Hebrew University of Jerusalem.
1. Early work on connections between politics and fluctuations in economic activity is reviewed in Kramer (1971).
2. Kalecki (1943) presented an early explicit model of the PBC; the political nature of economic fluctuations was recognized by Schumpeter (1939) in his study of business cycles. Simultaneously with Nordhaus, Lindbeck (1976) presented a similar idea; soon after, McRae (1977) also presented a formal model of the PBC.
3. Rogoff (1988) called Nixon "the all-time hero of political business cycles," at least in contemporary U.S. history. Tufte (1978) begins his famous book on the PBC with a quotation from 1814, "A Government is not supported a hundredth part so much by the

Subsequent to this flurry of research, there has been a large amount of further work. Theoretical research has concentrated on making both opportunistic and partisan models consistent with voters behaving rationally, both in forming expectations about future policy and in voting on the basis of those expectations. The success of opportunistic pre-electoral manipulation was rationalized by assuming that there is imperfect information about an incumbent's competence, with expansionary policy before an election taken as an indicator of high competence, as in the pioneering work of Rogoff (1990) and Rogoff and Sibert (1988), and in papers that followed. A partisan postelectoral cycle was argued to be consistent with rational expectations in the important work by Alesina (1987, 1988). On the empirical side there has been extensive work testing the original and subsequent models, and more generally, looking for empirical evidence of political determinants of business-cycle activity. In his *NBER Macroeconomics Annual* paper in 1988, Alesina presented an excellent summary of much of the work up to that time.

It is over a decade since Alesina's paper was published. It now seems like a good time to look at the past twenty-five years of work and to evaluate the state of the literature. What is our current state of understanding of the PBC, both theoretically and empirically? On what points is there agreement and on what points is there still significant disagreement? How well do the models explain the data? What does existing theory as well as data suggest about directions for future research?

The short answer to these questions is that we have learned quite a bit, with agreement on a number of issues, but still significant disagreement on others. On the empirical side, there are a number of clear electoral effects on macroeconomic variables. However, at least for the opportunistic model in developed countries, there is much less hard evidence than both the theoretical models and the conventional wisdom about the prevalence of "election-year economics" would suggest. Although there is wide (but not universal) agreement that aggregate economic conditions affect election outcomes in the United States, there is significant disagreement about whether there is opportunistic manipulation that can be observed in the macro data. There is a clear partisan effect in the United States (as well as in some other countries), with economic activity being lower in the first part of Republican than Democratic administrations, but still disagreement about the underlying driving mechanisms. On the theoretical side, many of the leading models have been criticized for implausibility of key assumptions. Two key

---

constant, uniform, quiet prosperity of the country as by those damned spurts which Pitt used to have just in the nick of time."

points, as I will discuss below, are: first, the assumption of seemingly irrational behavior by the public in some of the models; and, second, the reliance on monetary surprises as the driving force.

The purpose of this paper is twofold: first to present a short review and critical assessment of the existing literature, both opportunistic and partisan models, the principal aim being to point out what we know empirically and to what extent existing models explain the empirical regularities. A principal conclusion is that models based on manipulating the economy via monetary policy are unconvincing both theoretically and empirically, while explanations based on fiscal policy conform much better to the data and form a stronger basis for a convincing theoretical model of electoral effects on economic outcomes. Second, I present a new model of political cycles based on Rogoff's (1990) model of political budget cycles, extended to include monetary policy. The model is the first to incorporate both monetary and fiscal policy in a rational opportunistic framework with separate monetary and fiscal authorities.[4] This separation of monetary policy from the direct control of elected officials is crucial for a number of reasons. It is both in sharp contrast to existing PBC models and far more institutionally realistic than the policy-making structure in those models. Moreover, it is crucial to the nature of the electoral cycle, which depends on the interaction between the incumbent politician who can influence fiscal policy and an independent central bank that controls monetary aggregates and interest rates, but may be pressured to accommodate fiscal shocks. We also present some nonparametric empirical evidence in favor of the *active-fiscal, passive-monetary* (AFPM) model of the opportunistic PBC.

The roadmap for the paper is as follows. In the next section I quickly review the opportunistic PBC model based on expansionary monetary shocks and present a conceptual assessment. In Section 3 the empirical work on this approach is summarized. In Section 4 I move on to partisan models driven by monetary policy, both the original Hibbs model and Alesina's rational partisan model. In Section 5 the empirical evidence on partisan effects on macroeconomic outcomes is reviewed. In Section 6, I sum up what I consider to be the conceptual and empirical problems with monetary-based PBC models and present evidence in favor of a fiscal-based model. In Section 7 recent work on fiscal cycles in developing countries is summarized, both theoretical extensions of the political budget-cycle model of Rogoff (1990), and empirical results supporting the importance of fiscal influences in political business cycles in a wide

---

4. Rogoff and Sibert (1988) present a model of fiscal-based PBC with inflation effects, but where both tax and inflation policy are chosen by a single authority.

range of countries. In Section 8, two central questions related to a fiscal-based PBC model are posed; the answers presented motivate the AFPM model of Section 9, which combines election-influenced fiscal policy with accommodating monetary policy. In Section 10, I take a look at some data for the United States that are consistent with the AFPM model, and I present concluding comments.

2. The Monetary Opportunistic Model

Beginning with Nordhaus's (1975) model, early models of the PBC, whether opportunistic or partisan, were based on monetary policy as the driving force. Expansionary monetary policy led to a temporary increase in economic activity, followed with a lag, by an increase in inflation. Models differed in the motivation of policymakers, as well as in the modeling of expectation formation, and these differences led to very different types of politically induced economic cycles. Nonetheless, it is useful to review monetary-based models as a group in assessing their success in explaining a PBC. All are based on some variant of a basic three-equation framework, one equation representing the policymaker's objective, one giving the relation between changes in the rate of money growth or inflation on the one hand and economic activity on the other (a Phillips curve), and finally, one specifying how expectations of inflation are formed. We begin with a brief review of these models, brief because we simply want to point out some of their theoretical shortcomings and to summarize empirical tests of their ability to explain political business cycles. This review, contained in Sections 2, 3, 4, and 5, is based on Chapter 7 of Drazen (2000a), where a fuller treatment may be found.

2.1 NORDHAUS'S OPPORTUNISTIC MODEL

Nodhaus's model was meant to show that if voting were based on economic performance in the recent past and if expectations of inflation were backward-looking, an opportunistic incumbent who controlled monetary policy would find it optimal to induce an inflation–unemployment cycle corresponding to the length of his term, with a boom just before an election and a recession afterwards.

The structure of the economy is summarized by a nonstochastic, expectations-adjusted Phillips curve, yielding an inflation–output trade-off.

$$x_t = \pi_t - \pi_t^e, \tag{1}$$

where x_t is the deviation of actual from potential output and where the monetary authority is assumed to control the inflation rate π_t.[5]

The objective of the policymaker is to maximize his probability of re-election. Voting behavior is retrospective, in that it depends on economic performance under the incumbent in the past. Economic performance in a period is measured by the behavior of inflation and unemployment, so that voter dissatisfaction in any period can be represented by a loss function of the form

$$\mathcal{L}_t = \alpha \frac{(x_t - \tilde{x})^2}{2} + \frac{(\pi_t - \tilde{\pi})^2}{2}, \quad (2)$$

where $\tilde{\pi}$ is the electorate's target rate of inflation, $\tilde{x}$ is the target rate of economic activity (relative to potential output), and α is the relative weight the electorate puts on output fluctuations relative to inflation fluctuations. An opportunistic policymaker will choose the policy that attracts most voters, so that these parameters could be thought of as representing the preferences of the median voter.

In the basic model, one then posits a retrospective voting function for an election at the end of period t, of the form:

$$N_t = N\left(\sum_{s=0}^{T} \delta^s \mathcal{L}_{t-s}\right) + \epsilon_t, \quad (2a)$$

yielding the number of votes N_t as a function of voters's well-being, where $N'(\cdot) < 0$. The exogenous length of time between elections is $T + 1$ periods, $0 < \delta < 1$ is the factor with which voters discount past economic performance (a "forgetfulness coefficient"), and ϵ_t is a mean-zero stochastic term relating economic performance to electoral outcomes. The electoral mechanism is not made more specific. The standard opportunistic PBC model assumes that δ is small, in the sense that recent economic performance counts far more heavily in influencing voter choices than economic performance in the more distant past. The stochastic element is added to allow for the possibility of an incumbent losing the election.

To close the model one must specify the formation of expectations.

---

5. In order to reproduce the regularity of high inflation lagging the monetary expansion, one must decouple money growth and inflation. A simple assumption along these lines is that inflation reflects money growth in the previous period, that is, $\pi_t = \mu_{t-1}$, with μ_t being the monetary authority's control variable, and with the divergence of actual from potential output depending on the difference between the actual rate of money growth and the economy-wide expected rate of money growth μ_t^e. See Chapter 7.3 of Drazen (2000a) for precise details.

Crucial to the main results of the Nordhaus model is some form of adaptive expectations. A standard formulation of adaptive inflation expectations is:

$$\pi_t^e = \pi_{t-1} + \theta(\pi_{t-1}^e - \pi_{t-1}), \tag{3}$$

where θ is a coefficient between 0 and 1 representing the speed with which expectations adapt to past inflation. What is crucial in the formation of expectations is that π_t^e does *not* depend on the expectation of future policies, so that expectations are not rational. It is this characteristic (combined with the absence of any other connections between periods) which gives the incumbent policymaker an exploitable trade-off between inflation and unemployment in the attempt to affect election outcomes.

Voter behavior in the Nordhaus model is backward-looking in two dimensions: voting depends on past incumbent performance, and expectations of money growth depend only on past inflation rates. The incumbent policymaker elected at $t-3$ chooses inflation rates π_{t-3}, π_{t-2}, π_{t-1}, and π_t to maximize his expected vote in the next election. This simple structure yields the following behavior of incumbents who wish to maximize the probability of remaining in office. Immediately preceding an election the government stimulates the economy via expansionary monetary policy. The levels of monetary expansion and economic activity are those that maximize voter satisfaction in an election period taken alone. In the period immediately after the election, the government reverses course. It engineers a recession via contractionary monetary policy to bring down inflationary expectations. The incumbent keeps economic activity low to keep expected inflation low until the period immediately before the next election, so that a given rate of economic expansion (induced by a monetary surprise) can be obtained at a relatively low rate of inflation. In the next election cycle, the same behavior is repeated. Hence, we have a simple example in which the possibility of influencing the probability of re-election, combined with the structure of the economy, yields a cycle in economic activity. [The exact solution may be found in any treatment of the Nordhaus model, for example, Drazen (2000a, p. 233–236).]

2.2 CONCEPTUAL CRITIQUE

There are three general conceptual criticisms of the basic Nordhaus model as a tool for explaining a PBC. First, it assumes that the president controls monetary policy, an assumption that is inconsistent with the independence of the Federal Reserve. Although some observers argue that decisions on monetary policy in the United States are strongly influenced by the executive branch, the notion that the president can easily use monetary policy as an electoral tool does not fit the institutional facts. A more subtle argument is that an independent Federal Reserve may be especially willing to accommodate the executive branch's pressures for monetary policy during election years in order to prevent sharp movements in interest rates which would lead the Fed to be criticized. We return to this argument below.

A second, more serious problem with the Nordhaus model is its reliance on *irrational* behavior on the part of voters. Voters are naive, not simply in the way they form expectations of inflation, but also in the way they assess government performance. Any voter who has lived through an election cycle in Nordhaus's world should not be fooled into voting for an opportunistic, manipulative policymaker. He will know that the pre-election period of low inflation and high economic activity will be followed by a postelection period of both high inflation and high unemployment. He should therefore punish rather than reward an incumbent who engages in pre-electoral manipulation.

Finally, and more generally, one may question the central role assigned to moving along the Phillips curve to reduce unemployment via inflation surprises. Fiscal policy plays no role in the PBC in the model, though transfers and other types of fiscal policy appear to play an important role in some episodes of pre-electoral policy manipulation.

3. Empirical Tests of the Nordhaus Model

There have been many econometric tests of the monetary opportunistic PBC, both for economic outcomes and for policy instruments. The most common form of econometric test of these models in terms of outcomes is to run an autoregression of an economic performance measure on itself, a small set of economic variables, and political dummies to test a specific theory. Consider a regression of the form:

$$Y_t = \sum_{i=1}^{s} a_i Y_{t-i} + b_0 + \sum_{j} b_j X_{jt} + d\text{PDUM}_t + \epsilon_t, \qquad (4)$$

where Y is an outcome variable such as GDP, the X_j are other economic variables that may also affect Y, such as world economic activity, and PDUM is a political dummy variable (or set of variables) meant to represent a given political model. The autoregressive specification for Y_t is adopted as a parsimonious representation of the time-series behavior of

Y_t, instead of using a structural model. For example, as a test of the Nordhaus model on quarterly data, Alesina and Roubini (1992), Alesina, Cohen, and Roubini (1992), and Alesina, Roubini, and Cohen (1997) use a dummy variable that equals 1 in the election quarter and in the $T-1$ quarters before the election, and 0 otherwise, where T may equal 4, 6, or 8. As the measure of economic activity Y they take the year-over-year growth rate of GNP or an unemployment measure, the exact specification depending on the model and data set.

3.1 THE EFFECT OF ECONOMIC CONDITIONS ON ELECTIONS

Prior to discussing the effect of elections on macroeconomic variables, one must consider the effect of economic conditions on elections. A crucial assumption in the Nordhaus model, or in any model of pre-electoral manipulation, is that voters vote on the basis of economic variables. Kramer (1971) regressed votes received by the incumbent party in U.S. congressional elections on two measures of performance in the year of the election—the growth rate of real per capita income and the rate of inflation in that year—and found they were both significant determinants of vote totals. The importance of economic conditions for voting in congressional elections was confirmed by Tufte (1975).[6]

The most influential work was probably that of Fair (1978) [updated in Fiar (1982, 1988)], who found similar results for the United States. In his original article, Fair looked at presidential elections from 1916 through 1976, arguing that if voters hold the party that holds the presidency accountable for economic events, their influence should be seen most strongly in presidential elections. Fair found that the change in real economic activity in the year of the election, as measured either by the change in real per capita GNP or the change in unemployment in the election year, does appear to have an important effect on votes for president. Specifically, a 1% increase in the growth rate increases the incumbent's vote total by about 1%. (Further evidence suggests it may be the growth of real per capita GNP in the second and third quarters of the election year that is important, but data limitations prevent Fair from drawing any definitive conclusions about what part of the election year is most important in determining voter behavior.) Given the growth of economic activity, other measures of macroeconomic performance contribute little; the most important of the other measures is the inflation rate in the two-year period before the election, as measured by the change in the GNP deflator. A second key finding of Fair's is that voters

---

6. Though most studies confirm the basic results, Stigler (1973) concluded that congressional election results are not affected by economic fluctuations. See also Okun's (1973) comment on Stigler, as well as Arcelus and Meltzer (1975) and Bloom and Price (1975).

appear to have a high discount rate on past economic performance; they don't look back more than a year or two.[7]

Numerous other articles find similar results on the importance of pre-election conditions on voting patterns in both the United States and other countries. Looking at voting or popularity functions, Lewis-Beck (1988) found that the sort of results that Kramer and Fair report for the United States hold in Britain, France, West Germany, Italy, and Spain as well. Madsen (1980) reported similar results for Denmark, Norway, and Sweden.[8] We summarize this as:

REGULARITY 1 *Aggregate economic conditions before an election, specifically per capita output or income growth (and to a lesser extent inflation), have a significant effect on voting patterns in the United States and other countries.*

3.2 ECONOMIC ACTIVITY

Numerous econometric tests provide little support for the political cycle in economic activity predicted by the Nordhaus model. Studies for the United States began with McCallum's (1978) study of unemployment fluctuations before elections. Alt and Chrystal (1983) summarize early empirical studies as showing a striking lack of support, a point reinforced by results summarized in Alesina, Roubini, and Cohen (1997). Faust and Irons (1999), using more sophisticated techniques, come to a similar conclusion. Figure 1, showing mean rates of GNP growth (seasonally adjusted) by quarter of the president's term in the United States from 1948 to 1998, illustrates the point.[9]

Similarly, no evidence was found in developed economies outside the United States for a Nordhaus-style PBC for unemployment or economic growth (Paldam, 1979; Lewis-Beck, 1988). Alesina, Roubini, and Cohen

---

7. One should distinguish aggregate from individual economic conditions on voting. Lewis-Beck (1988) argues that individuals vote on the basis of national economic performance (sociotropic voting) rather than their own personal economic situation ("narrow pocketbook" voting).
8. What about the effect of economic conditions on the timing of elections when governments can call early elections? Ito (1990) finds evidence that governments in Japan do not manipulate policies in anticipation of upcoming elections, but that they opportunistically manipulate the timing of elections to take advantage of autonomous economic expansions. Specifically, high growth significantly increases the probability of an election, while high inflation significantly reduces it. Chowdhury (1993) reports similar results for India, with the government more likely to call early elections when economic times are good. On the other hand, Alesina, Cohen, and Roubini (1993), argue that for a sample of 14 OECD countries with endogenous election timing, there is no evidence of such an effect in countries other than Japan.
9. A plot of median growth rates, or of other measures of aggregate economic activity, for the United States would tell a similar story.

Figure 1 MEAN GNP GROWTH RATE, 1948–1998

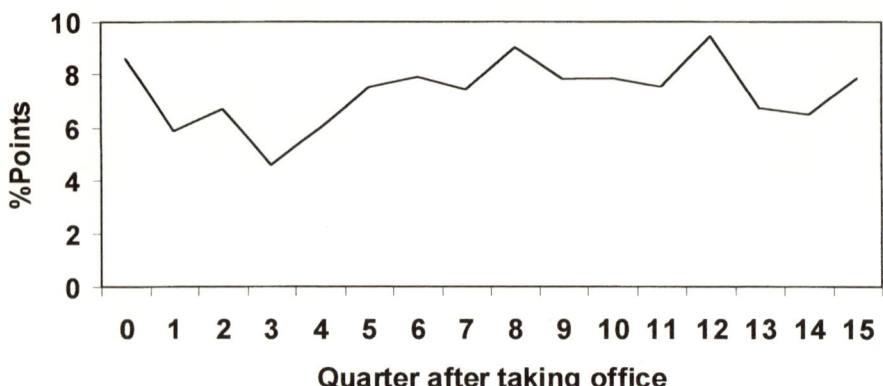

(1997) reject an opportunistic cycle in real activity for a sample of 18 OECD countries over the period 1960–1993.[10]

We summarize the general consensus that the opportunistic PBC receives little support in the pre-electoral behavior of GNP or unemployment as:

REGULARITY 2 *There is no significant increase in aggregate economic activity prior to elections in either the United States or other OECD countries.*

3.3 INFLATION

The postelectoral increase in inflation predicted by the Nordhaus model receives support in some countries and not in others. Alesina, Cohen, and Roubini (1992) and Alesina, Roubini, and Cohen (1997) test for a political cycle in inflation (measured as the growth rate of the CPI over the previous 4 quarters), using the same data set and methodology they used for GNP growth, and defining a political dummy equal to 1 in the election quarter and in the 3 quarters *following* the election, and 0 otherwise. In a pooled cross-section, time-series regression, they find a highly

10. If aggregate economic performance is important in determining the way people vote and governments want to win re-election, why don't we observe a clear opportunistic PBC? Lewis-Beck (1988) argues that it is because it is exceedingly hard to time economic manipulation. Monetary and fiscal policy can be used only with great imprecision, so that politicians cannot expect to time the aggregate stimulus to come right before an election, while the risks associated with a mistimed expansion are high. Another explanation is that opportunistic politicians target transfers to a fraction of voters with minor effect on aggregate economic activity. The AFPM model in Section 9 includes both of these possibilities.

Figure 2 MEAN INFLATION RATE (CPI), 1960–1978

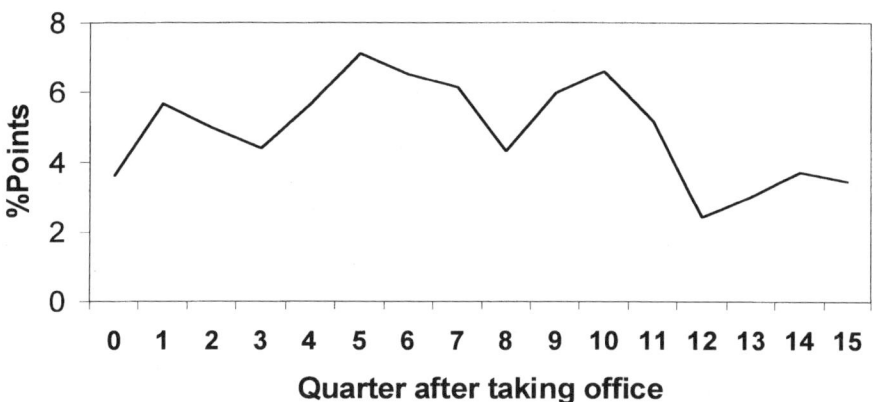

significant coefficient of the correct sign on the political dummy; in the individual country regressions, they find the coefficient is of the correct sign in almost all the regressions, and significant at the 10% or higher level for Denmark, France, Germany, Italy, and New Zealand. Overall, they conclude the PBC effect on inflation is widespread across OECD countries (on the basis of their pooled regression) and on a much stronger empirical footing than the effect on GNP and unemployment.

The evidence for the United States is less clear. In similar tests to those described above, Alesina, Roubini, and Cohen (1997) reject the existence of a postelectoral surge in inflation over the period 1947–1994. However, the behavior of inflation after elections changed over this sample period. After 1979 there is no evidence of a political inflation cycle, which corresponds to the timing of the change in Federal Reserve policy rules in 1979. (See, for example, the estimated policy rules in Clarida, Gali, and Gertler, 2000.) Prior to this however, there is more evidence of a possible postelectoral increase in inflation. This is consistent with other studies, and is illustrated in Figures 2 and 3, showing mean annualized CPI inflation (seasonally adjusted) from 1960 to 1979 vs. 1979 to 1998 by quarter of the president's term. (A graph for 1948–1979 looks very similar to 1960–1979, but the latter is used for better comparability with later figures.)

To summarize:

REGULARITY 3   *In many OECD countries there is a clear postelectoral increase in inflation. In the United States, there is evidence of such a postelectoral increase in inflation prior to 1979, but no evidence thereafter.*

Figure 3 MEAN INFLATION RATE (CPI), 1979–1998

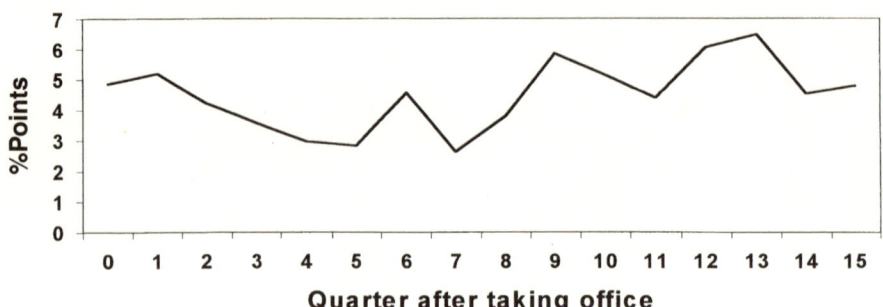

3.4 MONETARY INSTRUMENTS

Not surprisingly, the results for expansionary monetary policy before elections mirror those for inflation after elections. Using the same political dummy they did for inflation, Alesina, Cohen, and Roubini (1992) find a significant political effect for the yearly M1 growth rates in pooled cross-section, time-series regressions in their sample of OECD countries, with money growth being higher for the year to year-and-a-half before elections. In the country regressions, the results are less strong, though a number of countries display significant effects.

For the United States, the sensitivity of the inflation results to the time period considered is seen in money growth rates as well. Alesina, Cohen, and Roubini (1992) find only very weak evidence of a political monetary cycle in the postwar period, a conclusion reinforced in Alesina, Roubini, and Cohen (1997) for the period 1949–1994. In contrast, Grier (1989) and Beck (1987) both find significant support for an office-motivated model of monetary policy in the United States over the subperiod 1960–1980. Grier, using U.S. quarterly data from 1961 to 1982, regresses M1 growth on its previous value, the full-employment deficit, and a political dummy specified as a fifteen-quarter second-degree polynomial distributed lag on a dummy which takes a value of one in the election quarter and zero otherwise. (The polynomial distributed lag is chosen to conserve on degrees of freedom.) He finds that the timing of an election significantly influences money growth, even when fluctuations in output, interest rates, and the deficit are held constant. Beck (1987) also finds a political cycle in the money supply in the United States over the same period. Figures 4 and 5 present mean M1 growth rates (seasonally adjusted) by quarter of the president's term over the periods 1960–1979 and 1979–1998. Interestingly, Beck finds no similar cycle in monetary instruments, such as reserves or

Figure 4 MEAN M1 GROWTH RATE, 1960–1978

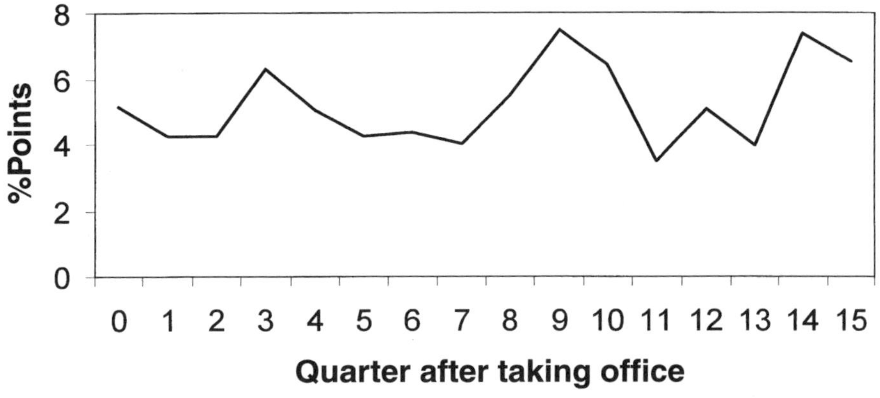

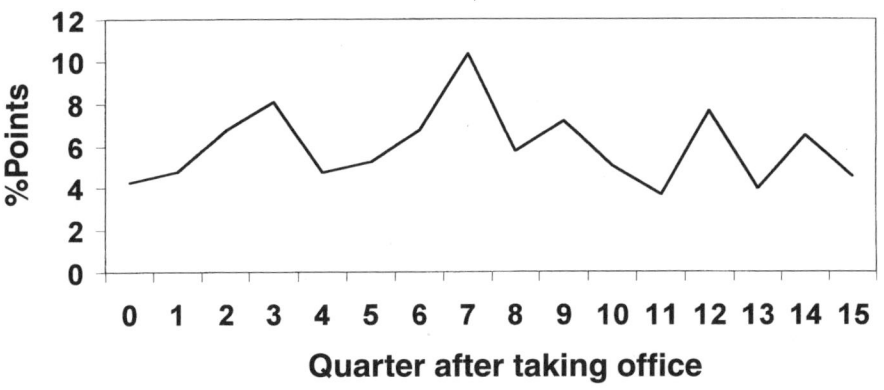

Figure 5 MEAN M1 GROWTH RATE, 1979–1998

the federal funds rate, a point made clear in Figure 6, giving the mean federal funds rate by quarter of term from 1959 to 1998. The difference in results for the behavior of money growth and instruments of monetary control will be central to our model of the PBC presented below. We summarize these results as:

REGULARITY 4 *There is evidence of a pre-electoral increase in money growth rates in many countries. In the United States, there is a pre-electoral effect from 1960 to 1980, but none thereafter. There is no evidence for the United States of an electoral cycle in the federal funds rate.*

Figure 6 MEAN FEDERAL FUNDS RATE, 1959–1998

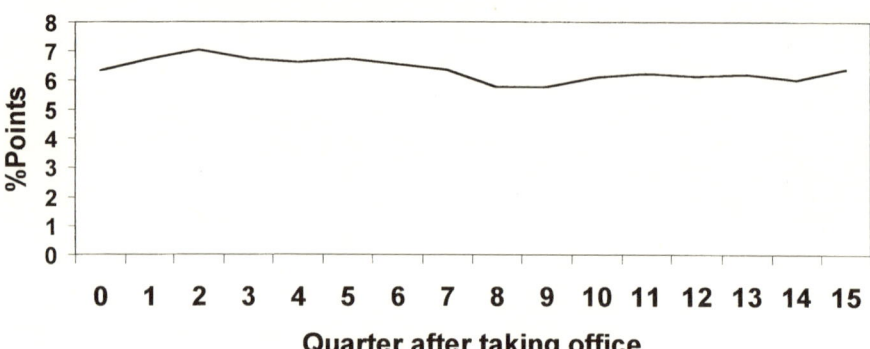

4. Monetary Partisan Models

The basic partisan model starts with the observation that right-wing and left-wing parties have different positions on economic issues and hence different macroeconomic objectives. In terms of the objective function (2), they have different preferences over inflation and unemployment, both in inflation and unemployment targets and the relative dislike of inflation vs. unemployment.

4.1 THE BASIC HIBBS MODEL

The partisan PBC model was introduced by Hibbs (1977). To represent the difference in interests, we replace the social loss function (2) by a partisan loss function:

$$\mathcal{L}_t^j = \alpha^j \frac{(x_t - \tilde{x}^j)^2}{2} + \frac{(\pi_t - \tilde{\pi}^j)^2}{2} \qquad (5)$$

for party j, where $\tilde{\pi}^j$ is party j's target rate of inflation, $\tilde{x}^j$ is party j's target for economic activity, and α^j is the relative weight put on output fluctuations relative to inflation fluctuations by party j. There are two parties, a left-wing party, denoted L, and a right-wing party, denoted R. The two parties are characterized by the following possible differences in their objectives. First, the left-wing party may have a higher target for economic activity than the right-wing party. Second, the left-wing party may assign a larger cost to deviations of economic activity from its target level than to deviations of inflation from the target. Finally, the left-wing party may have a higher inflation target than the right-wing party, *independent* of the effects on economic activity via the Phillips curve, which could reflect other effects of inflation viewed differently by the two parties. To summarize the difference between the parties:

$$\tilde{x}^L \geq \tilde{x}^R$$
$$\alpha^L \geq \alpha^R, \quad (6)$$
$$\tilde{\pi}^L \geq \tilde{\pi}^R.$$

To obtain the partisan cycles, at least one of these must hold with strict inequality.

Fluctuations in economic activity induced by these partisan differences are generated in the basic Hibbs model by movements along an exploitable Phillips curve, where it is assumed, as in the basic Nordhaus model, that expectations are not rational. Thus, the left-wing party will pursue a more expansionary monetary policy throughout its term.[11] How long these effects last depend on the exact specification of expectations. In an adaptive expectations framework, the more slowly inflation expectations adjust to actual inflation, the longer will be the partisan effect.

A basic criticism of the original Hibbs model is the same as the one that was applied to the Nordhaus model, namely that it relies on mistaken expectations of what policy will be in order to get real effects. Hence, to the extent that it is assumed that monetary policy is used to hit partisan unemployment and growth targets, the explanation of the political business cycle is unsatisfactory.

4.2 ALESINA'S RATIONAL-PARTISAN MODEL

Alesina (1987, 1988) introduced rational expectations into a monetary-based PBC, influenced by the criticism of models based on an exploitable Phillips curve. In his partisan model with rational expectations, only surprise inflation affects output, leading to Alesina's terming the approach the *rational-partisan* model. The rational-partisan model can be represented by a similar three-equation model to that used by Nordhaus, retaining the expectations-augmented Phillips curve (1) but changing the other two components. First, following Hibbs, the motivation of policymakers is quite different than in the Nordhaus model: they are purely partisan, with no opportunistic motives and hence no desire to manipulate outcomes. To represent the difference between economic effects in the early part and the latter part of an incumbent's term of office, Alesina divides a term of office into two periods and assumes that

---

11. As in the Nordhaus model, the key assumption here is that, in spite of the Federal Reserve's formal autonomy in the United States, monetary policy reflects the administration's macroeconomic goals.

there is an election every other period, say at t, $t+2$, $t+4$, ... It is assumed that a party cares only about its own term of office, so that the objective function of party j at time t may then be represented by an extended version of (5), namely

$$\Lambda_t^j = \alpha^j \frac{(x_t - \tilde{x}^j)^2}{2} + \frac{(\pi_t - \tilde{\pi}^j)^2}{2} \qquad (7)$$

$$+ \beta \left(\alpha^j \frac{(x_{t+1} + \tilde{x}^j)^2}{2} + \frac{(\pi_{t-1} - \tilde{\pi}^j)^2}{2} \right)$$

for party j, where $\tilde{\pi}^j$ and $\tilde{x}^j$ are the partisan targets, α^j is the relative weight put on output deviations by party j, and β is the discount factor. These are characterized, as in the Hibbs model, by (6) above, where, in order to obtain the cycles in the rational-partisan model, at least one of the inequalities in (6) must be strict.

The other crucial change, relative to both the Nordhaus and Hibbs models, is that Alesina replaces the assumption of adaptive expectations by rational expectations, so instead of (3), expected inflation π_t^e is given by

$$\pi_t^e = E_{t-1}(\pi_t). \qquad (8)$$

In determining the evolution of inflation and unemployment during a term of office, say t and $t+1$, the key variable in the model is expected inflation in those periods, this expectation being formed before the election in period t. Conditional on expected inflation in each half term, the party in power chooses its optimal policy, by maximizing (7) subject to (1). We retain the assumption from earlier models that the government has perfect control over inflation. In turn, expectations of inflation depend on the expectation of who will win the upcoming election. If outcomes were fully known, there would be no cycle, since a party's policy would be fully anticipated and hence have no effect on real activity.

The existence of a cycle thus depends on uncertainty about election outcomes. Expected inflation for the half term after the election is the weighted sum of the two parties' policies, weighted by the probability that each will win the election, namely,

$$\pi_t^e = q^L \pi_t^L + (1 - q^L) \pi_t^R, \qquad (9)$$

where q^L is the probability that the left-wing party will win the election, and where π_t^L and π_t^R are the optimal policies of the two parties in the first half of the term, which depend not only on their policy preferences (6), but also on the election probability q^L itself, as optimal policy depends on π_t^e. Since the left-wing party follows a more inflationary policy once in office than the right-wing party, expected inflation is between these two values. Hence, there is a positive inflation surprise if the left-wing party wins the election, implying unemployment below the natural rate, and a negative inflation surprise if the left-wing party wins the election, implying unemployment above the natural rate. In the second half of a president's term, there are no fluctuations in economic activity, as the identity of the party in power is known when contracts are signed (in the first part of the term). In contrast, Hibbs's partisan model suggests higher economic activity in left-wing administrations than in right-wing administrations over the life of the term.[12]

4.3 A CONCEPTUAL ASSESSMENT OF THE
RATIONAL-PARTISAN MODEL

The theoretical structure of the rational-partisan model raises a number of questions about the underlying driving forces. First, and most difficult, there is the question of whether the underlying microeconomic structure, namely nominal wage contracts signed before elections, makes sense in the context of the model. The question of microfoundations is often raised about models in which policymakers exploit an expectations-augmented Phillips curve, but the importance of electoral effects gives it special importance here. A standard argument, used also by Alesina, is that nominal wage contracts are signed at discrete intervals, where nominal wage increases reflect rationally anticipated inflation at the time the contract is signed, so that surprise inflation between contract dates can have real effects even when agents are rational. The basic problem, as Rogoff (1988) points out, is that, on the one hand, elections are an important source of fluctuations due to their outcomes being less than fully anticipated, but, on the other, the election date is fully known. The magnitude of the changes in inflation and unemployment the model is meant to explain are sufficiently large that there should be a large utility payoff to eliminating the uncertainty that leads to these fluctuations. But that is easy to do. To the extent there is a significant effect on unemployment,

12. Hibbs (1994) presents such a theory of adjustment of partisan objectives contingent on economic outcomes and learning, which predicts that unemployment and inflation outcomes across the two parties may diverge more in the first part of their terms than in the second, though not because of uncertainty about electoral outcomes. The key to Hibbs's model of changing objectives (and to the result on time-varying outcomes) is that *policymakers* are uncertain about the structure of the economy and the effects of policies. They use outcomes to refine their beliefs about attainable targets, leading to a feedback from outcomes to partisan objectives and thus policies.

old contracts should be timed to expire and the signing of new contracts postponed until just after an election, so that they can reflect the election results. Hence, the main driving force of the model would seem to depend on behavior of workers and unions that is less than rational, not in the formation of their expectations per se, but in their labor-supply behavior. A simple change in the timing of contract behavior would eliminate the political cycle. Garfinkel and Glazer (1994) present empirical evidence that for labor contracts of less than two years signed in a presidential election year, there is a clear tendency to delay the signing of labor contracts until after the election.[13]

A second crucial question concerns the electoral uncertainty that drives the model. The magnitude of the cycle depends on the degree of electoral uncertainty, as well as on the difference in the parties' desired inflation rates. One problem is that these key driving forces are exogenous. Far more troublesome is the predicted positive correlation between the extent of the electoral surprise and the size of postelectoral movements in real economic activity. As the key probability q^L approaches zero or one, the magnitude of the fluctuations will approach zero, with fluctuations being maximal (all else equal) for $q^L = \frac{1}{2}$. Hibbs (1992), among others, has argued that this prediction is not consistent with the empirical evidence for the United States. Consideration of individual elections reveals the problem. For example, the outcome of the 1964 presidential election is probably the closest we have seen to a sure thing in the postwar era, with Lyndon Johnson's victory widely anticipated. Yet the rate of real GNP growth in the first two years of the Johnson administration averaged 5.8% per year, the highest figure of any Democratic administration. In contrast, among postwar Republican victories through Regan's first election, Nixon's victory in 1968 was the closest and least certain, but corresponds to the smallest drop in real output in the critical second year of the administration.

Alesina, Roubini, and Cohen (1997, Chapter 5) construct an index of electoral surprise for the U.S. presidential elections from 1948 to 1992, with Republican victories entering as negative surprises. They use different variants as an explanatory variable in a real-GDP-growth regression of the form (4) and find that the coefficient on the surprise variable is significantly positive, meaning that larger Democratic (Republican) surprises imply higher (lower) postelection real growth rates. The construc-

---

13. Garfinkel and Glazer's results may be interpreted in two ways. One is that postponement of contract signing indicates that electoral uncertainty is important in forming inflation expectations, consistent with the basic thrust of the rational-partisan model. The other is that in industries where this is true, contract signing is postponed, undercutting the empirical relevance of the main driving force of the model.

tion of the variable is complicated, so that it is not easy to see why the results of the regression and of the simple case study do not agree. The relation of pre-electoral uncertainty and postelectoral fluctuations is an important question deserving further research.

A final question, which can be applied to all the models discussed so far, is the central role assigned to moving along the Phillips curve to reduce unemployment via inflation surprises. That is, even though real effects of monetary policy are consistent in this approach with rational expectations, the reliance on monetary policy as the driving force of cycles is inconsistent with the evidence on the important role of fiscal policy in PBCs. We return to this point in Section 6.

5. Empirical Tests of Partisan Models

The partisan PBC has been tested less than the opportunistic model. There is general agreement on the existence of partisan effects per se, especially on economic activity. However, there is far less consensus on the mechanism at work.

5.1 ECONOMIC ACTIVITY

Perhaps the strongest regularity in the U.S. data was first pointed out by Alesina (1988), with Faust and Irons (1999) confirming the effect over a longer time period using more sophisticated econometric techniques: For the United States, real GDP growth is substantially higher under Democrats than Republicans in years 2 and 3 of their administrations. Alesina, Roubini, and Cohen (1997) report that over the period from the first quarter of 1949 through the second quarter of 1994, growth rates during Democratic and during Republican administrations sharply diverge starting about the third quarter after the election. The quarterly growth rate averaged over Democratic administrations rises from about 3% per annum in quarter 3 to about 6% per annum by quarter 6 or 7 in the administration's term of office, and falls from the same level to zero by quarter 6 or 7 in the administration's term averaged over Republican administrations. Real GDP growth rates then improve under Republican and worsen under Democratic administrations, so that in the fourth year of the administration, the growth performance under the two parties is identical. Unemployment shows analogous partisan patterns in the expected direction. Alesina, Roubini, and Cohen (1997) present more formal econometric tests for the United States to confirm this result, using autoregressive equations like (4) in quarterly data from 1947:I through 1993:IV with a political dummy that equals +1 in the first part of a Republican administration, −1 in the first part of a Democratic administration, and 0 otherwise. They report results favorable to the rational partisan theory for real GDP growth and for unemployment. They find a significant political dummy over the whole life of an administration, but by dividing the variable into first and second halves of the administration, they reject Hibbs's version of the partisan theory. They run similar tests on a sample of 18 OECD countries over the period 1960–1993, also finding support for the rational-partisan model and lack of support for both the Hibbs and the Nordhaus model.

Faust and Irons (1999) find similar partisan differences in both output growth and unemployment, which are strongest in the first half of the term. However, they find this partisan difference remains even after controlling for observable economic variables and for political effects as in partisan models, suggesting that the data do not give support to any partisan model. Graphs of quarter-after-inauguration effects similar to those presented here may be found for a large group of variables. The key empirical regularity on which there is wide agreement is

REGULARITY 5   *There is a clear partisan effect on economic activity in the United States, with economic activity being significantly higher under Democrats than Republicans in the first half of their terms.*

5.2 INFLATION AND MONETARY POLICY

There are partisan differences in inflation (as measured by the rate of change in the Consumer Price Index), though they do not conform simply to the partisan theory, especially the rational-partisan theory. Democratic administrations have *lower* average inflation than Republican administrations in the first half of their terms, but that inflation is rising under Democrats and falling under Republicans, a finding reported both by Alesina, Roubini, and Cohen (1997) and by Faust and Irons (1999). Hence, the basic inflation data for the United States do not support a monetary partisan model, whereby the *level* of inflation should be higher under Democrats than Republicans.

In interpreting these results, Alesina, Roubini, and Cohen argue that the differences found in *changes* in inflation rates are consistent with their theory, though the argument is only partially convincing, since the rational-partisan theory based on the expectations-augmented Phillips curve is built on the rate of inflation, not on changes in that rate. The econometric tests for inflation cycles in the United States are far less favorable to partisan models, paralleling the nonparametric tests discussed above. Alesina, Roubini, and Cohen (1997) find that after 1973 (and the move to floating rates after the collapse of Bretton Woods), the difference in average inflation rates between Democratic and Republican administrations is only about 1.8% per year. They present no formal tests of the timing of inflation within administrations, that is, whether inflation rates are higher in the first half of Democratic than Republican administrations, with these differences narrowing in the second half.

In contrast to the work of Alesina and coauthors, Sheffrin (1989) finds the empirical evidence in favor of the rational-partisan theory to be weak for both the United States and other countries. For example, he argues that economic fluctuations following Republican presidential victories in the United States are generally inconsistent with the rational-partisan theory, postelectoral recessions often coming as a surprise. He argues that his weak results are due, among other things, to the importance for macroeconomic fluctuations of factors other than unanticipated monetary policy. Similarly, Faust and Irons (1999) find no support for partisan effects operating through monetary policy. We sum up these disagreements as:

"REGULARITY" 6   *There is no consensus on the role of monetary policy or inflation surprises in driving partisan effects, with views varying widely.*

6. From Monetary to Fiscal Policy

We have so far considered a number of theoretical and empirical issues raised by monetary models of the PBC. Each of the models had conceptual and empirical shortcomings, some more than others. I think it is fair to say that none of the three basic models considered so far receive overwhelming support in the data. This suggests that after twenty-five years, monetary surprises as a driving force of a PBC just do not provide a very convincing story.

I considered the basic opportunistic and partisan model and the rational model as a group to stress this point, that is, to stress their similarities rather than their differences. All three models mentioned above rely on a Phillips curve as the vehicle by which the economy is manipulated. Inflation, particularly when it is unanticipated, induces movements in unemployment, as the economy moves up or down the Phillips curve. Hence, *active monetary policy is the key driving force*. Second, *monetary policy is basically chosen by politicians* according to their desires—an incumbent facing re-election in the opportunistic models, or a newly elected administration with specific macroeconomic goals in the partisan models. The monetary authority is subservient to the politicians, and in no sense does it make independent monetary decisions. These two characteristics—activist monetary policy (more specifically, monetary surprises) as the driving force, and control of monetary policy by politicians—do not very well describe either PBCs or central-bank behavior. Countries in which political cycles are observed are often countries seen as having highly independent central banks. Hence, the view of monetary policy as being dictated by politicians doesn't sound right.

An alternative approach is that *fiscal policy* is the key driving force, especially in pre-electoral manipulation, in many countries. Tufte (1978) documents a number of clear incidents of pre-electoral opportunistic manipulation of fiscal transfers, both social security payments and veterans benefits. Keech and Pak (1989) found an electoral cycle for veterans' benefits in the United States between 1961 and 1978, but argued that it had subsequently disappeared. Similarly, Alesina (1988) shows that there was an electoral cycle in net transfers relative to GNP over the period 1961 to 1985, but that the electoral effect disappears if one extends the sample back to 1949. Alesina, Cohen, and Roubini (1992), as well as Alesina and Roubini (1990), find evidence for an opportunistic cycle in transfers, though they argue that there is no evidence of a fiscal cycle for instruments other than transfers.

These effects may be seen by looking at government transfers to individuals net of social insurance contributions relative to GNP (seasonally adjusted and detrended), as a function of the quarter of the president's term before, from 1960 to 1978 in Figure 7 and from 1979 to 1998 in Figure 8.

This evidence on fiscal policy suggests a last regularity for the United States and other developed countries:

REGULARITY 7   *There is evidence of pre-electoral increases in transfers and other fiscal policy instruments in a number of countries. In the United States, this effect appears strongest prior to 1980.*

7. Fiscal Cycles in Developing Countries

Before considering the implications of these regularities in the United States for modeling the business cycle, it is instructive to look at developing countries. Recent research has found that the fiscal cycle is especially strong in developing countries. As in the United States, there is much anecdotal evidence of fiscal manipulation before elections in other countries. For example, in Israel, Ben-Porath (1975) shows convincingly that opportunistic policymaking in light of elections was quite consistent over the period 1952–1973, with tax cuts implemented before elections, but tax increases only after. Pre-electoral fiscal manipulation was especially strong in the 1982 elections, and Brender (1999) finds evidence of

Figure 7 RATIO OF NET TRANSFERS TO GNP, 1960–1978

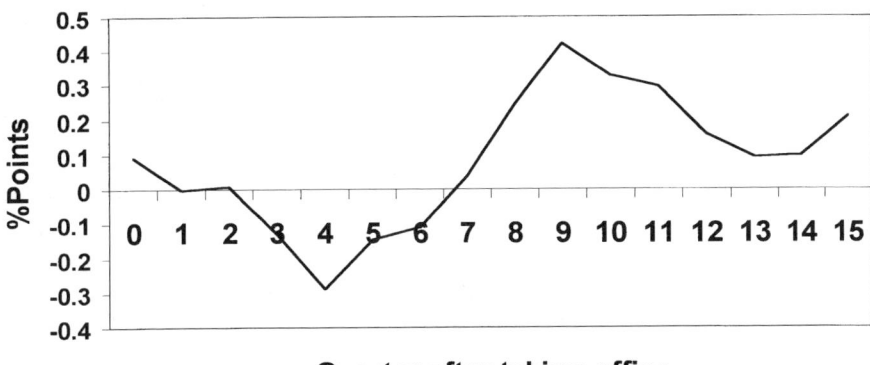

Quarter after taking office

Figure 8 RATIO OF NET TRANSFERS TO GNP, 1979–1998

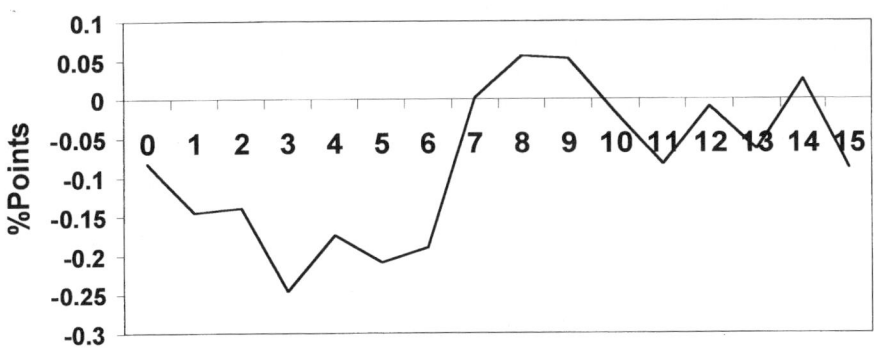

Quarter after taking office

fiscal manipulation before the most recent elections (although he argues that it hurt rather than helped the incumbents). Krueger and Turan (1993) argue that pre-electoral fiscal manipulation was common in Turkey in the period 1950–1980. Pre-electoral fiscal manipulation is common in Latin America, the increase in the quasifiscal deficit in Mexico before the 1994 elections being but one of many examples. [Gonzalez (1999b) shows the existence of an electoral cycle in government spending in Mexico over the period 1958–1997 in both presidential and congressional elections.] Several studies have found significant pre-electoral increases in public spending in India before elections.

Cross-country studies yield similar results. Ames (1987) presents a panel study of 17 Latin American countries in which he shows that over the period 1947–1982, government expenditures increased by 6.3% in the pre-election year and decreased by 7.6% in the year after the election. Block (2000) presents evidence of a political business cycle in both fiscal and monetary policy in a cross section of 44 sub-Saharan African countries. Schuknecht (1996) is probably the first comprehensive study of the political business cycle in 35 developing countries over the period 1970–1992. He argues that there should be more room for manipulation in developing countries, as checks and balances are weaker and the incumbent has more power over monetary and fiscal policy. He argues that in developing countries expenditure policies (such as distribution of free or subsidized goods or employment generation via public works programs) are probably more effective than tax cuts in affecting voter behavior. He uses a political dummy which is positive in the year of elections, negative in the year after, and zero otherwise in fiscal deficit and output autoregressions such as (4) and finds a clear, significant effect of elections on the fiscal balance, but no significant effect on output.

Gonzalez (1999a) and Shi and Svensson (2000) extend the Rogoff (1990) model of political budget cycles to study the effect of the degree of democracy on the magnitude of fiscal cycles. Gonzalez considers the fiscal model set out in a subsequent section (but without a monetary sector), including two further variables: the cost of removing a policymaker from office (the *degree of democracy*), and *transparency*, meaning the probability that voters learn the incumbent's competence costlessly, that is, independent of signaling. She finds that with a high enough cost of removing officeholders, incumbents will not be removed from office and will follow their full-information optimal policy. An electoral budget cycle emerges only if removing a politician from office is not too costly. Transparency also has intuitive effects: the higher the degree of transparency, the smaller the amount of distortion away from the first best in the political budget cycle. Interestingly, when there is a positive correlation between the degree of democracy and transparency, political budget cycles arise only where both measures are at intermediate levels. Shi and Svensson include a similar measure of transparency in a Rogoff political-budget-cycle model, but where government spending is chosen before the government learns its competence, so that no signaling occurs. (See their footnote 9.)

Gonzalez (1999b) considers the relation between the level of democracy and the strength of the political cycle in a sample of 43 countries over the period 1950–1997 and finds that the cycle is strongest in countries with intermediate levels of democracy. Shi and Svensson (2000) consider regressions such as (4) for a sample of 123 developed and developing countries over the period 1975–1995 and similarly include an index of democracy. They also find that a fiscal political business cycle is especially strong in developing countries.

8. An Initial Summing Up

The argument presented so far is twofold. First, both empirically and theoretically, a monetary-based PBC model—either of manipulation of aggregate economic activity via monetary surprises before an election, or of partisan effects after an election—is less than fully convincing. Second, there appears to be a strong role for fiscal policy in many countries, including the United States in certain time periods. This suggests basing PBC models on fiscal rather than monetary policy. Conceptually, this solves some basic problems for which monetary PBC models have been criticized. Fiscal policy has real effects on economic activity even if anticipated. Moreover, it can affect voting behavior even if there are no aggregate effects. Since monetary policy is not the driving force, one need not assume that the incumbent controls monetary policy.

However, basing a PBC model, or at least an opportunistic PBC model, on manipulation of fiscal policy raises two key questions. First, *how can the monetary effects that are observed be made consistent with a PBC driven by fiscal policy?* This question has at least two aspects: first, on a conceptual level, what is the role of an independent central bank in a fiscal induced PBC, and, on an empirical level, how can we reconcile the cycle in monetary aggregates that often does appear before an election? Second, *why do rational voters respond to pre-electoral manipulation?* We consider these questions in turn.

The key to the monetary effects is that, as Woolley (1984) and Beck (1987) have argued, an independent central bank may be willing to accommodate the executive branch's pressures for monetary policy during election years in order to prevent sharp movements in interest rates. They do so in order to avoid any appearance of interfering politically in the election process. Woolley, who has studied the political relation between the U.S. president and the Federal Reserve more than anyone else, puts it as follows (1984, p. 127):

> Sherman Maisel wrote that "Federal Reserve policy has always been to avoid, if possible, taking any major monetary actions as elections approach." This conclusion was echoed in several interviews with Federal Reserve officials. As Governor Partee put it, "if you were to ask a central banker about what he would want to see in a period prior to an election, he would say he wanted to

have stability." Stability in interest rates and the money supply would presumably keep the central bank from being dragged into partisan politics.

The Fed is not so much interested in pushing the re-election of the incumbent as in simply "lying low" during the election so as not to be subsequently criticized.[14]

The role of monetary policy in a political cycle is more probably passive rather than active, accommodating fiscal stimuli that opportunistic policymakers may employ to affect election outcomes. This distinction follows Beck (1987), who, as pointed out above, argued that there is a political cycle in the money supply in the United States, but no cycle in monetary instruments, such as reserves or the federal funds rate. The reason is that the Federal Reserve accommodates fiscal policy in an election year, so that there is a passive political monetary cycle caused by a political cycle in fiscal instruments, but the Fed does not actively induce a political cycle.[15]

Why do voters respond to pre-electoral manipulation if they are rational? The basic argument, first formalized by Rogoff (1990) and Rogoff and Sibert (1988), is that the enactment of policies that appear to be opportunistically short-sighted and the influence they have on voters may be due to a *signaling* effect: voters have imperfect information about relevant characteristics of potential policymakers, and what appear to be gimmicks have an effect because they are taken to provide relevant information about candidates for office. Specifically, a government signals its "type" by taking actions that worsen the budget situation with the notion that only someone who is very competent would put himself in that situation.

One criticism that has been raised of this approach is that it is the most competent who distort the economy, a result seen as unrealistic. A better

---

14. Both Beck and Woolley argue that the easy monetary stance of the Fed under Arthur Burns in the 1972 presidential election was due to something more complicated than giving Nixon the expansionary monetary policy he wanted to ensure his re-election. It must be seen against the backdrop of wage–price controls instituted the previous year. In October 1971, as part of Phase II, the White House asked Congress for the authority to control interest rates and corporate dividends, but to forgo use of the authority for the time being. This led to the formation of the Committee on Interest and Dividends (CID), of which Burns was chairman, responsible for monitoring interest rates. Burns was dead set against interest-rate controls, but aware of the political pressure for their imposition. He was therefore especially concerned about letting interest rates rise during 1972, and, according to Woolley, communicated to the FOMC his concerns about the political pressures for administrative controls that rising interest rates would induce. See Woolley (1984, Chapter 8).
15. Beck argues that this accommodation is why the monetary cycle that both he and Grier (1989) find peaks in the election quarter itself, when the monetary expansion shouldn't affect outcomes.

way to view this approach, in my opinion, is that a more "competent" policymaker can expand government spending or reduce taxes and still not induce the distortion that a less "competent" policymaker would induce.

9. The Active-Fiscal, Passive-Monetary Model

We now present a model of the PBC illustrating the approach suggested in the previous section. The fiscal side of the model follows Rogoff's (1990) model of political budget cycles, with an incumbent using fiscal policy to help his re-election prospects. Monetary policy is controlled by a separate monetary authority, which may nonetheless accommodate fiscal expansion. On a conceptual level the model differs from existing models in that political cycles reflect not a single authority that controls all macroeconomic policy, but elected officials who influence fiscal policy and an independent monetary authority that controls monetary policy. The political cycle reflects the interaction of these separate forces.

9.1 VOTERS

Voters are heterogeneous in two dimensions. First, the utility of every voter depends on aggregate economic variables, with this effect given by a loss function such as (2). Voters differ in the relative weight they assign to output fluctuations, the coefficient α in equation (2), but have the same targets for x and π. Second, the utility of a subset of voters is affected by some government-provided public goods, which are controlled by the incumbent president, and all such voters place the same utility value on public goods. (These play the role of targeted transfers to specific constituencies.) Since the incumbent does not control macroeconomic aggregates on his own (in fact, they are more influenced by the monetary authority), only those voters who receive public goods will have a preference over candidates.[16]

The implicit assumption of heterogeneous voters is made to highlight three issues crucial to a fiscal model of the PBC and to PBC models in general. First, heterogeneity of the population means that we cannot think of a policymaker as maximizing the utility of a "representative" agent. This insight formed the basis of partisan models and is more general. As I argue in Drazen (2000a), heterogeneity of interests is the

---

16. This structure is a much simplified version of the Dixit–Londregan (1996) model of targeted transfers in which voters differ in the relative weights they put on transfers and policy preferences, with those most susceptible to transfers being targeted by opportunistic politicians.

central concept of political economy.[17] Second, transfers can be targeted to specific groups, so that there can be a significant effect on voting as a result of fiscal manipulation without there necessarily being an effect on aggregate economic activity. Third, whether any fiscal electoral cycle has aggregate effects will depend, among other things, on the possible size of politically motivated fiscal expenditures relative to the economy as a whole. (It will also depend on the strength of the monetary authority relative to elected politicians.)

More specifically, there are two government-produced goods: g, a public consumption good (measured in per voter terms), and k, a public investment good. In any period, the utility of a voter i who is affected by public-good provision may be written:

$$U^i(x_t, \pi_t, g_t, k_t) = -\left(\alpha_i \frac{(x_t - \tilde{x})^2}{2} + \frac{(\pi_t - \tilde{\pi})^2}{2}\right) + g_t + v(k_t), \tag{10}$$

where $\tilde{x} \geq 0$, $\tilde{\pi} \geq 0$, and $v(\cdot)$ is an increasing concave function satisfying the Inada conditions. A voter of type i who is not affected by public goods has a utility function only containing the first expression on the right-hand side of (10). There are two periods, so that the expected utility of voter i over his horizon is

$$E(\Omega^i) = E_t\left(\sum_{t=1}^{2} \beta^{t-1} U^i(\cdot)\right), \tag{11}$$

where $\beta < 1$ is the voter's discount rate.[18]

9.2 AGGREGATE SUPPLY OF AND DEMAND FOR GOODS

The aggregate output gap x_t and inflation π_t are related by an aggregate supply relation as in (1), but with a stochastic element:

$$x_t = \pi_t - E_t \pi_{t+1} + s_t, \tag{12}$$

where s_t is a supply shock described by $s_t = \rho s_{t-1} + \hat{s}_t$, with $0 \leq \rho \leq 1$, and where $\hat{s}_t$ is an i.i.d. mean-zero random variable. Note the difference in

---

17. In Rogoff's (1990) paper, the key conflict of interest is between a voter who maximizes his utility and a politician who cares about social welfare but has the additional objective of staying in office. See equation (17) below.
18. As in Rogoff (1990), there may also be a nonpecuniary, leader-specific shock. Its role here would be to ensure that in a pooling equilibrium in which policy gives no information about competence, an incumbent is *not* elected with certainty. This is important for some of the proofs of equilibrium, but suppressed here.

the expected inflation term from (1), where it is expected future inflation, rather than current inflation, that enters. This change is to make the monetary side of the model consistent with recent work on interest-rate rules, as in Clarida, Gali, and Gertler (1999). This change is of crucial importance in how one interprets the Phillips curve (see Clarida, Gali, and Gertler, 1999), but has no qualitative effect on our basic argument about the interaction of the fiscal and monetary authorities. It is assumed that prices are sticky in the short run, which allows monetary policy to have short-run effects.

Output consists of public goods determined by the incumbent politician (as explained below) and all other goods; as shorthand, we term *nonpolitical* goods those that the politician cannot determine directly. The supply of public consumption goods is given by

$$g_t = \epsilon - k_{t+1}, \tag{13}$$

where ϵ is the *competence* of the President currently in office. A more competent leader is a better economic manager, able to increase a country's level of output. Competence is a given characteristic of a leader, which in this two-period setup is equivalent to the first-order moving-average structure assumed by Rogoff. Leaders are of two types: high competence (ϵ^H) and low competence ($\epsilon^L < \epsilon^H$). Competence ϵ is not observed by the voters; in the absence of any information, they assign a probability $0 < \gamma < 1$ to a leader being of high competence, where $\bar{\epsilon} = \gamma \epsilon^H + (1 - \gamma) \epsilon^L$.

The public-goods constraint is written in this way to highlight the fact that for public capital to be purchased in period $t+1$, funds must be allocated in period t.[19] Hence, though the decision on public investment is made at t, it only enters aggregate demand in $t+1$. Moreover, though k_{t+1} is chosen in period t, it is only observed in period $t+1$.

Following the monetary-policy literature, we assume that demand for nonpolitical goods (relative to potential output) is a decreasing function of the ex ante real interest rate with a stochastic term z_t, that is, it is $X(i_t - E_t \pi_{t+1}) + z_t$. We may then write the output gap as a function of the interest rate (the "IS curve"):

$$x_t = X(i_t - E_t \pi_{t+1}) + k_{t-1} + g_t + z_t - \epsilon. \tag{14}$$

In deriving the monetary authority's interest-rate rule, we will consider a linear version of (14):

19. Multiplying k_{t+1} by one plus the real interest rate to represent the cost of carry does not change the basic results, but makes the calculations more difficult.

$$x_t = -\varphi(i_t - E_t\pi_{t+1}) + \eta_t, \tag{15}$$

where $\varphi > 0$ and $\eta_t = k_{t-1} + g_t + z_t - \epsilon$.

9.3 THE PRESIDENT AND FISCAL POLICY

It is assumed that the incumbent president controls the determination of public (that is, political) goods g and k. The president cares about the social welfare of all voters. Given the form of the utility function (10) and the fact that voters don't hold the president directly accountable for macroeconomic performance, the single-period voter welfare measure he maximizes is the sum of (negative) macroeconomic loss over all voters plus $g + v(k)$ multiplied by the fraction of voters who are affected by public-good supply. This objective may be written as

$$U^V(\cdot) = -\left(\bar{\alpha}\frac{(x_t - \tilde{x})^2}{2} + \frac{(\pi_t - \tilde{\pi})^2}{2}\right) + n[g_t + v(k_t)], \tag{16}$$

where $\bar{\alpha}$ is the average value of α^i over the electorate and $0 < n < 1$ is the fraction of voters affected by provision of political goods.

The incumbent has two additional arguments in his objective function. First, as in Rogoff, he attaches a value to being in office per se, which we denote by Θ. Second, he may try to influence the central bank's choice of monetary policy; specifically, consistent with the discussion in the previous section, an incumbent may press the monetary authority to keep interest rates low in an election year, which he may value for re-election purposes or to satisfy important constituencies. Here, the second is modeled loosely by assuming that voters value economic activity more highly than the monetary authority [see equation (18) below], which is therefore important to the incumbent in an election year. However, applying pressure has a cost independent of its effect on interest rates or other observable variables. This cost may reflect the psychic costs to the executive of tension with the monetary authority or, more likely, the cost of reduced cooperation from the monetary authority in the future. The cost depends on the whole nature of the interaction between the monetary authority and the elected president, including the ability of the monetary authority to withstand such pressures. For now, we simply write the cost of such pressure as ζ, where ζ is increasing in the amount of pressure applied.

An incumbent's expected utility may then be written

$$\Omega^P = E\Omega^V + \sum_{t=1}^{2} \beta^{t-1} q_t(\Theta - \zeta), \tag{17}$$

where q_t is the probability of being in office in period t, and Ω^V is obtained from U^V in (16) via (11). For an incumbent, $q_1 = 1$; q_2 will be derived below. Equation (17) makes clear that since an incumbent places a value on being in office, he will be opportunistic and try to manipulate the economy to improve his re-election chances, but there are limits on how far he is willing to go.

In our model manipulation takes two forms. First, and most importantly, there is direct manipulation via fiscal policy (choice of g), where concern for social welfare puts a limit on the degree of manipulation. Second, he may put pressure on the central bank to lower interest rates, but there are costs of doing so, as summarized by ζ. For simplicity, it is assumed that the incumbent knows that fiscal policy affects interest rates but does not know exactly how the monetary authority will respond and therefore does not take into account the effect of g on interest rates in choosing his preferred value. This assumption, which simplifies the mathematical analysis, seems realistic and has no substantive effect on the nature of the results.

9.4 ELECTORAL STRUCTURE

The electoral structure is as follows. For simplicity, there are only two periods, with an election at the end of the first period. In the first period the incumbent observes ϵ and chooses g_1 and k_2. Voters observe g_1 and i_1 (but not ϵ or k_2) and use these observations to form an inference about competence. Based on their beliefs about competence, they then vote whether to retain the incumbent or replace him with a challenger of unknown competence, so that the expected competence of the challenger is $\bar{\epsilon}$. More specifically, the voters choose to retain the incumbent if expected utility under the incumbent is higher than expected utility under the challenger.[20] In the second period, the elected president chooses his first-best policy, as there is no election.

9.5 THE MONETARY AUTHORITY

We assume that the central bank's objective function can be represented by the loss function (2) (which also represents the loss that individuals

20. An alternative assumption is that the incumbent chooses g_1 *before* ϵ is observed, so there is no signaling of type. Suppose that output, which *is* observed by voters before an election, is the sum of competence ϵ and a random shock, both unobserved. Hence, when a high level of output is observed, optimal inference would lead voters to raise the probability that the incumbent is of high competence, and therefore make them more likely to vote to re-elect him. Incumbents, knowing this, are induced to increase government expenditures before an election. One would therefore obtain a preelectoral fiscal cycle, with all competence types raising spending before an election and voters voting on the basis of good economic times, but without signaling.

assign to aggregate fluctuations) but that the coefficient on output deviations or the target levels for the output gap and inflation need not be the same as the public's. Specifically, let the central bank's single-period loss function be

$$\mathcal{L}_t^{CB} = \sigma \frac{(x_t - \tilde{x})^2}{2} + \frac{(\pi_t - \tilde{\pi})^2}{2}, \tag{18}$$

where $\sigma < \bar{\alpha}$, that is, the monetary authority assigns a greater cost to inflation fluctuations than the "average" voter, as well as possibly having lower targets for output and inflation. Though there is considerable research aimed at deriving the central bank's objective from the utility function of the representative agent, the whole concept of a policymaker maximizing the utility of a representative agent misses the essence of political-economy models. Furthermore, using a loss function such as (18) follows both the PBC literature and the literature on monetary policy rules [see, for example, Clarida, Gali, and Gertler (1999) and the discussion therein], making it easier to compare results from those literatures.

The monetary authority chooses x_t and π_t to minimize its loss function subject to the aggregate supply relation (12) and the shocks s_t and η_t. (See the appendix for a derivation of optimal policy as well as the interest-rate rule.) By maximizing (18) subject to (12), and using (15) to derive the nominal interest rate, one obtains the monetary authority's optimal interest-rate rule:

$$i_t = \left(1 + \frac{1}{\rho\sigma\varphi}\right) E_t \pi_{t+1} + \frac{1}{\varphi} \eta_t, \tag{19}$$

where $E_t \pi_{t+1} = \rho s_t$ and it is assumed that this rule will be followed in the future. This rule gives the first-best response to supply shocks s_t and demand shocks η_t.[21] We consider below how pressure from the executive may force the monetary authority to follow a different rule implying a smaller interest-rate response to shocks.

To close the monetary sector, the money-supply growth rate consistent with the interest-rate target is given by the money-market equilibrium condition (the *LM curve*) when the price level is sticky in the short run. In the absence of money demand shocks, we obtain a simple relation between money growth and interest rates, namely,

---

21. As Clarida, Gali, and Gertler (2000) point out, this rule is consistent with the Taylor rule when lagged inflation or a linear combination of lagged inflation and the output gap is sufficient to forecast future inflation. It is also consistent with inflation targeting.

$$\mu_t = M(i_t, x_t) \tag{20}$$

where, given x_t, the money growth rate will be an increasing function of the interest rate. We assume that the money-supply growth rate is contemporaneously unobserved by voters. This prevents them from using interest rates and monetary growth rates together to infer the competence of the president.

9.6 EQUILIBRIUM FISCAL AND MONETARY POLICY UNDER FULL INFORMATION

We begin with the benchmark full-information equilibrium, where voters can observe ϵ before voting. If ϵ is observed, pre-electoral fiscal policy can have no effect on the election outcome. Taking q_2 as given in (17), the incumbent's decision problem over g_t and k_t becomes equivalent to maximizing the voters' utility U^V. Using the simplifying assumption that the president does not take into account the effect of g on interest rates in choosing his preferred value, one obtains a first-order condition:

$$\beta v'(k) \geq 1, \tag{21}$$

with equality if $\epsilon \geq (v')^{-1}(1/\beta)$. If ϵ is sufficiently large, then both public goods are supplied and (21) holds as an equality. We assume that ϵ^L (and hence ϵ^H) is high enough that this is the case. First-best government investment and consumption are then

$$k^* = (v')^{(-1)}(1/\beta), \qquad g^*(\epsilon^j) = \epsilon^j - k^*, \tag{22}$$

for $j = L, H$. This is the policy always chosen in the second period (when there is no election), and it is the policy chosen in the first period under full information. Clearly, g^* is increasing in ϵ, so that voter utility is increasing in ϵ as well.

To find monetary policy in a nonelection year (or under full information), we assume that the monetary authority knows (22), that is, that it knows that there is no electoral manipulation in a nonelection year. Combining (22) with (19) and (20), one finds that the interest rate and money growth rate will be the same under low- and high-competence policymakers in nonelection years, depending only on aggregate demand and supply shocks.

9.7 FISCAL POLICY UNDER ASYMMETRIC INFORMATION

We now consider the incumbent politician's decision problem when his competence is not observed. In this sort of signaling problem, there is generally a multiplicity of equilibria, both separating and pooling. We consider only pure strategies, and assume that voters are sufficiently sophisticated that they rule out incumbents following dominated strategies. This leaves only one separating equilibrium, on which we focus.[22] (Of course, the welfare the low-competence type gets in a pooling equilibrium will be important in deriving the separating equilibrium.) We show that in a separating equilibrium, the low-competence type chooses his full-information, first-best solution, while the high-competence type signals his type by choosing public consumption g higher than the full-information optimum (at the expense of low public investment, which is contemporaneously unobserved). The effect on interest rates depends on the choice of g_t, which is perceived by the central bank as a demand shock, and on the pressure the president is able to put on the monetary authority. High pre-electoral government consumption combined with effective pressure on the monetary authority will be seen in high money growth rates, even though it has no causative effect on the pre-electoral expansion.

Under asymmetric information, voters' beliefs about competence are a function of the observed fiscal policy. (The level of interest rates will give no additional information, given the unobservability of the money growth rate.) We represent these beliefs as $\hat{\gamma}(g)$, which is the probability a voter assigns to the incumbent being of high competence, given the observation of fiscal policy. These beliefs in turn determine the probability that an incumbent is re-elected. Given Equation (19), interest rates are determined by g and the incumbent's type as given above, so that we may write the incumbent's expected utility as a function of his chosen policy and his type as $\Omega^p(g, \hat{\gamma}(g), \epsilon)$.

To derive the equilibrium, we work backwards. In the second period, both competence types choose the fiscal policy according to (22), with government consumption g being higher under a high-competence than a low-competence type. Given the first-best fiscal solution, the central bank can meet both of its monetary targets. Voters will therefore always re-elect an incumbent they believe to be of high competence [$q_2(\hat{\gamma} = 1) = 1$] and vote to remove an incumbent they believe to be of low competence [$q_2(\hat{\gamma} = 0) = 0$]. When there is no information about the competence of the incumbent (for example, in a pooling equilibrium where both types chose the same policy), so that the incumbent is assumed to be of average competence γ, it is assumed that the probability that he is re-elected is positive, but less than one [$0 < q_2(\hat{\gamma} = \gamma) < 1$], for the reasons discussed in footnote 18 above.

---

22. In this sort of model, pooling equilibria are generally ruled out by the Cho–Kreps "intuitive" criterion. See the discussion in Rogoff (1990).

In the first period in a separating equilibrium, a low-competence type chooses his full-information optimum, since he gains nothing from choosing a distortionary public-expenditure combination that yields less utility but still allows voters to deduce his type. A high-competence type must therefore choose a policy that the low-competence type chooses not to mimic. More specifically, denote the policy of the high-competence type in a separating equilibrium by g^H, with an associated nominal interest rate. In order for the low-competence type not to mimic the high-competence type, he must receive lower utility from mimicking the high-competence type than from revealing himself. (In the case of equal utility, we assume that the low-competence type chooses to reveal himself.) We thus require in a separating equilibrium that

$$\Omega^P(g^H, \hat{\gamma}(g^H) = \gamma; \epsilon^L) \leq \Omega^P(g^*(\epsilon^L), 0; \epsilon^L). \tag{23}$$

That is, in a separating equilibrium, g^H (and the associated interest rate) is such that a low-competence incumbent would rather choose the full-information solution and be revealed (and hence defeated for sure) than choose to mimic the spending level g^H with the implied low level of public investment. In such a pooling equilibrium the low-competence type must put enough pressure on the central bank to hit the interest rate i^H that the high-competence type achieves, which is possible if the monetary authority chooses a high enough (unobserved) money growth rate. That is, the high-competence type must choose a high enough level of g^H that the low-competence type chooses not to mimic.

One possibility is that the high-competence type's full-information level of expenditure, namely $g^*(\epsilon^H)$, satisfies (23). That is, the high-competence type can separate himself by choosing his first-best point, because it is such that the low-competence will not find it optimal to adopt it. This would be the case, for example if the value Θ of being in office were low. In that case the distortion that a low-competence incumbent would have to undertake to match the high-competence type's nondistortionary solution would not justify the (low) value of winning reelection. Another case in which $g^*(\epsilon^H)$ would be a separating equilibrium is where the difference between ϵ^H and ϵ^L is very large, since it would be too costly for the low-competence type to adopt the high-competence type's first-best policy.

When $g^*(\epsilon^H)$ does not satisfy (23), then the high-competence type must choose a point which gives him less utility than $g^*(\epsilon^H)$ in order to separate himself. Since the cost to the high-competence type of signaling his type is higher for higher g^H relative to g^*, he will choose the lowest level of g^H consistent with separation. (That is, he will choose an undominated strategy.) This value is given by the value of g^H that satisfies (23) with equality.

A further condition for a separating equilibrium is that g^H must give the high-competence type utility no lower than the full-information expenditure level $g^*(\epsilon^H)$ gives him, that is,

$$\Omega^P(g^H,1;\epsilon^H) \geq \Omega^P(g^*(\epsilon^H),\hat{\gamma}(g^*(\epsilon^H)) = \gamma;\epsilon^H). \tag{24}$$

A separating equilibrium must satisfy both (23) and (24). One may show that since $\epsilon^H > \epsilon^L$ and $v(\cdot)$ is concave, a separating equilibrium exists. (See Drazen, 2000b.) In such an equilibrium, the low-competence type chooses $g^*(\epsilon^L)$, his full-information first-best level of expenditure, while a high-competence type chooses a level of expenditure g^H just high enough that the low-competence type does not find it optimal to adopt that policy instead of his first-best policy.

More realistically, there will be many different competence types, with all but the least competent choosing a level of expenditure above his first-best optimum to signal his competence level. [See Rogoff and Sibert (1988) for the derivation of this type of equilibrium with a continuum of competence types.] Hence, some degree of pre-electoral manipulation of fiscal policy will be the rule rather than the exception.

We may then summarize the characteristics of the political fiscal cycle. Before an election, a high level of spending signals an high-competence incumbent, so that a high level of spending leads the incumbent to be re-elected by rational voters. This high level of spending may be either nondistortionary [if $g^*(\epsilon^H)$ satisfies (23)] or distortionary (if it does not). When the optimal signal is distortionary, the central bank will partially accommodate high government spending to restrain the impact of fiscal expansion on interest rates. Hence, money growth will rise before an election, not to affect economic activity directly, but in response to expansionary fiscal policy.

9.8 MONETARY POLICY IN AN ELECTION PERIOD

In a nonelection period all competence types choose fiscal policy according to (22), so the demand stimulus is independent of competence; and, as was argued above, the monetary authority's preferred monetary policy, as determined by (19), is independent of competence as well. Moreover, there is no reason for a politician to put pressure on the monetary authority for electoral purposes. In contrast, neither of these conditions need hold in an electoral period.

As argued in the previous section, in an election period, the high-competence type (all but the lowest-competence type in a model of many types) will choose to signal, and this may require choosing a level of public consumption g_1 above the first-best optimum. If there are many competence types with two adjoining types having values of ϵ not far from one another, then signaling will almost certainly require increasing g_1 above the level given in (22).

How will the monetary authority react? In the absence of any knowledge of the president's competence, an increase in g in an election period is seen simply as a demand shock η_t, which the monetary authority would want to offset by increasing the nominal interest rate according to (19). However, when the "average" voter prefers higher and less variable output than the monetary authority, an incumbent president gains votes by limiting the increase in the interest rate, implying that the equilibrium output gap is below what the monetary authority prefers. Note that this is true even if the president shares the monetary authority's preferences over aggregate variables in (18), as long as the voters have different preferences.

To make this precise, one has to specify how much pressure the president puts on the monetary authority and how this is translated into limitations on interest rate. There are several ways of modeling this. For simplicity, suppose that the intervention takes the form of inducing the monetary authority to reduce proportionally the response to demand shocks (which means accommodating the fiscal stimulus of the incumbent, among other things), that is, to choose the interest rate in the election period according to

$$i_t = \left(1 + \frac{1}{\rho\sigma\varphi}\right) E_t \pi_{t+1} + (1 - w)\frac{1}{\varphi} \eta_t, \qquad (25)$$

for $0 \leq w \leq 1$ chosen by the incumbent president.[23] The higher w is, the greater is the incumbent's cost ζ. An incumbent will choose w optimally depending on the nature of the cost of pressure relative to the weight he puts on voters' welfare Ω^V. Interest-rate intervention will limit the increase in interest rates in response to fiscal shocks and hence increase output above what the monetary authority prefers, which is preferred by the voters. The aggregate effect of this will depend on the size of the fiscal stimulus. If it is targeted to a narrow group of voters (that is, if n, the fraction of voters who are affected by higher g, is small) or if the size

23. From the monetary authority's optimization problem, it is clear that even with intervention, conditions (A2) and (A3) in the appendix still hold. Since the monetary authority expects to be allowed to follow the first-best rule in period 2, (25) gives the response of interest rates to shocks when the monetary authority knows that its reaction is limited in the way it is.

of the fiscal stimulus is small relative to the economy, there will be little or no aggregate effect. If it is large, as in some of the developed-country cases discussed in Section 8, there may be a large aggregate effect.

The effect on money growth rates is obvious. The more pressure the incumbent puts on the monetary authority to keep interest rates from rising, the higher must be money growth relative to the monetary authorities' first-best. In the case of $w = 1$, interest rates don't rise at all in response to a fiscal stimulus, so that the money growth rate must increase before the election. Of course, this depends on the existence of a fiscal stimulus. In its absence, there is no higher-than-average pressure on interest rates and hence no need for a monetary accommodation of the politically induced fiscal stimulus. The possibility of accommodation in response to pressure, its implications for monetary policy, and its connection with the fiscal stimulus contain the essence of the AFPM model of the PBC.

10. A Look at the Data and Some Concluding Comments

We now take a quick look at the data to show that they are broadly consistent with the model. A clear difference between a money-based PBC model and the AFPM model is that in the former, monetary effects are the driving force of the political–economic cycle, while in the latter they are induced effects, due to the monetary authority wanting to offset fiscal effects that would otherwise drive up interest rates. Hence, money growth in a money-driven PBC model should be expansionary and drive down interest rates, while in the AFPM model it should be associated with stable or even slightly rising interest rates. Put another way, the monetary expansion in a money-driven model should be reflected in changes in the instruments of monetary policy in an expansionary direction, while in the AFPM world, we should see an expansion only in broad monetary aggregates, not in instruments of policy. This type of argument was first put forward by Beck (1987), as discussed in Section 8 above. He found that the opportunistic monetary growth cycle from 1960 to about 1980 was characterized by this distinction, and in regressions such as (4) he found no political effects on the fed funds rate to match the M1 political cycle. This distinction is summarized by the difference between the money growth over a president's term in Figures 4 and 5 and by the federal funds rate shown in Figure 6, where there is no clear political effect.[24]

---

24. In fact, in the post-1979 period, the fed funds rate actually rises in the quarter before the election.

A second broad prediction of the AFPM model is that monetary growth before an election should reflect fiscal impulses. Note that one is *not* testing whether fiscal manipulation or voters' responses are rational, but whether there is a causal connection between the fiscal and the monetary cycle. As reported in Section 6, both Keech and Pak (1989) and Alesina (1988) found an electoral cycle for transfers between 1961 and the late 1970s or early 1980s, which has since disappeared. The strongest evidence for an M1-growth-rate electoral cycle is over the same period, while there is no such cycle after 1980.

Of course, correlation is not causation. A stronger test is to show whether when an electoral monetary cycle exists, it can be explained by the fiscal cycle, as opposed to simply a political dummy. Beck (1987) performs such a test and argues that fiscal variables can in fact explain the 1960–1978 electoral cycle in M1 growth rates. In Drazen (2000b), I present regression results that show a money growth cycle over this time period (but the absence of a federal-funds-rate cycle) and an electoral cycle in both net transfers to GNP and the ratio of the fiscal surplus to GNP over the same period.[25] Moreover, when the ratio of the fiscal surplus to GNP is included as an explanatory variable in the money growth regressions, the political dummy to capture electoral effects loses much of its significance.

A broader question is whether there is significant evidence of an opportunistic PBC in the aggregate data for the United States. On the whole, the evidence is not strong for effects on many macroeconomic aggregates. A key point of the AFPM model is that there can be a significant electoral cycle in policy instruments—significant in that it affects voting—without there being clear aggregate implications. "Traces" of monetary effects that are observed may be simply an attempt by the central bank to aim for an *absence* of aggregate effects that can be attributed to monetary policy! Of course, if the fiscal manipulation is large, as is the case in some developing countries, we should expect to see large aggregate effects.

Though the empirical findings are only suggestive at this point, they should, at the very least, induce us to rethink our approach to PBCs. This paper was in part survey and in part new research induced by considering what we have learned from twenty-five years of research on PBCs. The survey was meant to convey a very clear message: monetary

---

25. One interesting result in this regard is that in the 1960–1978 sample, there appears to be a significant positive effect on money growth in the election quarter itself, which is too late if monetary policy is meant to increase economic activity before the election. On the other hand, if monetary policy is counteracting the effects of fiscal policy on interest rates, the timing is not puzzling.

surprises are an unconvincing driving force for political cycles, either opportunistic or partisan; research should concentrate on fiscal policy as the driving force, especially for opportunistic cycles. Political monetary cycles are more likely the effect of accommodation of fiscal impulses, that is, monetary policy is passive while fiscal policy is active in trying to affect election outcomes.

Appendix. Derivation of Interest-Rate Rules[26]

The monetary authority minimizes a loss function

$$\sigma \frac{x_t^2}{2} + \frac{\pi_t^2}{2} + F_t, \tag{A1}$$

where F_t represents future expected loss from inflation and output, subject to (12). This yields an optimal relation between x_t and π_t of the form

$$x_t = -\frac{1}{\sigma}\pi_t. \tag{A2}$$

Combining this condition with the aggregate supply curve (12) and imposing rational expectations yields x_t and π_t as functions of the supply shock s_t, namely,

$$x_t = hs_t, \qquad \pi_t = -\sigma hs_t, \tag{A3}$$

where $E_t\pi_{t+1} = \rho s_t$ and $h = [1 + \sigma(1 - \rho)]^{-1}$. The optimal interest-rate rule then follows from substituting the desired value of x_t into the linearized aggregate demand relation (15) to obtain the nominal interest rate consistent with the output target, which is equation (19).

REFERENCES

Alesina, A. (1987). Macroeconomic policy in a two-party system as a repeated game. *Quarterly Journal of Economics* 102:651–678.
———. (1988). Macroeconomics and Politics. In *NBER Macroeconomics Annual*, Stanley Fischer, (ed.). Cambridge, MA: The MIT Press.
———, G. Cohen, and N. Roubini. (1992). Macroeconomic policy and elections in OECD democracies. *Economics and Politics* 4:1–30.
———, ———, and ———. (1993). Electoral business cycles in industrial democracies. *European Journal of Political Economy* 23:1–25.

26. Following Clarida, Gali and Gertler (1999).

———, and N. Roubini. (1992). Political cycles in OECD economies. *Review of Economic Studies* 59, 663–88.

———, ———, and G. Cohen. (1997). *Political Cycles and the Macroeconomy.* Cambridge MA: The MIT Press.

Alt, J., and A. Chrystal. (1983). *Political Economics.* Berkeley, CA: University of California Press.

Ames, B. (1987). *Political Survival.* Berkeley, CA: University of California Press.

Arcelus, F., and A. Meltzer. (1975). The effect of aggregate economic variables on congressional elections. *American Political Science Review* 69:1232–1239.

Beck, N. (1987). Elections and the Fed: Is there a political monetary cycle? *American Journal of Political Science* 31:194–216.

Ben-Porath, Y. (1975). The years of plenty and the years of famine—a political business. *Kyklos* 28, 400–403.

Block, S. (2000). Political business cycles, democratization, and economic reform: The case of Africa. Medford, MA: Fletcher School, Tufts University. Working paper.

Bloom, H., and H. Price. (1975). Voter response to short-run economic conditions: The asymmetric effect of prosperity and recession. *American Political Science Review* 69:1240–1254.

Brender, A. (1999). The effect of fiscal performance on local government election results in Israel: 1989–1998. Bank of Israel Research Department Discussion Paper 99.04.

Chowdhury, A. (1993). Political surfing over economic waves: Parliamentary election timing in India. *American Journal of Political Science* 37:1100–1118.

Clarida, R., J. Gali, and M. Gertler. (1999). The science of monetary policy: A new Keynesian Perspective. *Journal of Economic Literature* 37:1661–1707.

———, ———, and ———. (2000). Monetary policy and macroeconomic stability: Evidence and some theory. *Quarterly Journal of Economics* 116:147–180.

Dixit, A., and J. Londregan. (1996). The determinants of success of special interests in redistributive politics. *Journal of Politics* 58:1132–1155.

Drazen, A. (2000a). *Political Economy in Macroeconomics.* Princeton, NJ: Princeton University Press.

———. (2000b). The AFPM model of the political business cycle: Theory and evidence. University of Maryland. Working Paper.

Fair, R. (1978). The effect of economic events on votes for president. *Review of Economics and Statistics* 60:159–172.

———. (1982). The effect of economic events on votes for president: 1980 results. *Review of Economics and Statistics* 64:322–325.

———. (1988). The effects of economic events on votes for president: 1984 update. *Political Behavior* 10:168–179.

Faust, J., and J. Irons. (1999). Money, politics, and the post-war business cycle. *Journal of Monetary Economics* 43:61–89.

Garfinkel, M., and A. Glazer. (1994). Does electoral uncertainty cause economic fluctuations? *American Economic Review* 84:169–173.

Gonzalez, M. (1999a). On elections, democracy and macroeconomic policy cycles. Department of Economics, Princeton University. Working Paper.

———. (1999b). Political budget cycles and democracy: A multi-country analysis. Department of Economics, Princeton University. Working Paper.

Grier, K. (1989). On the existence of a political monetary cycle. *American Journal of Political Science* 33:376–389.

Hibbs, D. (1977). Political parties and macroeconomic policy. *American Political Science Review* 71:1467–1487.
———. (1992). Partisan theory after fifteen years. *European Journal of Political Economy* 8:361–373.
———. (1994). The partisan model of macroeconomic cycles: More theory and evidence for the United States. *Economics and Politics* 6:1–24.
Ito, T. (1990). The timing of elections and political business cycles in Japan. *Journal of Asian Economics* 1:135–156.
Kalecki, M. (1943). Political aspects of full employment. *Political Quarterly* 7:322–331.
Keech, W., and K. Pak. (1989). Electoral cycles and budgetary growth in veterans' benefit programs. *American Journal of Political Science* 33:901–911.
Kramer, G. (1971). Short-term fluctuations in U.S. voting behavior, 1896–1964. *American Political Science Review* 65:131–143.
Krueger, A., and I. Turan. (1993). The politics and economics of Turkish policy reform in the 1980's. In *Political and Economic Interactions in Economic Policy Reform: Evidence from Eight Countries*, R. Bates and A. Krueger, (eds.). Oxford: Basil Blackwell.
Lewis-Beck, M. (1988). *Economics and Elections.* Ann Arbor: University of Michigan Press.
Lindbeck, A. (1976). Stabilization policy in open economies with endogenous politicians. *American Economic Review Papers and Proceedings* 66:1–19.
Madsen, H. (1980). Electoral outcomes and macroeconomic policies: The Scandinavian cases. In *Models of Political Economy*, P. Whitely, (ed.). London: Sage, pp. 15–46.
McCallum, B. (1978). The political business cycle: An empirical test. *Southern Economic Journal* 42:504–515.
McRae, D. (1977). A political model of the business cycle. *Journal of Political Economy* 85:239–263.
Nordhaus, W. (1975). The political business cycle. *Review of Economic Studies* 42:169–190.
Okun, A. (1973). Comments on Stigler's paper. *American Economic Review* 63:172–177.
Paldam, M. (1979). Is there an electoral cycle? A comparative study of national accounts. *Scandinavian Journal of Economics* 81:323–342.
Rogoff, K. (1988). Comment on "Macroeconomics and Politics." In *NBER Macroeconomics Annual*, Stanley Fischer, (ed.). Cambridge MA: The MIT Press.
———. (1990). Equilibrium political budget cycles. *American Economic Review* 80:21–36.
Rogoff, K., and A. Sibert. (1988). Elections and macroeconomic policy cycles. *Review of Economic Studies* 55:1–16.
Schuknecht, L. (1996). Political business cycles in developing countries. *Kyklos* 49:155–170.
Schumpeter, J. (1939). *Business Cycles: A Theoretical, Historical, and Statistical Analysis of the Capitalist Process.* New York: McGraw-Hill.
Sheffrin, S. (1989). Evaluating rational partisan business cycle theory. *Economics and Politics* 1:239–259.
Shi, M., and J. Svensson. (2000). Political business cycles in developed and developing countries. The World Bank. Working Paper.

Stigler, G. (1973). General economic conditions and national elections. *American Economic Review* 63:160–167.
Tufte, E. (1975). Determinants of the outcomes of midterm congressional elections. *American Political Science Review* 69:812–826.
———. (1978). *Political Control of the Economy.* Princeton, NJ: Princeton University Press.
Woolley, J.T. (1984). *Monetary Politics: The Federal Reserve and the Politics of Monetary Policy.* Cambridge, UK: Cambridge University Press.

Comment

ALBERTO ALESINA
Harvard University, NBER, and CEPR

1. Introduction

The purpose of Allan Drazen's fine paper is twofold: (1) to assess the literature on political business cycles, and (2) to provide a new model that combines monetary and fiscal policies as driving forces of opportunistic cycles. I will focus, as a discussant is supposed to do, on the points of disagreement.

Let me begin by noting that one should not expect that every election will create the same predictable pattern of policy choices. Some governments may use monetary instruments to achieve partisan or opportunist goals, others may use the fiscal instruments. Initial conditions may matter as well: in certain cases showing fiscal restraint may be a political plus, while fiscal expansions in election years may be punished. For instance Alesina, Perotti, and Tavares (1998) show that voters in OECD countries do not always reward governments that are fiscally expansionary. Alesina (2000) discusses the complex political economy of the current U.S. budget surplus. Spending more or taxing less in election years is only one of many aspects of the politics of fiscal policy. Drazen writes that "the reliance on monetary policy as the driving force of cycles is inconsistent with the evidence on the important role of fiscal policy." Why? I do not understand why it has to be one or the other. This fiscal-vs.-monetary "horse race" is a bit distracting from the main issues in this literature, namely whether voters behave rationally, whether opportunistic behavior is important (and in which countries and in which political systems), whether partisan motivations were and are still strong, which electoral systems are more or less prone to create cycles, what influence the degree of central-bank independence can have, what are the different issues arising in developed and developing countries, etc.

2. Review of the Literature

2.1 THE OPPORTUNISTIC CYCLE AND RATIONAL VOTERS

A striking feature of the opportunistic cycle of growth and unemployment is that while there is ample evidence that the state of the economy (especially GDP growth) affects electoral results, there is no evidence that in terms of growth and unemployment the economy does better than average in election years. This is clearly true for the United States and also for other OECD countries. Is this a puzzle? Not quite. The rational versions of the opportunistic model provide models consistent with these observations. Since this is a point that Drazen does not develop much, it is worth explaining. I will sketch the approach developed in Alesina and Rosenthal (1995). Consider an output equation

$$x_t = \pi_t - \pi_t^e + \eta_t + \epsilon_t, \tag{1}$$

where x is a measure of economic activity, π is inflation, and π^e is rationally expected inflation. The shock ϵ is a random noise that represent *luck*, and η represents government *competence* in managing the economy and evolves, for instance, with a MA(1) structure:

$$\eta_t = u_{t-1} + u_t, \tag{2}$$

where u is an i.i.d. shock. Higher competence means that output is higher for given inflation rate. Suppose that at the moment of the election that takes place at the end of period t the public observes x_t, π_t, and π_t^e but cannot distinguish between luck and competence. That is, the public observes the sum $\eta_t + \epsilon_t$ but not its components. Note that some form of persistence in competence is necessary; otherwise forward-looking voters would not care about the current state of the economy. Rational voters prefer to re-elect competent governments; therefore they will use observations on x_t (thus on $\eta_t + \epsilon_t$) as a noisy signal of competence. In this model the policymaker cannot engage in strategic manipulations of the economy using monetary or fiscal instruments (which would affect inflation); thus the rate of growth (or unemployment) in election years is not different from average. Nevertheless, the higher x_t is, the more likely it is that the incumbent will be elected. Thus the state of the economy affects electoral results, but opportunistic cycles à la Nordhaus are not present. This simple approach thus reconciles two features of the empirical evidence. Note that Wolfers (1999) has found considerable evidence of sophisticated voting behavior exactly in the sense that voters try to distinguish competence from luck. Alesina and Rosenthal (1995), on the other hand, find inconclusive results on voters' rationality in a competence-type model. In particular, American voters seem too sensitive to the rate of growth in election years.

In this version of the model there is no scope for manipulation, but Persson and Tabellini (1990) apply Rogoff's (1990) model of competence and, by assuming asymmetric information on the observation of inflation and output, show that even with rational voters one can have pre-electoral manipulations of inflation and growth. So one of the questions that Drazen raises in his Section 8 (summing up), namely, how rationality of voters can be consistent with opportunistic cycles, has received one answer already. Alesina and Rosenthal (1995) merge this model of retrospective voting with a partisan approach, so that the electorate votes on two grounds: competence and "ideology."

In summary: it should be clear that one can have retrospective voting based on competence without opportunistic manipulations. I am not saying that the latter do not occur, but it should be clear that retrospective voting and active manipulations do not necessarily go hand in hand. While I made this point using an inflation–output framework, the same applies in a fiscal-competence example.

2.2 OPPORTUNISTIC MONETARY AND FISCAL POLICY

Rational behavior of voters, plus the inherent difficulty in timing and controlling the business cycle, may restrict opportunistic behavior of policymakers with respect to instruments like monetary and fiscal policy. Drazen reviews carefully much empirical research on fiscal cycles both in OECD countries and in developing ones. My view of this empirical evidence is that in OECD countries there are several examples of fiscal relaxation in election years, in some cases accompanied by monetary relaxation. However, the evidence is not overly strong, and it should not be. If a policymaker went too far in the direction of election-oriented fiscal policy, the public would punish him because the electorate can be fooled only up to a point. Shi and Svensson (2000) in fact provide some interesting evidence that fiscal cycles may be more prevalent in countries where the voters have less access to a free press and other mechanisms to monitor the policymaker. Alesina, Perotti, and Tavares (1998) do not find that the timing of fiscal adjustments is particularly influenced by the timing of elections in OECD countries. In summary, opportunistic fiscal cycles are there in some countries and in some elections. As implied by rational models à la Rogoff (1990) and Rogoff and Sibert (1988), these cycles cannot be too large and predictable. I also agree that, as a vast literature on lobbying shows, favors to certain groups may be critical for electoral victory, even though these favors may not show up as large fluctuations of macro variables.

2.3 PARTISAN MODELS

The traditional partisan model due to Hibbs is based on an exploitable Phillips curve where left-wing and right-wing governments can choose permanently different levels of unemployment, growth, and inflation. In my work, started in the late eighties, I embodied partisan parties in models with rational expectations and consistent with a fairly standard neo-Keynesian model of the economy with wage contracts à la Fischer (1977). The idea was that if elections cannot be predicted, the future course of aggregate demand policy cannot be predicted. Thus electoral uncertainty is associated with policy uncertainty that leads to partisan cycles which are short-lived in real economic activity but may be longer-lived in inflation. I am probably not an impartial reader of the literature, but I find the partisan effects on growth and unemployment predicted by this model to be by far the strongest of all the regularities uncovered by the literature on political business cycles, in the United States in particular and in OECD countries more generally. As for the latter, the evidence is stronger in OECD countries with two-party (or two-bloc) systems. This last point reinforces the theory, since multiparty systems normally led by large centrist coalitions (as in Italy until recently) do not conform to the setup of the theory. For instance, Alesina, Roubini, and Cohen (1997) calculate that the difference between the rates of growth of GDP from the beginning of a left-wing government and of a right-wing government in a sample of 19 OECD countries reaches 2.2% about 6 quarters after a change of government (sample, 1960 to 1993). The same figure for the United States is larger, about 3.5%.[1] These partisan differences disappear about two years after an election.

Drazen raises several criticisms of this model that lead him to emphasize even in the abstract of his paper that "models based on monetary surprises . . . are unconvincing explanations of . . . partisan cycles." The first conceptual objection is that wage contracts could be adjusted ex ante to incorporate the electoral uncertainty, either by being contingent on the election result or by being signed after the election. This is an important issue that to some extent applies to all nominal-contract models. One could give the battery of standard answers to why agents may lock themselves in nominal contracts, such as menu-cost arguments.[2] More interesting is the direct evidence on this point raised by Garfinkel

---

1. See Alesina, Roubini, and Cohen (1997, p. 152).
2. See Alesina and Rosenthal (1995) for an extensive discussion of this point.

and Glazer (1994). As Drazen notes, these authors show that a fraction of wage contracts to be signed in election years are adjusted to be signed after the election. I find this very strong evidence in favor of the electoral uncertainty model. Note that Glazer and Garfinkel find that some, but not all, contracts are adjusted. Thus, according to these results, the agents recognize the role of electoral uncertainty but can protect themselves only partially. This seems to me one of the strongest direct confirmations of the theory. If these authors had found that nobody readjusts contracts, a critic of the rational-partisan theory would have said that the latter is irrelevant, since nobody cares about electoral uncertainty. If all contracts were readjusted, the same critic would say that the rational-partisan theory cannot work. The only result fully compatible with the rational-partisan theory is the one found by Garfinkel and Glazer (1994).

A second objection concerns direct tests of the role of electoral uncertainty. Chapter 5 of Alesina, Roubini, and Cohen (1997), which is based on the PhD thesis of Cohen (1993), is fully devoted to direct tests of the electoral uncertainty. Based on pre-electoral polls, Cohen calculates the ex ante probability of a Democratic or Republican victory for every postwar election. Note that ex post landslides may not always coincide with pre-electoral sentiments, especially if evaluated several months before an election, the timing relevant for a wage-contract (or a nominal-price rigidity) model. While some election outcomes may be very clear the day before, they were not six months ahead. For instance, the 1980 election was much more uncertain ex ante than the Reagan victory may indicate. The current election at this date (July 2000) is very unpredictable. By October 2000 it may appear as a sure bet, and 20 years from now we may just remember a landslide victory. These considerations suggest that impressions about electoral uncertainty ex post may be misleading.

Cohen discusses two types of evidence. One considers the expected inflation implied by the term structure of interest rates. This measure of expected inflation seems to be related to the ex ante anticipation of who is going to win the next election, in a way consistent with the partisan theory. The second set of tests relates electoral uncertainty to the size of fluctuations of growth, again with positive results for the theory. I am not arguing that the issue is settled by these results, but I am surprised that Drazen did not find it necessary to discuss these tests in more detail, given his serious objections to the theory on this point. He simply says, relative to the second test, that the computation is complicated and is not consistent with his (Drazen's) assessment of the data. As a test he mentions one election in the sixties. If this issue "requires further research" as Drazen writes (and I agree), then I do not understand how Drazen can be so sure that on this point the theory is flawed.

A third objection is that the pattern of inflation is not consistent with the partisan theory, because if, say, a Republican administration inherits a high inflation rate from the past, it may take a couple of years to reduce it. For example, according to this view the first Reagan administration in 1981–1984 would be a pro-inflation administration, since inflation was still high in 1981 and 1982. I find this the least convincing of Drazen's criticisms. Any model with some persistence in inflation would deliver this result.

Fourth, Drazen disagrees with the inflation-augmented Phillips curve, but if I understand correctly, his equation (12) is of the same family. It seems to me that a partisan structure which uses his equation (12) would also imply that electoral uncertainty is relevant.

Finally, it is true, as Drazen emphasizes, that the evidence on policy instruments is weaker for the partisan theory than the evidence on growth and unemployment. My reading of these results is that different administrations in the United States or governments of other countries may use different combinations of policies to achieve their goals, and by looking at one or the other one may find weaker results. For instance, suppose than one looks at monetary policy and some governments use fiscal policy as their main policy instrument. Evidence of partisan monetary policy may be weak not because partisan motivations are weak but because of difficulties in isolating one specific policy instrument. For instance, Perotti and Kontopoulos (1999) find evidence of partisan fiscal policy in OECD countries, while Alesina, Roubini, and Cohen (1997) find evidence of partisan monetary policy.

3. The AFPM Model

In the final part of the paper Drazen extends Rogoff's (1990) and Rogoff and Sibert's (1988) model of fiscal policy in order to incorporate a monetary accommodation. This is a Rogoff-type model with a monetary policy equation containing an exogenous parameter that captures the degree of pressure of the fiscal authority. There is some connection here with the literature on monetary–fiscal policy games originating from the unpleasant monetarist arithmetic by Sargent and Wallace. This connection would be worth exploring. Let me raise a few points:

1. A key assumption is that the money-supply growth rate is unobserved contemporaneously by the voters. Otherwise the voters could infer the competence of the incumbent and the model would not deliver interesting results. Some sort of asymmetric information is crucial to deliver opportunistic manipulations with rational voters. I

find Rogoff's assumption that the asymmetric information is about the composition of the budget more convincing than the one that the voters cannot figure out if the central bank is accommodating or not. More generally, assumptions about asymmetry of information seem to have a higher status than assumptions about imperfect nominal contracting. I see this simply as a matter of taste.
2. A key element of this model is the amount of pressure that the president puts on the central bank for accommodation. It seems to me that the obvious (and perhaps the only) way to test this model is to check whether this accommodation occurs more or less in countries with different levels of central-bank independence. This would be an interesting exercise.
3. A somewhat unfair criticism of the model would be to ask why the government would want to have an independent central bank at all here. But there are reasons outside the model why central-bank independence may be desirable. Perhaps one might try to bring in this point more directly, also in reference to empirical testing, as of my previous point. Also, an endogenous determination of the optimal degree of central-bank independence would provide a more solid derivation of the central bank's objective function, which in this version of the model is fairly arbitrary.

I am not quite sure what to make of the empirical evidence discussed in the last section of the paper. The author refers to another paper by him on more formal empirical tests on the United States. Based upon my previous work, I find it hard to believe that one can find strong evidence of large opportunistic cycles based on either monetary or fiscal policy in this country, because information circulation and central-bank independence are relatively high. In fact, one may argue that lack of strong evidence on the United States would be in favor of the spirit of the model. My sense is that in order to find evidence for the AFPM model, or of any other model of opportunistic cycles, I would look at other countries besides the United States and make cross-country comparisons.

In summary, I found things to like in this paper and things to disagree with. Three concluding points: First, my main general point of disagreement is with the attempt to emphasize a somewhat misleading contrast between those who argue that monetary policy is the driving force and those who argue that fiscal policy is. Second, I find the AFPM model a reasonable and interesting extension of Rogoff's work. I look forward to seeing it tested in cross-country data sets. Third, Drazen finds unconvincing both opportunistic and partisan models based on inflation surprises, but he did not offer an alternative and more convincing partisan model.

REFERENCES

Alesina, A. (2000). The political economy of budget surpluses. *Journal of Economic Perspectives*, forthcoming.

———, Perotti, and J. Tavares. (1998). The political economy of fiscal adjustments. *Brookings Papers on Economic Activity* 1:197–248.

———, N. Roubini, and G. Cohen. (1997). *Political Cycles and the Macroeconomy*, Cambridge Mass: The MIT Press.

———, and H. Rosenthal. (1995). *Partisan Cycles, Divided Government, and the Economy*, Cambridge UK: Cambridge University Press.

Cohen, D. (1993). Pre- and postelection macroeconomic fluctuations. Harvard University. PhD Dissertation.

Fischer, S. (1997). Long term contracts, rational expectations and the optimal money supply rule. *Journal of Political Economy* 85:191–206.

Garfinkel, M., and A. Glazer. (1994). Does electoral uncertainty cause economic fluctuations? *American Economic Review*, 84:169–173.

Perotti, R., and J. Kontopoulos. (1999). Fragmented fiscal policy. Unpublished.

Person, T., and G. Tabellini. (1990). *Macroeconomic Policy, Credibility, and Politics*. Chur, Switzerland: Harwood Academic Publishers.

Rogoff, K. (1990). Equilibrium political budget cycles. *American Economic Review* 80:21–36.

Rogoff, K., and A. Sibert. (1988). Elections and macroeconomic policy cycles. *Review of Economic Studies* 55:1–16.

Shi, M., and J. Svensson. (2000). Political business cycles in developed and developing countries. World Bank. Working Paper.

Wolfers, J. (1999). Are voters rational? Evidence from gubernatorial elections. Unpublished.

Comment[1]

CARL E. WALSH
University of California, Santa Cruz, and Federal Reserve Bank of San Francisco

1. Introduction

Allan Drazen achieves two objectives in his paper. First, he provides a brief but critical survey of the political-business-cycle (PBC) literature, managing to cover both the theoretical and empirical results on opportunistic and partisan models. This summary draws on material from his excellent new book (Drazen, 2000). Second, he develops a new model of the PBC, one that draws on the earlier work by Ken Rogoff and others focusing on fiscal policy as the source of politically driven macro effects.

---

[1]. Any opinions expressed are not necessarily those of the Federal Reserve Bank of San Francisco or the Federal Reserve System. I would like to thank Alina Carare for research assistance.

The model differs from earlier approaches in incorporating the notion of a passive Fed, trying to "keep its head down" during election years.

In achieving these two objectives, he has made me rethink the role of electoral factors in affecting monetary policy; I was left unconvinced that, at least from the perspective of U.S. macroeconomics and monetary economics, opportunistic PBCs with aggregate effects are of major importance.

2. What Are the Basic "Facts"?

To assess both the survey Drazen presents and the new model he develops, one needs to examine the basic "facts" the PBC literature has tried to explain. I will focus my attention on the United States, both because that is the country I know best, and because Drazen's discussion of the empirical evidence on PBCs draws primarily on findings from the United States. This focus has its drawbacks. The relevance of PBC models appears to be much greater in other countries, and Drazen does provide some discussion of the international evidence.

3. The Survey of the Previous Literature

Drazen organizes his survey round the distinction between monetary opportunistic and partisan models. As he stresses, the active manipulation of monetary policy for macro ends plays a critical role in both approaches. As he also stresses, the notion that the president is able to manipulate monetary policy to achieve his desired outcome is simply not plausible as a description of the relationship between the president and the Fed. This leads him to reject the standard opportunistic and partisan models that have relied on monetary surprises as the key transmission channel through which political factors influence the macroeconomy.

I agree with this assessment, at least as it applies to the United States. The evidence for strong political effects operating through monetary policy just isn't there. In part, this is because they are only one among many sources of macroeconomic fluctuations. Given the few elections and business cycles since 1960 (the period that is the focus of much of this literature), it would be hard to discern political effects using time-series econometrics. And the existing empirical work in this area has generally failed to deal with the important issue of simultaneity. Did the 1960 and 1990 recessions bring victory to Kennedy and Clinton, or did Kennedy and Clinton bring us the postrecession (and postelection) expansions?

In one of the most careful attempts to deal with the problem of simultaneity, Faust and Irons (1999) conclude the economic effects on election outcomes are more likely than election effects on the economy. According to Faust and Irons,

> There is, at best, weak and fragile evidence in favor of important presidential-cycle effects in US macroeconomic data. The strongest evidence seems to come from the first half of Republican administrations: recessions have followed the election of Republicans and macroeconomic factors alone may not account for this fact. There is little evidence, however, that the causal explanations of any political effects on the economy operates through changes in monetary policy. Thus, we find little support for the view that empirical monetary models should include political variables. (p. 84)

While causality cannot be reliably assessed in nonexperimental data, we cannot reject the view that the data show only causality from the economy to party and not the other way around. (p. 85)

Two points are worth noting. First, the evidence from Faust and Irons relates to aggregate variables, so it is consistent with either opportunistic or partisan manipulation of fiscal instruments that have distributional consequences but not aggregate effects. In fact, the current presidential election provides numerous examples of the incumbent-party candidate announcing spending programs that seem intended to reward specific constituents rather than to have any macroeconomic effects.

Second, the results are also consistent with isolated incidences in which fiscal manipulations might have had aggregate effects. The 1972 presidential election comes to mind as an example, and as Drazen mentions, it is not surprising that the PBC literature really starts in the mid-1970s with the work of Nordhaus and Hibbs. The Nixon–McGovern contest provided the key observation in the United States that motivated work designed to understand how elections might create incentives that distort policy and thereby the macroeconomy.

What I take from Faust and Irons's work is that there are no compelling facts against which to judge PBC models. If we focus on the post-1960 period as Drazen does in this paper, I am just not convinced there is anything at the aggregate level that needs to be explained via political models. Furthermore, Drazen's survey of the empirical evidence suggests that what electoral effects may have been present in the 1960s and 1970s have disappeared in the post-1980 period. The Volcker tenure really did represent a monetary policy regime shift. This doesn't mean there aren't electoral effects on government spending decisions. But evidence that spending fluctuates isn't necessarily evidence that this is a source of business-cycle behavior.

Let me contrast this with the time-inconsistency literature in monetary policy. There were at least two important puzzles facing monetary political economists in the late 1970s. First, why were many countries experiencing high inflation even though everyone seemed to agree that inflation was bad, most agreed that there were no permanent gains from higher average inflation, and we all knew how inflation could be reduced? And second, why did governments so often fail to carry through their announced intentions to reduce inflation?[2] These were real puzzles that needed understanding.

In contrast, one almost gets the sense that, when applied to the United States, PBC literature is theory in search of an application. There are many intellectually appealing game-theoretic models, but what puzzle are these models trying to address? What are the empirical regularities they need to explain?

4. The AFPM Model

Given the weaknesses he identifies in the basic opportunistic and partisan models, Drazen's proposed alternative is the active-fiscal, passive-monetary (AFPM) model. This model combines a signaling model with a specification of monetary policy that differs significantly from that used in previous work.

The basic intuition is borrowed from the budget-cycle model of Rogoff (1990). Elected officials differ in their ability to provide public goods. Their competence, however, is not observed directly by voters. During the runup to an election, a competent incumbent may distort the provision of public goods in an attempt to signal her competency. Allan combines this with a model of passive monetary policy. The monetary authority wants to stabilize output and inflation, but the target levels for output and inflation in the monetary authority's loss function differ from those of the public (and the politicians). If a competent fiscal authority tries to signal to voters by increasing government consumption, the monetary authority is forced to boost interest rates to offset the fiscal effect on output. By itself, this would imply we should observe political cycles in the policy instruments of both the fiscal and monetary authorities but no cycle in output. If the monetary authority implements policy through control of a nominal interest rate, then prior to an election, nominal rates should rise and money growth should fall.

To generate outcomes more in line with the empirical evidence, Drazen makes two further assumptions. First, the public has a higher

---

2. There are similar puzzles on the fiscal side. Persson and Tabellini (2000) summarize these, but they are not related to business-cycle issues.

output target than the monetary authority. This implies that the incumbent politician can gain votes by lobbying the monetary authority to limit interest-rate increases and to allow output to expand. And second, such lobbying is assumed to be costly to the politician—this serves to limit the extent of the pressure brought to bear on the monetary authority. Together, these two assumptions imply that a competent incumbent boosts fiscal spending to signal competence and pressures the monetary authority so that interest rates are not raised sufficiently to completely offset the aggregate impact of the fiscal spending. As a consequence, prior to an election, fiscal spending, interest rates, output, and money growth should all rise, but only if the incumbent is competent (at least in the separating equilibrium).

4.1 THE IMPLICIT VIEW OF MONETARY POLICY

One aspect of the AFPM model that is a real improvement on many of the earlier PBC models is its recognition that the institutional structure in many countries separates responsibility for monetary policy from the direct control of elected officials. This is certainly the case in the United States. The president can bring pressure to bear on the Fed—witness the role played by the White House in 1972 that John Woolley (1995) has documented—but this is far from having actual control over monetary policy.

In the AFPM model, the monetary authority has its own agenda, but its ability to achieve its own goals is compromised by the stance of fiscal policy. The fiscal authority can lobby the monetary authority, but doing so is costly (the exact nature of this cost is not specified). If the high-competence type wishes to signal to voters by increasing the provision of government consumption goods, it must also lobby the monetary authority to expand money growth, thereby limiting the interest-rate effects of the increased government spending.

I think this gets at the right relationship between the fiscal and monetary authorities, at least in the United States and in other countries with relatively independent central banks. Recognizing the institutional structure within which policy decisions are made is important. Institutional characteristics, such as central-bank independence, do seem to matter. Much of the PBC literature has ignored the role of institutions other than in the timing of elections; this made it poorly framed for addressing many interesting issues about how institutional structure affects economic outcomes. It would be interesting to use the AFPM model to explore the implications of the degree of central-bank independence for opportunistic cycles, much as Alesina and Gatti (1995) and Waller and Walsh (1996) have done for partisan models.

In the general literature on discretionary monetary policy that builds on the work of Kydland and Prescott (1977) and Barro and Gordon (1983), a positive inflation bias is generated under discretion because the central bank has an output objective that is too high relative to the economy's natural rate of output. In contrast, the AFPM model assumes the central bank has an output target that is lower than that of the public. The fiscal authority, because he must face elections, shares the public's output target. It would be interesting to explore whether the AFPM specification is consistent with a positive average rate of inflation. Many recent authors have suggested the inflationary bias of discretionary monetary policy can be eliminated if the central bank simply uses the natural rate of output as its output target. This is essentially what the central bank does in the AFPM model, yet policy is still distorted (potentially) in the face of political pressures.

While the separation of the monetary and fiscal authorities is a nice feature of the AFPM model, other aspects of monetary policy in the model seem incomplete. For example, why do the output and inflation preferences of the monetary authority differ from those of the public? The utility of voters does not enter into the monetary authority's objective function. Perhaps it doesn't because the monetary authority is unelected.[3] But even for the unelected Fed, there is evidence that Fed policy does reflect the changing concerns of the public (Tootell, 1999).

The view of monetary policy adopted in the AFPM model can be contrasted with the trend in the monetary-policy literature. There, the literature has moved progressively away from ad hoc loss functions, basing policy evaluation on the utility of the representative agent in a general equilibrium framework. In the AFPM model, the monetary authority cares about output and inflation, but neither is connected in any way to the welfare of the public.

4.2 IS THE AFPM MODEL PLAUSIBLE?

Drazen provides "a quick look at the data" to assess whether the AFPM model appears consistent with the basic PBC facts discussed in the survey part of his paper. The key to distinguishing the AFPM model from a standard PBC model based on the direct manipulation of monetary policy lies in the correlation between interest rates and the cycle. Under either an opportunistic or a partisan model, expansionary monetary policy lowers interest rates—this is the key transmission mechanism through which political influences on monetary policy induce an economic expansion. In contrast, when monetary policy simply reacts passively in the face of a

---

3. Which raises a different question in political economy—why isn't the Fed chair elected?

fiscally induced expansion, interest rates rise or remain unchanged. They do not fall.

Figures 4–6 of Drazen's paper present the basic evidence for passive monetary policy in the United States. Figures 4 and 5 show M1 growth rates by quarter of presidential terms for 1960–1979 and 1979–1998. Figure 6 shows the funds rate by quarter of presidential terms for 1959–1998. To my eyes, there does not appear to be much evidence that either M1 or the funds rate is related to the electoral cycle. However, Drazen concludes from his review of the existing empirical literature that there is a pre-election increase in money growth rates from 1960 to 1980, and this forms one of the observations that the AFPM model is designed to account for. Figure 4 does show some increase in money growth in the last two quarters prior to an election, but it also shows a similar increase about seven quarters prior to an election. Given the lags in the impact of monetary policy actions on the macroeconomy, this timing seems more consistent with a traditional opportunistic model in which money growth increases early enough to generate a boom during the election year.

More interesting is the evidence on the funds rate, as this has been the instrument used to implement monetary policy over most of the last few decades. Figure 6 reveals that the funds rate is unrelated to the election cycle over the 1959–1998 period. Under the AFPM model, this would be consistent with a very strong political influence on the Fed. Recall that the basic idea is that the Fed will want to boost interest rates to offset the expansionary impact of the fiscal signaling. The president is assumed to pressure the Fed to limit the rate increases. The evidence seems to suggest presidents succeed completely. But this would mean output should rise prior to elections, a prediction that Drazen concludes does not hold (his Regularity 2). Of course, the alternative interpretation is that the fiscal manipulations are too small to have macro impacts, and therefore there is no need for the Fed to adjust its policy instrument. This hypothesis, however, cannot account for the rise in money growth prior to elections.

In measuring the impact of monetary policy on the economy, it is the real interest rate that should be relevant. Figure 1 shows, by quarter of presidential terms, the average nominal and real funds rate. Averages are shown for the 1961–1980 and 1961–1999 periods.[4] Looking at the real funds rate is appropriate because average inflation (and therefore the average funds rate) differed significantly over this time period. The time

---

4. The first quarter of a term is taken to be quarter 1 of the year following an election. So, for example, Carter's terms runs from 1977:1 to 1980:4.

Figure 1 AVERAGE FUNDS RATE AND ELECTIONS

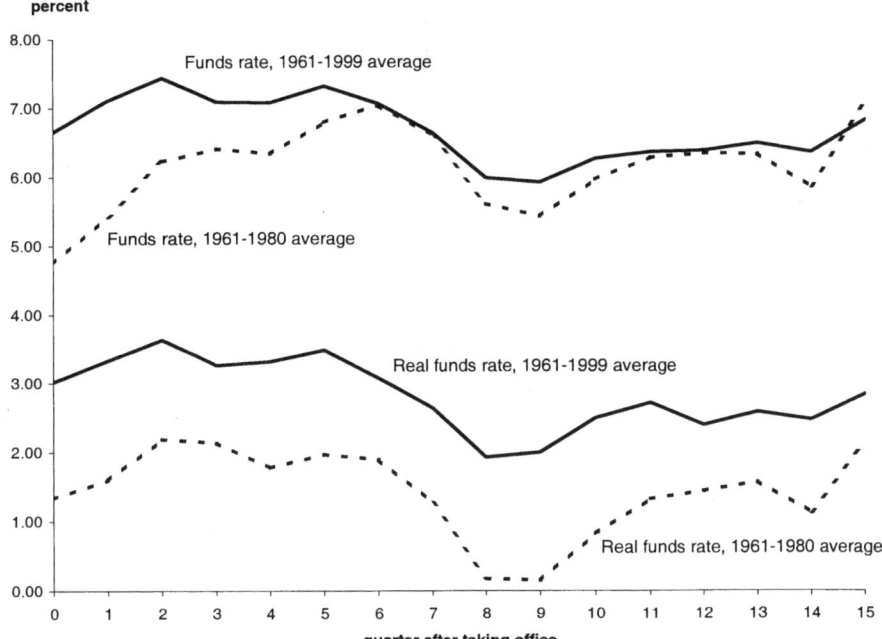

series on the real funds rate appears to be most consistent with a pre-election manipulation of policy. On average, the real funds rate starts to fall a little more than two years prior to an election. Again, given that the lags of monetary policy are on the order of 18 to 24 months, this timing is consistent with a traditional opportunistic political business cycle.

Recall, however, that the 1961–1980 period contains only five presidential elections, so the average behavior might easily be driven by a single presidential term. To investigate this possibility, Figure 2 shows the behavior of the real funds rate over each presidential term. As the figure shows, the average in the previous figure reflects a wide range of experience across the individual presidential term. Two aspects are of particular note. The decline in the average real funds rate two years prior to an election that was suggestive of pre-election monetary expansions is almost entirely due to the 1973–1976 Nixon–Ford administration. What this really reflects is the Fed's countercyclical response to the 1975 recession. That leaves only Nixon's first term (1969–1972) as providing evi-

Figure 2 REAL FUNDS RATE BY PRESIDENTIAL TERM

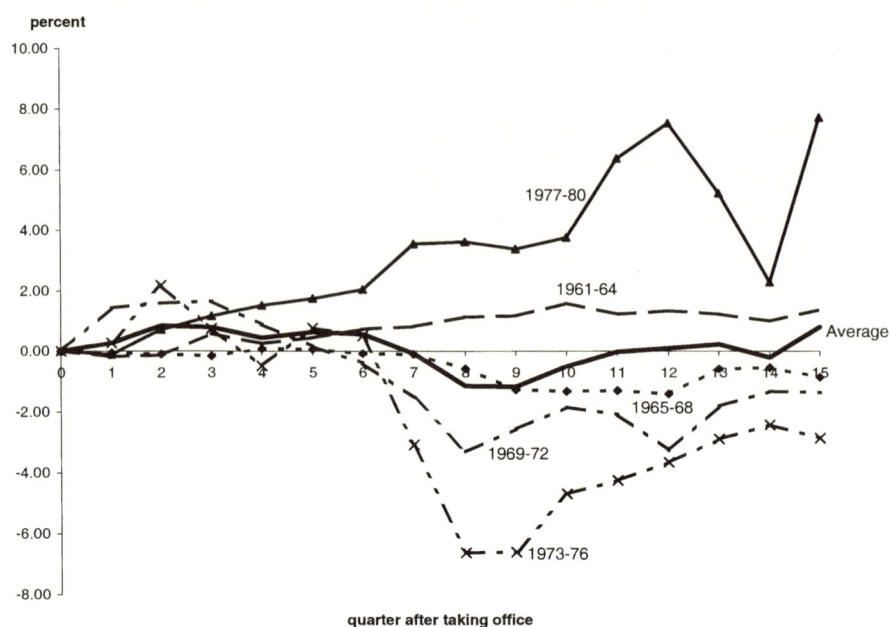

dence of a political impact on Fed policy related to elections. I interpret this to mean the evidence for a traditional opportunistic monetary policy that was suggested in Figure 1 is largely spurious.

Is there evidence that expansionary fiscal policy, combined with political pressures, led the Fed to reduce rates immediately prior to an election? The most dramatic swing in rates occurred in 1980 when Jimmy Carter was running for re-election. The real funds rate, which reached record highs as the Fed under Paul Volcker moved to fight inflation, suddenly plummeted in early 1980. This episode was associated with the short-lived credit controls that the White House pressured the Fed to implement. So this could be taken as evidence in support of the AFPM model, but the mechanism is somewhat different than that implied by the basic theory. And note that the credit controls were removed well before the 1980 election.

5. What Is the Benchmark for Measuring a Passive Policy?

As I indicated earlier, the relevance of PBC models is likely to be much greater in countries other than the United States, so it would be interesting to focus on a larger sample of countries. I think the empirical analysis could also be strengthened if a clearer benchmark were established against which to measure political influences on monetary policy. This lack of a benchmark is a problem with much of the empirical work in the PBC literature, so this comment applies both to Drazen's work on the opportunistic model and to the existing work on partisan models.

In general terms, we can write the funds rate i as a function of macroeconomic variables y and political variables x:

$$i = F(y(x,z),x),$$

where the macroeconomic variables may be affected directly by x as well as by other, exogenous variables z. We know that the funds rate responds to economic conditions, usually summarized in terms of the unemployment rate and the rate of inflation, so these would be part of y. How should we measure the impact of political variables on monetary policy? Do we want to measure the partial derivatives of F with respect to x? Or should we measure the total differential, taking into account the effects of x on i operating through y?

Most regression work on PBCs tends to focus on estimating what corresponds to the partial derivative of F with respect to x. That is, in most regressions, a list of potential y-variables are also included. The list is often short, consisting of lagged unemployment rate, for example, as well as own lags of the funds rate. But if electoral factors affect unemployment, as in the standard opportunistic model, this would indirectly lead to a monetary policy reaction—a reaction one would also presumably want to label as "passive."

The empirical evidence in Alesina, Roubini, and Cohen (1997) displays similar shortcomings. In testing for postelection partisan effects on interest rates (see their Table 4.9, p. 99), they regress nominal interest rates on own lags and a dummy for the party holding the presidency. Finding that interest rates are higher under Democratic administrations, they interpret this as evidence of greater expansionary policies and higher inflation under Democratic presidents. But is this the right interpretation? If unemployment is higher under Republicans, as the partisan model implies, then the lower interest rates under Republicans might reflect the normal Fed reaction to unemployment. Regressing i on political dummies alone will correctly measure the total effect (i.e., the total differential of F) only if the other omitted factors, the things in z, are uncorrelated with political factors. But if politics responds to the economy, this won't be the case.

My general conclusion is that to investigate political effects on monetary policy, we need a benchmark—what would monetary policy have been in the absence of electoral influences?

6. Summary

Let me briefly summarize my reactions to the two components of Drazen's paper. The survey provides an excellent assessment of the literature. The AFPM model is an attractive model in that it recognizes that monetary policy in most countries is not simply the tool of the fiscal authority. By taking account explicitly of the separation of monetary and fiscal policy, the model can provide a framework for investigating how changes that affect the central bank's incentives might affect the political business cycle.

The evidence that the AFPM model applies to the United States is weak, however. I don't find this surprising. There is evidence that some fiscal instruments (transfers being the prime candidate) are manipulated for election effects. The problem for the AFPM model is that there is little evidence that this fiscal activism has any macro effect, and if it doesn't affect the macro economy, it cannot account for an induced reaction by a passive monetary authority.

Econometric time-series analysis can, at times, be a powerful tool for testing hypotheses suggested by economic theory. However, the contributions of econometrics to our understanding of political influences on U.S. economic policy may be limited. We have only 9 elections (soon to be 10) if we restrict attention to the post-1960 period. Combined with the fact that most economic fluctuations are at best loosely connected to elections, the lack of degrees of freedom is daunting.

So how can we test political theories? Here, I think the tools of the historian are more enlightening than econometrics. John Woolley, for example, has explored in great depth the influence the Nixon White House brought to bear on Arthur Burns in 1972, and he does so not with econometrics but by reading the diaries of H. R. Haldeman, Nixon's chief of staff. Further case studies might be the most informative means for exposing the "facts" that political business cycle theories will then need to explain.

REFERENCES

Alesina, A., and R. Gatti. (1995). Independent central banks: Low inflation at no cost? *American Economic Review* 85(2):196–200.
———, and N. Roubini, with G.D. Cohen. (1997). *Political Cycles and the Macroeconomy*. Cambridge: The MIT Press.
Barro, R. J., and D. B. Gordon. (1983). A positive theory of monetary policy in a natural rate model. *Journal of Political Economy* 91:589–610.

Drazen, A. (2000). *Political Economy in Macroeconomics*. Princeton: Princeton University Press.
Faust, J. and J. S. Irons. (1999). Money, politics and the post-war business cycle. *Journal of Monetary Economics* 43(1):61–89.
Kydland, F., and E. C. Prescott. (1977). Rules rather than discretion: The inconsistency of optimal plans. *Journal of Political Economy* 85(3):473–491.
Persson, T., and G. Tabellini. (2000). Political economics and macroeconomic policy. In *Handbook of Macroeconomics*, J. Taylor and M. Woodford (eds.). Amsterdam: North-Holland.
Rogoff, K. (1990). Equilibrium political budget cycles. *American Economic Review* 80(1):21–36.
Tootell, G. M. B. (1999). Whose monetary policy is it anyway? *Journal of Monetary Economics* 43(1):217–235.
Waller, C. J., and C. E. Walsh. (1996). Central bank independence, economic behavior and optimal term lengths. *American Economic Review* 86(5):1139–1153.
Woolley, J. (1995). Nixon, Burns, 1972, and independence in practice, University of California, Santa Barbara.

Discussion

Responding to the discussants, Allan Drazen agreed that the empirical literature on the political business cycle remains somewhat unsettled. However, defending his view that research should concentrate on fiscal policy manipulation rather than monetary surprises, Drazen cited the work of Faust and Irons as support for the position that partisan effects exist but are not due to monetary policy, as well as Maria Gonzalez's evidence for fiscal cycles in developing countries. He argued that we need something other than the Phillips curve—other than monetary policy—to make progress in this area. Drazen agreed with discussant Carl Walsh that his AFPM model is rudimentary at this stage, but he argued that it opens new directions for research, including attention to comparative institutions. He suggested also that less ad hoc loss functions could be adopted without losing the general flavor of the model's results.

Michael Klein observed that one should be careful in cross-country studies that include countries where elections can be called, as the election dates may be affected by economic conditions. Ken Rogoff praised work by Gonzalez and others that examine cross-sectional data; he noted the interesting prediction of Gonzalez's work that political budget cycles will be largest in middle-income countries with intermediate levels of democracy. Richard Portes claimed that in Europe there is evidence that economic cycles are becoming synchronized though election timing is not. Drazen replied that evidence does exist for political fiscal cycles, though perhaps these are stronger in middle-income countries (as Gonzalez suggests) than in Europe or the United States.

Rick Mishkin noted that an important issue is now to set up central banks so that they are able to resist government pressure not to raise interest rates when they know they need to do so to keep inflation under control. He gave the example of Paul Volcker's targeting of monetary aggregates, which he interpreted as a smokescreen that allowed Volcker to raise interest rates as needed to subdue inflation. More recently, central banks have adopted inflation targeting in part to deflect pressure for short-run accommodation and to permit them to focus on long-run issues. Drazen replied that his focus was on the nature of short-run pressure on the central bank; were central banks being asked to actively stimulate the economy for electoral purposes, or only to accommodate fiscal policy to prevent swings in the interest rate? On the other hand, he argued that his approach, which recognizes the separation of fiscal and monetary policy-making, provides a framework for discussing optimal policy institutions. For example, if we conclude that fiscal policy is most prone to political pressure, we may then want to look for remedies that deal most directly with that problem.

Ben Bernanke found it odd that the competent policymaker is the one who creates the distortion in the fiscal signaling model. He pointed out that one might question the assumption that both types of policymakers put the same weight on social welfare. He asked how we would know that someone who overspent is not putting a lower weight on social welfare and a higher weight on being in office, rather than demonstrating competence. Ken Rogoff noted that this issue is an artifact of the model with two types which does not apply when there is a continuum of types, as in Rogoff and Sibert's original paper. Drazen replied that his idea is that the competent policymaker is more able to economize on low-visibility or routine spending, and is thus more able to introduce spending initiatives that attract votes. Carl Walsh agreed with the thrust of Bernanke's remark by saying that a lot of political signaling seems to be about policymakers' preferences, rather than their competence; for example, a candidate's promises are often designed to reveal which interest groups he is likely to favor and wants to attract.

Olivier Blanchard distinguished two empirical questions. The first is how much of movements in fiscal policy can be attributed to political reasons; the second is whether these induced movements in fiscal policy are of any consequence at the macroeconomic level. He thought there was some evidence for political effects on fiscal choices but that politically induced fiscal decisions seem too small to explain macroeconomic fluctuations. Drazen agreed that there are two separate questions but suggested that the effects of politically induced fiscal changes on macroeconomic variables remain an open question.

Daron Acemoglu said the opportunistic model does not sit as comfortably with fiscal policy as with monetary policy. He noted that fiscal policy actions such as appropriations are easily observable, even before the direct effects are seen. Alesina disagreed, suggesting that fiscal policy is the area where we have more uncertainty and asymmetry of information. For example, we know more or less whether the Fed has moved or not, but it's realistic to assume that voters do not understand the intricacies of budget projections and legislation. He thought that this difference lends some support to the fiscal model. Acemoglu suggested that, because of the two-term limitation of U.S. presidents, the model would imply testable differences between the first and second terms of a given president.

Stephen Morris and Hyun Song Shin
YALE UNIVERSITY AND OXFORD UNIVERSITY

Rethinking Multiple Equilibria in Macroeconomic Modeling

1. Introduction

It is a commonplace that actions are motivated by beliefs, and so economic outcomes are influenced by the beliefs of individuals in the economy. In many examples in economics, there seems to be an apparent indeterminacy in beliefs in the sense that one set of beliefs motivate actions which bring about the state of affairs envisaged in the beliefs, while another set of self-fulfilling beliefs bring about quite different outcomes. In both cases, the beliefs are logically coherent, consistent with the known features of the economy, and borne out by subsequent events. However, they are not fully determined by the underlying description of the economy, leaving a role for *sunspots*.

Models that utilize such apparent indeterminacy of beliefs have considerable intuitive appeal, since they provide a convenient and economical prop in a narrative of unfolding events. However, they are vulnerable to a number of criticisms. For a start, the shift in beliefs which underpins the switch from one equilibrium to another is left unexplained. This runs counter to our theoretical scruples against indeterminacy. More importantly, it runs counter to our intuition that bad fundamentals are somehow "more likely" to trigger a financial crisis, or to tip the economy into recession. In other words, sunspot explanations do not provide a basis for exploring the *correlation* between the underlying fundamentals and the resultant economic outcomes. Finally, comparative-statics analyses and the policy implications that flow from them are only as secure as the equilibrium chosen for this exercise.

We are grateful to the editors for their guidance during the preparation of this paper, and to our two discussants Andy Atkeson and Hélène Rey for their perceptive comments.

The literature on multiple equilibria is large and diverse. The recent book by Cooper (1999) provides a taxonomy for a selection of examples from macroeconomics. Technological complementarities (as in Bryant, 1983), demand spillovers (as in the "big push" model of Murphy, Shleifer, and Vishny, 1989), and thick-market externalities [as in Diamond's (1982) search model] are some of the examples. Models of financial crises, encompassing both banking crises and attacks on currency pegs, have a similarly large and active research following. Obstfeld and Rogoff (1997) and Freixas and Rochet (1997) are good stepping-off points for this literature.

Our objective in this paper is to encourage a re-examination of the theoretical basis for multiple equilibria. We doubt that economic agents' beliefs are as indeterminate as implied by the multiple-equilibrium models. Instead, the apparent indeterminacy of beliefs can be seen as the consequence of two modeling assumptions introduced to simplify the theory. First, the economic fundamentals are assumed to be common knowledge; and second, economic agents are assumed to be certain about each other's behavior in equilibrium. Both assumptions are made for the sake of tractability, but they do much more besides. They allow agents' actions and beliefs to be perfectly coordinated in a way that invites multiplicity of equilibria. We will describe an approach where agents have a small amount of idiosyncratic uncertainty about economic fundamentals. Even if this uncertainty is small, agents will be uncertain about each other's behavior in equilibrium. This uncertainty allows us as modelers to pin down which set of self-fulfilling beliefs will prevail in equilibrium.

To elaborate on this point, it is instructive to contrast a single-person decision problem with a game. In a single-person decision problem, payoffs are determined by one's action and the state of the world. When a decision maker receives a message which rules out some states of the world, this information can be utilized directly by disregarding those states in one's deliberations. However, the same is not true in an environment where payoffs depend on the actions of other individuals as well as on the state of the world. Since my payoff depends on your actions and your actions are motivated by your beliefs, I care about the range of possible beliefs you may hold. So, when I receive a message which rules out some states of the world, it may not be possible to disregard those states in my deliberations, since most of them may carry information concerning your beliefs. Even for small disparities in the information of the market participants, uncertainty about others' beliefs may dictate a particular course of action as being the uniquely optimal one. In this way, it may prove possible to track the shifts in beliefs as we track the shifts in the economic fundamentals. There is no longer a choice of what beliefs to hold. One's beliefs are dictated by the knowledge of the fundamentals and the knowledge that other agents are rational.

In this paper, we provide an elementary demonstration of why adding noise to a game with multiple equilibria removes the multiplicity. The analysis builds on the game-theoretic analysis of Carlsson and van Damme (1993) for two-player games and on the continuum-player application to currency attacks of Morris and Shin (1998). We develop a very simple continuum-player example to illustrate the argument, and show by example why this is a flexible modeling approach that can be applied to many of the macroeconomic models with multiplicity discussed above. In doing so, we hope to show that the indeterminacy of beliefs in multiple-equilibrium models is an artifact of simplifying assumptions that deliver more than they are intended to deliver, and that the approach described here is not merely a technical curiosity, but represents a better way of understanding the role of self-fulfilling beliefs in macroeconomics.

We also outline the principal benefits of the approach. One is in generating comparative statics, which in turn aids policy analysis. The other is in suggesting observational implications. Here we summarize those benefits in a general way; below, we will discuss them in the context of particular applications.

Multiple-equilibrium models in macroeconomics are often used as a starting point for policy analysis, despite the obvious difficulties of any comparative-statics analysis with indeterminate outcomes. The unique equilibrium in the approach described here is characterized by a marginal decision maker who, given his uncertainty about others' actions, is indifferent between two actions. Changing parameters in the model then delivers intuitive comparative-statics predictions and implications for optimal policy. In general, we show that inefficiencies are unavoidable in equilibrium. The question is how large such inefficiencies are. The answer turns on the underlying fundamentals of the economy as well as on the information structure of the economic agents. Thus, the notion of a *solvent but illiquid borrower* can be given a rigorous treatment, and the extent of the welfare losses associated with such illiquidity can be calculated.

The theory offers a different perspective on existing empirical work. One traditional approach in the literature is to attempt to distinguish empirically between multiple-equilibrium models and fundamentals-driven models. These ultimately reduce to tests of whether observed fundamentals are sufficient to explain outcomes or whether there is a significant unexplained component that must be attributed to self-fulfilling beliefs. We argue that correlation between fundamentals and outcomes is exactly what one should expect even when self-fulfilling beliefs are playing an important role in determining the outcome. One will be pessimistic about others' beliefs exactly when fundamentals are weak. The standard sunspot approach, by contrast, offers no theoretical rationale as to why good outcomes should be correlated with good fundamentals (although admittedly this is consistent with the theory and often assumed).

We also suggest one distinctive observational implication. Consider an environment where agents' actions are driven by their beliefs about fundamentals and others' actions. Suppose agents are slightly uncertain about some fundamental variable when they make their decisions, but that ex post the econometrician is able to observe the actual realization of that fundamental variable as well as some public signal concerning it that was available to agents at the time. The theory suggests the prediction that the public signals will have an apparently disproportionate impact on outcomes, even controlling for the realization of fundamentals, precisely because it signals information to agents about other agents' equilibrium beliefs.

We start in the next section by analyzing a simple model of bank runs, in the spirit of Diamond and Dybvig (1983), to illustrate the approach in the context of a particular application. Goldstein and Pauzner (1999) have developed a richer model; we abstract from a number of complications in order to bring out our methodological message. In Section 3, we show how the insights are more general and can be applied in a variety of contexts. In particular, we discuss models of currency crises and pricing debt in the presence of liquidity risk.

2. Bank Runs

There are three dates, $\{0, 1, 2\}$, and a continuum of consumers, each endowed with 1 unit of the consumption good. Consumption takes place at either date 1 or date 2. There is a measure λ of *impatient* consumers who derive utility only from consumption at date 1, and a measure 1 of *patient* consumers for whom consumption at date 1 and at date 2 are perfect substitutes. The consumers learn of their types at date 1. At date 0, the probability of being patient or impatient is proportional to the incidence of the types. Thus, there is probability

$$\frac{\lambda}{1 + \lambda}$$

of being an impatient consumer, and complementary probability of being the patient consumer. All consumers have the log utility function, and the utility of the impatient type is

$$u(c_1) = \log c_1,$$

where c_1 is consumption at date 1, while the utility of the patient type is

$$u(c_1 + c_2) = \log(c_1 + c_2)$$

where c_2 is consumption at date 2.

The consumers can either store the consumption good for consumption at a later date, or deposit it in the bank. Those consumers who have invested their wealth in the bank have a decision at date 1, after learning of their type. They can either leave their money deposited in the bank, or withdraw the sum permitted in the deposit contract (to be discussed below). The bank can either hold the deposits in cash (with rate of return 1) or invest the money in an illiquid project, with gross rate of return $R > 1$ obtainable at date 2. We assume that this technology is only available to the bank. If proportion ℓ of the resources invested in the illiquid investment are withdrawn at date 1, then the rate of return is reduced to $R \cdot e^{-\ell}$, reflecting the costs of premature liquidation. Writing $r \equiv \log R$, this rate of return can be written as $e^{r-\ell}$. We assume that $0 < r < 1$.

2.1 OPTIMAL CONTRACT

We proceed to solve for the optimal contract in this context. The aim is to maximize the ex ante expected utility

$$\frac{\lambda}{1+\lambda} u(c_1) + \frac{1}{1+\lambda} u(c_2) \qquad (2.1)$$

by choosing the amount c_1 that can be withdrawn on demand at date 1. We assume that the bank is required to keep sufficient cash to fund first-period consumption under the optimal contract. Thus, the first constraint is

$$\lambda c_1 + \frac{c_2}{R} \leq 1 + \lambda, \qquad (2.2)$$

which states that the amount held in cash (λc_1) plus the amount invested in the project (c_2/R) cannot exceed the total resources. The second is the incentive compatibility constraint

$$u(c_1) \leq u(c_2), \qquad (2.3)$$

which states that patient consumers will, indeed, choose to leave their money in the bank. Ignoring the incentive compatibility constraint, we obtain $c_1 = 1$ and $c_2 = R$. Then,

$$u(c_1) = 0 < r = u(c_2),$$

so that the incentive compatibility constraint is satisfied strictly. Thus, the optimal deposit contract stipulates that any depositor can withdraw the whole of their 1 unit deposit at date 1. Because the investment is assumed to be available only to the bank, such a contract can only be implemented through the bank. Under such a contract, it is a weakly dominant action for every consumer at date 0 to deposit their wealth in the bank. At worst, they will get their money back at date 1, and possibly do better if the consumer turns out to be a patient type. Thus, at date 0, all consumers deposit their money in the bank.

2.2 THE COORDINATION GAME BETWEEN PATIENT CONSUMERS

Diamond and Dybvig (1983) observed that, unfortunately, the optimal contract gives rise to multiple equilibria at date 1. At date 1, the impatient consumers will clearly have a dominant strategy to withdraw. Given this behavior, the patient consumers are playing a coordination game. If a patient consumer withdraws, he gets a cash payoff of 1, giving utility of $0 = u(1)$. This payoff is independent of the number of patient consumers who withdraw. If a patient consumer does not withdraw, then the payoff depends on the proportion of patient consumers who withdraw. If a proportion ℓ withdraw, his cash payoff to leaving money in the bank is $e^{r-\ell}$, which gives utility $r - \ell$. Thus, utility is linearly decreasing in the proportion of patient consumers who withdraw. If a patient consumer expects all other consumers *not* to withdraw (i.e., $\ell = 0$), then his utility from not withdrawing is $r > 0$. Thus there is an equilibrium where all patient consumers conform to the optimal deposit contract and leave their money in the bank. But if a patient consumer expects all other patient consumers to withdraw (i.e., $\ell = 1$), then his utility from not withdrawing is $r - 1 < 0$. Thus there is also an equilibrium where all patient consumers withdraw.

2.3 UNCERTAIN RETURN AND UNIQUE EQUILIBRIUM

Postlewaite and Vives (1987) and Chari and Jagannathan (1988) both examine how bank runs become a unique equilibrium when asymmetric information is added to the model. We follow Goldstein and Pauzner (1999) in introducing a small amount of uncertainty concerning the log return r, holding fixed the deposit contract described above. It should be noted that as soon as we depart from the benchmark case, there is no guarantee that the existing deposit contract is optimal. Neither the portfolio choice of the bank nor the amount that can be withdrawn at date 1 need be optimal in the new context. The objective here is to examine the equilibrium outcome and the welfare losses that result when the benchmark contract is imposed on an environment with noisy signals.

Suppose that r is a normal random variable, and that r has mean $\bar{r}$ and precision α (i.e., variance $1/\alpha$). We carry forward the assumption that the return is neither too small nor too large—we assume that $\bar{r}$ lies in the range:

$$0 < \bar{r} < 1.$$

The depositors have access to very precise information about r before they make their withdrawal decisions, but the information is not perfect. Depositor i observes the realization of the signal

$$x_i = r + \epsilon_i, \tag{2.4}$$

where ϵ_i is normally distributed with mean 0 and precision β, and independent across depositors.

With the introduction of uncertainty, we need to be explicit about what is meant by equilibrium in the bank-run game. At date 1, depositor i not only observes his type, but also observes his signal x_i, and forms the updated belief concerning the return r and the possible signals obtained by other depositors. Based on this information, depositor i decides whether to withdraw or not. A *strategy* for a depositor is a rule of action which prescribes an action for each realization of the signal. A profile of strategies (one for each depositor) is an equilibrium if, conditional on the information available to depositor i and given the strategies followed by other depositors, the action prescribed by i's strategy maximizes his conditional expected utility. Treating such realization of i's signal as a possible "type" of this depositor, we are solving for the Bayes Nash equilibria of the imperfect-information game. To economize on the statement of the results, we assume that if withdrawal yields the same expected utility as leaving money in the bank, then the depositor prefers to leave money in the bank. This assumption plays no substantial role in what follows.

Since both r and x are normally distributed, a depositor's updated belief of r upon observing signal x is

$$\rho = \frac{\alpha \bar{r} + \beta x}{\alpha + \beta} \tag{2.5}$$

In contrast to the benchmark case in which there is no uncertainty, the introduction of uncertainty eliminates multiplicity of equilibrium if private signals are sufficiently accurate. The result depends on the prior and posterior precision of r. Specifically, let

$$\gamma \equiv \frac{\alpha^2 (\alpha + \beta)}{\beta (\alpha + 2\beta)}, \tag{2.6}$$

and write $\Phi(\cdot)$ for the standard normal distribution function. Our main result states that there is a unique equilibrium in this context, provided that γ is small enough.

THEOREM. *Provided that $\gamma \leq 2\pi$, there is a unique equilibrium. In this equilibrium, every patient consumer withdraws if and only if $\rho < \rho^*$, where ρ^* is the unique solution to*

$$\rho^* = \Phi\left(\sqrt{\gamma}(\rho^* - \bar{r})\right).$$

In the limit as γ tends to zero, ρ^* tends to $\frac{1}{2}$.

Provided that the depositors' signals are precise enough (β is high relative to α), every depositor follows the switching strategy around the critical value ρ^*. This critical value is obtained as the intersection of a cumulative normal distribution function with the 45° line, as depicted in Figure 1. In the limiting case when the noise becomes negligible, the curve flattens out and the critical value ρ^* tends to 0.5. The critical value ρ^* then divides the previously indeterminate region [0, 1] around its midpoint.

Let us sketch the argument behind this result. For ρ^* to be an equilibrium switching point, a depositor whose updated belief is exactly ρ^* ought to be indifferent between leaving his money deposited in the bank and withdrawing it. The utility of withdrawing is zero, and is nonrandom. The utility of leaving money in the bank is

Figure 1 SWITCHING POINT ρ^*

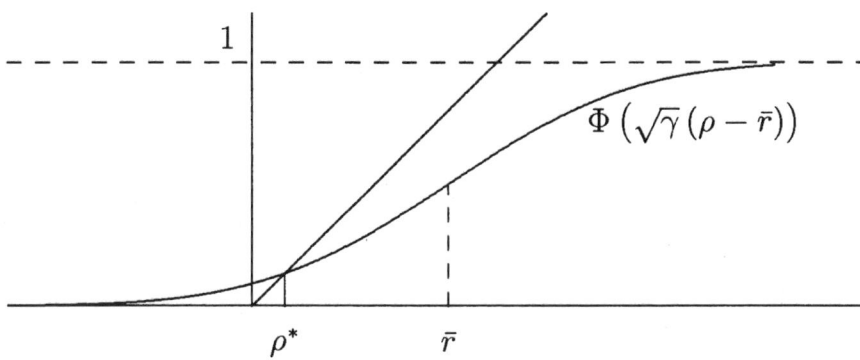

$$r - \ell \tag{2.7}$$

which is random and depends on ℓ, the proportion of the patient depositors that withdraw. At the switching point ρ^*, the expectation of $r - \ell$ conditional on ρ^* must therefore be zero. The expectation of r conditional on ρ^* is simply ρ^* itself. Thus, consider the expectation of ℓ conditional on ρ^*. Since noise is independent of the true return r, the expected proportion of patient depositors who withdraw is equal to the probability that any particular depositor withdraws. And since the hypothesis is that every depositor follows the switching strategy around ρ^*, the probability that any particular depositor withdraws is given by the probability that this depositor's updated belief falls below ρ^*.

When patient depositor i has posterior belief ρ_i, what is the probability that i attaches to some other depositor j having posterior belief lower than himself? Figure 2 illustrates the reasoning.

Conditional on ρ_i, return r is normal with mean ρ_i and precision $\alpha + \beta$. Since $x_j = r + \epsilon_j$, the distribution of x_j conditional on ρ_i is normal with mean ρ_i and precision

$$\frac{1}{\frac{1}{\alpha+\beta} + \frac{1}{\beta}} = \frac{\beta(\alpha + \beta)}{\alpha + 2\beta}. \tag{2.8}$$

But $\rho_j = (\alpha \bar{r} + \beta x_j)/(\alpha + \beta)$, so that the distribution of $\rho_j | \rho_i$ is as depicted in Figure 2, and the probability that ρ_j is less than ρ_i conditional on ρ_i is given by the shaded area. Moreover,

Figure 2 BELIEFS CONDITIONAL ON ρ_i

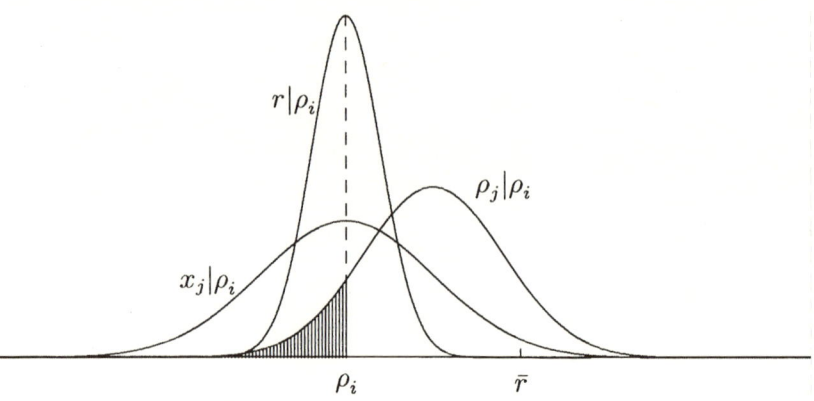

$$\rho_j < \rho_i \Leftrightarrow \frac{\alpha \bar{r} + \beta x_j}{\alpha + \beta} < \rho_i \Leftrightarrow x_j < \rho_i + \frac{\alpha}{\beta}(\rho_i - \bar{r}), \tag{2.9}$$

so the question of whether ρ_j is smaller than ρ_i can be reduced to the question of whether x_j is smaller than $\rho_i + (\alpha/\beta)(\rho_i - \bar{r})$. Hence,

$$\text{Prob}(\rho_j < \rho_i | \rho_i) = \text{Prob}\left(x_j < \rho_i + \frac{\alpha}{\beta}(\rho_i - \bar{r}) \Big| \rho_i\right)$$

$$= \Phi\left(\sqrt{\frac{\beta(\alpha+\beta)}{\alpha+2\beta}}\left(\rho_i + \frac{\alpha}{\beta}(\rho_i - \bar{r}) - \rho_i\right)\right)$$

$$= \Phi(\sqrt{\gamma}(\rho_i - \bar{r})). \tag{2.10}$$

So the shaded area in Figure 2 can be represented in terms of the area under a normal density which is centered on the ex ante mean $\bar{r}$. Figure 3 illustrates.

If ρ^* is an equilibrium switching point, the expectation of $r - \ell$ conditional on ρ^* must be zero. Since

$$E(r - \ell | \rho^*) = \rho^* - \Phi(\sqrt{\gamma}(\rho^* - \bar{r})), \tag{2.11}$$

ρ^* must be the point at which $\Phi(\sqrt{\gamma}(\rho - \bar{r}))$ intersects the 45° line, exactly as depicted in Figure 1. Provided that γ is small enough, the slope of $\Phi(\sqrt{\gamma}(\rho - \bar{r}))$ is less than one, so that there can be at most one point of intersection. Since the slope of the cumulative normal is given

Figure 3 DENSITY $\phi(\sqrt{\gamma}(\rho_i - \bar{r}))$

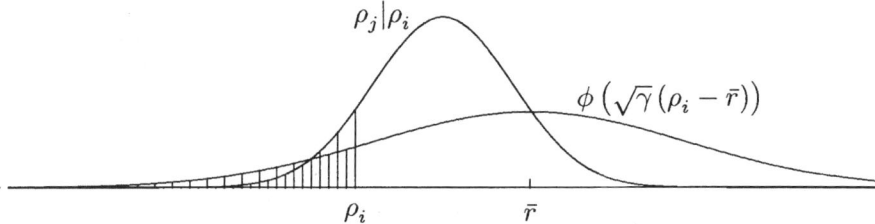

by the corresponding density function (which has the maximum value of $\sqrt{\gamma/2\pi}$), we can guarantee that there is a unique intersection point provided that γ is less than 2π. All that remains is to show that if there is a unique symmetric equilibrium in switching strategies, there can be no other equilibrium. Appendix A completes the argument.

2.4 COMPARATIVE STATICS AND POLICY ANALYSIS

The uniqueness of equilibrium makes it possible to perform secure comparative-statics analysis. We will illustrate this with a simple exercise in our example, where an early-withdrawal penalty t is imposed on consumers who withdraw in period 1.

In order to set a benchmark to measure our results against, consider the case with no uncertainty. The log return r is commonly known, and there is multiplicity of equilibria. The introduction of the early-withdrawal penalty has little effect in this case. The only effect is to shift the range of returns where multiple equilibria exist from [0, 1] to [log (1 − t), log (1 − t) + 1]. Without a theory guiding us as to which outcome results in the game, it is hard to evaluate the welfare consequences of this policy. The most we can say is that when r is close to 1 [i.e., in the marginal interval (log (1 − t) + 1,1)], the tax will remove the multiplicity of equilibrium, and the efficient outcome that consumers do not withdraw will occur for sure. When r is slightly less than 0 [i.e., in the marginal interval (log (1 − t), 0)], the tax will allow multiple equilibria.

In contrast to the lack of meaningful comparative statics when r is common knowledge, we can say much more when r is observed with noise. In particular, contrast the case with no uncertainty with the case in which noise is negligible (i.e. the limiting case where $\gamma \to 0$). The theorem tells us that patient consumers will withdraw if and only if $\rho <$ log (1 − t) + $\frac{1}{2}$. This allows us to calculate the incidence of withdrawals at any realized value of r. Policy affects outcomes for interior values of the parameters, by shifting the boundary of the two populations, not merely at extremal parameter values.

We can also use this unique equilibrium to examine policy trade-offs. Recall that the efficient outcome at date 1 is for withdrawal by patient consumers to take place only if $r < 0$. If noise concerning r is very small, we achieve this outcome with very high probability by setting $t = 1 - e^{-1/2}$ [so that $\log(1 - t) + \frac{1}{2} = 0$]. But of course achieving efficiency in the withdrawal decision comes at the cost of reducing the value of the contract to consumers. The explicit form for the equilibrium allows us to calculate the ex ante expected utility of consumers. For any given t, it is $1/(1 + \lambda)$ times

$$[\lambda + \Phi(\sqrt{\alpha}(\log(1 - t) + \tfrac{1}{2} - \bar{r}))]\log(1 - t)$$
$$+ \int_{\log(1-t)+1/2}^{\infty} r\phi(\sqrt{\alpha}(r - \bar{r}))\sqrt{\alpha}\, dr,$$

while the revenue from the penalty is

$$[\lambda + \Phi(\sqrt{\alpha}(\log(1 - t) + \tfrac{1}{2} - \bar{r}))]\, t.$$

An increase in the penalty can be welfare-enhancing for consumers (even if they derive no benefit from the tax revenue). Goldstein and Pauzner (1999) examine contracts where early-withdrawal penalties are received by consumers who leave their money until date 2. This further enhances the desirability of early-withdrawal penalties from the consumers' point of view.

2.5 OBSERVABLE IMPLICATIONS

We have presented a highly simplified model of bank runs. Even in this model, though, we can start thinking about observable implications of this theory. The main prediction is that despite the self-fulfilling aspect of the bank run, each depositor will withdraw his money exactly when his beliefs about the riskiness of bank deposits crosses some threshold, implying that the size of equilibrium bank runs will be negatively correlated with returns. Consider the incidence of deposit withdrawals as given by the equilibrium value of ℓ. This incidence is a random variable that depends on the realized return r. A depositor withdraws whenever his posterior belief falls below the critical value ρ^*, which happens whenever

$$\frac{\alpha \bar{r} + \beta x_i}{\alpha + \beta} < \rho^*.$$

Figure 4 PROPORTION $\ell(r)$ OF WITHDRAWALS

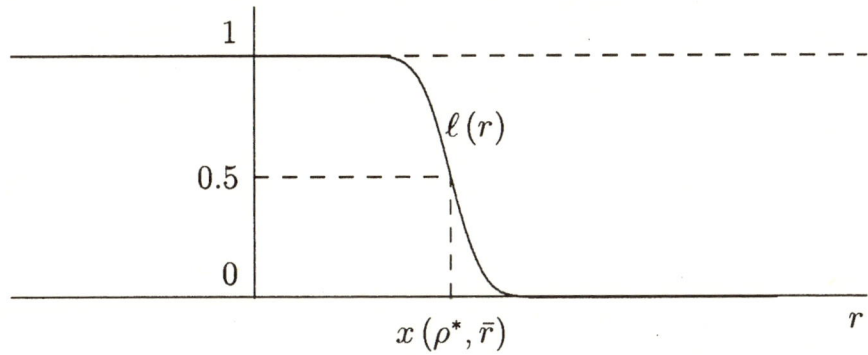

In other words, a depositor withdraws whenever the realization of his signal x_i falls below the critical value

$$x^*(\rho^*, \bar{r}) \equiv \frac{\alpha + \beta}{\beta} \rho^* - \frac{\alpha}{\beta} \bar{r}. \tag{2.12}$$

Since $x_i = r + \epsilon_i$, the incidence of withdrawal is a function of the realized return r, and is given by

$$\ell(r) = \Phi(\sqrt{\beta}\,(x^*(\rho^*, \bar{r}) - r)). \tag{2.13}$$

Figure 4 illustrates.

Clearly, the incidence of withdrawal is high when the return is low. Fundamentals plays a key explanatory role. Gorton (1988) studies bank panics in the U.S. national-banking era (1863–1914). He interprets the data in the light of the traditional dichotomy between fundamentals and sunspots as a cause of panics:

> A common view of panics is that they are random events, perhaps self-confirming equilibria in settings with multiple equilibria, caused by shifts in the beliefs of agents which are unrelated to the real economy. An alternative view makes panics less mysterious. Agents cannot discriminate between the riskiness of various banks because they lack bank-specific information. Aggregate information may then be used to assess risk, in which case it can occur that all banks may be perceived to be riskier. Consumers then withdraw enough to cause a panic. . . . [This latter] hypothesis links panics to occurrences of threshold value of some variable depicting the riskiness of bank deposits.

He concludes that the latter theory performs well. The highly simplified model of bank runs presented here suggests a reinterpretation of the evidence. The theory suggests that depositors will indeed withdraw their money when the perceived riskiness of deposits crosses a threshold value. But nonetheless, the banking panic is self-fulfilling in the sense that individual investors only withdraw because they expect others to do so. The theory suggests both that banking panics are correlated with poor fundamentals and that inefficient self-fulfilling panics occur. Of course, it is possible to make assumptions about sunspots that mimic these predictions; but the theory presented here places tighter restrictions on outcomes than sunspot theory.

One would like to come up with distinctive implications that are harder to mimic with judiciously chosen sunspots. We will suggest one example in this bank-deposit context. Suppose that we were able to observe both the prior mean of the log return $\bar{r}$ and the realized log return r; the prior mean $\bar{r}$ is a public signal that is observable by all depositors when they make their withdrawal decisions. Our theory predicts that for any given level of fundamentals r, the proportion of consumers running would be decreasing in $\bar{r}$. This is apparent from our theorem, since a fall in the ex ante mean $\bar{r}$ shifts the curve $\Phi(\sqrt{\gamma}(\rho - \bar{r}))$ to the left, so that its intersection with the 45° degree line is shifted to the right. Figure 5 illustrates this shift. Thus, when the fundamentals are commonly known to be weak (i.e. $\bar{r}$ is low), the equilibrium strategy dictates much more aggressive withdrawals, even controlling for one's posterior belief about r.

A prediction of the model, then, would be that if we could divide the fundamentals variables in Gorton's analysis into those that were most

Figure 5 SHIFT IN ρ^*

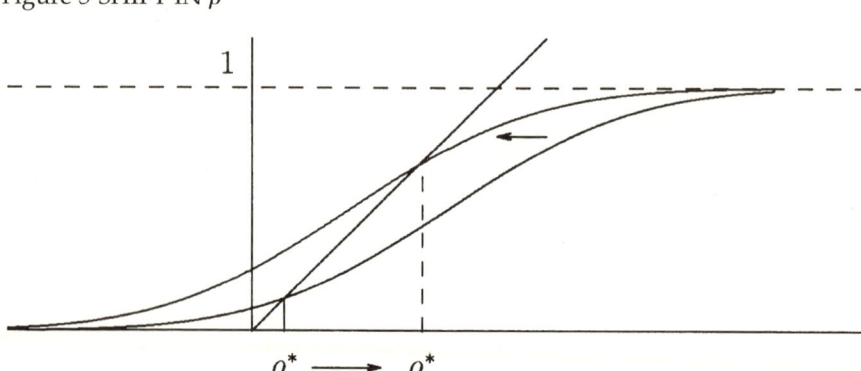

readily available to depositors contemporaneously and those that were not, we should expect the most readily available variables to have the biggest effect. We will come across another instance of the impact of public information below.

3. Complementarities and Macroeconomics

The example above was constructed around a simple coordination game played by a continuum of players. Much of the macroeconomics literature on complementarities, multiple equilibria, and sunspots similarly reduces in the end to coordination games played by large populations. In this section, we illustrate how other issues can be addressed using similar methods.

Consider the following class of problems. A continuum of individuals must choose between a safe action and a risky action. If an individual chooses the safe action, his payoff is a constant. If he chooses the risky action, his payoff is an increasing function of the "state of fundamentals" r but a decreasing function of the proportion of the population who choose the safe action, ℓ. In the bank-run example above, the payoff was linear in both r and ℓ. This linearity allowed us to give simple characterizations of the equilibrium. But as long as the payoff to the risky action is increasing in r and decreasing in ℓ, there will be a unique equilibrium of the type described above when information is sufficiently accurate. We will give an informal description of two applications that fit this general setup that we have analyzed elsewhere.

3.1 CURRENCY CRISES

A continuum of speculators must decide whether to attack a fixed exchange rate. The cost to the monetary authority of defending the peg depends on the fundamentals of the economy and the proportion of speculators who attack the currency. If the monetary authority has some fixed benefit of maintaining the peg, then for each realization of fundamentals, there will be some critical mass of speculators sufficient to induce abandonment of the currency. If the peg is abandoned, the exchange rate will float to some level that depends on the fundamentals. A speculator may choose to attack by selling a fixed amount of the currency short. If he attacks, he must pay a transaction cost but receives the difference between the peg and the floating rate if the attack is successful and there is a devaluation.

This stylized model is in the spirit of the self-fulfilling-attacks literature (see, for example, Obstfeld, 1996). If the state of fundamentals is common knowledge, there are three ranges of fundamentals to consider. If fundamentals are sufficiently low, devaluation is guaranteed. If fundamentals are sufficiently high, there will be no devaluation. But for some intermediate range of fundamentals, there are multiple equilibria. Morris and Shin (1998) show how if there is a small amount of noise concerning fundamentals, there is a unique equilibrium.

Now consider a policy that makes it harder for an attack to be successful. For example, the monetary authority might accumulate reserves. A naive calculation of the value of those reserves might involve calculating the likelihood of contingencies in which those extra reserves would make the difference in the authority's ability to defend against an attack. This is analogous to seeing when a tax on early withdrawals would remove the existence of a withdrawal equilibrium in the bank-run model. But taking into account the strategic analysis, we see that the true benefit of accumulating reserves is as a confidence-building measure. If the accumulation of reserves is publicly observed, speculators will anticipate that other speculators will be less aggressive in attacking the currency. So in regions of fundamentals where a self-fulfilling attack is in fact feasible, it will not occur.

The theory also generates intuitive predictions about which events lead to currency attacks. Deteriorating fundamentals, even if observed by most participants, will have less effect if the fact that fundamentals are deteriorating is not common knowledge. Very public signals that fundamentals have deteriorated only a small amount may have a large impact. This is because a speculator observing a bad signal not only anticipates that the monetary authority will have a harder time defending against an attack, but also anticipates that other speculators will be attacking. This explanation is quite commonplace. But the theoretical model that we have described captures this argument exactly.

3.2 PRICING DEBT

Our methods may also help us to understand some of the anomalies noted in the empirical literature on the pricing of defaultable debt. One influential approach has been to note that a lender's payoff is analogous to the payoff that arises from holding a short position in a put option on the borrower's assets. Hence, option-pricing techniques can be employed to price debt, as shown in the classic paper by Merton (1974). Nevertheless, the empirical success of this approach has been mixed, with the usual discrepancy appearing in the form of the overpricing (by the theory) of the debt, and especially of the lower-quality, riskier debt. The anomaly would be explained if it can be shown that the default trigger for asset values actually *shifts* as the underlying asset changes in value, and shifts in such a way that disadvantages lower-quality debt.

The incidence of inefficient liquidation seen in our bank-run example suggests that similar inefficiencies might arise in the coordination problem between creditors facing a distressed borrower. This would give us a theory of *solvent* but *illiquid* borrowers, enabling us to address the empirical anomalies. This is attempted in Morris and Shin (1999).

When the fundamentals are bad, coordination to keep a solvent borrower afloat is more difficult to achieve, and the probability of inefficient liquidation is large. This is another manifestation of the importance of public information in achieving coordination alluded to in the previous section. The disproportionate impact of public information can be illustrated in the following example of a borrower in distress.

Consider a group of lenders who are funding a project. Time is discrete, and advances by increments of $\Delta > 0$. The fundamentals of the project at date t are captured by the random variable r_t. Conditional on its current realization, the next realization of r_t is i.i.d., normally distributed around its current realization, with variance Δ. In other words, $\{r_t\}$ is a sequence of snapshots of a simple Brownian motion at time intervals of Δ. To economize on notation, we denote by r the current value of the fundamentals, and by r_+ its value in the next period. At each date, every lender chooses whether or not to continue funding the project. The project fails if and only if

$$\ell > r,$$

where ℓ is the proportion of creditors who pull out of the project. Hence, when $r > 1$ the project is viable irrespective of the actions of the creditors. If $r < 0$, the project fails irrespective of the actions of the creditors. However, when r lies between 0 and 1, the fate of the project depends on how severe the creditor run is. At each date, a lender receives a payment of 1 if the project has survived. When the project fails, a lender receives zero. By pulling out, a lender receives an intermediate payoff λ, where $0 < \lambda < 1$. We also suppose that a creditor who withdraws when the project is still viable rejoins the project in the next period (having missed a single payment of 1). This assumption ensures that the creditors face a sequence of one-shot games.

None of the creditors observe the current fundamentals perfectly. Each has signal

$$x_i = r + \epsilon_i,$$

where ϵ_i and ϵ_j are independent for $i \neq j$, and ϵ_i is normal with mean 0 and variance Δ^2. The noise in the signal x is thus small compared to the underlying uncertainty. The lenders, however, observe the previous realization of r perfectly. This will serve as the public information on which much of the analysis will hinge. As the time interval Δ becomes small, the noise disappears at a faster rate than the overall uncertainty governing r. Each lender chooses an action based on the realized signal x and the (commonly known) previous realization of r.

This game has a unique equilibrium (the proof if sketched in Appendix B) in which there is a critical value of fundamentals r_+^* for which the project fails next period whenever $r_+ < r_+^*$. We call r_+^* the *collapse point* for the project. It is given by the (unique) solution to

$$r_+^* = \Phi\left(r_+^* - r + \Phi^{-1}(\lambda)\sqrt{1+\Delta}\right). \tag{3.1}$$

The collapse point is obtained as the intersection between the 45° line and the distribution function for a normal with unit variance centered on $r - \Phi^{-1}(\lambda)\sqrt{1+\Delta}$. The following points are worthy of note.

1. r_+^* is a function of the current realization r. Hence, public information plays a crucial role in determining the trigger point for collapse.
2. The continuous time limit as $\Delta \to 0$ is well defined.
3. r_+^* is a *decreasing* function of r. So, when fundamentals deteriorate, the probability of collapse increases not only because the fundamentals are worse, but also because the trigger point has moved unfavorably.

This last feature is possibly quite significant. For an asset whose fundamentals are bad (i.e., r is low), the probability of default is higher than would be the case in the absence of coordination problems among creditors. Such a pattern would explain why one would misprice such an asset in a model that assumes a fixed default point. The mispricing takes the form of *overpricing* the riskier bonds—exactly the empirical anomaly discussed in the literature.

There is a more general lesson. The onset of financial crises can be very rapid, and many commentators note how the severity of a crisis is disproportionate to the deteriorating fundamentals. In our account, such apparently disproportionate reactions arise as an essential feature of the model. When fundamentals deteriorate, coordination is less easy to achieve. We can explore this effect further by examining the comparative statics of the probability of collapse. The probability of collapse next period conditional on the current fundamentals r is

$$\Phi\left(\frac{r_+^* - r}{\sqrt{\Delta}}\right).$$

As r falls, the probability of collapse increases at the rate

$$\frac{\phi}{\sqrt{\Delta}\,(1-\phi)},$$

where ϕ is the standard normal density at $(r_+^* - r)/\sqrt{\Delta}$. The increase in the probability of collapse can be quite large when r hovers close to the collapse point, and the onset of failure can thus be quite rapid. As compared to the naive model which does not take into account the dependence of the collapse point on the current fundamentals, this is larger by a factor of $1/(1-\phi)$. When r is close to the collapse point r_+^*, this is roughly $\sqrt{2\pi}/(\sqrt{2\pi}-1) \approx 1.66$.

The inverse relationship between the current value of fundamentals and the collapse point is suggestive of the precipitous falls in the price of defaultable securities during financial crises.

The continuous time limit of the model makes possible further simplifications in the analysis. Taking the limit as $\Delta \to 0$, the fundamentals r evolve as a simple Brownian motion, and the collapse point r_+^* for the next period converges to the collapse point in the current period. So (3.1) can be written

$$r^* = \Phi\left(r^* - r + \Phi^{-1}(\lambda)\right)$$

Collapse occurs when r hits r^*, i.e. at $r^* = \lambda$.

3.3 HOW SPECIAL IS THE ANALYSIS?

In this paper, we have described stylized examples with normally distributed states and signals, binary choices by a symmetric continuum of players, and payoffs linear in the state and proportion of players choosing each action. These assumptions allowed us to give simple characterizations of the unique equilibrium. However, the analysis is arguably quite general. If one is only interested in the limiting case where noise in signals is very small, the exact shape of the noise or prior beliefs about the state do not matter. Asymmetries among the players can also be incorporated. Corsetti et al. (1999) examine the role of a large trader in currency markets in an asymmetric game. The qualitative features of the analysis are very similar between continuum and finite player cases. Indeed, in the special case of the payoffs in the bank-run model, where only the proportion of other players choosing each action matters, the analysis is literally unchanged. That is, if we had a finite number of depositors, with proportion $\lambda/(1+\lambda)$ impatient and proportion $1/(1+\lambda)$

patient, the unique equilibrium would have patient consumers using the same cutoff point for withdrawals. Dealing with many actions is more delicate (see Frankel, Morris, and Pauzner, 2000), although the analysis extends straightforwardly in some instances. Carlsson and Ganslandt (1998) describe what happens when noise is added to Byrant's (1983) model of technological complementarities.

4. Concluding Remarks

We draw two conclusions from our analysis. The first is that applied theorists should be wary of selecting an arbitrary outcome for further attention when conducting comparative-statics exercises and in drawing policy implications. The mere fact that an outcome is Pareto-superior to another is no good reason for it to be selected, and we should expect to see some inefficiencies as a rule. The notion of a "solvent but illiquid bank" can be given a rigorous treatment, and we hope that our discussions can contribute to policy debates in the area.

Our second conclusion is a methodological one. Contrary to the impression given by multiple-equilibrium models of the apparent autonomy of beliefs to float freely over the fundamentals, we believe that such autonomy of beliefs is largely illusory when information is modeled in a more realistic way. No doubt some researchers may find this regrettable, since one degree of freedom is lost in the exercise of providing a narrative of unfolding events. However, there are compensations for this loss, and we hope that these benefits will be recognized by researchers. One promising line of inquiry is to explore the correlations between the underlying fundamentals and the degree of optimism of the economic agents. Empirical investigations will then have a much firmer basis.

Appendix A

When there is a unique symmetric equilibrium in switching strategies, there can be no other equilibrium. An argument is sketched here. Denote by $u(\rho, \hat{\rho})$ the expected utility from leaving one's money in the bank conditional on posterior ρ when all other patient depositors follow a switching strategy around $\hat{\rho}$. Conditional on ρ, the expected proportion of depositors who withdraw is given by the probability that any particular depositor receives a signal lower than the critical value $\hat{\rho}$. From the argument in the text, this probability is given by

$$\Phi\left(\sqrt{\tfrac{\beta(\alpha+\beta)}{\alpha+2\beta}}\left(\hat{\rho}+\tfrac{\alpha}{\beta}(\hat{\rho}-\bar{r})-\rho\right)\right)=\Phi\left(\sqrt{\gamma}\left(\hat{\rho}-\bar{r}+\tfrac{\beta}{\alpha}(\hat{\rho}-\rho)\right)\right). \tag{A.1}$$

Hence, $u(\rho,\hat{\rho})$ is given by

$$u(\rho,\hat{\rho})=\rho-\Phi\left(\sqrt{\gamma}\left(\hat{\rho}-\bar{r}+\tfrac{\beta}{\alpha}(\hat{\rho}-\rho)\right)\right). \tag{A.2}$$

If r is negative, the utility from withdrawing is higher than that from leaving money in the bank, irrespective of what the other depositors decide. So, if the posterior belief ρ is sufficiently unfavorable, withdrawing is a dominant action. Let $\underline{\rho}_1$ be the threshold value of the belief for which withdrawal is the dominant action. Any belief $\rho < \underline{\rho}_1$ will then dictate that a depositor withdraws. Both depositors realize this, and each rules out strategies of the other depositor which leave money in the bank for signals lower than $\underline{\rho}_1$. But then, leaving money in the bank cannot be optimal if one's signal is lower than $\underline{\rho}_2$, where $\underline{\rho}_2$ solves

$$u(\underline{\rho}_2,\underline{\rho}_1)=0. \tag{A.3}$$

This is so because the switching strategy around $\underline{\rho}_2$ is the best reply to the switching strategy around $\underline{\rho}_1$, and even the most optimistic depositor believes that the incidence of withdrawals is higher than that implied by the switching strategy around $\underline{\rho}_1$. Since the payoff to withdrawing is increasing in the incidence of withdrawal by the other depositors, any strategy that leaves money in the bank for signals lower than $\underline{\rho}_2$ is dominated. Thus, after *two* rounds of deletion of dominated strategies, any strategy that leaves money in the bank for signals lower than $\underline{\rho}_2$ is eliminated. Proceeding in this way, one generates the increasing sequence

$$\underline{\rho}_1 < \underline{\rho}_2 < \cdots < \underline{\rho}_k < \cdots, \tag{A.4}$$

where any strategy that leaves money in the bank for a signal $\rho < \underline{\rho}_k$ does not survive k rounds of deletion of dominated strategies. This sequence is increasing, since $u(\cdot,\cdot)$ is increasing in its first argument and decreasing in its second. The smallest solution $\underline{\rho}$ to the equation $u(\rho,\rho)=0$ is the least upper bound of this sequence, and hence its limit. Any strategy that leaves money in the bank for signal lower than $\underline{\rho}$ does not survive iterated dominance.

Conversely, if ρ is the largest solution to $u(\rho,\rho) = 0$, there is an exactly analogous argument from "above," which demonstrates that a strategy that withdraws for signals larger than ρ does not survive iterated dominance. But if there is a *unique* solution to $u(\rho,\rho) = 0$, then the smallest solution just *is* the largest solution. There is precisely one strategy remaining after eliminating all iteratively dominated strategies. Needless to say, this also implies that this strategy is the only *equilibrium* strategy.

Appendix B

The posterior belief of the current value of r is normal with mean

$$\rho = \frac{x_i + \Delta r_-}{1 + \Delta}$$

and precision $(1 + \Delta)/\Delta^2$, where r_- denotes the previous realization of r. Denote by $U(\rho)$ the payoff to continuing with the project conditional on ρ when all creditors are following the ρ-switching strategy. It is given by

$$U(\rho) = \Phi\left(\frac{\sqrt{1+\Delta}\,(r^* - \rho)}{\Delta}\right), \tag{B.1}$$

where r^* is the trigger value of fundamentals at which the project collapses. r^* satisfies $r^* = \ell$. But if other speculators follow the ρ-switching strategy, ℓ is the proportion of creditors whose signal is lower than the marginal value of x that implies the switching posterior ρ. This gives

$$r^* = \Phi\left(\rho - r_- + \frac{\rho - r^*}{\Delta}\right). \tag{B.2}$$

From these two equations, we can show by implicit differentiation that $U'(\rho) > 0$. There is a unique solution to $U(\rho) = \lambda$, and the equilibrium is unique for the same reasons as cited for the main theorem. To solve explicitly for the collapse point r^*, we solve the pair of equations given by (B.2) and $U(\rho) = \lambda$. This gives

$$r^* = \Phi\left(r^* - r_- + \Phi^{-1}(\lambda)\sqrt{1+\Delta}\right),$$

as required.

REFERENCES

Bryant, J. (1983). A simple rational expectations Keynes type model. *Quarterly Journal of Economics* 98:525–529.

Carlsson, H., and M. Ganslandt. (1998). Noisy equilibrium selection in coordination games. *Economic Letters* 60:23–34.

Carlsson, H., and E. van Damme. (1993). Global games and equilibrium selection. *Econometrica* 61:989–1018.

Chari, V. V., and R. Jagannathan. (1988). Banking panics, information and rational expectations equilibrium. *Journal of Finance* 43:749–761.

Cooper, R. (1999). *Coordination Games: Complementarities and Macroeconomics.* Cambridge: Cambridge University Press.

Corsetti, G., A. Dasgupta, S. Morris, and H. S. Shin. (1999). Does one Soros make a difference? A theory of currency crises with large and small traders. Yale University.

Diamond, D., and P. Dybvig. (1983). Bank runs, deposit insurance and liquidity. *Journal of Political Economy* 91:401–119.

Diamond, P. (1982). Aggregate demand management in search equilibrium. *Journal of Political Economy* 90:881–894.

Freixas, X., and J.-C. Rochet. (1997). *Microeconomics of Banking.* MIT Press.

Frankel, D., S. Morris, and A. Pauzner. (2000). Equilibrium selection in global games with strategic complementarities. Yale University.

Goldstein, I., and A. Pauzner. (1999). Endogenous probability of bank runs in a rational expectations model. Tel Aviv University.

Gorton, G. (1988). Banking panics and business cycles. *Oxford Economic Papers* 40:751–781.

Merton, R. C. (1974). On the pricing of corporate debt: The risk structure of interest rates. *Journal of Finance* 29:449–470.

Morris, S., and H. S. Shin. (1997). Approximate common knowledge and coordination: Recent lessons from game theory. *Journal of Logic, Language and Information* 6:171–190.

———, and ———. (1998). Unique equilibrium in a model of self-fulfilling currency attacks. *American Economic Review* 88:587–597.

———, and ———. (1999). Coordination risk and the price of debt. Unpublished paper. http://www.nuff.ox.ac.uk/users/Shin/working.htm.

Murphy, K., A. Schleifer, and R. Vishny. (1989). Industrialization and the big push. *Journal of Political Economy* 97:1003–1026.

Obstfeld, M. (1996). Models of currency crises with self-fulfilling features. *European Economic Review* 40:1037–1047.

———, and K. Rogoff. (1997). *Foundations of International Macroeconomics.* MIT Press.

Postlewaite, A., and X. Vives. (1987). Bank runs as an equilibrium phenomenon. *Journal of Political Economy* 95:485–491.

Comment

ANDREW ATKESON
Federal Reserve Bank of Minneapolis and University of Minnesota

1. Introduction

Macroeconomists have used coordination games with multiple equilibria to describe any number of phenomena in which we appear to see large changes in economic outcomes with little or no apparent change in the underlying economic fundamentals. Usually, in macroeconomic applications, these games are shown to have multiple equilibria and the argument is made that large changes in economic outcomes can follow from changes in agents' expectations about what other agents will do rather than from changes in economic fundamentals alone.

Morris and Shin present a simple and dramatic insight into the structure of simple coordination games. With only a few assumptions, they show that if agents see a noisy signal of the true state of the world and thus have some uncertainty about the exact structure of the coordination game that they are playing as well as some uncertainty about what every other agents knows about the coordination game that they are playing, then these games in fact have a unique equilibrium corresponding to each underlying state of the world. This result suggest that macroeconomists should reassess whether their previous findings of multiple equilibria in these coordination games are robust to small changes in the structure of information available to agents.

Morris and Shin go on to show that if the noise introduced into the coordination game is small, the selected equilibrium has the feature that there is a threshold state of the world around which the economic outcome changes very rapidly with small changes in the state, while in the other regions of the state space, the economic outcome is quite stable as the underlying state of the world varies. This second feature of the equilibrium selected by Morris and Shin's apparatus suggests that their work may be more than a criticism of the robustness of previous multiple-equilibrium literature and may, in fact, have important implications for a number of applications.

My discussion of this paper by Morris and Shin has four parts. First, I present what I think is the simplest environment in which to apply their apparatus. Second, I go over a proof of their result in this environment that is slightly different than the proof presented in the paper. I hope that it will help any reader interested in understanding the logic of Morris and Shin's results to see the argument from a different angle. Third, I describe what I find to be the most interesting feature of the equilibrium that is selected and also go over an example of how one might use this technology to do comparative statics. Fourth, I describe what I believe is the main impediment to use of this technology for modeling macroeconomic phenomena.

To jump ahead for a moment, this fourth and final part of my discussion does not focus on the applied question of whether the models that Morris and Shin have proposed for currency crises and the pricing of corporate debt in related papers are relevant for analyzing those phenomena. Instead I focus on the broader question of whether one can introduce markets and prices, clearly essential parts of any macroeconomic application, into what, to date, has been a purely game-theoretic analysis. Morris and Shin, in their introduction, criticize previous applications of coordination games in macroeconomics for relying on assumptions that "allow agents' actions and beliefs to be perfectly coordinated in a way that invites multiplicity of equilibria." The noise that they introduce into coordination games has the effect of preventing coordination of agents' actions and beliefs. In a market economy, however, prices serve precisely to coordinate actions (so that supply equals demand), and in a dynamic market economy, asset prices play an important role in coordinating agents' beliefs, since these prices tend to aggregate information across individuals.

It is not clear to me how the argument presented by Morris and Shin would carry over to a model with markets. Their arguments require agents to have diverse beliefs about the probabilities of future outcomes in equilibrium, and this typically does not happen in models in which agents see the market signals about those probabilities embodied in asset prices. The nature of this difficulty in translating Morris and Shin's technology to a market environment should become clearer after we review the details of how this technology works.

2. A Simple Coordination Game

Let us review how Morris and Shin's technology works in the context of what seems a natural application of the game theory. Consider a crowd that faces riot police in the street. Individuals in the crowd must decide whether to riot or not. If enough people riot, the riot police are overwhelmed, and each rioter gets loot $W > 0$. If too few people riot, the riot police contain the riot, and each rioter gets arrested with payoff $L < 0$. Individuals who choose not to riot leave the crowd and get safe payoff 0. The strength of the riot police depends on the state of the world, θ, and the strictly increasing function $a(\theta)$ indexes the fraction of the crowd that must riot to overwhelm the police. Let $\underline{\theta}$ denote the point at which $a(\theta)$ crosses 0, and $\bar{\theta}$ the point at which $a(\theta)$ crosses 1.

The equilibria of this game when the state θ is common knowledge are as follows. If $\theta \leq \underline{\theta}$, then it is a dominant strategy for each individual to riot, since the riot police in this case are so weak that they cannot stop even a single rioter [$a(\theta) \leq 0$]. Thus, if θ is in this region of the state space, everyone riots and gets payoff W for sure. If $\theta > \bar{\theta}$, then it is a dominant strategy for each individual not to riot, since the police can contain the crowd even if everyone riots [$a(\theta) > 1$]. Thus, if θ is in this region of the state space, no one riots and everyone gets payoff 0 for sure. In the middle of the state space, with $\underline{\theta} < \theta \leq \bar{\theta}$, there are two possible equilibria corresponding to each value of the state θ. In the first of these equilibria, everybody riots. In this case, the fraction of the crowd that riots is $1 \geq a(\theta)$, so the police are overwhelmed and everybody gets payoff $W > 0$. In the second of these equilibria, nobody riots. In this case the fraction of the crowd that riots is $0 < a(\theta)$, so the police contain the crowd and any individual who riots is arrested. Hence, nobody riots, and everybody in the crowd gets $0 > L$. This game clearly has multiple equilibria in a region of the state space, and when the state variable is in this region, the economic outcome depends on agents' expectations of what other agents will do and not on the underlying economic fundamental $a(\theta)$.

3. An Alternative Presentation of the Proof of Their Result

Morris and Shin introduce the following changes into this coordination game. They assume that individuals do not know the state of the world, θ. Instead, each individual starts with a common prior that θ is normally distributed with some mean m_θ and variance $1/\alpha$ (precision α). (I think of the randomness in θ as arising from the problem that the precise strength of the squad of riot police available to any particular crowd in any particular street at any particular time depends somewhat on chance.) Each individual in the crowd then receives an idiosyncratic signal $x_i = \theta + \epsilon_i$ of the state θ, where ϵ_i is normally distributed with mean 0 and variance $1/\beta$ (precision β) and is i.i.d. across individuals. Given these assumptions, we have two distributions that play a key role in the analysis. First is the distribution of signals x_i across agents conditional on the realization of the state θ. With the assumptions above, this is a normal distribution, but we can write it more generally as a c.d.f. $\text{Prob}(x \leq x^*|\theta)$, which we will assume to be a strictly positive, continuous, decreasing function of θ for any value of x^*. Second is the posterior distribution over θ for an agent who has seen signal x. This is obtained from Bayes's rule and, under the assumptions above, is a normal distribution; but it can also be written more generally as a c.d.f. $\text{Prob}(\theta \leq \theta^*|x)$. We also assume that this is a continuous and decreasing function of x for any value of θ^*.

Morris and Shin's result in the context of this simple game can then be stated as follows. Assume that there is a unique solution x^*, θ^* to the following two equations:

$$\text{Prob}(x \leq x^*|\theta) = a(\theta^*), \tag{1}$$
$$\text{Prob}(\theta \leq \theta^*|x^*)W + [1 - \text{Prob}(\theta \leq \theta^*|x^*)]L = 0. \tag{2}$$

Then there is unique equilibrium described by x^* and θ^*. The signal x^* is a threshold signal such that all individuals who get signals $x \leq x^*$ riot, and those who get signal $x > x^*$ do not riot. The state θ^* is a threshold state such that the crowd overwhelms the police, so that rioters get payoff W if $\theta \leq \theta^*$ and the police contain the crowd, and rioters are arrested and get payoff L if $\theta > \theta^*$.

In the paper, Morris and Shin make assumptions on the precision of the signal relative to the precision of the prior in stating the result. In proving their proposition they show that there is a unique solution to the analogues to equations (1) and (2) if we assume that the precision of the signal, denoted β, is sufficiently high relative to the precision of the prior, denoted α, and the slope of the function $a(\theta)$. The necessary and sufficient condition for their result, however, appears to be that these two equations have a unique solution.

One way to prove this proposition is by iterated deletion of dominated strategies. I find this proof the easiest to understand. It goes as follows.

First observe that individuals who get sufficiently low and high signals, which I denote x_0 for the low signal and x^0 for the high signal, are so confident of their posterior beliefs that $\theta \leq \underline{\theta}$ or $\theta > \bar{\theta}$, that they find it a dominant strategy to riot or not riot, respectively, regardless of what everyone else does. The low signal x_0 is the highest value of x such that

$\text{Prob}(\theta \leq \underline{\theta}|x)W + \text{Prob}(\theta > \underline{\theta}|x)L \geq 0.$

The interpretation here is that, even if one believed that everyone else in the crowd was not going to riot, and thus any individual rioter would be arrested in the event that $\theta > \underline{\theta}$, the posterior probability that $\theta \leq \underline{\theta}$ for someone who saw $x \leq x_0$ is high enough to make it worthwhile to run the risk of rioting.

Analogous reasoning defines x^0. Even with the belief that everyone else always riots and thus that rioters will get W if $\theta \leq \bar{\theta}$, someone who saw signal $x > x^0$, where x^0 is the smallest x such that

$$\text{Prob}(\theta \leq \bar{\theta}|x)W + \text{Prob}(\theta > \bar{\theta}|x)L \leq 0,$$

would not find the potential reward of rioting likely enough to justify the risk. These two observations give us the first round of deletion of dominated strategies: any equilibrium strategy must have all agents with signals $x \leq x_0$ rioting and those with signals $x > x^0$ not rioting, because, for agents with such signals, rioting and not rioting are optimal strategies regardless of what everyone else does.

In the subsequent rounds of our iterated deletion of dominated strategies, we take as given the restriction on dominated strategies obtained from the previous round. That is, any individual contemplating the actions of others must believe that everyone who has signals $x \leq x_0$ will riot and no one who has signals $x > x^0$ will riot. If everyone who has signals $x \leq x_0$ riots, then the fraction of the crowd that riots in state θ must be at least $\text{Prob}(x \leq x_0|\theta)$. Given our assumptions on this c.d.f., this fraction of rioters is always positive and is a continuous and declining function of θ. Thus, there is a maximum value of the state, which I denote $\theta_0 > \underline{\theta}$, such that

$$\text{Prob}(x \leq x_0|\theta) \geq a(\theta).$$

Accordingly, a rational individual must realize that at least in all states of nature $\theta \leq \theta_0$, enough of the crowd will riot to overwhelm the police, and such an individual thus finds it a dominant strategy to riot as long as his signal $x \leq x_1$, where x_1 is the largest signal x such that

$$\text{Prob}(\theta \leq \theta_0|x)W + \text{Prob}(\theta > \theta_0|x)L \geq 0.$$

Likewise, each agent realizes that at least a fraction $\text{Prob}(x > x^0|\theta)$ of the crowd will not riot in state θ, and thus the rioters must lose and be arrested in all states greater than or equal to θ^0, where $\theta^0 < \bar{\theta}$ is the maximum value of θ such that

$$\text{Prob}(x \leq x^0|\theta) \geq a(\theta).$$

Accordingly, it is a dominant strategy for a rational agent not to riot when his signal exceeds x^1, where x^1 is the smallest x such that

$$\text{Prob}(\theta \leq \theta^0|x)W + \text{Prob}(\theta > \theta^0|x)L \leq 0.$$

With these observations we iteratively delete dominated strategies: given x_0 and x^0 as threshold signals below which everyone riots and above which no one riots, we have shown that any equilibrium strategy must have the crowd winning at least in states $\theta \leq \theta_0$ and losing at least in states $\theta > \theta^0$, and thus rational agents should riot when their signals $x \leq x_1$ and not riot when their signals $x > x^1$. These new threshold signals x_1 and x^1 then take the place of x_0 and x^0 as restrictions on the behavior of every other agent, and we go through these calculations again, deriving new restrictions on the equilibrium strategies.

This iterative procedure of restricting the equilibrium strategies defines increasing sequences $\{x_n, \theta_n\}_{n=0}^{\infty}$ and decreasing sequences $\{x^n, \theta^n\}_{n=0}^{\infty}$ that progressively put tighter and tighter bounds on the equilibrium strategies. To finish the proof of Morris and Shin's proposition, we need only show that these sequences converge to common limit points, which I will denote x^* and θ^*. Showing this proves the proposition because it forces the conclusion that all agents with signals $x \leq x^*$ riot, while no agents with signals $x > x^*$ riot, and that the crowd wins the riot in all states $\theta \leq \theta^*$, and loses in all states $\theta > \theta^*$.

To show that the sequences above have common limit points, we observe that any limit points x^* and θ^* of either of these two sequences must be a solution to the two equations (1) and (2). But, if these two equations have a unique solution, then we are done, since that forces the conclusion that these two sequences have a common limit point.

The algebra behind Morris and Shin's result that equations (1) and (2) have a unique solution when the signals x are precise relative to the prior is straightforward. To do the algebra under the assumption of normality, observe that the term

$$\text{Prob}(x \leq x^* | \theta^*) = \Phi\left(\sqrt{\beta}(x^* - \theta^*)\right),$$

where Φ is a standard normal c.d.f., and use the fact that an agent who sees signal x has a posterior over θ that is normal with mean $(\alpha m_\theta + \beta x)/(\alpha + \beta)$ and precision $\alpha + \beta$, to get that

$$\text{Prob}(\theta \leq \theta^* | x^*) = \Phi\left(\sqrt{\alpha+\beta}\left(\theta^* - \frac{\alpha m_\theta + \beta x^*}{\alpha + \beta}\right)\right).$$

Use equation (2) to get

$$x^* = \frac{\alpha + \beta}{\beta}\theta^* - \frac{\alpha}{\beta}m_\theta - \frac{\sqrt{\alpha+\beta}}{\beta}\Phi^{-1}\left(\frac{-L}{W - L}\right), \tag{3}$$

and plug this into (1) to get one equation in the threshold state θ^*:

$$\Phi\left(\frac{\alpha}{\sqrt{\beta}}(\theta^* - m_\theta) - \frac{\sqrt{\alpha+\beta}}{\sqrt{\beta}}\Phi^{-1}\left(\frac{-L}{W-L}\right)\right) = a(\theta^*). \quad (4)$$

Equation (3) gives us the threshold signal x^* at which an agent is indifferent between rioting and not rioting given threshold state θ^*, and the left-hand side of equation (4) gives us the fraction of the crowd who receives signals less than or equal to x^*. Any solutions to equation (4) must lie in the interval $[\underline{\theta}, \overline{\theta}]$. Both sides of this equation are increasing functions: the left-hand side looks like a normal c.d.f. with steepness determined by $\alpha/\sqrt{\beta}$, and the right-hand side has whatever slope is assumed to reflect how the strength of the police varies with the state. The fact that there is at most one solution when β is large relative to α follows from the fact that the left-hand side becomes flat in θ over the interval $[\underline{\theta}, \overline{\theta}]$ in the limit as $\alpha/\sqrt{\beta}$ goes to zero. Note that if $\alpha/\sqrt{\beta}$ is large, then this equation typically has three solutions in the interval $[\underline{\theta}, \overline{\theta}]$ (since the c.d.f. looks more like an S over this interval), and thus the iterated deletion of dominated strategies does not pin down a unique equilibrium.

4. The Selected Equilibrium and Comparative Statics

Consider now what the unique equilibrium outcome looks like as a function of the state of nature θ. Note first that, whatever θ is, some portion of the crowd will riot and some portion of the crowd will not. All that varies with the state θ is the size of the fraction of the crowd that riots and whether the rioters overwhelm the police or are arrested.

The fraction of the crowd that riots in state θ is Prob($x \leq x^*|\theta$) = $\Phi(\sqrt{\beta}(x^* - \theta))$. This fraction, as a function of the state θ, is one minus a normal c.d.f. and thus looks like a reverse S-curve. If the noise ϵ has a small variance, then this fraction begins to look like a step function: close to 1 for $\theta < x^*$ and close to 0 for $\theta > x^*$, with a steep transition from high to low as θ crosses the threshold signal x^*. Thus, the equilibrium relationship between the actions of the crowd and the strength of the police is highly nonlinear. For large ranges of values of the state θ, we have changes in the strength of the police, $a(\theta)$, but little or no change in the fraction of the crowd that riots. On the other hand, for values of θ close to the threshold signal x^*, we have a large and sudden change in the number of people rioting. This is a very interesting result, since it suggests that sudden shifts in agents' expectations with small changes in the state may play an important role in determining equilibrium outcomes despite the fact that the equilibrium is unique.

Now let us go through an example of how to use this technology to do comparative statics. The natural exercise in this example is to ask what effect changes in the average strength of the police (parametrized by m_θ) have on the equilibrium incidence of riots, computed as the ex ante probability that the state θ is below the threshold θ^*, or $\Phi(\sqrt{\alpha}(\theta^* - m_\theta))$. Differentiating equation (4) gives us the result that as long as the left-hand side of (4) is flatter in θ than the right-hand side (the same condition that ensures uniqueness of the solution), then $d\theta^*/dm_\theta < 0$. What this implies, of course, is that strengthening the police has two beneficial effects: first, it lowers the probability that the crowd will win the riot, holding fixed the threshold state θ^*, and second, it leads to a reduction in the threshold state θ^*, further reducing the probability that the crowd will overwhelm the police. Morris and Shin play up this shift in the threshold state in their application of this technology to the pricing of corporate debt. Note, of course, that this second effect, this shifting of the threshold state, is smaller, the larger is β relative to α. In the limit as $\alpha/\sqrt{\beta}$ goes to zero, this second effect disappears.

5. *The Problem with Introducing Prices into the Model*

So far in our analysis, individuals in this crowd have no information other than their own signal to consider when they decide whether to riot or not. This would be different, of course, if we introduced markets and prices into the model. Imagine, for the sake of this discussion, that individuals also could see asset prices, and assume specifically that there is a traded asset with payout contingent on the claims that the insurance company that covers the property threatened by the rioters must pay. For simplicity, assume that the claims that the insurance company would have to pay following a riot take on only two values: a large value in the event that the crowd overwhelms the police, and a small value in the event that the police keep the crowd under control. Imagine, as well, that assets trade continuously, so that individuals in the crowd can see asset prices after θ is realized but before they need to decide whether to riot.

On the one hand, if this asset ends up being priced in equilibrium in a way that accurately reflects its subsequent payout, it will have one price in all states $\theta \leq \theta^*$ (reflecting that the insurance claims will be large) and another price in all states $\theta > \theta^*$ (reflecting that the insurance claims will be 0). This, of course, will be a problem for our previous analysis. Every individual should be able to look at this asset price and know whether the crowd is going to overwhelm the police or not. Depending on the price, then, either every individual should strictly prefer to riot, or to not riot. Agents' actions and beliefs would be coordinated, since there would be no reason for any individual to act differently on the basis of his own signal. The logic of Morris and Shin's argument goes out the window.

On the other hand, if this asset does not get priced in equilibrium in a way that allows agents to infer whether the crowd will overwhelm the police or not, we must ask why it is not priced that way. How do we set up the model so that the asset price does not aggregate the information that all of the individuals in the economy have and thus reveal the true state?

The idea that individuals in a crowd considering whether to riot or not would consult asset prices via the newspaper or their handy wireless Internet connections seems farfetched. That, in part, was my motivation for picking this example for my discussion. The analysis of Morris and Shin seems as if it might work pretty well for this example. In the macroeconomic examples that Morris and Shin point to in their paper, however, asset prices are clearly a necessary part of the picture, and it is not at all clear how their arguments apply.

In Morris and Shin's example regarding speculative attacks on currencies, one would think that forward exchange rates (interest-rate differentials) and options on exchange rates are readily observed by all market participants when they consider whether to attack or not. Their example in their earlier paper (Morris and Shin, 1988), like the riot example above, has agents holding diverse beliefs about the probability that the currency will be devalued and deciding whether or not to attack on the basis of those beliefs. But, if, given the fundamentals today, the equilibrium uniquely pins down whether the currency will soon be devalued or not, then it seems that those interest-rate differentials and exchange-rate option prices should reflect today which of the two outcomes will occur. If those prices do accurately reflect which outcome will occur, agents should coordinate their decision to attack or not according to them: everyone should attack if the asset prices indicate a devaluation will occur, and no one should attack if they indicate that a devaluation will not occur. It does not make sense in this application to assume that agents will take different actions (attacking or not) on the basis of their private signals if publicly observed asset prices accurately reveal which outcome will actually occur. It thus does not make sense to apply the argument proposed by Morris and Shin to the analysis of currency attacks unless we can tell some story as to why interest-rate differentials and exchange-rate options do not reveal an imminent devaluation of the currency even if that devaluation must occur in equilibrium with probability one.

In Morris and Shin's example regarding corporate debt, discussed in detail in a cited working paper (Morris and Shin, 1999), the price of the firm's equity and the secondary market price of the firm's debt will clearly reflect some market assessment of the likelihood that the firm will be liquidated in equilibrium. If the outcome, liquidation or not, is uniquely pinned down by the fundamentals, then these prices should reveal that, and agents should be able to coordinate their actions accordingly.

Finally, in the bank-run example presented in this paper, the price of the bank's equity should reveal whether there will be a run or not, since this outcome is pinned down in equilibrium. Accordingly, agents should look at this price in deciding whether to run or not, and it seems natural to suspect that their actions and beliefs might be coordinated upon the observation of this price.

The question then stands, how do we integrate prices into the analysis and yet preserve the diversity of posterior beliefs across agents that is key to pinning down a unique equilibrium? Perhaps the answer to this question will depend on the specific application: it seems plausible that rioters are not integrating asset prices into their analysis of whether to riot or not; it seems less plausible to assume that currency traders are ignoring interest-rate differentials and option prices in deciding whether to attack a currency or not. Finding an answer to this question seems to me to be the obvious next step in refining this potentially useful technology for analyzing macroeconomic coordination games.

Comment[1]

HÉLÈNE REY
London School of Economics and CEPR

1. Introduction

It is a real pleasure to comment on a paper which is of great interest, addresses a fundamental issue in macroeconomics, and is also very elegant.

In a series of articles, Steve Morris and Hyun Song Shin have developed a fruitful line of research that extends and applies sophisticated game-theoretic concepts to traditional macroeconomic problems. In this paper, which may be seen to some degree as a synthesis of their approach, they use a simple bank-run model as a framework to ask a very

---

1. These comments benefited from discussions with Harald Hau, Thomas Philippon, Richard Portes, David Romer, and Mike Woodford.

important question: Are multiple equilibria in economics the unintended consequence of too simplistic assumptions?

The answer provided by the paper is unambiguously yes. The authors write, for example: "We doubt that economic agents' beliefs are as indeterminate as implied by the multiple-equilibrium models. Instead, the apparent indeterminacy of beliefs can be seen as the consequence of two modeling assumptions introduced to simplify the theory. First, the economic fundamentals are assumed to be common knowledge; and second, economic agents are assumed to be certain about each other's behavior in equilibrium." The paper then claims that introducing a small amount of idiosyncratic uncertainty is enough to destroy the perfect coordination of agents' actions and beliefs and therefore to eliminate the possibility of multiple equilibria. Since our world seems indeed to be one of imperfect and asymmetric information, this realistic generalization of our traditional macroeconomic models appears to banish multiple equilibria once and for all. They become an "artifact of simplifying assumptions that deliver more than they are intended to deliver," as the authors put it.

In my discussion, I will emphasize that Morris and Shin's paper does not in fact eliminate the possibility of multiple equilibria. I will also discuss the robustness of their results more precisely and perform some comparative-statics exercises. Finally, I will comment on the empirical applicability of their model and its relations to the literature on multiple equilibria.

2. Unique Equilibrium?

Morris and Shin set up a Diamond–Dybvig bank-run model with a slightly more sophisticated information structure than usual. Returns follow a normal distribution with a given precision α; this is *public information*. On the other hand, each agent gets a signal with precision β regarding the realization of the return; this is *private information*. When the fundamentals are common knowledge, it is well known that the Diamond–Dybvig model gives rise to multiple equilibria. By introducing a little bit of noise (a very small degree of asymmetric information), the authors show that the equilibrium is unique. So a very minor modification to an otherwise standard model is able to eliminate the multiplicity of equilibria.

This is a very strong result. I will argue, however, that the minor deviation from the benchmark model chosen by the authors brings with it a lot of interesting and sometimes puzzling results, some of them not emphasized in the paper. In particular, if one does not look exclusively at the limiting case on which the authors are focusing but at the general case of their own model, the possibility for multiple equilibria reappears very naturally.

In Morris and Shin's paper, the condition characterizing the equilibrium is

$$\rho^* = \Phi(\sqrt{\gamma}(\rho^* - \bar{r})),$$

where ρ^* is the cutoff point below which patient consumers withdraw their money from the bank, $\bar{r}$ is the mean of the returns, $\Phi(\cdot)$ is the cumulative normal distribution, and γ is a constant given below. Graphically, this equilibrium is illustrated in Figure 1 of the paper. It is immediately apparent that the 45° line and the cumulative normal distribution will intersect only once if the slope of the cumulative normal is "not too steep." Formally, a sufficient condition for this to happen is

$$\gamma = \frac{\alpha^2(\alpha+\beta)}{\beta(\alpha+2\beta)} \leq 2\pi.$$

When the precision of the private information, β, is very high (β goes to infinity for a given α, meaning that γ becomes very small), the authors interpret their model as being a very small deviation from the standard Diamond–Dybvig model with common knowledge. In that case the Morris–Shin model gives the discontinuity result emphasized in the paper: If private information is very precise, then the two curves intersect only once and we have a unique equilibrium. If, on the other hand, private information is infinitely precise, then we are in the standard Diamond–Dybvig case and there are multiple equilibria. This is an interesting and surprising result, and the authors present it very well in the paper.

But this is not the end of the story. Note that there are two different ways to approach the common knowledge case from within the Morris–Shin framework (Figure 1). We can approach common knowledge either by letting the precision of the *private* signal go to infinity, as in the paper, or by letting the precision of the *public* information go to infinity. In that latter case, α would be going to infinity for a given β and the slope of the cumulative normal distribution would become very steep as in Figure 2. In that case, there can be multiple equilibria. More generally, it is obvious that as long as the precision of the public information is high compared to that of the private signal, multiple equilibria will still exist. This result is intuitive: the more precise public information is, the closer we

Figure 1 COMMON KNOWLEDGE AS A LIMIT

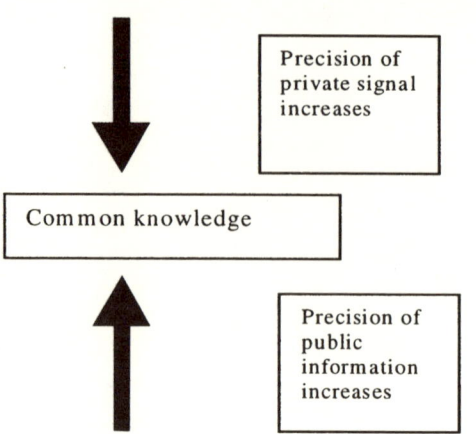

Figure 2 MULTIPLE EQUILIBRIA IN THE MORRIS–SHIN FRAMEWORK

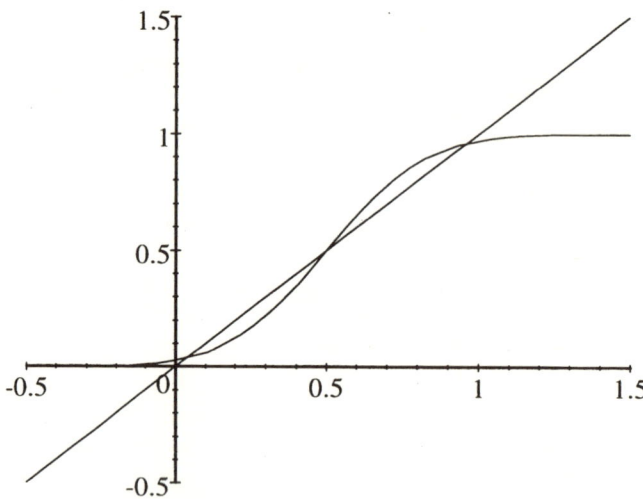

are to the standard case of common knowledge among economic agents, which is known to generate multiple equilibria. At another level, it is however somehow paradoxical to think that the economies that are generating the more accurate publicly available information are also the ones that are the more prone to multiple equilibria. And, conversely, it is also puzzling that for a given degree of precision of the private signals, economies with very diffuse public information will converge to a unique equilibrium.

To summarize, the central claim of the paper (the discontinuity result), that a very minor deviation from the standard models with common knowledge is enough to eliminate the possibility of multiple equilibria, is not the whole story: if one does accept that the Morris–Shin framework is a better representation of reality, one has to recognize that this model also delivers multiple equilibria for some parameter domains. Furthermore, common knowledge can be seen as a limiting case in two different ways: in one case, one converges towards common knowledge with a unique equilibrium, in the other case, one converges towards common knowledge with multiple equilibria.

3. Comparative-Statics Results and Dynamics

If we limit ourselves to the parameter region where uniqueness of equilibrium prevails, we can perform comparative-statics exercises, which pave the way towards policy recommendations. A first thing to look at is the effect of the precision of private and public information on the cutoff signal x^* below which patient depositors will withdraw their money from the bank. It turns out that an increase in the precision of either type of information may either lower or raise the value of the critical signal for a given return. This result is puzzling.

Another interesting exercise is to look at the impact of a change in public information versus the impact of a change in private information. One can even characterize by how much a private signal should change to balance the impact of a change in public information so that the strategies of the agents are kept unchanged. Since one of the key aspects of public information in Morris and Shin's paper is that it coordinates the expectations of agents, one would expect that public news would have a bigger relative effect than private news. This intuition is correct provided one is able to control for the relative precision of the private and public informations, which requires knowing the magnitudes of α and β.

The model presented is a one-shot game (a repetition of one-shot games in the second part of the paper). It would obviously be very nice to do a dynamic extension of the framework. Careful thought should then be given to the process of information revelation. Let us imagine that economic agents play the game presented in the paper at date t. At date $t + 1$, they will have observed the number of people having run on the bank at date t, which is given by

$$\ell(r) = \Phi\left(\sqrt{\beta}\left((\rho^* - r) + \frac{\alpha}{\beta}(\rho^* - \bar{r})\right)\right).$$

As soon as the proportion of people withdrawing money is observed, the realized return becomes common knowledge, since all the other parameters are known. If there is some persistence in the return variable, then the precision of the public information is increasing over time (α is increasing for a given β), and we may exit the unique equilibrium region. Extending the model dynamically therefore requires keeping enough "fuzziness" in the public information.

4. Empirical Applicability

An interesting feature of Morris and Shin's approach is the ability to address policy issues, thanks to the comparative-statics exercises performed around the unique equilibrium. For practical purposes, it is therefore very important to know whether the economy is in a unique- or a multiple-equilibrium region, which depends on the value of the parameter γ. Since γ is not homogeneous in α and β, figuring out the relative precision of the two types of information is not enough. It matters whether α is 17 rather than 13 or whether β is 9 rather than 10. Moreover, just like the number of equilibria themselves, we have seen that the comparative-statics results depend on the absolute magnitude of the precision of the public and the private information. Unfortunately, it seems extremely difficult to get an idea of what these numbers are in reality. They partly depend on the interpretation one has of the model itself. Should we think of the private-information element of the model as differences in psychology across individuals, so that traders reading the same economic news may form different views on the economy depending on their temperament? Or should we think of it as the degree of precision of "inside information"?

This aspect put aside, we should ask ourselves whether Morris and Shin's approach has empirical implications which can clearly be distinguished from those of the models exhibiting multiple equilibria. The authors argue that their model provides testable implications so that it suggests a correlation between fundamentals and outcomes, unlike multiple-equilibrium models, where the shift from one equilibrium to the other may be due to pure sunspots. This point is interesting. Note, however, that multiple-equilibrium models also provide some correlations between fundamentals and outcomes. In a self-fulfilling speculative-attack model, for example, the parameter space is divided into three regions: one where the fundamentals are so good that there can be no attack, one where the fundamentals are so bad that there is an attack for sure, and an intermediate region where there are multiple equilibria.

Therefore I would argue that the key empirical implication of the Morris–Shin model is not that fundamentals are correlated with outcomes, nor that multiple equilibria do not exist—as discussed above—but rather that the degree of information aggregation matters. Having recognized this fact, there are nice natural experiments which could be used to test the model. One could for example look at the role of polls or surveys in a situation with strategic complementarities (like foreign-exchange traders). One could also study the impact of the introduction of a futures market on the evolution of spot prices, the idea being that prices of futures would aggregate the information of market participants. The difficulty of putting numbers on the precisions of public and private information and therefore of pinning down the exact implications of the model—which vary across parameter regions—will, however, remain.

5. Interpretation of Multiple Equilibria

The main message of multiple-equilibrium models may be that even when the fundamentals of the economy are almost the same, outcomes can be very different. The sense of this basic message seems empirically quite relevant. The ERM crisis of 1992, for example, has often been given as an example of self-fulfilling speculative attack. By fundamentals we usually mean all the variables describing the economy (GDP, prices, exchange rates, etc.) except the information structure. A great virtue of the Morris–Shin model is that it introduces the information structure into the set of the fundamental variables. The question is then whether the model can deliver the flavor of the multiple-equilibrium models while keeping the uniqueness of the equilibrium.

The paper shows that for some parameter values, introducing some noise makes the equilibrium unique. In that uniqueness region, small changes in the information structure do change the threshold value below which an attack occurs, but not dramatically so (in general). In Figure 1 of the paper, for example, one can see that a small change in the information structure (or in the mean return) will change the slope of the normal distribution (or shift it, respectively). But this will not result in a big variation in ρ^*, the posterior belief below which the patient consumers withdraw their money, unless the slope of the normal distribution is quite steep, which is exactly the case when one is close to the region where multiple equilibria exist. In other words, the Morris–Shin model can have the flavor of multiple-equilibrium models, but that is only provided one is in a parameter region away from the limit case considered by the authors and close to the multiplicity domain.

In the absence of even more sophisticated ways to model information aggregation and the endogeneity of the information structure, we are still left with a multiple-equilibrium region where we cannot say much about equilibrium selection. Perhaps a phenomenon like the 1992 ERM crisis could be modeled as unique equilibrium if dramatic shifts in information aggregation were incorporated explicitly. One way forward could be to think harder about the information aggregation process: here private information is costless to acquire and is automatically given to all agents. Costly and voluntary information acquisition should ideally be related to the other fundamentals of the economy.

6. Conclusion

The paper makes a very important contribution to the literature on strategic complementarities. First, Morris and Shin's approach can be applied to a wide spectrum of issues. We have many macroeconomic models which exhibit multiple equilibria, whether they are used to discuss bank runs, speculative attacks, industrialization, inflation, poverty traps, or thick-market externalities. As the authors point out, this multiplicity is a problem if one wants to perform comparative-statics exercises. What is the impact of increasing a tax rate, for example, when the system can switch from one equilibrium to another in a random fashion? Determining the equilibrium to which an economic system will converge is a key issue for policy makers, and this is where the Morris and Shin's approach is so valuable. But as I have pointed out, the Morris–Shin model is not as opposed to the multiple-equilibrium literature as the authors claim. This is not a criticism, and it underlines that the model has many interesting and rich features, which can be exploited further. The model is not very operational yet as far as empirical tests are concerned, mainly because it is hard to pin down the magnitude of the key parameters which determine the domain of existence of equilibria as well as the comparative-statics results. It also lacks true dynamics. The Morris–Shin framework has however already been (rightly) very influential in the way we think about coordination and information aggregation in macroeconomic models and will certainly generate a lot of interesting new results in very diverse areas.

Discussion

In responding to the discussants' comments, Stephen Morris agreed that there are two ways of proving the existence of a unique equilibrium in their framework. The first, employed in their paper, is the direct approach of showing that no equilibrium other than the one they find can exist. The other approach is discussant Andrew Atkeson's iterated elimination of dominated strategies. Morris noted that Atkeson's approach makes the equilibrium a little less mysterious but may give the impression that agents in the model need to do sophisticated reasoning, which is not the case, as no other threshold will work as an equilibrium. Morris agreed with the discussant Hélène Rey that the implications of alternative assumptions on the information structure, especially the distinction between public and private information, are the most important area of future research. On the importance of public information, he attributed to Robert Shiller the claim that "bubbles started when newspapers became widely available." The importance of financial news networks of all kinds is not only that an individual receives information, but that he knows that others are also receiving that information.

Daron Acemoglu began the general discussion by suggesting that one way of interpreting multiple-equilibrium results is that they arise from sparse formal models with limited fundamentals. The fact that models with few fundamentals imply multiple equilibria does not imply necessarily that multiple equilibria are a feature of the real world. The virtue of this paper is that it suggests that minimal increases in the complexity of our models may reduce or eliminate multiple equilibria. Acemoglu also offered an intuition about why the model works: In discrete choice models there are multiple equilibria because when everybody else does something the return is sufficiently high, and when everybody else doesn't do something the return is sufficiently low, so that "following the crowd" is a winning strategy for everyone. Noise creates a thick tail of people who will always do or not do something independently of others' actions, leading ultimately to a unique equilibrium. This reasoning suggests why we want the parameter β to be large but not α, because when α is large, tails are not thick enough relative to common information. The authors agreed with this intuition.

Mike Woodford argued against making the inference that any finding of multiple equilibria depends on extreme assumptions. He said the paper does not show that multiple-equilibrium models are not robust; it only shows that one can construct examples with private signals where there is a unique equilibrium. Woodford suggested that minor perturbations of private-information models will yield multiple equilibria that are qualitatively similar to those in common-knowledge models; hence Morris and Shin's analysis does not demonstrate that the conclusions of models without private signals are not robust. Woodford also thought the authors overstressed the finding that, in their model, a small change in the public signal can have a large effect on the equilibrium outcome, even though the equilibrium is unique. He observed that this result requires the parameter γ to be large, which means that the model is very close to one with multiple equilibria, implying in turn that the unique equilibrium is very fragile. Fundamentally, then, the mechanisms that generate big swings are similar in this model and in models exhibiting multiple equilibria.

The authors agreed with Woodford that there are many ways to perturb the common-knowledge model that preserve multiple equilibria. However, Shin argued that their model is special (and not a small perturbation) in its result that people remain uncertain in equilibrium about the actions of others, so that common knowledge is destroyed. Shin suggested that their model should be viewed as a cousin of the "second-generation" models, which preserves the flavor of those models but includes a rigorous equilibrium argument that pins down the model's prediction. Morris added that finding out under what information structures equilibrium is unique is a worthwhile project in itself. He noted that models with strategic complementarities will already have a strong multiplier effect, so that interpreting a crisis as a switch from one equilibrium to another amounts to throwing in an extra, and perhaps unnecessary, strategic complementarity. Their approach eliminates this extra degree of freedom.

Pierre Gourinchas suggested that in multiperiod models there might be a feedback process: agents may observe fundamentals and get very precise information. Asset prices that efficiently aggregate information may have the same effect. If precise information on fundamentals becomes publicly available, the results of the paper are undermined. Morris agreed there would be progressive information revelation through prices in a dynamic model; he thought a useful direction would be to write down a more complicated model in which this happens, but in which people also receive private information over time.

Paolo Pesenti was enthusiastic about the approach, arguing that it represents the best chance so far to build the foundations of a theory of confidence crises. Such a theory would have far-reaching implications about how we think about financial stability and other important issues. He hoped that this approach would eliminate the current dichotomy in the literature between fundamentals-based and non-fundamentals-based models of crises.

Ken Rogoff recalled that, in his Ely lecture, Larry Summers complained about models of crises that have the implication that, in certain regions, economics can say nothing. Summers called for a model with the feature that the worse the fundamentals are, the more likely a crisis. Rogoff noted that, at a formal level, the Morris–Shin model has this desirable property. But, he asked, suppose we establish at a theoretical level that equilibrium is unique but can't connect it to any fundamental that we can plausibly observe. Then would our empirical approach be in any way different, relative to the case in which we are guided by models with multiple equilibria?

Harold L. Cole and Lee E. Ohanian
FEDERAL RESERVE BANK OF MINNEAPOLIS; AND FEDERAL RESERVE BANK OF MINNEAPOLIS AND U.C.L.A.

Re-examining the Contributions of Money and Banking Shocks to the U.S. Great Depression

1. Introduction

Many economists argue that deflation can account for much of the Great Depression (1929–1933) in the United States. According to this story, a sharp decline in the money supply caused rapid deflation, which in turn reduced output. Empirical research has documented large decreases in money, prices, and output between 1929 and 1933. But there is much less work assessing whether this shock can plausibly account for the Depression within fully articulated general equilibrium models. This paper quantitatively evaluates the deflation hypothesis with dynamic, general equilibrium business-cycle models.

Evaluating the deflation hypothesis with general equilibrium models requires an explicit theory of why deflation reduced output so much in the 1930s. Since there are several explanations for this in the literature, we first narrow the field by requiring that any successful deflation theory of the Depression also be consistent with macroeconomic activity during other major deflations. We therefore determine which deflation theories satisfy this criterion by comparing the Great Depression with

We thank Andy Atkeson, Ben Bernanke, Narayana Kocherlakota, Stanley Lebergott, Axel Leijonhufvud, Ken Rogoff, Art Rolnick, and our discussants Michael Bordo and Mark Gertler for helpful comments. We thank Daniel Hammermesh for CPS wage data, and Jonathon Parker for estimates of compositional wage changes. Special thanks go to Ed Prescott for many discussions about the Great Depression. We have also benefited from the outstanding research assistance of Jesus Fernandez-Villaverde. The views expressed herein are those of the authors and not necessarily those of the Federal Reserve Bank of Minneapolis or the Federal Reserve System.

macroeconomic activity during the early 1920s, which is a period of comparable deflation, but a much less severe downturn in economic activity.

We find that two of the four most popular explanations are ruled out by this consistency criterion. These are the *surprise-deflation story* of Lucas and Rapping (1969), which argues that the Great Depression was severe because the deflation was unexpected, and the *debt–deflation story* of Irving Fisher (1933), which argues that the Great Depression was severe because deflation substantially raised the real value of private debt. The two stories that are not ruled out are the high-wage story and the banking story. According to the *high-wage story*, deflation, combined with imperfectly flexible wages, raised real wages and reduced employment and output. A number of economists report evidence in favor of this story, including Eichengreen and Sachs (1985), Bernanke and Carey (1996), and Bordo, Erceg, and Evans (2000). According to the *banking story*, deflationary money shocks contributed to bank failures and to a reduction in the efficiency of financial intermediation, which in turn reduced lending and output. Bernanke (1983) reports evidence in favor of this story.

Following this empirical analysis, we develop two general equilibrium models to separately evaluate the wage shock hypothesis and the banking shock hypothesis. We ask two questions: Can these shocks drive down output per adult nearly 40% relative to trend between 1929 and 1933? Are the other predictions of the theories consistent with the data?

Our main finding is that wage shocks and banking shocks account for a small fraction of the Great Depression. We also find that some other predictions of the theories are at variance with the data. We conclude that these results raise questions about the deflation and banking hypotheses as explanations of the Great Depression in the United States.

The paper is organized as follows. Section 2 presents the comparison between the Great Depression and the 1921–1922 Depression, and the evaluation of the four popular deflation stories for the Great Depression. We then go on to develop general equilibrium models for the two stories that are not ruled out by this comparison—the high-wage story and the banking story. Section 3 presents a general equilibrium model with above-market wages, and also presents a quantitative assessment of the wage hypothesis. Section 4 presents a general equilibrium model with an intermediation sector to assess the macroeconomic impact of bank failures. Since our results support neither the wage nor banking story, Section 5 briefly discuss two other possible contributing factors to the Great Depression: changes in asset prices and changes in productivity. Section 6 presents a summary and conclusion.

Table 1 DEFLATION AND OUTPUT—OUTPUT AND ITS COMPONENTS[a]

Depression of 1921–1922 (1920 = 100)				Great Depression (1929 = 100)				
Year	P	Y	C	I	Year	P	Y	C	I
1921	85.2	93.9	102.4	86.1	1930	97.5	86.9	90.0	73.2
1922	80.6	96.2	102.7	114.4	1931	88.5	77.6	84.3	48.5
					1932	79.5	64.0	74.3	26.7
					1933	77.5	60.9	70.8	23.0

[a] The price level is from Romer (1988) for 1921–1923, and from Bureau of the Census (1975) for 1929–1933. The output data for 1920–1922 are from Kendrick (1961, p. 294). Romer (1988) argues that the Kendrick series is a better output measure for the 1920s than the Commerce Department measure, which is based on preliminary work of Kuznets and Kendrick. The output data for 1929–1933 are from the National Income and Product Accounts. The population data are from Bureau of the Census (1975, p. 10).

2. An Empirical Puzzle about the Deflation Hypothesis

A successful theory of the Great Depression based on deflation should account for macroeconomic activity during 1929–1933 and should also be consistent with macroeconomic activity during other major deflations. This section empirically evaluates this consistency requirement by comparing changes in prices and real output during 1929–1933 to those during a period of comparable deflation: 1920–1922.

Table 1 shows the percentage change in the GNP deflator (P), real GNP (Y), real consumption (C), and real investment (I) during these two episodes. The three quantity variables are deflated by their specific deflators, are measured relative to the adult (16 and over) population, and are detrended.[1] Deflation is similar during these two periods: the price level fell about 20% between 1920 and 1922, and also fell about 20% between 1929 and 1932. Despite these similar deflations, however, output fell much more between 1929 and 1932 than between 1920 and 1922. Real GNP fell 36% between 1929 and 1932, but just 4% between 1920 and 1922.

These data raise a puzzle about the deflation hypothesis: If the 20% deflation of the 1930s caused the Great Depression, why didn't the 20% deflation of the 1920s also cause a major depression? Resolving this puzzle requires finding some other shock(s) that magnify the depressing effects of deflation and that were present in the 1930s, but not in the 1920s. There are several stories for why the 1930s deflation had such

1. We detrended these three quantity variables at a rate of 1.9% per year. We define this rate as normal growth, because it is the growth rate of output per adult both before the Great Depression (1919–1929), and after World War II (1947–1997), and because it is close to the 2% average growth rate between 1900 and 1997. It is also worth noting that output per adult in 1929 is very close to an OLS trend line fitted to this series between 1900 and 1997. This suggests that output was close to its normal trend value in 1929.

large, negative real effects. But can these stories explain why the Great Depression was so much worse than the 1921–1922 Depression? We address this question in the next section.

2.1 CAN THE STANDARD STORIES EXPLAIN THE SEVERITY OF THE GREAT DEPRESSION?

Four popular deflation stories for the Great Depression are: (1) the deflation was unexpected, (2) nominal debt levels were high, (3) nominal wages were imperfectly flexible, and (4) there were many bank failures in addition to the deflation. We consider each of these stories in turn and ask whether they might be consistent with both the Great Depression and the 1921–1922 Depression. For each story, this consistency requires that the shock that magnified the real effect of deflation in the 1930s not be present in the 1920s.

2.1.1 Differences in Deflation Predictability between the 1920s and the 1930s Some theories predict that only unanticipated deflation depresses real economic activity. Lucas and Rapping (1969) argue that the 1930s deflation was unexpected and that this was an important factor behind the severity of the Great Depression. Can differences in the predictability of the 1920s and 1930s deflations explain the difference in the severity of these two depressions? We address this question by comparing nominal and ex post real interest rates between these two periods.[2] If differences in the predictability of deflation can explain both the Great Depression and the Depression of 1921–1922, we should observe very low nominal interest rates in the 1920s, but relatively high nominal and ex post real interest rates during the 1930s.

Table 2 shows average annual nominal and real interest rates on 3- to 6-month U.S. Treasury notes and certificates. The real rate is the nominal rate minus the percentage change in the annual GNP deflator. The most striking feature of these data is that both nominal and real interest rates are higher during the Depression of 1921–22. The average nominal rate on Treasury securities is 4.35% between 1921 and 1922, compared to an average of 1.1% between 1930 and 1933. The average real rate on these securities is 14.25% between 1921 and 1922, compared to an average of 7.21% between 1930 and 1930.[3] These data suggest that the 1930s defla-

---
2. There is some work addressing the predictability of the 1930s deflation (see Hamilton, 1992, and Cecchetti, 1992), but we are unaware of any studies of the predictability of the deflation of the early 1920s, or any comparison of the predictability of deflation between the two periods.
3. It may seem surprising that the deflation of the early 1920s was more unexpected, since monetary policy after wars traditionally produced deflation. However, the timing and rates of those deflations were probably much less certain.

Table 2 NOMINAL AND EX POST REAL INTEREST RATES: 1920s AND 1930s[a]

	Depression of 1921			Great Depression	
	Interest rate (%)			Interest rate (%)	
Year	Nominal	Real	Year	Nominal	Real
1921	4.83	19.63	1930	2.23	4.73
1922	3.47	8.87	1931	1.15	10.38
			1932	0.78	10.95
			1933	0.26	2.78
Avg.	4.35	14.25	Avg.	1.10	7.21

[a]The data are from Board of Governors of the Federal Reserve System (1943). The results are very similar using 4–6-month prime commercial paper.

tion was *more* predictable than the 1920s deflation, rather than *less* predictable. We conclude from these data that unexpected deflation is not the key factor behind the relative severity of the Great Depression.[4]

2.1.2 Differences in Private Debt and Deflation between the 1920s and 1930s
Fisher (1933) suggested that deflation and high private debt levels contributed to the Great Depression by reducing borrower wealth and constraining lending. This is known as the *debt–deflation* view of the Great Depression. Before asking whether this story is consistent with both depressions, it is important to note that there are two separate macroeconomic effects from this redistribution. We call one the *debt-burden effect* of debt and deflation, which is Fisher's original view. The other is the *wealth-transfer effect,* in which unexpected deflation transfers wealth from debtors to creditors. On average, creditors are older and borrowers are younger. This transfer increases the old generation's consumption, but changes their labor input little in absolute terms, since their labor endowment is low. The wealth transfer will tend to increase the hours of the young generation. Overall, the wealth-transfer effect should increase aggregate hours and output and thus will tend to offset the debt-burden effect. Thus, there is no theoretical presumption that wealth redistributions between debtors and creditors reduce aggregate employment and output.

If the debt–deflation story can explain the severity of the Great Depression, the debt-burden effect must be quantitatively much more impor-

---

4. Some economists have also suggested that high real interest rates were an important contributing factor to the Great Depression. The fact that real interest rates were substantially higher during the 1921–1922 Depression casts doubt on this explanation.

Table 3 INCREASE IN THE PRIVATE DEBT BURDEN DUE TO DEFLATION: THE DEPRESSION OF 1921–1922 VS. THE GREAT DEPRESSION[a]

Year	Private debt relative to output	Δ (price level) in first 2 years of deflation (%)	Increase in debt burden in first 2 years of deflation	Δ GNP in first 2 years of deflation (%)
1920	1.20	−19.4	0.29	−3.8
1929	1.56	−11.5	0.20	−22.4

[a] The increase in the debt burden is given by

$$\frac{100 D/Y}{100 + \%\Delta P} - D/Y,$$

where D is the debt-to-output ratio. There are two basic sources of data on business liabilities in the Historical Statistics (Bureau of the Census, 1975). The first is the nominal debt series put out by the BEA, which we have used. The second is from IRS data on corporate tax returns (see series V 108–140). The IRS data only begin in 1926, and there appears to be a significant difference in the indicated increase in corporate debt levels between the two sources. The IRS data indicate that corporate debt in the form of bonded debt and mortgages rose 47% between 1926 and 1929. This figure seems too large and suggests that the coverage level was initially low when the IRS was first collecting the returns data. This view is supported by the observation that according to the IRS data the total debt of the corporate sector—including notes, accounts payable, bonded debt, and mortgages—was only $55.8 billion in 1926, while the net debt from the BEA for the total corporate sector in 1926 was $76.2 billion.

tant in the 1930s than in the 1920s. Two factors that affect the quantitative extent of the debt-burden effect are the size of the stock of debt at the start of the deflation and the pattern of deflation. A larger initial stock of debt and a rapid deflation will tend to increase the effect. We measure the increase in the debt burden as the increase in the real value of debt (relative to output) due to deflation over the first two years of each depression.

Table 3 shows the initial stock of debt relative to output at the price-level peak prior to each depression, as well as the percentage change in prices in the first two years of each depression, the implied percentage increase in the debt burden relative to initial output, and the percentage change in real output. The most striking feature of these data is that the debt-burden channel rises *more* in 1921–1922 than in 1929–1931. The more rapid 1920s deflation increased the debt burden by 0.29 between 1920 and 1922, compared to 0.20 between 1929 and 1931. This larger debt-burden increase, however, is associated with a much smaller decrease in output. Real GNP falls 3.8% between 1920 and 1922, but falls 22.4% between 1929 and 1931.

Explaining the severity of the Great Depression through debt and deflation thus requires a model in which an initial debt stock of 1.2, with 19% deflation, is associated with only a 4% decrease in output, while an initial debt stock of 1.56, with 11% deflation, drives down output by more than 22%.[5] We are unaware of any quantitatively plausible model that is consistent with these observations. We conclude from these data that the debt–deflation story does not explain why the Great Depression was worse than the 1921–1922 Depression.[6]

2.1.3 Differences in Wages between the 1920s and the 1930s Some economists believe that wage changes increased the depressing effects of deflation in the 1930s. Before addressing whether differences in wages can explain the difference between the Great Depression and the Depression of 1921–1922, it is important to recognize that there is disagreement over *how* wage changes may have contributed to the Great Depression. Some economists, for example Lucas and Rapping (1972) and Lucas (1983), argue that the Great Depression was severe because nominal wages fell so *much*. Others, for example Bernanke and Carey (1996), Bordo, Erceg, and Evans (2000), and Eichengreen and Sachs (1985), argue that the Great Depression was severe because nominal wages were imperfectly flexible and did not fall *enough*.

Since Lucas and Rapping's view is based on unexpected deflation, and it is unlikely that unexpected deflation is responsible for the severity of the Great Depression, we focus on the inflexible-wage hypothesis. According to this hypothesis, inflexible nominal wages, combined with deflation, raised real wages, which reduced employment and output.

Explaining the relative severity of the Great Depression through high wages requires: (1) real wages well above the trend in the 1930s, and significantly higher than wages in 1921–1922, and (2) a theory of labor market failure during the 1930s—if the Great Depression was caused by high real wages, there would have been enormous competitive pressure for wages to fall.

We begin by examining wages between the two depressions. Unfortunately, there are few survey wage data that are both of reasonable quality and consistently available during both the 1920s and the 1930s. Two sectors for which such data are available are agriculture and manufacturing. Tables 4 and 5 show that detrended wage changes are fairly similar

5. Olney (1999) argues that high consumer debt levels and extreme default penalties help account for the large drop in consumption in 1930. If this indebtedness was key, we would expect a larger than normal decrease in consumer durables spending in 1930. However, the decrease in the ratio of durables to output in 1930 is small relative to postwar recessions. The major decrease in consumption in 1930 is due to nondurables and services.
6. It is worth noting that the difference in debt levels between the two periods—1.2 vs. 1.56—may overstate the actual difference in the debt-burden channel, since financial markets were probably more sophisticated in the 1930s, and as a consequence might have managed larger debt levels more efficiently.

Table 4   FARM WAGES[a]

Depression of 1921–1922		Great Depression	
Year	Real wage (1920 = 100)	Year	Real wage (1929 = 100)
1921	71.9	1930	93.0
1922	73.1	1931	76.8
		1932	64.7
		1933	60.2

[a]Source: Bureau of the Census (1975, p. 468). The farm wage rate is the daily wage without room and board. It is deflated by the GNP deflator and is detrended at 1.4%/yr, as that is the average growth rate of real hourly compensation between 1947 and 1997.

Table 5   MANUFACTURING AVERAGE HOURLY EARNINGS[a]

Depression of 1921–1922		Great Depression	
Year	Real wage (1920 = 100)	Year	Real wage (1929) = 100)
1921	101.5	1930	102.1
1922	101.2	1931	106.8
		1932	106.5
		1933	104.2

[a]These data are deflated by the GNP deflator. We detrended manufacturing wages at a 1.4% annual rate, as that is the average growth rate of real hourly compensation between 1947 and 1997. The average growth rate of real manufacturing wages between 1923 and 1929 was slightly higher at 1.6%/yr.

between the two episodes and that wage changes differed significantly across sectors of the economy. Some real wages fell substantially during both depressions, while others remained near trend. The wage in the farm sector is an example of one real wage that fell significantly during both depressions. Table 4 shows that, on average, it is about 28% below trend during both periods.

In contrast, the real manufacturing wage rose modestly during the Great Depression and remained near trend in 1921–1922. Table 5 shows the manufacturing wage during these two depressions. The basic data for the Great Depression are from surveys conducted by the National Industrial Conference Board, and are considered to be among the best wage measures during the Great Depression.[7] The real manufacturing

7. The 1930s data are from Hanes (1996). The 1920s data are from the National Industrial Conference Board (1928) and Beney (1936) and include average hourly earnings of all wage earners in 25 industries plus anthracite mining, railroads, and building trades. Industries include metal, textiles, leather, paper, furniture, lumber, meat, and rubber. The data are on p. 25, Table 2.

wage, on average, was roughly 5% above trend during 1930–1933 and about 1% above trend during the Depression of 1921–1922.

These manufacturing wage differences between the 1920s and 1930s do not seem large enough to account for the relative severity of the Great Depression. But without a formal model we do not know how much of the Great Depression these differences can explain. We therefore construct a two-sector general equilibrium model in Section 3 to assess the quantitative contribution of high wages in some sectors to the Great Depression.

2.1.4 Differences in Bank Closings between the 1920s and the 1930s Many banks either temporarily suspended operations or failed during the early 1930s. Bernanke's (1983) widely cited work shows that the number of banks that either closed temporarily or failed is a significant predictor of output during the Great Depression. Bernanke's work has led a number of economists to conclude that bank closings were an important contributing factor to the Great Depression. For example, Romer's (1993) survey of the Great Depression argues that these closings were responsible for much of the fall in output between 1930 and 1933. According to the bank-closing hypothesis, bank suspensions and failures destroyed private information about borrowers, which in turn reduced the efficiency of financial intermediation (see Romer, 1993).

Can bank closings explain the difference between the Great Depression and the 1921–1922 Depression? Table 6 presents a comparison of bank closings in the 1920s and 1930s. Since the importance of a bank suspension or failure depends on the size of the bank, we measure bank closings not by the number of banks that closed, but rather by the fraction of deposits in banks that either suspended operations or failed. The table thus shows the fraction of total deposits in commercial banks that either suspended operations or failed, and shows the fraction of total deposits lost by depositors.[8]

Bank suspensions and failures were higher during the Great Depression. About 0.5% of banks, measured by deposits, either suspended operations or failed during the Depression of 1921–1922, and about 0.2% of total deposits was ultimately lost. In comparison, an average of 2.6% of banks either suspended operations or failed between 1930–1932, and an average of 0.4% of total deposits was ultimately lost during that

---

8. Since deposits at failed and suspended banks are only available for commercial banks, we show this ratio relative to commercial deposits. Commercial deposits accounted for over 85% of total deposits during 1919–1923 and over 80% during 1929–1934. We include failures and suspensions together because we are unaware of any data that separate these two categories.

Table 6 BEHAVIOR OF COMMERCIAL BANK DEPOSITS[a]

	Depression of 1921–1922				Great Depression		
Year	Susp. / total (%)	Loss / total (%)	Total output	Year	Susp. / total (%)	Loss / total (%)	Total output
1921	0.5	0.2	0.52	1929	0.4	0.1	0.58
1922	0.3	0.1	0.55	1930	1.7	0.5	0.64
				1931	4.3	0.8	0.65
				1932	2.0	0.4	0.78
				1933	11.0	1.3	0.75

[a]Source: Board of Governors of the Federal Reserve System (1943).

period. Both of these ratios rose significantly in 1933 when President Franklin Roosevelt declared a bank holiday. An explicit economic model is needed to determine the quantitative importance of these differences for the severity of the Great Depression. We develop a model for this purpose in Section 4.

The final data we present are on the ratio of total commercial bank deposits to output during these two depressions. This ratio rises significantly during the Great Depression. We present these data because they will be a key in the model that we develop for assessing the macroeconomic impact of bank closings.

2.2 SUMMARY

This section has assessed whether four popular deflation stories for the Great Depression can explain why the 20% deflation of the 1930s produced the Great Depression, and why the 20% deflation of the 1920s produced a much milder downturn. For any of these stories to be consistent with both depressions requires that the story be quantitatively important during the 1930s, but quantitatively unimportant during the 1920s. We found that two of these four stories—unexpected deflation, and debt plus deflation—do not satisfy this criterion, and therefore do not seem capable of explaining the relative severity of the Great Depression. For the other two stories—imperfectly flexible wages and bank failures—we did find some differences between the 1920s and 1930s. We now develop two models—one for assessing the role of inflexible nominal wages, and one for assessing the role of banking shocks—to evaluate quantitatively how much these two factors contributed to the Great Depression.

3. How Much of the Great Depression Was Due to High Wages?

3.1 A TWO-SECTOR GENERAL EQUILIBRIUM MODEL

This section presents a general equilibrium model to quantitatively assess the macroeconomic effects of high wages. Since wages in some sectors, such as agriculture, were flexible, we develop a two-sector model in which the wage in one sector is fixed above the market-clearing level, and the wage in the other sector is flexible. We assume that the fixed wage in the distorted sector is equal to the manufacturing wage; this assumption is discussed in detail below. All labor hired in that sector must be paid the above-market wage. This approach captures the basic distorting effects of above-market wages but allows us to abstract from other monetary features that would complicate the environment. All other prices in the economy, including the wages in the nondistorted sector, adjust to equate supply and demand in the other markets.

We first summarize the physical environment. We then analyze the pure market-clearing version of the model with no wage distortions, and then analyze the model with above-market wages in the manufacturing sector.

3.1.1 Environment Time is denoted by $t = 0, 1, 2, \ldots$. There is a representative family with many members. Family members supply labor, consume a single physical good, and accumulate physical capital. There are two distinct types of physical goods: *Final goods* are the numeraire, and can be either consumed or invested to augment the capital stock. These final goods are produced using two types of *intermediate goods*. Each intermediate good is produced from a distinct sector. We denote the sector that will be distorted by the above-market wage as *sector m*, and the nondistorted sector as *sector n*. We denote the output of the final good by Y, and the output of the two intermediate goods by Y_i, where $i = m, n$. These two intermediate goods are produced using identical Cobb–Douglas technologies with capital, denoted by K_i and labor, denoted by H_i, for $i = m, n$. The parameter A is labor-augmenting technological change.

Capital and labor are both sector-specific—neither labor nor capital can move from one sector to the other. Thus, workers who are unable to work as much as they wish in the distorted sector are not permitted to move to the nondistorted sector. This assumption amplifies the distorting effects of the high wage.

3.1.2 Technologies
The technology for producing the intermediate good m is

$$Y_m = (AH_m)^{1-\theta} K_m^{\theta}.$$

The same technology is used to produce the intermediate good n:

$$Y_n = (AH_n)^{1-\theta} K_n^{\theta}.$$

The technology for final goods is a CES aggregate of the two intermediate goods:

$$Y = [\alpha Y_m^{\phi} + (1 - \alpha) Y_n^{\phi}]^{1/\phi}. \tag{1}$$

3.1.3 The Market-Clearing Model

THE HOUSEHOLD'S PROBLEM There is a representative household with many members. At date 0, it is assumed that half of the family members work in the m sector, and half work in the n sector. The household's preferences over sequences of consumption of the final good c_t and market time in the two sectors is given by[9]

$$\max \sum_{t=0}^{\infty} \beta^t \{\log(c_t) + B[\log(1 - h_{mt}) + \psi \log(1 - h_{nt})]\}. \tag{2}$$

The household owns the capital stock and chooses consumption (c_t), work effort in the two sectors (h_{mt} and h_{nt}), and investment (x_{mt} and x_{nt}) to maximize (2) subject to the following present-value budget constraint, capital accumulation constraint, and time constraint:

$$\sum_{t=0}^{\infty} Q_t [w_{mt} h_{mt} + w_{nt} h_{nt} - c_t + r_{mt} k_{mt} + r_{nt} k_{nt} - x_{mt} - x_{nt}] \geq 0, \tag{3}$$

$$k_{it+1} = x_{it} + (1 - \delta) k_{it}, \quad i \in \{m, n\}. \tag{4}$$

The wage rates in the m and n sectors are denoted w_m and w_n, respectively, and the rental prices of capital in the two sectors are analogously

---

9. This preference specification with different utility weights on leisure permits us to retain the tractability of a representative-agent formulation. The different utility weights are required when employment is different between the two sectors (e.g. $\alpha \neq 0.5$). It can be shown that this specification is equivalent to an environment with agents who work in either sectors m or sector n, and who are perfectly insured against idiosyncratic shocks to their specific sectors.

denoted r_m and r_n. Note that the parameter ψ captures the relative size difference in employment for the household. The date-t price of the physical good in terms of date-0 goods is denoted by Q_t.

THE INTERMEDIATE-GOOD FIRMS' PROBLEM   We assume that there is a single producer of the m intermediate good, and a single producer of the n intermediate good, both of whom behave competitively.[10] The intermediate-good producer in sector i, $i \in \{m, n\}$, maximizes profits given (p_i, w_i, r_i):

$$\max_{n_i, k_i} p_i k_i^\theta h_i^{1-\theta} - w_i h_i - r_i k_i. \tag{5}$$

The first-order conditions for hiring the inputs imply that factor prices are equated to the value of marginal products.

THE FINAL-GOOD FIRMS' PROBLEM   The final-good producer also is competitive. The maximization problem is:

$$\max_{Y_m, Y_n} [\alpha Y_m^\phi + (1-\alpha) Y_n^\phi]^{1/\phi} - p_m Y_m^d - p_n Y_n^d. \tag{6}$$

EQUILIBRIUM CONDITIONS   A competitive equilibrium for this economy consists of sequences of allocations and a price system such that the allocations solve the household's problem subject to its budget constraint and given prices; that the allocations solve the firm's problem, given prices; that the labor market, the capital-services market, and the intermediate-good markets all clear; that the resource constraint is satisfied; and that prices are equal to marginal productivities.

3.1.4 The Model with Some Wages above the Market-Clearing Level   We now modify our model so that the wage in sector m is set above its market-clearing level. Rather than develop a monetary model with fixed nominal wages and deflation, we adopt a much simpler specification that captures the distorting effects of above-market wages. At the start of period t the wage is fixed exogenously for that period at a level above its normal market-clearing level. We denote this fixed wage by $\bar{w}_{mt}$. All labor hired in this sector at date t must be paid this wage. The above-market wage is a completely unexpected shock each period.[11]

---

10. We assume a single firm that behaves competitively, rather than a large number of competitive firms, to economize on notation.
11. There are many ways to model household beliefs about future distortions to manufacturing wages. Our approach, in which households believe that the fixed manufacturing wage does not recur, treats each wage shock as a completely unexpected event. As we

The fixed wage changes our model in one key way: labor input in this sector is no longer a choice variable for the household.[12] The households are rationed in terms of their labor supply to this sector:

$$\frac{B}{1-h_{mt}} > \frac{\bar{w}_{mt}}{c_t}.$$

Labor input in the distorted sector is determined by firms' labor demand. The representative firm hires labor until the fixed wage is equated to labor's value of marginal product:

$$(1 - \theta)p_{mt}(K_{mt}/H_{mt})^\theta = \bar{w}_{mt}. \tag{7}$$

The high wage has *direct* and *indirect* effects on aggregate output. We define the direct effect as the change in aggregate output from the increase in the distorted wage, holding all other prices fixed. This effect is measured by solving for y_m from (7), given $\bar{w}_{mt}$ and holding p_{mt} fixed, and then solving for aggregate output, holding y_n fixed. The indirect, or general equilibrium, effects of the high wage operate through changes in prices and the other wage. These indirect effects depend not only on $\bar{w}_{mt}$, but also on all the model parameters. Assessing the quantitative effects of the high manufacturing wage on the economy thus requires choosing parameter values and numerically computing the equilibrium path of the model economy.

3.2 CHOOSING PARAMETER VALUES AND COMPUTING AN EQUILIBRIUM

3.2.1 Technology and Preference Parameter Values Several of the parameters in our model are commonly used in the equilibrium-business-cycle literature. We choose values for these parameters that are similar to values in other studies. Since the data are available at an annual frequency, we define the unit of time in the model to be one year.

The common parameters in our model are β, A, B, δ, and θ. We set $\beta = 0.96$, which is comparable to values used in other studies. We assume that the level of technological progress, A, is given by $A_t = (1 + g)^t$, and choose $g = 0.02$. Our values for β and g imply a steady-state interest rate of about

---

show later, this approach simplifies computing the equilibrium considerably. This approach is also consistent with the prevailing view that the Great Depression was the result of unexpected shocks.

12. Since no other markets are distorted, all other equations in the model will continue to be satisfied.

6%. We choose B such that the household works about one-third of its discretionary time in the steady state. The additional leisure parameter ψ is chosen so that in the undistorted version of the model, the household chooses to allocate the appropriate fraction of labor to each sector at a common wage. We set $\theta = 0.33$, and the depreciation rate to 7%.

The final parameter we discuss in this section is ϕ, which governs the substitution elasticity between the two sectors in final-good production. Since manufacturing appears to be a key sector distorted by the high wage during the Depression, we use postwar data on changes in manufacturing's expenditure share and relative price to choose a value for ϕ. Manufacturing's expenditure share and relative price have both fallen over the postwar period, which is consistent with a substitution elasticity between manufacturing and nonmanufacturing of less than one. We choose a benchmark value of $\phi = -1$, which implies a substitution elasticity of 0.5. We also conduct our analysis with a low substitution elasticity of 0.1 to assess the robustness of our results.

3.2.2 The Distorted Wage and the Relative Size of the Distorted Sector Finally, we need to choose a measure of how much real wages rose in the distorted sector, and we need to choose a value for the fraction of the economy distorted by the high wage.

We use Hanes's (1996) compilation of the Conference Board's manufacturing wage data as the measure of the wage for the distorted sector. This wage is shown in Table 5 for each year of the Great Depression. The Conference Board wage data have also been used in some other analyses of the Great Depression, including O'Brien (1989), Lebergott (1991), Bernanke (1986), and Bernanke and Carey (1996). This wage is the most natural choice for a distorted wage in this study, because the data are of relatively high quality, and because there is a plausible economic explanation for why manufacturing wages were above market clearing despite the downturn in economic activity: government intervention. This intervention comes from President Herbert Hoover's belief that maintaining nominal wages would *prevent* a major depression by keeping demand high. In a White House meeting, Hoover asked the CEOs of major manufacturing corporations to not cut their wages. They agreed to maintain wages, and seem to have honored that agreement during the first two years of the Great Depression—manufacturing wages fell only 4.4% between December 1929 and September 1931. [See Lamont (1930) for a description of the meeting.[13]]

---

13. The effect of this intervention, however, weakened during the last two years of the Depression. By late 1931, Gerard Swope, CEO of General Electric, circulated an industrial plan that would have cartelized much of the U.S. economy. Hoover denounced

It is worth noting that there are also manufacturing-wage surveys produced by the Bureau of Labor Statistics (BLS) that could be used to measure the distorted wage, but these surveys do not cover all manufacturing industries, and they suffer from sampling problems. In particular, large firms, which tend to pay higher wages than small firms, were oversampled.

We now turn to choosing the fraction of the economy distorted by the high wage. In our model, this fraction is governed by the parameter α. Unfortunately, we do not know of any established measures of the fraction of the economy distorted by the high wage. The data we presented earlier suggest that on average, manufacturers paid high wages, but farmers did not. But since we do not have wage measures across the entire economy of the same quality as the Conference Board's wage data, it is difficult to estimate how much of the economy was subject to high wages.[14]

To address this uncertainty over the fraction of the economy distorted by the high wage, we conduct our analysis for two values of the parameter α. We first assume that the entire manufacturing sector was subject to the distorted wage. Given Hoover's view about the importance of maintaining high wages, we also assume the federal government paid the high wage. These two sectors account for about 28% of employment in 1929. We therefore choose a benchmark value for α such that this sector accounts for 28% of employment in the deterministic, flexible-price steady state of the model. We also conduct the analysis for $\alpha = 0.50$, which implies that the distorted sector was 50% of the economy. This choice seems to be a plausible upper bound on the fraction of the economy distorted by the high wage. This is because at least 30% of workers were not paid the high wage (farming and sole proprietors), and because there do not seem to be direct measures of wages of sufficient quality that indicate that half of all workers were paid wages above trend values.

3.2.3 Computing the Equilibrium Computation of the equilibrium of the model with high manufacturing wages is facilitated by our assumption

---

this plan and refused to recommend it to Congress. Nominal manufacturing wages began to fall significantly after Hoover's condemnation of the Swope plan.

14. There are wage measures in some nonmanufacturing sectors, and there are also BLS payroll and employment data outside of manufacturing that can be used to construct average employee compensation. A difficulty with these BLS payroll data is that the coverage is narrow in some sectors, the data do not include hours, and in some sectors the data combine all classes of workers, including executives. This last fact suggests that constructing measures of compensation per employee from these data is subject to significant compositional bias. We discuss compositional bias, and how it may have affected different wage measures during the Depression, at the end of this section.

that each wage shock is a completely unexpected, one-time event—the household expects at each date that the economy will return to pure market clearing the following period. This permits us to compute the equilibrium for each year of the Depression (1930–1933) recursively.

Since households expect the economy to return to market clearing in the following period, the value of capital next period is a function of the single state variable in the economy, the aggregate capital stock. To compute the equilibrium at date t when the manufacturing wage is higher than its competitive level, we use a log-linear approximation of the right-hand side of the Euler equation from the pure market-clearing model around its steady state. This approximation allows us to estimate the marginal value of an additional unit of capital and is used with the static first-order conditions of the model to compute the equilibrium for each year of the Depression. This involves solving N nonlinear equations in N unknowns for each year. We feed our measures of the manufacturing wage for 1930–1933 into the model and compute the equilibrium path of the economy for these years. Our findings are presented in the next section.

3.3 MACROECONOMIC EFFECTS OF HIGH WAGES: 1930–1933

Tables 7–9 show the predicted path of the U.S. economy between 1930 and 1933 for our model with benchmark parameter values and alternative parameter values. We find that the predicted depression for all these parameter values is much less severe than the actual U.S. Great Depression.

Table 7 shows the equilibrium path of output, consumption, and investment from our benchmark model with about 28% of the economy distorted by the high wage. Predicted real output is about 1% below trend in 1930 and about 2% to 3% below trend between 1931 and 1933. Most of the decrease in economic activity occurs in the distorted sector. The high wage reduces employment in the distorted sector about 7% below trend. In contrast, employment in the nondistorted sector falls

Table 7 PREDICTED GREAT DEPRESSION (1929 = 100), BENCHMARK MODEL

Year	Y	C	I	h_m	h_n
1930	99.2	99.8	96.9	97.8	99.3
1931	97.3	99.3	90.4	93.1	97.8
1932	97.2	98.9	91.1	93.3	98.0
1933	97.8	98.7	94.6	95.4	98.8

Table 8 DECOMPOSITION OF PREDICTED OUTPUT: DIRECT AND INDIRECT EFFECTS, BENCHMARK MODEL

Year	%ΔY	Effect (%)	
		Direct	Indirect
1930	−0.8	−1.5	0.7
1931	−2.7	−6.4	3.7
1932	−2.8	−6.3	3.5
1933	−2.2	−4.2	2.0

Table 9 PREDICTED GREAT DEPRESSION: LARGE DISTORTED SECTOR (1929 = 100)

Year	Y	C	I	h_m	h_n
1930	98.7	99.7	95.0	97.2	98.9
1931	95.6	98.9	84.2	91.2	96.4
1932	95.2	98.2	84.9	91.1	96.5
1933	96.1	97.8	90.1	93.6	97.8

only about 2% to 3% below trend. These predicted decreases in economic activity are much smaller than the observed decreases in output, consumption, investment, and employment that occurred between 1929 and 1933.

There are two reasons why predicted economic activity falls so little compared to the actual decrease in economic activity. First, the distorted sector is relatively small, which means that the direct effect of the high wage on aggregate output is small. Second, the indirect, general equilibrium effects tend to reduce, rather than amplify, the direct effects.

The most important indirect effect is the increase in the relative price of manufactured good, which rises 3% to 4% above its steady-state level after 1930. The relative price rises because the manufactured good is in relatively scarce supply and is not highly substitutable with the non-manufactured good. This increase offsets some of the distorting effects of the high manufacturing wage. Equation (7) shows that each percentage-point increase in the relative price of the manufactured good effectively reduces the fixed wage by one percentage point. Thus, the 4.4% increase in the relative price of manufactured goods in 1931 effectively reduces the manufacturing wage from 6.8% above trend to just 2.4% above trend.

Table 8 shows a decomposition of the change in output due to the direct and indirect effects. This decomposition shows that the negative direct effects are partially offset by the indirect effects.

The effects of the high wage depend on all the model parameters, but in particular depend on the share parameter α. We therefore assess the robustness of the results by increasing the distorted share of the economy to 50%, which in our view is a reasonable upper bound on the distorted share of the economy.

Table 9 shows the equilibrium path of the model economy with $\alpha = 0.5$. This higher value in the model produces a larger decrease in economic activity, but the decrease is still much smaller than the actual Great Depression. Real output is predicted to be 4.8% below trend in 1932 with $\alpha = 0.5$, compared to 2.8% below trend in the benchmark version of the model. We thus find that raising the share of the economy that must pay the high wage to 50% does not materially change the findings.

We also conducted the analysis by reducing the elasticity of substitution between the two sectors from 0.5 to 0.1. We do not present these results, because this change did not significantly affect the results. Output falls about one percentage point more than in the benchmark model, and the relative price of the good from the distorted sector rises more.

These results suggest that the high wage was not the primary cause of the Great Depression. Given our measure of the wage from the manufacturing sector, our benchmark model shows that this wage accounts for about a 3% decline in output at the trough of the Great Depression, compared to an actual 38% decline. Increasing the size of the distorted sector to 50% or reducing the substitution elasticity to 0.1 did not significantly change the results.

This simple model focused on the basic distorting effects of an above-market wage through two channels—the direct reduction in sectoral labor input, and the general equilibrium effects of the high wage through prices to the other sectors of the economy. One reason why the model doesn't generate a large depression is that the general equilibrium effects offset some of the distortion of the high wage. In particular, the sectoral high wage reduces output primarily in the distorted sector, and this drives up that sector's relative price and reduces the macroeconomic effect of the distortion.

This result raises the possibility that the wage story might have a better chance if the theory could be modified to eliminate the relative price increase. This approach is not likely to be successful, however. Eliminating the relative price increase arising from the wage distortion requires substantially reducing the demand for the output of that sector. This reduction in demand requires a second shock. In our model, this second shock is a decline in the parameter α, which governs the distorted sector's share of aggregate output. Reducing α would reduce the demand for goods from the distorted sector and would prevent the relative price of the distorted good from rising. But this higher real wage won't generate a major depression, because the reduction in α also reduces the quantitative importance of the distorted sector and thus reduces the macroeconomic effect of that sector.[15]

Finally, our model indicates another difficulty with the wage hypothesis: the timing of the depression and the timing of wage increases. With the exception of 1931, real wage increases do not occur at the same time as output declines. Real output fell 13% in 1930, yet the real manufacturing wage remained close to trend. Similarly, real output fell more than 17% between 1931 and 1932, yet the real manufacturing wage was roughly unchanged between 1931 and 1932. This lack of coincidence between the timing of output changes and wage increases suggests that some other shock reduced output in those years.

Accounting for the Depression through imperfectly flexible manufacturing wages is difficult—the real wage increase is too small and affects too little of the economy, and wage increases coincide with lower output only in 1931. The hypothesis would have a better chance if wages were significantly higher and affected more of the economy, and if there were more coincidence between the timing of wage increases and the Great Depression. But as the next section describes, these factors are unlikely.

3.4 MEASURED WAGES ARE PROBABLY BIASED UPWARDS

We are skeptical that actual wages were as high as the manufacturing-wage measures suggest. This is because the composition of employees changed during the Depression, and this compositional shift likely induces upward bias in the wage measures. Researchers who analyze the cyclical pattern of real wages argue that cyclical changes in the composition of employment leads to wage measures that are biased upward during recessions and biased downward during expansions. This is because hours of low-wage earners tend to be much more sensitive to the business cycle than hours of high-wage earners. Consequently, the average employed worker during a recession tends to be a higher-wage earner than the average employed worker during an expansion.

Lebergott (1991) and Margo (1993) argue that compositional effects may have been particularly important during the Great Depression. Lebergott argues that compositional shifts in employee quality and in the quality of operating establishments may result in measured wages substantially

---

15. This discussion highlights the problems associated with focusing on the product wage instead of the real wage. In particular, high product wage results from a combination of a positive shock to real wages and a negative shock to product demand.

overstating actual wages. He indicates that layoffs were concentrated among low-wage, young workers, which tends to increase the average measured wage of those individuals remaining employed. He also notes that relatively young firms, rather than older established firms, failed during the Depression, and that these younger firms tended to pay significantly lower wages. This compositional change also raises the average measured wage of those individuals remaining employed. Margo makes a very similar point regarding compositional bias.[16]

How large are these biases? Lebergott cites some microeconomic evidence which, he argues, points to significant upward bias arising from changes in employee quality. He notes that Westinghouse and General Electric retained their most productive employees during the Depression, and also cut these employees' wages by 10% between 1929 and 1931. However, the Conference Board's wage survey for this industry, which was heavily influenced by these two firms, shows that wages were unchanged during this period. This deviation between the wages paid by these two firms and the survey wage is likely due to changes in the composition of employees at the two firms.[17] While this microeconomic example suggests the possibility of important compositional biases, we do not have the necessary individual wage and employment data to measure aggregate compositional effects. To obtain a rough idea of how compositional shifts may have affected measured wages more broadly, we compute estimates of compositional bias from the Current Population Survey (CPS) and the Panel Study of Income Dynamics (PSID). We estimate the bias using two separate computations. The first computation is motivated by Lebergott's argument that employment loss was concentrated among the lowest-wage earners. Determining how this compositional shift affects the wage requires specifying how

---

16. There is also evidence that some firms reclassified workers down (e.g., a foreman works as an assembly-line worker); see Bernanke and Carey (1996) and Lebergott (1991). This would tend to bias wages in the opposite direction if the individual's wage was unchanged, but the value of the individual's marginal product fell. It is unclear, however, whether reclassified workers' wages were changed as a consequence of the reclassification.

17. Lebergott notes that these two firms laid off low-productivity workers, reassigned some higher-skilled workers, and assigned the retained workers to either 2-, 3-, or 4-day workweeks, depending on worker ability, with the most productive workers receiving 4-day workweeks. Lebergott clearly interprets these personnel decisions and their impact on the measured wage as an example of upward compositional wage bias. As we noted above, this interpretation is clearly warranted provided that those reclassified employees who performed different tasks were paid their value marginal product. If these employees were paid in excess of their value marginal product, however, this effect would tend to offset the upward wage bias resulting from the change in the composition of employees and the allocation of work towards the most productive employees.

employment loss was distributed during the Depression. To capture Lebergott's argument, we assume that the bottom 20% of wage earners lost employment and that the remaining employment loss was evenly distributed across all other workers. Using CPS data from 1998 for all full-time workers, we find that the average wage for the top 80% of wage earners is about 15% higher than for all full-time wage earners. This implies that the average wage during the Great Depression may have been overstated by 15% if the distribution of employment loss was concentrated among low-wage earners in this fashion, and if the wage distribution in the 1930s was similar to the wage distribution today.[18]

Our second computation uses measures of cyclical compositional wage bias from postwar data to estimate the compositional bias in the Depression. Solon, Barsky, and Parker (1994) estimate the difference between the response to fluctuations in output relative to trends between aggregate wages and individual wages from the PSID. This difference is a direct measure of the compositional bias from using aggregate wages as a measure of an average wage, and the bias is an increasing function of the magnitude of the decrease in output. Applying their estimates to the Depression suggests that compositional shifts biased measured wages up by about 18%.[19]

While we cannot draw a firm conclusion about the quantitative magnitude of compositional wage bias during the Depression, these estimates suggest that measured wages may be substantially upward biased.[20] This suggests that manufacturing wages may have been significantly below trend at the trough of the Great Depression after correction for compositional bias.[21]

18. We thank Daniel Hamermesh for performing this computation. The data are from the CPS-ORG 1998. Full-time workers are defined as those working 35 or more hours per week.
19. Solon, Barsky, and Parker (1994) only reported the differences in the coefficient between the fluctuations in the coefficient on the unemployment rate relative to trend. We thank Jonathon Parker for computing their estimates using real chain-weighted GDP rather than unemployment. The measure of the compositional bias is $(0.558 - 0.0896) \log[dGDP(1933)/dGDP(1929)]$, where $dGDP$ is the deviation of real GDP per adult from trend.
20. It is interesting to note that the cross-sectional differences in employment and wages between manufacturing and farming are consistent with significant compositional bias. Since the bias should be most severe for sectors in which employment fell substantially, we should observe relatively high wages associated with low employment. Manufacturing hours fell more than 40%, and measured wages were about 5% above trend. In contrast, farm hours remained near trend, and measured wages fell substantially.
21. Bordo, Erceg, and Evans (BEE, 2000) construct a measure of hourly employee compensation that rises about 4 percentage points more than the Conference Board's measure of hourly manufacturing wages, and use changes in this measure as a proxy for changes in the average wage during the Great Depression. There are two reasons why the change in their average compensation measure may deviate considerably from the

4. How Much of the Great Depression Was Due to Banking Shocks?

This section asks how much banking shocks contributed to the Great Depression. Unfortunately, there is no standard version of the neoclassical growth model with financial intermediation to use for this purpose, nor is there a standard definition of the banking shock—at least not as an explicit shock to primitives (technologies or endowments) that can be used in a general equilibrium model. We therefore develop a simple benchmark neoclassical model in which banking output, which is produced with deposits and information capital, is an input into production of the economy's final good. We define the banking shock to be the stock of information capital lost as a consequence of bank closings. This definition is consistent with the literature which associates the banking shock with bank failures and the destruction of information capital. We use the model to address three questions: How much did bank closings reduce intermediation capital? How much did this loss of intermediation capital reduce output? Are the predicted effects of bank closings on other variables consistent with the data?

4.1 A MODEL WITH FINANCIAL INTERMEDIATION

Our model extends the standard neoclassical growth model by requiring that some investment be *intermediated*. This modifies the standard model to include both internally and externally financed investment. In our model, a fraction of the capital stock is transferred from households to firms by an intermediation technology that uses real resources. This technology gives rise to borrowing and lending rates. The model allows us to analyze the effects of shocks to the intermediation technology on output, intermediated and internally financed investment, and borrowing and lending rates.

---

change in the average person's wage during the Depression. First, as we noted before, it is difficult to infer *individual* wage changes from an aggregated compensation measure because of compositional shifts in employment. Thus, their compensation measure is also subject to upward bias under the assumption that layoffs were concentrated among low-wage earners. Second, there is an inconsistency in their construction of total hours worked which is used in measuring average hourly compensation. In particular, their measure of total hours worked is equal to the number of full-time equivalent employees (from the NIPA) multiplied by Kendrick's (1961) average hours worked for full-time equivalent workers, which includes not only employees, but also proprietors and unpaid family workers. These latter two groups are quantitatively important, accounting for about 38% of Kendrick's full-time equivalent workers in 1929 (see p. 304). For BEE's calculation, this measure of hours would be correct only if fluctuations in proprietor and unpaid family hours were identical to fluctuations in employee hours.

We now describe the model in detail. There are two plants that produce a single physical good using capital. At the beginning of the period there are three types of capital: *installed physical capital* at each plant, which we denote by K_1 and K_2, respectively; *uninstalled physical capital*, which is held by households and is denoted by D; and *intermediation capital*, which we denote by Z. Intermediation capital is in fixed supply.

The capital stocks at each plant can be increased during the period with uninstalled capital. We denote by x_1 and x_2 the amounts that are installed during the period. This uninstalled capital must be intermediated, and some of this capital is used up during the intermediation process. The capital available for production is thus $K_j + x_j$. At the end of each period, some output is used to costlessly augment the capital stock at each plant, and the remainder is distributed to households who either consume it or hold it as uninstalled capital for the following period.

The plant technologies are subject to an i.i.d. shock, which is realized at the beginning of each period. The production shock can take on two levels: ϵ_h and ϵ_l, where $\epsilon_h > \epsilon_l > 0$. One plant receives the high shock ϵ_h, and one plant receives the low shock ϵ_l. Each plant has an equal probability of receiving the high productivity level, and we normalize the shocks so that $0.5(\epsilon_h + \epsilon_l) = 1$.

After the idiosyncratic plant productivity shock has been realized, uninstalled capital is allocated to the two production plants according to

$$\sum_{j=1}^{2} x_j \leq G(D, Z).$$

We will assume that G exhibits constant returns to scale (CRS) and that $G(D,Z) \leq D$. The resources used in the intermediation process are the quantity $D - G(D,Z)$.

Plant output is produced from a CRS Cobb–Douglas technology that uses capital and labor. For simplicity, we assume that there is one unit of labor at each plant, and that labor is in fixed supply. Plant output is given by

$$y_j = A\epsilon_j(K_j + x_j)^\gamma.$$

Plant output is used for either consumption or investment. Investment from retained output has no intermediation cost. The resource constraint for this economy is

$$\sum_j \left[A\epsilon_j(K_j + x_j)^\gamma - K_j' \right] \geq c + D',$$

where D' denotes the next period's level of uninstalled capital and K'_j the amount of capital installed at plant i at the beginning of the next period. We require that output net of retained investment be nonnegative.

The social planning problem for this economy is given by

$$\text{P1:} \quad \max_{\{c_t, x_{i,t}, K_{i,t+1}, D_{t+1}\}} \sum_{t=0}^{\infty} \beta^t u(c_t) \tag{8}$$

subject to

$$G(D_t, Z) \geq \sum_j x_{j,t}, \tag{9}$$

$$\sum_j [A\epsilon_{t,j}(K_{t,j} + x_{t,j})^\gamma - K_{t+1,j}] \geq c_t + D_{t+1}, \tag{10}$$

$$A\epsilon_{jt}(K_{jt} + x_{jt})^\gamma - K'_{jt} \geq 0 \quad \text{for each} \quad j = 1, 2 \text{ and } t, \tag{11}$$

$$x_{jt} \geq 0 \quad \text{for each} \quad j = 1, 2 \text{ and } t. \tag{12}$$

We assume that the difference in the ϵ_h and ϵ_l is small enough that the nonnegativity constraint on retained earnings given in equation (11) never binds. Since the productivity shocks are i.i.d., it is optimal to set $K_1 = K_2 = K/2$. Thus, we aggregate plant capital and define the state variables to be (K, D).

The solution to this planning problem can be decentralized as a competitive equilibrium. This allows us to solve for equilibrium borrowing and lending rates. We assume competitive profit-maximizing firms operate each plant. We also assume that there is a competitive profit-maximizing intermediary who operates the intermediation technology. This intermediary receives funds from the household at the savings rate $1 + r_s$ and loans it out at the borrowing rate $1 + r_b$.

In equilibrium, the marginal cost of additional capital to the high productivity plant, $1 + r_b$, must be equal to its marginal productivity:

$$1 + r_b = \gamma A \epsilon_h \left(\frac{K}{2} + G(D_t, Z) \right)^{\gamma - 1}.$$

Similarly, the interest rate on savings must be just equal to the return on uninstalled capital:

$$1 + r_s = \gamma A \epsilon_h \left(\frac{K}{2} + G(D_t, Z) \right)^{\gamma-1} G_D(D_t, Z).$$

The *spread* between these two rates is

$$r_b - r_s = \gamma A \epsilon_h \left(\frac{K}{2} + G(D_t, Z) \right)^{\gamma-1} G_Z(D_t, Z).$$

Note that this spread is a decreasing function of the level of intermediation capital, Z. Thus, a decrease in Z will raise the spread between these two rates. It can also be shown that a decrease in Z will reduce output and the quantity of intermediated capital, but will increase the quantity of internally financed capital as firms substitute out of intermediation into internal finance. These results are presented in the Appendix.

4.2 HOW MUCH DID BANK CLOSINGS REDUCE INTERMEDIATION CAPITAL?

Our model provides a measure of the banking shock—the loss of intermediation capital as a consequence of bank closings. Assuming that intermediation capital is in fixed supply and is bank-specific, the fraction of intermediation capital lost due to bank closings is equal to the fraction of deposits in suspended or failed banks. This implication follows directly from the CRS intermediation technology. We therefore infer from the deposit data presented in Table 6 that bank closings cumulatively reduced intermediation capital about 8% between 1930 and 1932, and about 19% between 1930 and 1933.

4.3 HOW MUCH DID THE BANKING SHOCK REDUCE OUTPUT?

We now use our model to evaluate the contribution of this decrease in intermediation capital to the Depression. Fixing (K_t, D_t), the elasticity of output with respect to intermediation capital is given by

$$\frac{dY_t}{dZ_t} \frac{Z_t}{Y_t} = \frac{A \epsilon_h [K_t/2 + G(D_t, Z_t)]^{\gamma-1} \gamma G_Z(D_t, Z_t) Z_t}{Y_t}.$$

The numerator of the right-hand side is the total return to intermediation. Therefore, the left-hand side of this equation is the intermediation sector's share of value added. This value-added-share elasticity result is not specific to our model. In fact, *any* model with a CRS technology for producing final goods has the feature that, to a first-order approximation, the elasticity of the final good with respect to any intermediate good is equal to that good's share of value added.

Banking's share of value added was about 1% in the 1930s. In fact, the value-added share of an entire finance, insurance, and real estate (FIRE) sector was only about 13% in 1929, and dropped to 11% in 1933.[22] Note that this value-added measure actually overstates the elasticity, since our model attributes all of banking's value added to intermediation capital. Some of this sector's value added will be paid to labor, which means that the elasticity of output with respect to intermediation capital is actually lower than the share of value added. With this small elasticity, our model predicts that the decrease in intermediation capital caused by bank closings reduced output less than 1% between 1929 and 1933.

4.3.1 Can a Low Substitution Elasticity Plausibly Magnify the Shock? The macroeconomic effect of destroyed intermediation capital would be larger if bank finance and alternative forms of finance or other inputs were poor substitutes. A low substitution elasticity, however, is inconsistent with the data. If banking shocks were an important contributing factor to the Depression *and* this substitution elasticity was very low, the cost share of banking and of FIRE should have increased considerably during the 1930s. In contrast, the cost share of FIRE falls from 13% in 1929 to 11% in 1933, and banking's cost share falls from about 1.4% to about 1% over the same period.[23]

4.3.2 Can Externalities Magnify the Impact of the Shock? Evidence from State-Level Data An externality associated with intermediation capital could increase the economic impact of an intermediation shock. One drawback to the externality story is that there are many different ways of putting externalities into models, but often these externalities do not have strong micro foundations, nor are they straightforward to evaluate quantitatively. The banking/depression literature, however, suggests a specific type of externality that is straightforward to assess. This literature argues that bank failures reduced output by destroying local bank information, and thus suggests a productive externality associated with intermediation capital that affects local production. We therefore consider a version of our model in which there are N regions, and aggregate output is the sum of regional outputs.

Suppose that output in region i is given by

$$Y_i = Z_i^\delta \sum_{j=1}^{2} A\epsilon_{t,ij}(K_{t,ij} + x_{t,ij})^\gamma H_{ij}^{1-\gamma},$$

---

22. Banking accounted for 10% of value added in FIRE in 1947. Kuznets (1941) reports a similar number for the period 1919–1938.
23. The data on banking's cost share are from Kuznets (1941, p. 731).

Figure 1 PERSONAL INCOME VS. SUSPENSIONS BY STATE DURING THE DEPRESSION

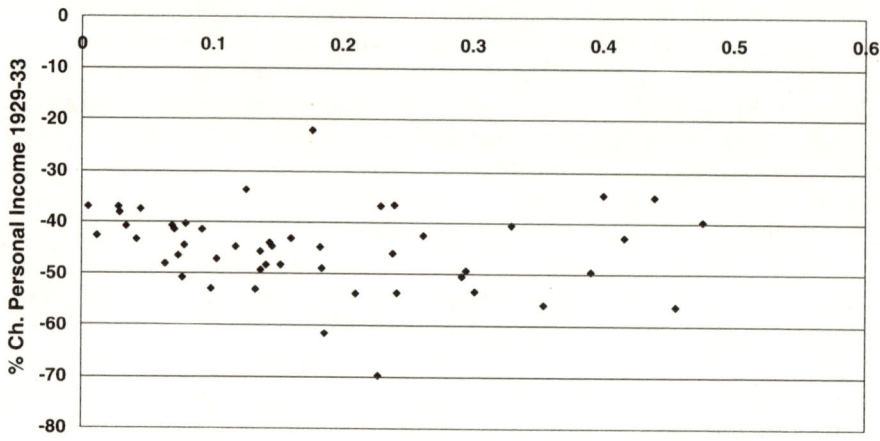

Commercial Bank Suspension 1929-33 / Total Deposits 1929

Where Z_i^δ is the productive externality from intermediation capital in region i. This version of our model predicts that regions that experience many bank closings should also experience relatively large depressions. We assess this prediction by first defining a region as a state and then computing the correlation between bank suspensions or failures and economic activity across the 48 U.S. states during the Great Depression. Note that this comparison is a regional extension of Bernanke's (1983) influential paper, which found that *aggregate* bank suspensions and failures were negatively correlated with *aggregate* output.

Figure 1 shows a scatterplot of the sum of suspended and failed deposits from 1929 to 1933 relative to total deposits in 1929 vs. the percentage change in nominal personal income between 1929 and 1933 by state. The most striking feature of these data is that the significant negative correlation between bank closings and output documented by Bernanke (1983) at the aggregate level does not emerge at the state level.[24] The plot shows no systematic relationship between the concentration of banking shocks and the severity of the Depression across states. The correlation between suspended deposits and nominal income is −0.15 and is not significantly different from zero. A regression of the percentage change in personal income divided by the aggregate GDP deflator on the fraction of deposits in suspended and failed banks yields an R^2 of 0.014 and a slope

---

24. Temin (1989) also notes that some bank-failure episodes were very regionally concentrated.

Figure 2 MANUFACTURING WORKERS VS. BANK SUSPENSIONS BY STATE DURING THE DEPRESSION

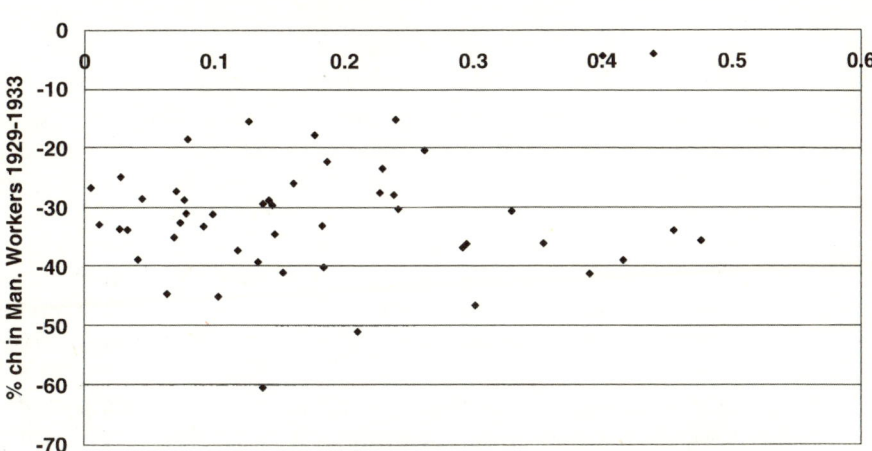

Commercial Bank Suspension 1929-33 / Total Deposits 1929

coefficient that is not significantly different from zero.[25] We also examined the relationship between the same measure of deposits and an alternative statewide measure of real economic activity—the percentage change in manufacturing employment between 1929 and 1933.[26] Figure 2 shows a scatterplot between these two variables. The correlation between these data is, in fact, positive rather than negative: 0.12.[27]

These data do not support the standard banking story for the Great Depression: that bank closings reduced output by destroying local information capital. The relatively small bank shock, combined with banking's small share in the production function, and the lack of any correlation between state-level bank closings and economic activity indicate that if banking was an important contributing factor during the Great Depression, it must have operated through some alternative mechanism in which the shock was much larger and was operative at the aggregate

25. We estimated two other versions of this equation. To control for level affects, we defined a dummy variable that takes the value of 1 if a state's per capita income was above the median. We used this dummy variable to analyze (1) an intercept shift and (2) an intercept shift and a slope coefficient shift. The results were quite similar to those for the simpler specification.
26. These data are from the biannual Census of Manufacturers.
27. The lack of a systematic pattern between bank closings and economic activity at the state level raises the possibility that the correlation between aggregate bank closing and aggregate output may indicate that aggregate bank closings are proxying for another variable. This is consistent with Green and Whiteman (1992).

level rather than the regional level. We analyze an alternative mechanism in the following section.

4.4 OTHER SHOCKS TO BANK CAPACITY

An alternative banking story is that depositors were afraid of bank runs and consequently withdrew deposits from all banks. This alternative story would have a better chance than the bank-failure story if the decrease in deposits resulting from depositor fear was substantially larger than the decrease in deposits at closed banks. This story is difficult to evaluate, however, because it is unclear how much of the decrease in total deposits was due to depositor fear and how much was an endogenous response to the large decrease in overall economic activity. Consequently, we can't measure the size of this shock associated with depositor fear.

Despite this measurement problem, our model makes one specific prediction about this story that can be evaluated. According to this story, banking services are in relatively scarce supply because of deposit withdrawal. The model predicts that an exogenous decrease in deposits will decrease the deposit/output ratio. This result is not specific to our model, but follows directly from CRS in production and the relative scarcity of deposits. The actual deposit/output ratio, however, differs considerably from this prediction. Table 6 shows that the ratio *rises* from 0.58 to 0.78 between 1929 and 1932. This increase implies that deposits were not relatively scarce during the Great Depression.

Even if deposits were relatively scarce because of depositor fear, however, there is no theoretical presumption that this would generate a massive depression, because banking's share of value added is small. In fact, these cost-share statistics suggest a presumption that banking shocks should tend to have small, rather than large, macroeconomic effects. The Irish bank strikes of the 1960–1970s provide evidence that is consistent with this latter view. Murphy (1978) reports that on three occasions between 1966 and 1976, industrial disputes led to the shutdown of the Associated Banks, which accounted for over 80% of Irish M2. These strikes, the longest of which was six months, represent negative, exogenous shocks to the banking sector that are larger than any plausible bank capacity shock that might have occurred during the U.S. Great Depression. The macroeconomic effects of these strikes, however, were small. During the longest strike, detrended retail sales fell about 4%, and real output rose over the full calendar year of 1970. Murphy argues that the strike did not have important effects because households and firms developed substitutes for bank services, including private trade credit. These "natural experiments" show that a long-term shutdown of most of a country's banking system—a shutdown much larger than that which occurred during the Great Depression—need not substantially reduce economic activity.

These data are inconsistent with the view that the Depression was caused by a large exogenous decrease in deposits. Instead, they are consistent with the view that the decrease in deposits may have been primarily an endogenous response to the overall decline in economic activity.

4.5 OTHER IMPLICATIONS OF A BANKING SHOCK

Our analyses of the banking story—through an explicit shock based on bank closings and through an alternative story based on a decrease in overall bank capacity—do not support the view that banking was an important contributing factor to the Great Depression. Of course, any explicit analysis along these lines depends on a definition and measure of the banking shock. Some other aspects of the banking story can be assessed without an explicit definition and measure of this shock. Our model makes two such predictions. The first prediction is that any reduction in banking capacity should increase the spread between deposit and loan interest rates. The second is that any reduction in the availability of intermediated loans, or any increase in the cost of intermediated loans, should lead firms to substitute out of external finance and into internal finance.

4.5.1 Impact of the Banking Shock on the Cost of Intermediation Our model predicts that a negative shock to the banking sector increases the spread between the interest rate on intermediated debt and the bank's cost of funds. Before examining changes in interest spreads, it is important to recognize that these spreads are affected not just by intermediation shocks, but also by changes in loan maturity, changes in the composition of borrowers, and changes in default risk. Since these other factors may have changed significantly during the Great Depression, it is very difficult to separately identify changes in interest spreads that are due to changes in the intermediation technology.

This identification problem leads us to make two comparisons of interest-rate spreads. We first examine an interest-rate spread between a collateralized, short-term obligation and short-term Treasuries during the Great Depression. This comparison permits us to reasonably control for some of the other factors affecting interest spreads: both securities have roughly constant maturities, and the collateralized nature of the private obligation limits the effect of changes in either default probability or the composition of borrowers.

Our second comparison presents the spread between long-term, quality-rated corporate securities and government bonds during the Great Depression. This analysis has been conducted in the previous literature for low-quality corporate debt. However, the change in this low-quality spread cannot be solely attributed to intermediation shocks, because the default risk on these lower-quality securities increased during the Great Depression. Consequently, it is unclear how much of the change in the spread was due to intermediation, and how much was due to higher default risk. To confront this identification problem, we present spreads on high-quality securities whose default risk may not have changed much during the Depression. If a negative intermediation shock was important, spreads on all types of securities would be expected to rise in the 1930s. Alternatively, if the spread on low-quality debt was higher largely because of changes in default risk, the spread should be roughly unchanged for the highest-quality securities, but should rise for lower-quality securities.

We first analyze our measure of the short-term spread. Table 10 presents the spread between 3- to 6-month banker's acceptances and 3- to 6-month Treasury notes. The banker's acceptances are collateralized, which controls for changes in default risk. Since the bank that originally discounted the bill stood as the guarantor of its ultimate payment, it is important to note that the bank performed an important intermediation function in the production of this asset. Consequently, a negative shock to the intermediation technology should have increased the spread between these two securities. The table shows that the spread between the rate on banker's acceptances and Treasuries does not change much during the Depression. The stability of this interest-rate spread therefore

Table 10 BANKER'S ACCEPTANCE RATES AND GOVERNMENT SECURITY YIELDS[a]

Year	Interest rate (%/yr)		(1) − (2)
	(1) Banker's acceptances	(2) Short-term govt. debt	
1928	4.09	3.97	0.12
1929	5.03	4.42	0.61
1930	2.48	2.23	0.25
1931	1.57	1.15	0.42
1932	1.28	0.78	0.50
1933	0.63	0.26	0.37

[a]The data are from Board of Governors of the Federal Reserve System (1943).

Table 11 INTEREST-RATE SPREADS BETWEEN CORPORATE AND GOVERNMENT BONDS[a]

Year	Spread (%/yr)			
	Aaa − Gov	Aa − Gov	A − Gov	Baa − Gov
1929	1.13	1.33	1.68	2.30
1930	1.26	1.48	1.84	2.61
1931	1.24	1.71	2.67	4.28
1932	1.33	2.30	3.52	5.62
1933	1.18	1.92	2.78	4.45
Avg.	1.25	1.85	2.70	4.24

[a]The data are from Board of Governors of the Federal Reserve System (1943).

indicates that the efficiency of this type of intermediation was not impaired during the Depression.[28]

We next examine the spread between the rates on corporate bonds, which are a substitute for bank finance for large firms, and U.S. government bonds. Table 11 shows the spread for corporate bonds of different qualities—Aaa (lowest default risk), Aa, A, and Baa. There are two striking features of these data. First, the average increase in interest spreads is fairly small. Second, the magnitude of the increases in the spread is directly related to the quality of the debt: the average spread changes very little for high-quality debt, but increases for lower-quality debt.

These data are consistent with the view that changes in default risk were an important contributing factor to higher spreads. To illustrate how these changes could have affected spreads, suppose that Baa securities pay off 60% of the principal if the firm defaults. With this assumption, the 230-basis-point spread between Treasuries and Baa bonds in 1929 implies that the default probability for Baa bonds was about 5% at that time. It also implies that the average 424-basis-point Baa spread during the Depression can be *completely* explained by an increase in this default probability from 5% to 8%. This increase does not seem implausible during this period.[29]

While we cannot draw a firm conclusion about the quantitative impor-

28. The gap between commercial loan rates and short-term government securities rose about 250 basis points during the Depression. The gap between commercial loans and government bonds, however, narrowed by about 120 basis points. Given the caveats mentioned above, plus a steepening in the yield curve, it is not clear how to interpret these changes.
29. Cole and Ohanian (2000) present a monthly analysis of those spreads, which permits a closer examination of changes in spreads with the onset of banking crises. We did not find much evidence of large increases in interest spreads around these periods.

Figure 3 DOMESTIC INDUSTRIES: PROFITS, DIVIDENDS, AND RETAINED EARNINGS (WITHOUT IVA)

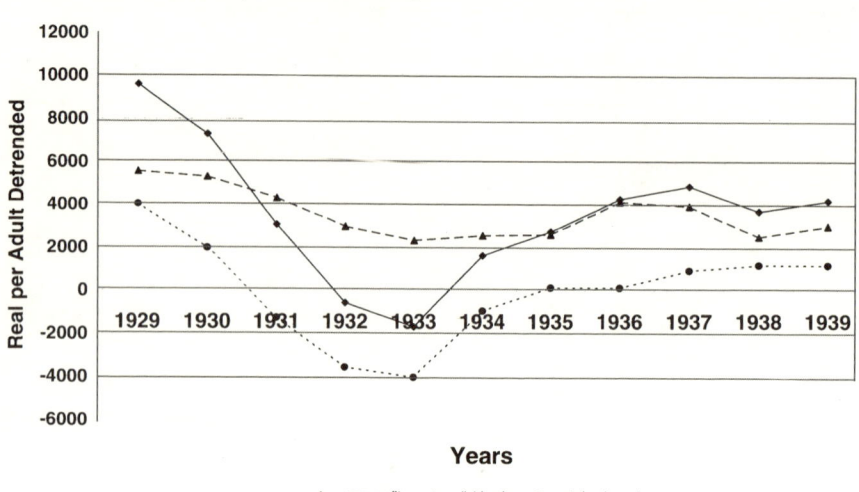

tance of changes in default risk, it is certainly true that default risk rose during the Depression and thus contributed to higher spreads. But even if we abstract from default risk and completely attribute these higher spreads to negative intermediation shocks, it seems unlikely that these increases—ranging from 12 to 194 basis points—can plausibly explain the Great Depression. If higher spreads were the key to understanding the Great Depression, they should have increased much more during the Depression than during milder recessions. But this is not the case. The average rise in the Baa–Treasury spread for all post–World War II recessions is more than 200 basis points. This includes several recessions in the 1970s and early 1980s in which this spread rose as much as 500 basis points. All of these recessions were much milder than the Great Depression, despite these much larger interest-spread increases.

In summary, interest spreads did not rise much outside of low-quality corporate securities, and it is unclear how much of this increase is due to intermediation shocks. Moreover, the average increase in spreads does not seem to be nearly large enough to account for the magnitude of the Great Depression. In the following section, we present the second prediction of our model that does not rely on an explicit definition of the banking shock. Our model shows that *if* a negative banking shock increased the cost of funds and disrupted economic activity, firms should have increased retained earnings.

Figure 4 MANUFACTURING INDUSTRIES: PROFITS, DIVIDENDS, AND RETAINED EARNINGS (WITHOUT IVA)

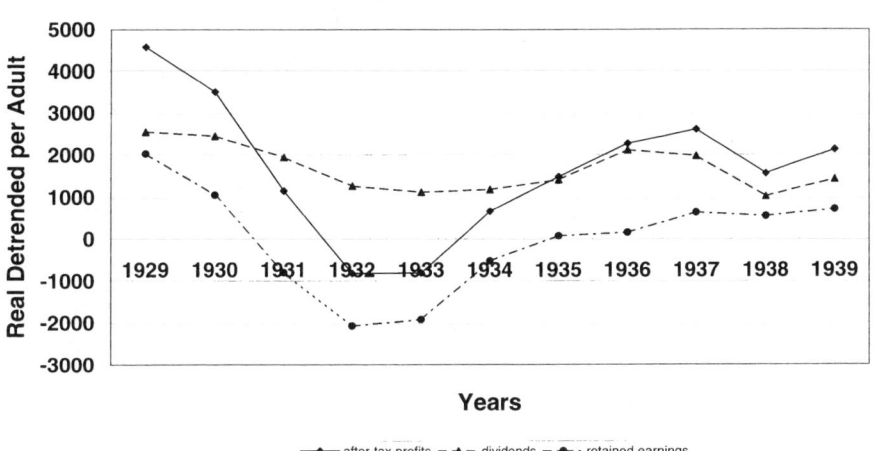

———— after-tax profits — ▲ — dividends — ● - retained earnings

4.5.2 Impact of Banking Shocks on Other Sources of Finance The theory predicts that a reduction in the availability of intermediated finance, or an increase in the cost of intermediated finance, should lead firms to substitute out of intermediated finance and increase retained earnings. Figures 3 and 4 show real profits, dividends, and retained earnings per adult relative to trend in the entire corporate sector and in the manufacturing subsector, respectively. The most striking feature of these data is that firms were not increasing retained earnings as the theory predicts. In sharp contrast, retained earnings fell substantially as firms maintained high dividend payments. Corporate profits fell by nearly 40% between 1929 and 1930, but dividend payments fell by only about 4%. Profits decreased by over 70% between 1929 and 1931, but dividend payments fell by only 25% during that period. By 1932, corporations experienced substantial losses, but retained earnings fell even more as firms maintained dividend payments equal to 51% of their 1929 level. This pattern also emerges at the sectoral level. Figure 4 shows that a very similar pattern prevailed among manufacturing corporations, and Table 12 shows that this pattern continues among durable and nondurable manufacturers and among mining corporations.[30]

30. There was some variation in dividend payouts at the industry level. For example, dividends in the tobacco industry were particularly high during the Depression. These outliers did not affect the sectoral-level statistics much. Real nondurable manufacturing dividends in 1933 were 66% of their 1929 level. Excluding tobacco, these dividends in 1933 were 62% of their 1929 level.

Table 12 PROFITS AND DIVIDENDS IN KEY SECTORS[a]

	Mining		Durable Mfg.		Nondurable Mfg.	
Year	Profits	Divs.	Profits	Divs.	Profits	Divs.
1929	430	309	2247	1335	2332	1213
1931	−75	118	−155	811	1303	1133
1933	−115	66	−721	314	−85	803

[a]The data are from NIPA and are measured without inventory valuation adjustment. They are in real dollars per adult, and are detrended at the average rate of growth of output per adult: 1.9%. We thank Mark Gertler for suggesting this measure of cash flow (net of depreciation).

The maintenance of dividend payments at the expense of retained earnings throughout the Depression suggests that firms were liquidating their enterprises, rather than finding substitutes for costly bank finance. Reconciling this large drop in retained earnings with the banking story seems difficult. To do so requires explaining why firms drained their coffers and increased their exposure to negative banking shocks.

5. Interactions between the Wage and Banking Shocks

Even though we find that neither banking shocks nor wage shocks account for much of the Great Depression, is it possible that the interaction between these two shocks has a large macroeconomic effect? There are two reasons why we do not think this is very likely. If there was an important connection between the two types of shocks, we should observe a strong negative correlation between the incidence of banking crises and economic activity in sectors distorted by high wages. Manufacturing was ostensibly distorted by the high wage, but the correlation between manufacturing employment and bank closings was positive at the state level, rather than negative. Moreover, the correlation between state per capita income and bank failures in states with large manufacturing sectors—those with above-median ratios of manufacturing employment to population—is roughly the same as that for all the states, and is not significantly different from zero.

There are also theoretical reasons for doubting that an interaction between the two shocks would have large effects. To illustrate this point, consider the simplest possible method of incorporating the banking shock into the wage model. Suppose that intermediation capital is another input into production, and denote the sectoral level of intermediation capital by Z_i. Sectoral output is now given by the production function $Y_i = (AH_i)^{1-\theta-\gamma} K_i^\theta Z_i^\gamma$, where θ is unchanged and $\gamma = 0.01$ to match banking's value-added share. Given this specification, it is straightforward to show that the 18% decrease in Z that occurred between 1929 and 1933 would reduce output in the wage model an additional 0.18%. This result partially reflects the fact that the decrease in intermediation capital leads to general equilibrium changes in factor prices that moderate the impact of the factor change.

6. What Else was Different about the Great Depression?

The two candidate shocks we have considered—bank failures and imperfectly flexible wages—don't seem capable of plausibly explaining the Great Depression. So if it wasn't banking or wages, what other factors might have been responsible?[31]

6.1 LOWER ASSET PRICES

The first alternative shock we examine is lower asset prices. The stockmarket crash of 1929 is considered by some economists to have contributed to the Great Depression (see Romer, 1993). It is difficult to evaluate this story, since there currently is no generally accepted theory of asset price fluctuations. Without such a theory, one cannot establish that asset price changes contributed significantly to the Great Depression.[32] But we can take a first step by empirically assessing whether other periods of large and prolonged decreases in asset prices also coincide with major depressions. One of the best known of these episodes is Japan in the 1990s. We therefore compare changes in stock prices and output in the U.S. in the 1930s with Japan in the 1990s. Tables 13 and 14 show real stock prices and output for these two countries. We find some important similarities in asset price changes between the two countries, but very different output changes after share prices fall.

Stock prices in both countries roughly doubled during the three-year period before their respective market peaks. Output growth relative to respective trends is also very similar in the two countries during these three-year periods of rising stock prices. Following their respective market peaks, stock prices fell sharply in both countries. U.S. share prices fell about 68%, and Japanese share prices fell about 55%. Despite these similar stock price patterns, output growth differs substantially after

---

31. One difference between these two episodes is that the deflation of 1921–1922 immediately followed a significant inflation, whereas that 1929–1933 followed a period of roughly stable prices. If nominal prices were more flexible during the early Depression, the deflation may have had smaller real effects. Little is known, however, about the differences in price flexibility during these two downturns.
32. Without a good theory of asset price fluctuations, it is unclear what shock drove down asset prices, or how asset prices interacted with employment, consumption, and investment decisions.

Table 13   REAL U.S. DETRENDED STOCK PRICES AND OUTPUT (1929 = 100)

Year	S&P index[a]	Output index
1926	50.4	102.8
1927	61.7	100.1
1928	78.2	97.7
1929	100.0	100.0
1930	81.4	86.9
1931	57.1	77.6
1932	31.6	64.0

[a]Source: Board of Governors of the Federal Reserve System (1943, Table X, pp. 492–498).

Table 14   REAL JAPANESE DETRENDED STOCK PRICES AND OUTPUT[a] (1989 = 100)

Year	Nikkei index	Output index
1986	55.1	96.2
1989	100.0	100.0
1990	81.6	101.4
1991	63.1	101.5
1992	44.6	98.9

[a]Quantities are *not* per adult. They have been detrended using a 3.7% growth rate, which is the average for real output between 1979 and 1989. Data are from the DRI International Database.

prices begin to fall. U.S. output is 36% below trend three years after its stock-market peak, whereas Japanese output remains on trend three years after its stock-market peak.[33]

These data show that large asset price decreases are not always associated with big depressions. Japanese stock prices fell nearly as much in the 1990s as U.S. share prices fell in the 1930s, but Japanese output remained close to trend while stock prices fell.[34] These Japanese data and

33. Japan did experience a *growth* slowdown after 1991, and by 1998 was 15% below trend. However, note that this decrease comes 9 years after the decrease in asset prices.
34. Land values in Japan also followed the same roller-coaster pattern as stock prices in the 1990s. Commercial real estate values doubled during the same period that stock prices doubled, and fell 35% three years after the market peak. These data are thus inconsistent with the view that Japan maintained high macroeconomic activity because other asset values remained high. (See commercial real estate prices in the six largest cities from the Japan Real Estate Institute: http://www.reinet.or.jp/index-e.htm.)

the pattern of retained earnings during the U.S. Great Depression raise questions about the asset-price story. First, if lower asset prices contributed to the U.S. Great Depression, why didn't a similar decrease produce a Great Depression in Japan? Second, if the macroeconomic impact of lower prices is through lower borrower net worth, as is often presumed in the literature, then why did firms continue to pay such dividends during the 1930s rather than increase retained earnings? Finally, if decreases in asset values have a substantial negative effect on output, through either borrower or consumer net worth, then why did the increase in asset prices have so little effect in either Japan or the United States? Any theory of the Depression based on lower asset values should be able to explain why lower asset prices don't always produce major depressions, and explain why retained earnings fell in the 1930s.[35]

6.2 THE FALL IN TOTAL FACTOR PRODUCTIVITY

The second alternative shock we consider is a total factor productivity (TFP) shock. This shock is much different during the Great Depression than other periods and in particular differs sharply from 1921–1922. TFP rose about 5% relative to trend in 1921, but fell about 14% below trend between 1929 and 1933.[36]

It is unlikely that this TFP decrease during the Great Depression reflects technological regress or is solely due to factor measurement error. To see this latter point, consider three types of measurement error: capital utilization, changes in labor quality, and changes in capital quality. The utilization of the capital stock was low during the Great Depression, and this overstatement of the capital input will bias down TFP measurement. But the other two sources of factor mismeasurement will tend to offset mismeasured capital input. The average quality of labor input probably rose during the Depression, as the least productive workers were probably the first to be laid off. This indicates that measures of labor input based on employment or hours worked will understate labor input in efficiency units. Similarly, the oldest, least efficient capital was idled during the Depression (Bresnahan and Raff, 1991). This "vintage effect" implies that measures of capital input based on the number of

---

35. These data cast doubt on the ability of theoretical models in which financial-market imperfections amplify the effects of macroeconomic shocks by reducing net worth to explain a significant portion of the Great Depression. [See Kiyotaki and Moore, 1997, and Bernanke, Gertler, and Gilchrist, 2000 (BGG).] According to these models, output should have expanded significantly when stock prices were rising. Moreover, these models predict that enterprises should have substantially increased internal cash when share prices began falling. Both of these predictions stand in contrast to the data.
36. Romer (1988) argues that there was a favorable supply shock during the 1921–1922 Depression, although she does not discuss TFP changes.

idle factories will understate capital input in efficiency units. Both of these compositional effects will tend to understate the true decline in TFP and tend to offset the effect of capital utilization.

Since labor's share is about twice as large as capital's share, considerable mismeasurement of capital utilization is required to bias the TFP measure. For example, if true capital input was 20% lower than measured capital input after correcting for vintage effects, and true labor input in efficiency units was 5% higher than measured labor input due to compositional shifts, TFP would have decreased by 11%, compared to the measured decrease of 14%.

Negative productivity shocks also show up in disaggregated data. Bernanke and Parkinson (1991) report negative productivity shocks in manufacturing and argue that the shocks reflect labor hoarding or increasing returns to scale. But there are good reasons to question these two explanations. Recent research indicates CRS in manufacturing, rather than increasing returns. And at least the traditional reason given for labor hoarding—the cost of laying off and subsequently rehiring a worker exceeds the cost of retaining the worker—seems unlikely during this period. Managers seem to have been liquidating their enterprises during the Great Depression, rather than planning for an upcoming expansion that would have productively utilized the hoarded labor.

The TFP decrease may not be adequately explained by technological regress, factor mismeasurement, or returns to scale. More research is needed to determine the sources of and reasons for this large change and how much it may have contributed to the Great Depression. Since a decrease in productivity reduces marginal productivity, this shock may represent the best chance for the wage hypothesis to account for a reasonable fraction of the output decrease.

7. *Summary and Conclusion*

Our results suggest that two popular stories for the Great Depression—the inflexible-wage deflation story and the banking-shock story—account for only a small fraction of the output fall that occurred between 1929 and 1933. The problem with the inflexible-wage story is that measured wages were above trend in only a subset of the economy, and that a reasonable correction for shifts in the composition of employment would reduce those wage measures below trend. The problem with the banking-shock story is that the shock is small, and the elasticity of aggregate output with respect to a banking shock is also small. Moreover, three important auxiliary predictions of the banking story don't line up with the data. The theory predicts that states that had worse banking crises should have had worse depressions. But there is no systematic relationship between state economic activity and the number of bank closings. The theory also predicts that firms should have increased internal cash in response to the banking shock. In contrast, firms reduced retained earnings substantially during the Great Depression. The theory also predicts that the ratio of bank deposits to output should have decreased during the Depression. This ratio increased substantially during the Depression. Any successful financial intermediation theory of the Depression should be consistent with these three facts.

We conclude that the Great Depression remains a puzzle. The paper suggests two directions for future research. One direction is to analyze money (deflation) shocks through alternative channels. The second direction is to analyze real shocks. The fact that real output per adult fell 13% in 1930 without any significant deflation suggests the possibility that a real shock contributed to the initial downturn. And the large decrease in TFP suggests the possibility that some shock may have affected productivity during the Great Depression.

Appendix. Characterizing the Equilibrium of the Financial-Intermediation Model

In what follows, we will assume that the difference in the idiosyncratic productivity shocks is small enough that the nonnegativity constraint on retained earnings never binds. Under this assumption, the f.o.c.s that characterize a solution include

$$\beta^t u'(c_t) = \lambda_t, \tag{13}$$

$$\lambda_t \gamma A \epsilon_{t,i}(K_{t,i} + x_{t,i})^{\gamma-1} = \mu_t - \xi_{t,i}, \quad \text{where} \quad x_{t,i}\,\xi_{t,i} = 0, \tag{14}$$

$$\lambda_{t+1}\gamma A E_t[\epsilon_{t+1,i}(K_{t+1,i}+x_{t+1,i})^{\gamma-1}] = \lambda_t, \tag{15}$$

$$\mu_{t+1} G_1(D_{t+1}, Z) = \lambda_t, \tag{16}$$

where μ_t, λ_t, and $\xi_{t,i}$ are the Lagrange multipliers on the constraints (9) and (10) and the nonnegativity constraints on x_i, respectively.

It is easy to see from the f.o.c. on plant capital, (15), that $K_1 = K_2$. Hence we can aggregate plant capital and treat (K, D) as the state variables, where $K/2$ is plant capital. It is easy to see that x_l cannot be positive, since condition (14) would imply that x_h was also positive, and hence at both plants the marginal product of capital would be greater than λ_{t-1}, which would contradict (15).

The steady state of this model will be given by (K, D), where

$$\beta\gamma A\left[\epsilon_h\left(\frac{K}{2}+G(D,Z)\right)^{\gamma-1}+\epsilon_l\left(\frac{K}{2}\right)^{\gamma-1}\right]=1, \tag{17}$$

$$\beta\gamma A\epsilon_h\left(\frac{K}{2}+G(D,Z)\right)^{\gamma-1}G_1(D,Z)\leq 1, \tag{18}$$

with strict equality if $D > 0$, and c is given by

$$c=\frac{1}{2}A\epsilon_h\left(\frac{K}{2}+G(D,Z)\right)^{\gamma}+\frac{1}{2}A\epsilon_l\left(\frac{K}{2}\right)^{\gamma}-(K-D).$$

We can develop the analysis further by assuming an explicit functional form for G. the Leontieff specification allows us to obtain closed-form solutions for the variables D and K:

$$G(D, Z) = \min(\alpha D, Z),$$

where $\alpha < 1$, and $(1 - \alpha)D$ is the cost of intermediation.

If D is positive and interior, that is, less than Z, it is straightforward to show that

$$D=\frac{1}{\alpha}(\beta A\gamma)^{1/(1-\gamma)}\left[\epsilon_h^{1/(1-\gamma)}-\left(\frac{\alpha\epsilon_l}{2\alpha-1}\right)^{1/(1-\gamma)}\right]. \tag{19}$$

If the value of D is such that $D \in [0, Z/\alpha]$, then the steady-state level of K is

$$K=\left(\frac{\alpha\beta A\gamma\epsilon_l}{2\alpha-1}\right)^{1/(1-\gamma)}.$$

If the value of D implied by (19) is negative, then it is easy to show that in the steady state $D = 0$, and

$$K=\left(\frac{\beta\gamma A}{2}(\epsilon_h+\epsilon_l)\right)^{1/(1-\gamma)}.$$

If the value of D implied by (19) is greater than Z/α, then in the steady state $D = Z$ and K is the solution to (17) when we set $G(D, Z) = Z$.

This allows us to conduct some comparative statics on what happens to K and D when intermediation capital changes. If Z binds, then $dK/dZ < 0$

and $d(K + \alpha D)/dZ > 0$. Furthermore, if $D > 0$, then $d(\alpha D)/d\alpha > 0$, and hence $dK/d\alpha < 0$, while $d(K + \alpha D)/d\alpha > 0$. Our model predicts that a decrease in intermediation capital increases internally installed capital, but significantly reduces intermediated investment. Similarly, an increase in the cost of intermediation $(1 - \alpha)$ increases internally installed capital and reduces intermediated investment. It is also easy to see how the spread in the lending and borrowing rate is affected by a change in Z. In this example, the marginal cost of funds to the high-productivity plant must be

$$1 + r_b = \gamma A \epsilon_h (K/2 + \alpha D)^{\gamma-1}.$$

The interest rate on savings must be

$$1 + r_s = \gamma A \epsilon_h (K/2 + \alpha D)^{\gamma-1} \alpha.$$

This implies that the spread between these two rates is given by

$$r_b - r_s = \gamma A \epsilon_h (K/2 + \alpha D)^{\gamma-1}(1 - \alpha).$$

A decrease in intermediation capital that binds will lower the quantity of intermediated capital, αD, and raise the quantity financed out of retained earnings, K. It also raises both the borrowing and lending interest rates and the spread between them, since the marginal productivity of capital at the high-productivity plant is raised. The spread also is decreasing in α, which governs the fraction of capital consumed by the intermediation process.

Finally, assume that $G_D, G_Z, G_{DZ} > 0$ for all $D, Z > 0$. In this case, a reduction in Z works like an increase in intermediation costs. Since G is CRS, $G(D,Z) = g(Z/D)D$, where $g' > 0$. In response to a decrease in Z, the equilibrium level of Z/D will increase. This indicates that the relevant factor for intermediation costs is not the level of intermediation capital per se, but the level relative to the quantity of intermediated capital.

REFERENCES

Beney, A. (1936). *Wages, Hours, and Employment in the United States 1914–36*. New York: National Industrial Conference Board.

Bernanke, B. S. (1983). Nonmonetary effects of the financial crisis in propagation of the Great Depression. *American Economic Review* 73(June):257–276.

———. (1986). Employment, hours, and earnings in the Depression: An analysis of eight manufacturing industries. *American Economic Review* 76(March):82–107.

———, and Carey, K. (1996). Nominal wage stickiness and aggregate supply in the Great Depression. *Quarterly Journal of Economics* 111(August):853–883.

———, Gertler, M., and Gilchrist, S. (2000). The financial accelerator in a quantitative business cycle framework. *Handbook of Macroeconomics*, J. Taylor and M. Woodford (eds.). Amsterdam: North-Holland.

———, and Parkinson, M. L. (1991). Procyclical labor productivity and competing theories of the business cycle: Some evidence from interwar U.S. manufacturing industries. *Journal of Political Economy* 99(June):439–459.

Board of Governors of the Federal Reserve System. (1943). *Banking and Monetary Statistics, 1914–1941*. Washington.

Bordo, M., C. Erceg, and C. Evans. (2000). Money, sticky wages, and the Great Depression. *American Economic Review*, forthcoming.

Bresnahan, T., and D. Raff. (1991). Intra-industry heterogeneity and the Great Depression: The American motor vehicles industry, 1929–35. *Journal of Economic History*, June, pp. 317–331.

Bureau of the Census. (1975). *Historical Statistics of the United States*. Washington.

Cechetti, S. (1992). Prices and the Great Depression: Was the deflation of 1930–32 really unanticipated? *American Economic Review*, March, pp. 80–102.

Cole, H., and L. Ohanian. (2000). New Deal policies and the persistence of the Great Depression: A general equilibrium analysis. Federal Reserve Bank of Minneapolis. Discussion Paper.

Eichengreen, B., and J. Sachs. (1985). Exchange rates and economic recovery in the 1930s. *Journal of Economic History*, December, pp. 925–946.

Fisher, I. (1933). The debt deflation theory of the Great Depression. *Econometrica* 1:337–357.

Green, S., and C. Whiteman. (1992). A new look at old evidence: On "Nonmonetary effects of financial crisis in the propagation of the Great Depression. University of Iowa.

Hamilton, J. (1992). Was the deflation during the Great Depression anticipated? Evidence from the commodity futures market. *American Economic Review*, March, pp. 157–178.

Hanes, C. (1996). Changes in the cyclical behavior of real wage rates, 1870–1990. *Journal of Economic History* 56(December):837–861.

Kiyotaki, N., and J. Moore. Credit Cycles. *Journal of Political Economy*, 105(2):211–248.

Kendrick, J. W. (1961). *Productivity Trends in the United States*. Princeton, NJ: Princeton University Press.

Kuznets, S. (1941). *National Income and its Composition, 1919–1938*. New York: NBER.

Lebergott, S. (1991). "Wage rigidity" in the depression: Concept or phrase? Wesleyan University. Discussion Paper.

Lamont, R. (1930). The White House conferences. *Journal of Business* III(3):269–271.

Lucas, R. (1983). In *Conversations with Economists*, Arjo Klamer (ed.). Rowman and Allanheld.

———, and Rapping, L. (1969). Real wages, employment and inflation. *Journal of Political Economy.* 77(5):721–754.

———, and L. Rapping (1972). Unemployment in the Great Depression: Is there a full explanation? *Journal of Political Economy* 80(1):186–191.

Margo, R. (1993). "Employment and unemployment in the 1930s. *Journal of Economic Perspectives*, Spring, pp. 41–59.
Murphy, A. E. (1978). Money in an economy without banks: The case of Ireland. *The Manchester School of Economic and Social Studies*, pp. 41–50.
National Industrial Conference Board. (1928). *Wages in the United States, 1914–1927.* New York.
O'Brien, A. (1989). Behavioral explanation for nominal wage rigidity during the Great Depression. *Quarterly Journal of Economics* 104(November):719–735.
Olney, M. (1999). Avoiding default: The role of credit in the consumption collapse of 1930. *Quarterly Journal of Economics*, February, pp. 319–335.
Romer, C. D. (1988). World War I and the postwar depression. *Journal of Monetary Economics* 22:91–115.
———. (1993). The nation in depression. *Journal of Economic Perspectives* 7(Spring):41–59.
Solon, G., R. Barsky, and J. Parker. (1994). Measuring the cyclicality of real wages: How important is composition bias?" *Quarterly Journal of Economics* 109(1):1–25.
Temin, P. (1989). *Lessons from the Great Depression.* Cambridge, MA: The MIT Press.

Comment[1]

MICHAEL BORDO, CHRISTOPHER ERCEG, AND CHARLES EVANS
Rutgers University, Board of Governors of the Federal Reserve System, Federal Reserve Bank of Chicago

1. Introduction

Cole and Ohanian's paper is both ambitious and provocative. It is ambitious because it investigates the ability of several alternative and widely cited explanations of the Great Depression to explain the quantitative magnitude of the output downturn that occurred in 1929–1933. It is provocative because it concludes that none of the standard battery of explanations can account for more than a small fraction of the observed output decline.

One explanation that Cole and Ohanian test is the sticky-wage hypothesis: that the massive deflation of 1929–1933 depressed output by driving up real wages. Their results are very different from our findings in "Money, sticky wages, and the Great Depression" (Bordo, Erceg, and Evans, 2000), in which we find that the sticky-wage channel accounts for

1. This paper represents the views of the authors and should not be interpreted as reflecting the views of the Board of Governors of the Federal Reserve System, the Federal Reserve Bank of Chicago, other members of their staff, or the National Bureau of Economic Research.

about 70% of the output decline over 1929–1933. In this comment, we focus on several key problems with the authors' formulation that account for the divergence in our results. We conclude by discussing their comparison of the postwar disinflation in 1920–1921 with the disinflation over 1929–1933. In the subsequent comment, Mark Gertler focuses on Cole and Ohanian's test of the bank-failure explanation for the Depression.

2. Evaluation of Cole and Ohanian's Model for Testing the Sticky-Wage Hypothesis

In our paper "Money, sticky wages, and the Great Depression," we construct a dynamic general equilibrium model to evaluate whether the monetary contraction over 1929–1933 can account for the output decline. Our model has only one productive sector, with capital and labor the only inputs. The representative agent makes consumption–investment decisions based on the permanent-income hypothesis, and has rational expectations. Persistent negative shocks to money growth over 1930–1933 cause a largely unanticipated fall in the price levels. Because wages are sluggish to adjust to the employment gap, real wages rise, causing hours worked and output to contract progressively. The negative effects of the real-wage rise on hours worked are exacerbated by the decline in the capital stock.

Our simple model accounts surprisingly well for the joint behavior of output, hours worked, and our measure of the real wage over the downturn phase of the Depression, particularly over 1929–1932. We interpret our results as providing support for the null hypothesis that (unexpected) contractionary shocks to money operating through a sticky-wage channel played a substantial role in the output downturn. As always, "support" is taken to mean nonrejection: it is possible that other explanations may perform as well or better at accounting for the same stylized facts, in which case we would need an additional basis to differentiate between the models.

Cole and Ohanian develop a two-sector model in order to allow for potentially different real-wage behavior across the manufacturing and nonmanufacturing sectors. Aside from this formal difference, there are several key features that account for their rejection of the null that nominal wage stickiness accounts for a sizeable fraction of the output downturn. First, Cole and Ohanian assume that real wages adjust flexibly (in a spot labor market) in the nonmanufacturing sector, which comprises 72% of employment in their baseline calibration (government is also included in their manufacturing sector). Second, the shock to the real product wage in manufacturing implied by their model greatly understates the observed increase. Third, Cole and Ohanian simply assume that trend productivity grew at 2% per year over the 1929–1933 period. We consider each of these restrictions in turn below. We argue that they appear unjustified empirically, and thus strongly bias Cole and Ohanian's model against the sticky-wage hypothesis.

2.1 WERE WAGES IN THE NONMANUFACTURING SECTOR PERFECTLY FLEXIBLE?

Cole and Ohanian motivate modeling wage behavior outside the manufacturing sector as perfectly flexible, based on wage behavior in the farming sector. In the upper panel of Table 4 of their paper, they show that real farm wages (deflated by the GNP deflator) collapsed during the Great Depression, falling over 40% between 1929 and 1933.[2]

While it is probably reasonable to model the farming sector as having flexible wages, there is little support for extending this characterization to the remainder of private nonmanufacturing. First, the farming sector was quite small at the onset of the Depression, accounting for only 10% of national income, or about 14% of the national income attributable to the private nonmanufacturing sector. Moreover, according to Kendrick (1961), the farm sector constituted about 11% of the total labor input to the private nonmanufacturing sector on a quality-adjusted basis (Table A-5, p. 267).

Second, the farming sector appears to have behaved very differently from the remainder of the private nonmanufacturing sector. Table 1 compares employment in farming to employment in the (private) non-farm non-manufacturing sector. While employment in farming remained nearly stable, employment in nonfarm nonmanufacturing fell 30% by 1933. Table 2 considers the relative price of farm output, derived by deflating the wholesale price index (WPI) for farm products by the GNP deflator. Real farm prices collapsed during the 1929–1933 period, declining by somewhat over 40% by 1933 (about the same fall as in the real wage). On the other hand, the decline in relative farm prices and the relative price of manufactured goods over the 1929–1933 period (discussed below) imply that the real price of nonfarm nonmanufactured goods must have risen over the period.

Even without considering wage data directly, the data on employment and relative prices suggest very different wage behavior across the farm and nonfarm nonmanufacturing sectors. The fact that employment in farming remained almost stable despite a massive fall in the product

---

2. Data on real wages and output reported by Cole and Ohanian are adjusted by deterministic trends. In this note, we report all data without making any trend adjustments.

Table 1 EMPLOYMENT IN THE NONMANUFACTURING SECTOR (CHANGE FROM 1929)

Year	Change (percentage pts.)	
	Farm[a]	Nonfarm[b]
1930	−2.1	−4.8
1931	−0.1	−14.2
1932	0.4	−26.9
1933	−0.2	−30.4

[a]Kendrick (1961, Table B-1).
[b]United States Department of Commerce (1981, Table 6.8A).

Table 2 REAL PRICE OF FARM OUTPUT[a] (CHANGE FROM 1929)

Year	WPI[b] (percentage points)
1930	−14.0
1931	−35.5
1932	−53.3
1933	−44.8

[a]Source: Bureau of Labor Statistics, *Wholesale Prices*, June 1934, Table 1.
[b]For farm products, divided by GNP deflator.

price would require a corresponding collapse in the real wage (measured relative to the GNP deflator). This is exactly what was observed. By contrast, the sharp decline in employment in the nonfarm nonmanufacturing sector despite a rise in the relative price of its output would suggest that the real wage in that sector rose.[3]

Table 3 compares a measure of the aggregate real wage that we constructed in our paper (2000) with the manufacturing real wage. The nonmanufacturing real wage behaves quite similarly to the manufactur-

---

3. Our argument implicitly assumes—as in Bernanke and Parkinson (1991)—that there was not a sizable fall in total factor productivity during the 1929–1933 period. In this case, the nonfarm nonmanufacturing sector's labor demand curve would be reasonably stable, except for movements in the capital stock. Thus, a large observed fall in sectoral employment (despite a relative price rise) would require a rise in that sector's real wage.

Table 3 REAL WAGES (USING GNP DEFLATOR)[a] (CHANGE FROM 1929, IN PERCENTAGE POINTS)

	1930	1931	1932	1933
Aggregate (all industries)	2.4	7.2	9.7	5.8
Manufacturing	3.5	9.2	10.7	10.6

[a]These real wage measures are derived by deflating average hourly earnings by the GNP deflator. The average hourly earnings series are described in Bordo, Erceg, and Evans (2000), footnote 2.

ing real wage (when wages are deflated by a common deflator), at least through 1932. We admit that there are important reasons to be cautious about drawing inferences from the aggregate wage data, particularly given that information about average hours worked is sparse in most sectors outside of manufacturing. Nevertheless, at the very least there is direct evidence suggesting that wages in the nonfarm nonmanufacturing sector rose somewhat, and the behavior of sectoral relative prices and that of employment seem consistent with the real wage movement. Thus, Cole and Ohanian's decision to assume flexible wages in the nonmanufacturing sector based on evidence of wage behavior in farming seems difficult to justify. This choice biases their model against finding an important role for the sticky-wage channel.

2.2 DOES THE IMPLIED BEHAVIOR OF THE PRODUCT REAL WAGE IN MANUFACTURING FIT THE DATA?

In Cole and Ohanian's model, manufacturing output depends on the product real wage, the capital stock in manufacturing, and the level of technology. The form of the dependence can be seen by taking the logarithm of the representative manufacturing firm's first-order condition for choosing hours worked:

$$h_{mt} = k_{mt} - \frac{1}{\theta}(w_{mt} - p_{mt} - a_t). \tag{1}$$

Here h_{mt} is the (natural) log of hours worked in manufacturing, k_{mt} is the log of the manufacturing capital stock, w_{mt} is the log of the manufacturing wage deflated by the GNP deflator (the "consumer" real wage), p_{mt} is the log of the price of the manufactured goods deflated by the GNP deflator, and a_t is the log of an index of technology. The product real wage in manufacturing is simply the difference between the consumer real wage in manufacturing and the real price of manufacturing output ($w_{mt} - p_{mt}$).

Cole and Ohanian interpret the sticky-wage model as implying a se-

Table 4 REAL WAGES AND RELATIVE PRICES IN MANUFACTURING[a] (CHANGE FROM 1929)

Year	Change (percentage points)		
	Consumer real wage in manufacturing, w_{mt}	Real price of manufactured good, p_{mt}	Product real wage in manufacturing, $w_{mt} - p_{mt}$
1930	3.5	−5.1	8.6
1931	9.2	−9.7	18.9
1932	10.7	−6.8	17.5
1933	10.6	−3.7	14.4

[a] The deflator for manufacturing output is the WPI for nonagricultural products, from the Bureau of Labor Statistics, *Wholesale Prices*, June 1934, Table 3.

quence of unanticipated shocks to the consumer real wage in manufacturing (w_{mt}). The shock in each period is assumed to equal the deviation of the observed consumer real wage from its 1929 value, except for an adjustment for "trend" productivity growth that we discuss below. The unadjusted consumer real-wage series is shown in the first column of Table 4 (it is identical to the second column of Table 3). While w_{mt} is taken as exogenous, the relative price p_{mt} is endogenously determined, depending inversely on the output of the manufactured relative to the nonmanufactured good. Cole and Ohanian's model generates a substantial rise in the real price of the manufactured good, and thus implies a rise in the product real wage that is much smaller than the rise in the consumer real wage.

This implication is contradicted by the data. The second column of Table 4 shows the real price of manufacturing output, defined as a deflator for manufacturing output divided by the GNP deflator. The real price of manufacturing output had fallen by 10% in 1931 relative to its 1929 level. This implies that the product real wage (column 3) rose 10 percentage points *more* than the consumer real wage in that year. By contrast, Cole and Ohanian report that their model implies a rise in the product real wage that is 4.4% *less* than the rise in the consumer real wage in 1931.

Thus, Cole and Ohanian's model appears to seriously understate the shock to the product real wage in manufacturing. Even ignoring their subtraction of "trend productivity growth" from the product real wage implied by their model, their model understates the rise in the product real wage by 10–15 percentage points over the Depression downturn. Holding manufacturing capital constant, this would translate into a serious understatement of the effects of a rise in the real product wage on manufacturing output.

To gauge the effects of understating the shock to the product real wage, note from (1) that the elasticity of labor demand in manufacturing is $1/\theta$, where θ is the capital share in manufacturing. Since $\theta = \frac{1}{3}$ in their calibration, we can take this elasticity to equal 3. Thus, relative to a model that simply took the product real wage as exogenous and equal to our values in column 3, their model understates the decline in manufacturing output by 30–45%. Moreover, because this understatement of the rise in the product wage greatly reduces the effect of the wage shock on aggregate output in their model, it also mitigates the fall in the manufacturing capital stock. Thus, their model's understatement of the wage shock may have a considerably larger effect on manufacturing hours worked and output through the capital channel.

2.3 IS IT APPROPRIATE TO SCALE FOR TREND PRODUCTIVITY GROWTH?

Cole and Ohanian assume that productivity grows at a constant rate of 2% per year over the 1929–1933 period. Given this assumption, they take the wage shock to manufacturing to be the consumer wage (in column 1 of Table 4) scaled down for trend productivity growth, i.e., $w_{mt} - a_t$.

The assumption of trend productivity growth obviously makes it more difficult to account for an output downturn, particularly in 1932–1933. Given the preference specification, this means that output and real wages in each sector would grow 2% per year in the absence of any shocks. Moreover, the size of the exogenous shock to the consumer real wage in the manufacturing sector is scaled down from what is reported in column 1 of Table 4. As a result, the baseline parameterization of Cole and Ohanian's model implies that while GDP falls below trend in 1929–1933, the level of GDP rises continuously over the period. Even output in manufacturing, the sticky-wage sector, rises above its 1929 level by 1933!

We believe that the inclusion of this trend term lacks justification, at least over the period considered. It seems especially puzzling given that the authors argue that "[aggregate] total faster productivity fell about 14% percent below trend between 1929 and 1933." If total factor productivity in fact declined, it may be more appropriate to extract a negative trend, or to allow for negative shocks to productivity. Allowing for a negative trend would of course allow sticky wages in manufacturing to exert much larger output effects (even more so if the relative-price problem in the current model were rectified). The authors seem to acknowledge this near the conclusion of the paper when they state that "a decrease in productivity . . . may represent the best chance for the wage hypothesis to account for a reasonable fraction of the output decrease."

In our own model, we take a conservative approach and assume that productivity remained unchanged over 1929–1933. However, we agree with Cole and Ohanian that it would be interesting to further investigate the implications of a possible fall in total factor productivity, despite the obvious difficulties in constructing a convincing measure over this period.

2.4 SUMMARY OF KEY PROBLEMS WITH MODEL

Cole and Ohanian claim to be testing the null hypothesis that wage stickiness accounted for the Great Depression. A convincing test requires building a model that is favorable to the null, subject to the constraints imposed by the data. We argue that Cole and Ohanian construct a model that is unduly biased against the null hypothesis, and this accounts for their rejection.

It is important to emphasize that the different results they derive are primarily driven by the three features of the model discussed (in Sections 2.1–2.3) above, and not from other features of their setup, e.g., the fact that their model has two sectors instead of one. Some preliminary work that we have done suggests that a multisector model can account for a very substantial output downturn if it: (1) takes the product real wage in manufacturing as exogenous (fitting it to the observed product-real-wage series), (2) allows for some degree of rigidity in the product real wage in the nonmanufacturing sector, even if considerably less than in manufacturing, and (3) assumes total factor productivity growth is zero over the 1929–1933 period.

From a methodological perspective, the authors' introduction of a multisectoral model to study the Depression period is innovative and welcome. The authors highlight how the farm sector behaved differently over that period, and future research may identify sectoral differences that have important consequences for the effects of a shock on aggregate activity. Regarding the monetary transmission mechanism, our preference is to model it directly rather than take the reduced-form approach of assuming an exogenous real wage shock. The authors' approach involves an unpalatable assumption about how agents in the model assume the real wage will eventually adjust to equilibrate the labor market (viz., the manufacturing real wage is expected to adjust flexibly in the subsequent year). The transmission mechanism, including the process by which wages are expected to adjust, has critical implications for the response of the capital stock to a shock.

3. Why Was the Disinflation of 1920–1921 Different from the Disinflation of 1929–1933?

The authors emphasize that for an explanation linking the large output contraction of 1929–1933 to deflation to be plausible, it should be able to explain why a similar-sized deflation in 1920–1921 had different real effects. In our NBER Working Paper version of "Money, sticky wages, and the Great Depression" (1997), we proposed the same "consistency check" to evaluate the plausibility of the sticky-wage channel. It is worthwhile briefly restating our interpretation of the two periods, since it is strongly at variance with that proposed by Cole and Ohanian.

In our estimation, two key differences mainly account for why deflation in 1920–1921 induced a smaller and less prolonged downturn in real activity than the deflation of 1929–1933. First, the deflation in 1920–1921 was more predictable than in 1929–1933, and considerably shorter-lived. Second, wage-setting practices in the early 1920s were more flexible than later in the decade.

Our contention that the deflation of 1920–1921 was more predictable requires some clarification. The disinflation was predictable insofar as contemporaries of the period expected that the authorities would pursue a monetary policy that supported the gold standard at the prewar parity. Since prices had risen rapidly during both World War I and into the early interwar period, it was clear that tight monetary policy and deflation would be required to maintain the gold standard after the embargo on gold exports was lifted in June 1919. The main uncertainty involved the timing and speed of the eventual disinflation. The authorities compounded this uncertainty by pursuing an accomodative monetary policy through late 1919, despite substantial gold outflows. The authorities then abruptly tightened policy, inducing a price decline that was much sharper than in 1929–1933. The GNP deflator fell 24% between 1920:3 and 1921:2, and an additional 8% by 1922:1 before roughly stabilizing. Output began contracting in 1920:1, and fell by 17% over the subsequent year—slightly more than the 14% decline that occurred during the first year of the Great Depression.[4] Friedman and Schwartz (1963, p. 232) characterize the downturn as "one of the severest on record. Its brevity makes annual data misleading guides to its severity."

Thus, the 1920–1921 depression was in fact quite severe. According to Friedman and Schwartz, the real effects were exacerbated by a twofold error of the monetary authorities: first, their refusal to move to a tighter policy stance immediately following the end of the world war; and sec-

---

4. Our source for the quarterly real GNP and the GNP deflator series is Balke and Gordon (1986).

ond, by tightening policy too sharply once they finally decided to disinflate. However, the policy of disinflation rapidly gained credibility once in place. Agents realized that it was crucial for maintaining the gold standard, and was in fact similar to the policies being pursued by other central banks. Thus, the disinflation episode was relatively short-lived, prices stabilized, and a rapid recovery ensued. Output recovered to its predepression peak within a year and a half of the trough. Relatively flexible wage-setting policies—in which wages fell quickly with prices—aided in the quick recovery.

By contrast, the price deflation in the Great Depression was drawn out over a considerably longer period. It is much less plausible that the deflation was anticipated: it occurred after a long period of price stability, and was associated with a large drop in the money multiplier due to bank failures and policy inaction. Moreover, the real effects of the disinflation were likely exacerbated by the adoption of less flexible wage-setting practices in the late 1920s. As O'Brien (1989) has emphasized, this change in wage-setting is in part attributable to the mistaken belief that maintaining consumer purchasing power (through keeping nominal wages high) was the key to ameliorating the effects of business cycles.[5]

Thus, we disagree with the basic thrust of Cole and Ohanian's characterization of the two disinflation episodes: namely, that the 1920–1921 disinflation was both less anticipated than the disinflation of 1929–1933, and yet associated with a very mild output downturn. It is true that the disinflation of 1920–1921 had a surprise component, as the timing and speed of the monetary tightening weren't known ex ante. This contributed to a sharp downturn in real activity, the severity of which is understated by Cole and Ohanian (due to their reliance on annual data). However, we have argued that a much larger component of the overall disinflation was predictable in 1920–1921, that the disinflation in any event was short-lived, and that these factors helped output to bounce back quickly. While the authors use annual data on both nominal and ex post real interest rates as the basis for concluding that the disinflation of 1920–1921 was less anticipated, we believe that using such data to make inferences about inflation expectations is highly problematic. The 1920–1921 period was very turbulent, as a large inflation was followed by a

---

5. The theory that sharp wage cuts during the 1920–1921 depression had induced a more severe output downturn by reducing household purchasing power became quite popular in the 1920s, even among the business community. Individual firms were urged to sacrifice their private gain (cutting wages) to help secure the overall benefit of maintaining household purchasing power. Thus, while Cole and Ohanian are correct that President Hoover encouraged employers to avoid wage cuts, there was substantial support for such a policy during the first two years of the Depression. Moreover, pressure on employers to keep wages high appears to have extended well beyond the manufacturing sector.

quick deflation. Real interest rates swung wildly, with the (annualized) ex post short-term real interest rate fluctuating from roughly −20% in the first half of 1920 to 45–50% in the second half of that year. In such circumstances, the usual difficulties of disentangling the effects of shifts in inflation expectations on nominal rates from the effects of changing real rates and risk premia are greatly exacerbated.

REFERENCES

Balke, N. S., and R. J. Gordon. (1986). Appendix B: Historical data. In *The American Business Cycle: Continuity and Change*, R. J. Gordon (ed.). Chicago: University of Chicago Press, pp. 793–794.

Bernanke, B. S., and M. L. Parkinson. (1991). Procyclical labor productivity and competing theories of the business cycle: Some evidence from interwar U.S. manufacturing industries. *Journal of Political Economy* 99(June):439–459.

Bordo, M., C. Erceg, and C. Evans. (1997). Money, sticky wages, and the Great Depression. Cambridge, MA: National Bureau of Economic Research. NBER Working Paper 6071.

———, ———, and ———. (2000). Money, sticky wages, and the Great Depression. *American Economic Review*, forthcoming.

Friedman, M., and A. J. Schwartz. (1963). *A Monetary History of the United States, 1867–1960*. Princeton: Princeton University Press.

Kendrick, J. W. (1961). *Productivity Trends in the United States*. Princeton, Princeton University Press.

O'Brien, A. (1989). Behavioral explanation for nominal wage rigidity during the Great Depression. *Quarterly Journal of Economics* 104(November):719–735.

United States Department of Commerce, Bureau of the Census. (1981). *The National Income and Product Accounts of the United States, 1929–76*.

Comment

MARK GERTLER
New York University and NBER

1. Introduction

Cole and Ohanian have produced an interesting and provocative paper. On one point I am in complete argument: Any explanation of the Great Depression should ultimately involve writing down a quantitative model that captures the magnitude of the contraction. At the same time, it is important to note that in this paper the authors do not provide a model that rationalizes the Depression. Rather they present a set of particular models with the objective of rejecting certain monetary and financial theories. I will argue below that neither of the two models they develop is adequate for providing a robust evaluation of the theories in question.

In addition, despite the (welcome) appeal to formal modeling, much of the analysis is in fact based on informal descriptive evidence. The authors' empirical strategy is to evaluate theories on the basis of simple comparisons of two different episodes. The authors, for example, rule out debt deflation as a factor in the Great Depression by repeating the familiar argument that the deflation during 1920–1921 did not produce a contraction of similar magnitude in the early 1930s (see, e.g., Kindleberger, 1986). Here the entire strategy rests on controlling for other relevant differences across the two episodes. I will argue below that the authors have not done this control adequately. Indeed, the problem of omitted factors is an issue of concern in virtually the entire descriptive analysis.

To be clear, identification of causal factors during the Great Depression is a difficult task. However, recent literature, beginning with Choudri and Kochin (1980), Eichengreen (1992), and Bernanke and James (1991), has made considerable progress by focusing on cross-country evidence. It is puzzling that the authors completely ignore this literature. While the authors draw inferences from just two data points—the 1920–1921 and 1929–1933 downturns in the United States—the cross-country analysis instead exploits a panel of twenty to thirty observations. On this score, using the cross-country data, Bernanke and James show formally that debt-deflation was indeed associated with major contractions.

The paper is similarly silent on the well-known work of Eichengreen (1992) and others that emphasize the role of the gold standard. This work puts monetary factors at the center of the Depression by showing that the countries that suffered severe contractions were precisely those that constrained their monetary policy to defend the gold standard. Countries that freed up their monetary policies by abandoning gold early fared much better.

Beyond presenting a compelling case for monetary factors, the issue of the gold standard circles directly back to debt-deflation: The countries in Bernanke and James's sample that experienced simultaneously deflation, financial crisis, and severe depression were also those that stayed on the gold standard. That is, the attempt to maintain the gold standard by monetary tightening was apparently at least one of a number of possible forces (in conjunction with other factors, e.g. wage rigidity and a weak financial system) that helped propagate deflation and depression. I would certainly agree that to complete the argument a formal model is necessary. On the other hand, I don't see how the authors can dismiss debt-deflation and other monetary and financial forces as possible factors without confronting this research.

In Section 2 below I fill in some important missing context to the authors' descriptive analysis by providing a brief discussion of the main events of the Depression. One theme I wish to emphasize is that, in contrast to 1920–1921, the period 1929–1933 was one of sustained contractionary forces. The Great Depression was likely the cumulative effect of these forces, as opposed to being the consequence of any single factor in isolation.

The initial downturn of 1929–1930 was due in large part to a collapse in household spending, including residential investment. It is reasonable to infer that monetary and financial factors had an influence on this early spending contraction. However, as stressed by Friedman and Schwartz (1963), the most significant effect of monetary and financial factors in the Depression likely came after the economy had already been weakened substantially by the initial downturn.[1] At this time, the combined forces of debt–deflation, strains in the banking system, and asset price contractions, along with subsequent tightening of monetary policy, likely helped turn what had been a severe recession into a depression. By contrast, the debt deflation and high real rates during 1920–1921 occurred in the wake of a release of pent-up consumption demand following the end of World War I and in the midst of a more favorable international economic climate (see, e.g., Temin, 1989). Nor, during 1920–1921, as Eichengreen emphasizes, was U.S. monetary policy constrained by gold.

In Sections 3 and 4 I discuss the models of wage rigidity and banking. I argue that from the start the authors' model does not give the wage-rigidity hypothesis a fair hearing, because it does not allow for nominal-wage stickiness and, accordingly, precludes the possibility of the kind of contraction in aggregate demand that is the essence of this hypothesis. I argue similarly that the banking model is too specialized to provide a robust assessment and, among other things, discuss why in general the cost share of banking in GDP is unlikely to provide a measure of the effects of a banking crisis. In Section 5, I take issue with the authors' interpretation of the evidence on each of the following three topics: (1) risk spreads, (2) dividends, and (3) the Japanese stock-market collapse. Concluding remarks are in Section 6.

2. Overview of the Depression

I now provide a brief description of the events of the Depression. My goal here is to outline the case for monetary and financial factors and also to show that simple comparisons with 1920–1921 can be misleading.

1. This timing consideration is highly pertinent. Most historical analyses stress debt–deflation not as a causal factor in the 1929–1930 downturn, but rather as a factor that helped turn this downturn into a protracted depression. The authors, however, focus on its role in the early stages of the Depression. I elaborate in the next section.

Figure 1 INDUSTRIAL PRODUCTION

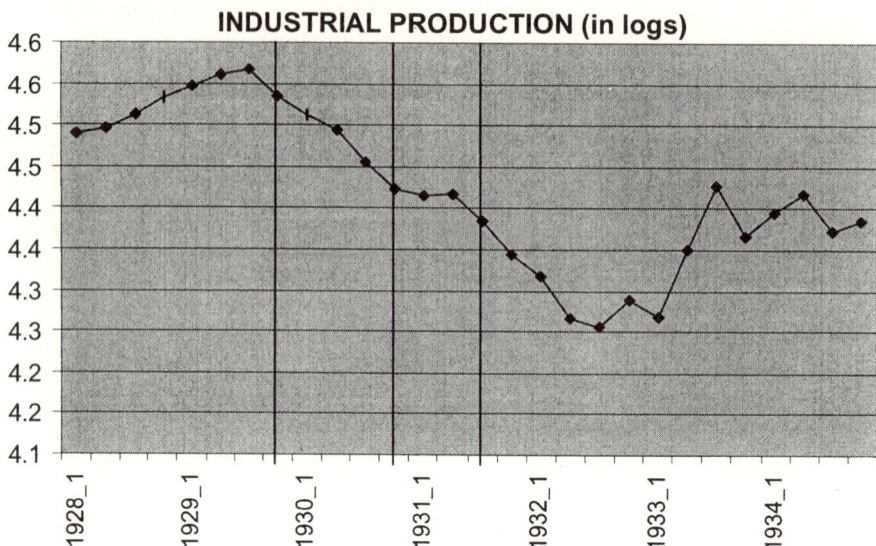

Figure 1 plots the behavior of log industrial production over the period 1928:1–1934:4. Figure 2 plots the behavior of the nominal commercial-paper rate along with two measures of inflation: the log difference of the GNP deflator and the log difference of the wholesale price index (WPI). In each figure, the three vertical lines mark dates associated with the three critical phases of the Depression, as described in Friedman and Schwartz: (1) October 1929 (the stock-market crash); (2) October 1930 (the beginning of the banking crisis); (3) September 1931 (Britain's abandonment of the gold standard). I discuss each phase in turn.

2.1 OCTOBER 1929

After a period of robust economic growth, a slowdown set in just prior to the stock-market crash. As argued by Hamilton (1987) and Romer (1993), tightening of monetary policy over the prior year was likely a contributing factor to this slowdown.[2] Following the crash, as Figure 1 indicates, there is a sharp slide in industrial production that does not level until the summer of 1930. A notable aspect of this initial output contraction was the sharp collapse in household spending, including residential investment as well as consumption demand. As Table 1

---

2. Hamilton cites the gold standard and a desire by the Federal Reserve to curb stock-market speculation as the motive for the tightening.

Figure 2 NOMINAL CP RATE VS. WPI AND GNPD INFLATION

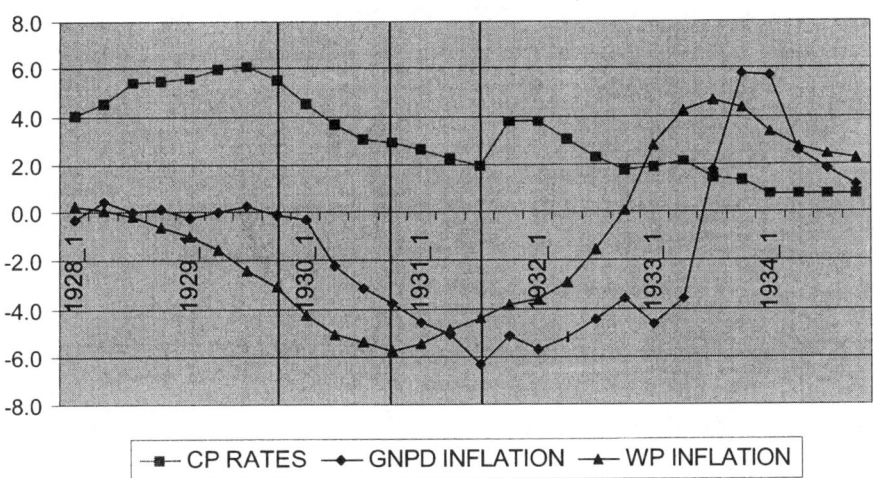

Table 1 COMPOSITION OF OUTPUT DROP

	GNP	Nondur. cons. and services	Dur. cons.	Residential investment	Inventories	Nonresid. invest.
% change, 1929–1930	−9.9	−4.8	−20.9	−39.4	−117.1	−18.1
% contribution to total: 1929–1930	100.0	29.4	16.9	20.4	20.4	23.9
% Ave. over postwar recessions	100.0	21.5	8.7	14.7	30.7	21.1

shows, between 1929 and 1930, durable-goods consumption dropped 20% and residential investment plummeted nearly 40%. Overall, the two spending components accounted for 37% of the output decline in 1930. Total household spending (obtained by adding in nondurables and services) accounted for nearly two-thirds of the output drop. As the table indicates, relative to the norm provided by postwar recessions, the relative contribution of household spending was unusually large across all categories (i.e., durable, housing and nondurable, and services).[3]

3. The average contribution of each GDP component to postwar recessions is taken from Romer (1996).

242 · GERTLER

Several pieces of evidence suggest that monetary and financial factors played a role. First, as Figure 2 indicates, the short-term nominal interest rate rose steadily over the preceding year, reflecting the monetary tightening. Real interest rates climbed to roughly 6% based on the GDP deflator and 9% based on the WPI. While the former is a broader-based index, the latter is likely measured with more precision, especially at the quarterly frequency.[4] In addition to monetary tightening, credit conditions—particularly the weakness in consumer balance sheets and general household illiquidity in the wake of the stock-market crash—likely also contributed to the household spending drop, according to evidence presented by Mishkin (1978) and Olney (1999).

To be sure, accounting for the huge decline in household spending remains an unsolved problem. My point here is simply that there is sufficient evidence to believe that monetary and financial factors had at least some role of significance. In addition, frictions in financial markets seem a natural avenue to pursue to help account for the sizable drop in household spending, particularly the drop in consumer durables and residential investment.

The sharp drop in household spending stands in sharp contrast to the downturn between 1920 and 1921. As noted in the introduction, the end of World War I likely released a pent-up demand for household spending, particularly for durable goods. Temin provides more detail on the factors that contributed to strong household demand. The contractionary forces of debt deflation and high real rates were thus partly offset by this strong postwar consumption demand.[5] Some support for this general story comes from the authors' Table 1. Observe that consumption actually rises in 1921.

2.2 OCTOBER 1930

Around this time the drop in industrial output slows, but financial conditions steadily deteriorate. Deflation picks up momentum: As Figure 2 suggests, the GNP deflator begins a protracted decline. Due to the combined effects of the deflation and the initial economic downturn, the debt burden rises significantly: The ratio of private debt to output rises

---

4. Romer (1993) similarly finds that real rates reached roughly 9% at this time, by constructing a measure of expected inflation based on the producer price index.
5. Also relevant according to Temin were differences in the international economic climate: In the early 1920s the United States benefited from strong demand to facilitate reconstruction from the war. By contrast, export demand tanked during the Depression as the industrialized world fell into recession along with the United States in the early 1930s. Eichengreen (1992) further emphasizes that the absence of the gold standard in 1920–1921 reduced the synchronization of downturns in 1920–1921 across countries, relative to 1929–1931.

Table 2 ANNUAL INCREASE IN THE PRIVATE DEBT BURDEN DUE TO DEFLATION: THE DEPRESSION OF 1920–1921 VS. 1930–1931 AND 1931–1932

Years	Initial private debt relative to output	Annual Δ (%) in		
		Price level	Debt burden	GNP
1920–21	1.20	−14.80	20.85	−6.10
1930–31	1.78	−9.23	18.12	−10.70
1931–32	1.96	−10.17	22.16	−17.53

from 1.5 in 1929 to 2.0 in 1931. Loan defaults significantly weaken the capitalization of commercial banks. One manifestation of this distress is a rise in the number of bank failures. During this time, Friedman and Schwartz argue, the Federal Reserve could have taken action to stem the tide, but failed to do so.

As I noted in the introduction, unlike 1920–1921, which featured a transitory period of simultaneous falling prices and output, the deflation of 1929–1933 sets in largely when the economy has already weakened considerably, after the initial contraction of 1929–1930 described above. The authors instead focus on the role of the debt deflation in the first part of the Depression. To underscore the significance, I redid the authors' calculation of the impact of the declining price level on the debt burden (see their Table 3), this time beginning in 1930, after the initial downturn. Also, I consider 1920–1921 as the relevant period to analyze the deflation of that time, in keeping with conventional historical analysis.[6] To keep the period length consistent, I compare 1920–1921 with 1930–1931 and 1931–1932.

Table 2 reports the calculations. Note that the rise in the debt burden is roughly similar across years. The percentage output contraction in each of the Depression years exceeds the output contraction of 1920–1921— 10.7% and 17.53% versus 6.1%. But the difference is far less stark than what obtains from the authors' analysis.[7] After allowing for other differ-

6. Virtually every historical account I have read refers to the contraction of 1920–1921, and not 1920–1922 as do the authors. Note from the authors' Table 1 that private spending is actually up relative to trend in 1922—overall output is down only because of a contraction in government spending due to the demilitarization following World War I. My guess is that the historical literature presumes that given that the decline in military spending likely reduced potential output, it does not seem right to treat 1922 as a recession year.
7. Also, Friedman and Schwartz (1963, p. 232) argue that the use of annual data greatly understates the severity of the 1920–1921 recession. Specifically, they state: ". . . although this contraction was relatively brief—the National Bureau dates the trough in

ences between the two episodes (e.g., vastly different initial behavior of household spending, different monetary policy regimes, different banking conditions), the relative experiences with deflation are far less anomalous than the authors' analysis suggests.[8]

An additional key difference from 1920–1921—one highlighted by the authors—is the development of the banking crisis. In the next section I address the authors' contention that banking problems were unimportant. In the meantime, I simply observe that there is considerable evidence to suggest that bank-dependent borrowers, including unincorporated businesses and corporations with imperfect access to credit, as well as households, were hit particularly hard during the first two years of the Depression. According to Fabricant (1934, 1935), business losses were concentrated mainly among small and medium-sized firms. Large firms on average made profits throughout the Depression.[9] Further, it is not the case that firms with imperfect access are "small potatoes." It is not unreasonable to suggest that unincorporated businesses and small and medium-sized corporations accounted for between half to two-thirds of GDP.[10] Thus, the disruption of credit markets affected a sizable component of the business sector along with households.

2.3 SEPTEMBER 1931

At this point, as noted above, Britain abandoned the gold standard. The Federal Reserve chose to defend, despite the severely weakened economy and despite very high ex post real interest rates. As a consequence, nominal interest rates rose 200 basis points and ex post real rates (using the GNP deflator) climbed to 10% (see Figure 2). Shortly afterward, as Figure 1 shows, industrial production began a free fall, and what had been a severe recession turned into a depression. Of course, trying to

---

July 1921—it ranks as one of the severest on record. Its brevity makes annual data misleading guides to its severity."

8. An additional difference was that the deflation in 1920–1921 was preceded by a large run-up in prices. To the extent debt contracts were long-term, a good fraction of the effect of the deflation on real debt burdens simply offset the effect of the earlier inflation. By way of contrast, the deflation during the Depression followed a long period of price stability.
9. The positive relationship between size and profitability during the Depression holds even after controlling for industry. See Table 6 in Fabricant (1935). Bernanke (1983) also emphasizes the heterogeneous performance of firms across size class during the Depression.
10. Unincorporated businesses accounted for roughly a third of GDP. Small and medium-sized corporations accounted for anywhere between a quarter and a half of overall corporate business. For example, firms under $50 million in assets—Fabricant's threshold for large firms—accounted for 53% of total corporate receipts in 1931 and 40% of the total corporate capital stock. Firms under $5 million in assets—clearly smaller firms—accounted for 40% of total corporate receipts and 25% of total corporate capital. Source: *Historical Statistics*.

infer causality with a single time-series observation is dangerous. It is precisely at this juncture, however, that the cross-country evidence provided in Eichengreen (1992) and Bernanke and James (1991) helps resolve the identification problem: Countries such as the United States that failed to abandon the gold standard early suffered more severe economic distress, greater deflation, and more severe banking and financial crises than countries such as Britain that moved relatively quickly to free up their monetary policy. These facts held not only for OECD countries; Campa (1990) showed that the connection between adherence to the gold standard and the severity of the Depression applied equally well to Latin American countries.

Again it is important to stress differences from 1920–1921. Unlike the tightening in this earlier period that came on the heels of an economic boom, the monetary tightening in late 1931 was the culmination of a series of contractionary shocks to the economy over the previous two years that had left both real and financial economic conditions in a highly fragile state. A tightening that follows a long period of duress may have a more potent effect than otherwise, since precautionary asset holdings and other insurance mechanisms that can help borrowers with imperfect access to credit weather bad times may have dried up. It is arguable that the tightening in late 1931 occurred exactly at this kind of point.

2.4 SUMMARY

To briefly recapitulate: To me, the evidence suggests that the authors' simple comparisons of 1920–1921 and the Depression are not adequate to rule out debt–deflation or other monetary and financial factors as having a role in the Depression. In addition to completely ignoring the international evidence, the authors do not take account of critical differences between 1920–1921 and 1929–1933, including the vastly different initial conditions influencing household spending and differences in the monetary policy regime, as well as the sustained and cumulative nature of the contractionary forces that was a feature of the latter period, but not the former.

3. *The Wage-Rigidity Model*

Here I argue that by not allowing for any kind of nominal rigidity the authors do not give the wage-rigidity hypothesis fair due. In particular, the authors consider a two-sector intertemporal general equilibrium model. Real wages are fixed exogenously in one sector, but flexible in the other. Otherwise, the model is completely frictionless. To capture the effect of rising real wages during the Depression, the authors consider a transitory increase in the real wage in the fixed wage sector. Not much happens in the aggregate, because the flexible wage sector soaks up a fair amount of the displaced workers.

It is not at all clear why the authors choose this particular model to evaluate the effect of wage rigidity. Because the model does not allow for nominal wage rigidity, it does not permit the kind of contraction in aggregate demand that advocates of the wage-rigidity hypothesis emphasize as a way to help explain the Depression. In contrast, Bordo, Erceg, and Evans (2000) show that by allowing for staggered nominal wage setting, a simple monetary model can help explain a good fraction of the output decline.

The authors also treat the increase in the real wages as if it came out of thin air. One might think *a priori* that the source of the wage increase should be relevant to the choice of model used to evaluate the issue. Here the international evidence sheds some light. The countries that experienced the largest increases in real wages were—as might be expected—those that stayed longest on the gold standard. One interpretation then is that contractionary monetary policy, interacting with nominal wage rigidities, produced the real wage increases. Specifically, contractionary monetary policy helped induce the contraction in aggregate activity and a corresponding deflation. With nominal wages a bit stickier than nominal prices, real wages increased. If this interpretation is indeed correct, then a model along the lines of Bordo, Erceg, and Evans would seem more appropriate than the authors' to study the effect of wage rigidity.[11]

4. The Banking-Crisis Model

I now address the authors' contention that the banking crises were unimportant. I have three basic concerns, involving: (1) potential measurement of the overall contraction in banking, (2) assumptions of the model that constrain its ability to produce a crisis, and (3) identification issues in the cross-state banking analysis.

4.1 MEASUREMENT OF THE DECLINE IN BANK LENDING CAPACITY

The authors use deposits of failed banks to measure the decline in banking services. A problem with this measure is that it does not take account of the decline in lending capacity of banks that continue to operate.

---

11. It may also be necessary to allow for countercyclical markups and/or some form of labor-market friction that produces real-wage rigidity in order to generate a sufficiently high elasticity of output with respect to the real wage.

Indeed, the convention in the banking literature is to use the decline in bank capital as an indicator of the contraction in lending capacity.

To see the relevance of capital, consider a typical bank balance sheet. On the asset side are loans and securities. Liabilities consist of deposits plus capital. Capital serves as a buffer to protect the return on deposits against loan losses. In practice, the quantity of bank capital influences a bank's ability to acquire uninsured deposits. In this way, it affects its lending capacity. Evidence from bank-level panel data from both the modern era (eg., Bernanke and Lown, 1991) and the Depression (e.g., Calomiris and Berry, 1998) suggests a quantitatively significant link between bank capitalization and bank lending. Accordingly the contraction of bank capital likely provides a better measure of the decline in bank lending services than the deposit measure the authors use.

One complication is that bank capital is usually measured in book- rather than market-value terms. However, recent work by Calomiris and Berry (1998) obtains evidence on the contraction of both market and book values during the Depression for a sample of New York City banks. If we use the New York City data as a guide to correcting the aggregate book-value numbers, then a crude estimate of the decline in the market value of bank capital is approximately 50%. Accordingly, using capital as a measure of lending capacity, as is consistent with the banking literature, suggests a much larger decline than the authors' deposit-based measure of 15%.

4.2 THE MODEL

While the authors' framework may be interesting as a model of financial intermediation, it is not clear that it is particularly useful for studying crises. Within the model, a particular input requires bank finance. A key limitation—if the model is to be used to study crises—is that all other factors (labor, etc.) remain fixed in the wake of the shock. This greatly constrains the ability of a banking crises to generate a contraction in real activity.

I illustrate this point with a very simple model. Let X denote a variable factor that requires bank finance (e.g., inventories), and θ be the service flow from this input. Let L (e.g. labor) be another variable input. Output Y is then given by a simple Cobb–Douglas production function, as follows:

$$Y = (\theta X)^\alpha L^{1-\alpha}.$$

Note that, holding L constant, the elasticity of output with respect to X is given by the cost share:

$$\left(\frac{\partial Y}{\partial X}\frac{X}{Y}\right)\bigg|_L = \alpha.$$

The authors then proceed to analyze a banking crisis, as follows. Suppose that B is the quantity of available bank loans. A shock to banking arises that reduces B below its frictionless equilibrium value. X, accordingly, is constrained to equal B, and the decline in B exactly matches the decline in X. Importantly, no other factors adjust during the crisis. Given this assumption, the percentage decline in output due to a percentage contraction in bank lines is simply given by the cost share; in simple terms, $X = B$ implies

$$\left(\frac{\partial Y}{\partial B}\frac{B}{Y}\right)\bigg|_L = \alpha.$$

To compute the overall decline in output from the banking crisis, the authors multiply the cost share α by their measure of the percentage decline in banking of x percent. Since the cost share of banking in the GDP is a tiny number, the authors conclude that the banking crisis did not have much effect.

I stress, however, that the assumption that all other factors are held constant is key to justifying the cost share as the measure of the output elasticity with respect to bank loans. Suppose instead that labor is perfectly elastic in supply at the wage w. Then it is easy to show that the effect of a banking crisis on output may be considerably larger. In this instance the relevant output elasticity is given by

$$\frac{\partial Y}{\partial B}\frac{B}{Y} = 1.$$

Here output drops proportionally with bank loans.[12] Further, if the elasticity of lending with respect to capital is roughly unity (which presumes that banks maintain a stable ratio of capital to loans), then given my estimate of a roughly 50% decline in bank capital and my (overly) simple model, the banking crisis could have produced a decline in output of up

---

12. The elasticity is lower if there are diminishing returns. It is higher, however, if the elasticity of substitution between the bank-financed input and the other variable inputs is lower. It will also be higher if there are overhead financing costs, since in this instance a given percentage reduction in banking lending will imply a proportionally greater decline in funds available to finance the variable input.

to 50% for bank-dependent firms. I would add that this calculation ignores the potential impact on household spending.

I am not suggesting that anyone take my model seriously. My point is only to illustrate that the authors' connection between the cost share and the impact of a banking crisis rests on the assumption that the crisis makes no impact on other factors of production. True, my assumption of perfectly elastic factor supply is extreme. On the other hand, during the Great Depression there was a huge contraction in employment with relatively little movement in real wages. This elastic-like behavior of employment was surely not a simple consequence of preferences. Rather, it likely reflected labor-market frictions in conjunction with other forces. The key point is that a proper evaluation of the banking crisis likely requires taking into account other frictions, such as labor-market rigidities, possibly including nominal as well as real rigidities, that open up the possibility of large output fluctuations. The mere fact that a banking shock doesn't do much in an otherwise frictionless framework does not imply that it will be unimportant once the frictions outside the banking sector are properly taken into account.

4.3 CROSS-STATE BANKING EVIDENCE

Examining the link between banking performance and output across states is in principle a good idea. Several problems confound the identification, however. As I have mentioned, the loss of bank capital is likely a better measure of the decline in lending capacity than are the deposits of failed banks. A state could have a banking industry in poor health due to low capitalization, but few banks that actually fail. (This is more likely to be true for states with large banks, since regulators are more likely to let small banks fail than large ones.) Accordingly, measurement error in the authors' independent variable (banking lending capacity) could be one factor responsible for the lack of explanatory power.

Second, there is likely unobserved heterogeneity across states. For example, midwestern states are dominated by durable-goods industries. Not controlling for this difference will bias the results. Finally, high integration of state economies also inhibits identification. A contraction in bank activity in Illinois that reduces demand for automobiles will lead to a contraction in Michigan output.

The authors' case would be more compelling if they set up the hypothesis test so that the argument they prefer requires a finding of statistical significance. But doing it the other way around—having victory depend on the absence of statistical significance—implies a test of low power: Absence of statistical significance could reflect a variety of factors having nothing to do with the authors' argument.

Figure 3 Baa GOVERNMENT-BOND SPREAD

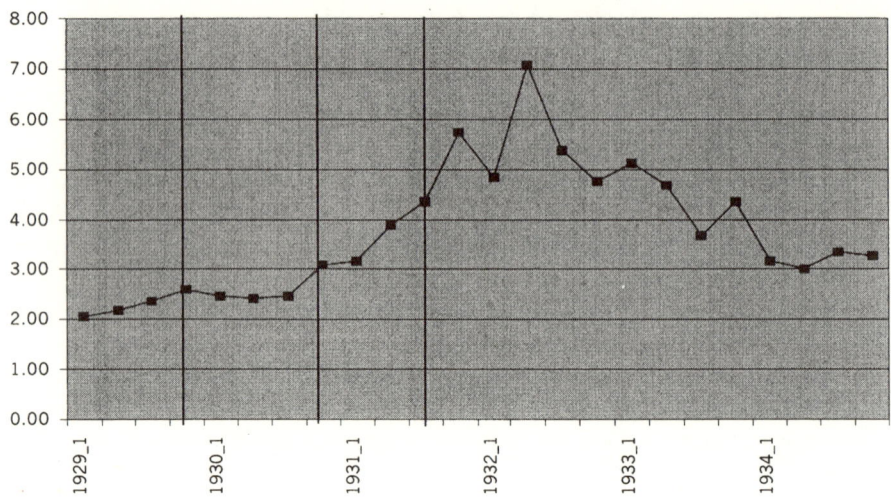

5. Risk Spreads, Dividends, and Japan

I now tie up some loose ends regarding the authors' discussion of financial factors involving risk spreads and dividend behavior during the Depression and also the Japanese stock-market crash of the early 1990s.

5.1 RISK SPREADS

One traditional indicator of the steady deterioration of financial conditions throughout the Depression is the behavior of the spread between Baa corporate bonds and long-term government bonds. As Figure 3 indicates, this spread rises from roughly 200 basis points in early 1929 to between 600 and 700 basis points in the wake of the September 1931 monetary tightening. The rise in the spread correlates well with the onset of debt deflation and the banking crises. Note further the nearly 300-basis-point jump in the spread in the interval between the banking crises and the wake of the subsequent monetary tightening.

The authors argue that the movement in the spread simply reflects expected default costs. This observation alone, however, does not rule out a role for financial factors. To the extent there are losses associated with bankruptcy, expected default costs entail an agency premium for external finance.[13]

---

13. In this instance, the agency cost of external finance equals the default probability times the deadweight cost associated with bankruptcy.

Figure 4 DEFAULT RATES (%)

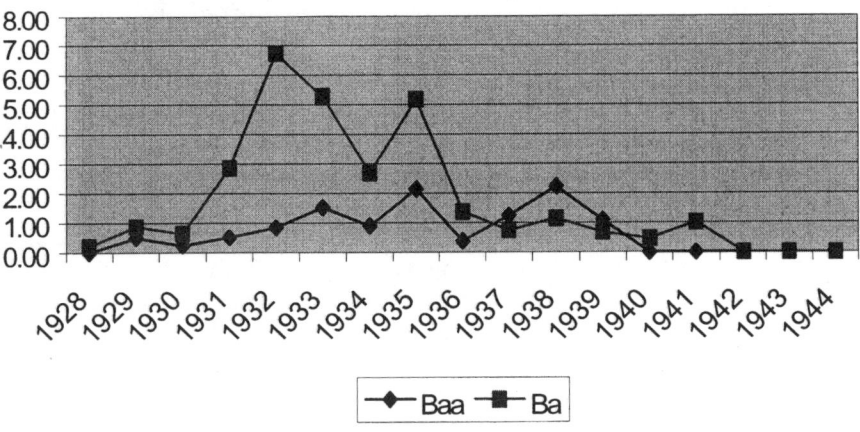

Leaving aside the question of whether there are significant bankruptcy costs, however, it is very unlikely that expected default costs alone could account for the sharp rise in the spread. As Figure 4 indicates, default rates on Baa bonds were relatively low during the Depression, peaking at just 1.5% in 1933.[14] This low default rate should not be surprising: Even though Baa is not the highest rating possible, it is nonetheless an investment-grade classification, a status achievable only if the likelihood of default is quite small.[15] It is also important to recognize that the bonds are long-term—the average maturity in Moody's sample is between twenty and thirty years—implying that the spread depends not only on the expected default probability in any given year, but rather on the expected average annual default probability over the life of the bond.[16] The low average annual default probabilities portrayed in Figure 4 sug-

14. I thank Richard Cantor for supplying me with the Moody's default-rate data.
15. To gain some perspective, the default rate on Aaa bonds was effectively zero during the Depression. Defaults were concentrated mainly among speculative (non-investment-grade) securities.
16. To get some sense of the significance of maturity for the spread, consider a discount bond that pays either 1.0 with probability $1 - \pi$ after T periods or 0.5 with probability π. Suppose further that investors are risk-neutral and that the riskless rate is fixed at $R > 1$. Then it is straightforward to show that the rate spread between the risky bond and riskless security may be expressed as $\pi/T \times 0.5$. Note that π is the cumulative default probability and that π/T is the annual average default probability. For $T = 20$, for example, an annual average default probability of 1.5%—a number well above the annual average for Baa-rated bonds—would generate a spread of only 75 basis points.

gests that expected defaults cannot come close to explaining 300–400-basis-point jump in the spread.[17]

One possibility is that the spread might have reflected the likelihood of a Baa-rated firm being reclassified into a higher default-rate category. However, the risk associated with non-investment-grade Ba bonds (the quality-level below Baa) appears too low to rationalize downgrade risk being a factor in the Baa spread. As Figure 4 illustrates, the Ba default rate peaked at 7% in 1932, before settling back to a low level by 1936. Annual default rates on Ba bonds of this magnitude do not appear able to raise expected default costs on Baa bonds sufficiently to explain the spread for the highest-rated Baa bonds, especially given that the probability of being reclassified from Baa to Ba was likely not huge.[18] Finally, note that the issue of ratings downgrades also cuts the other way: The measured spread may significantly understate the true rise in the spread to the extent that firms in distress were downgraded from Baa and thus dropped from the sample used to construct the average Baa rate.

What then accounts for the sharp rise in the spread over this period? Friedman and Schwartz argue that much of it reflected an increasing liquidity premium that was due to capital-constrained banks unloading their holdings of Baa bonds on the open market, especially in the wake of the banking crises and subsequent monetary tightening.[19] Apparently, the same Baa bonds intermediated by banks commanded a larger premium when floated on the open market. This suggests that the movements in the spread indeed reflected financial distress and, among other things, that the contraction in banking was indeed affecting real credit costs.

5.2 DIVIDENDS

The authors argue that firms on the whole greatly smoothed dividends throughout the Depression, suggesting an absence of financial distress. I agree that dividend behavior is an important issue, but question the

---

17. The idea that expected default costs explain little of the movement in the risk spread on corporate bonds is consistent with recent evidence. See, for example, Elton et al. (2001).
18. The increase in the probability of default from downgrade risk equals the probability of downgrade times the difference in the default rate between the higher and the lower risk class. Elton et al. show that the annual probability of a downgrade from Baa to Ba was only 5.4% over 1987–1996, the period when the corporate default rate was the highest since the time of the Depression. While this transition probability was surely higher in the Depression, it is safe to say that it was still considerably less than unity, particularly for the bonds in the Moody's sample (since the latter tends to drop bonds selling at a deep discount.)
19. Friedman and Schwartz (1963, p. 312) state: "Interest rates clearly show the effects of the banking crisis. . . . The yield on corporate bonds rose sharply, the yields on government bonds began to fall. The reason is clear. In their search for liquidity, banks and others were inclined first to dispose of their lower grade bonds."

authors' claim, for three basic reasons: (1) Though there was considerable smoothing in the early stages of the Depression, firms did cut dividends significantly after 1930. (2) A simple comparison of total dividends with total corporate profits significantly overstates the degree of dividend smoothing, due to an aggregation bias. Firms with positive profits, mainly large firms, accounted for most of the aggregate dividend payments; small and medium-sized firms that experienced substantial losses could not cut dividends below zero. (3) The residual dividend smoothing (mainly by large firms) may have in part reflected pressures from shareholders who themselves faced financial distress.

To gain some perspective, Table 3 reports the behavior of nominal dividends relative to nominal personal income. Consistent with conventional wisdom, a buildup of retained earnings over the late 1920s permitted corporations to keep dividends relatively stable between 1929 and 1930. After 1930, however, dividends dropped sharply not only in absolute terms, but also in comparison with the overall drop in personal income. In 1930, dividends were roughly 7.1% of total personal income. By 1933 the ratio drops by roughly 40%, to 4.3%. Thus, the aggregate evidence does suggest significant dividend cuts.

Why didn't dividends fall to zero? First, the aggregation bias is relevant. Even though total profits became negative after 1930, a significant fraction of firms continued to earn positive profits. Table 4, for example, shows that corporate income-tax payments remained positive throughout the Great Depression, suggesting that a core of firms were indeed earning money over this entire time period. Fabricant (1934) presents direct estimates of total earnings of corporations with non-negative profits along with total losses by firms with negative profits. As the Fabricant data make clear, the drop in aggregate profits over the period in part reflected a fraction of firms each year drifting from positive to negative profits. Since dividends are bounded below at zero, total dividends may drop less than proportionally to total profits simply in part due to aggre-

Table 3 CORPORATE DIVIDENDS AND PERSONAL INCOME

Year	Corporate dividends ($million)	Personal income ($million)	Ratio (%)
1929	5801	85,905	6.75
1930	5468	77,015	7.10
1931	4066	65,896	6.17
1932	2544	50,150	5.07
1933	2038	47,004	4.34

Table 4 CORPORATE TAXES, PROFITS, AND DIVIDENDS[a]

Year	Aggr. profits before taxes	Corp. taxes	Aggregate profits		Aggr. profits (Y > 0) −taxes −divs.
			Y > 0	Y < 0	
1929	9,990	1,369	13,841	−3,851	6,671
1930	3,697	842	7,987	−4,290	1,677
1931	−372	498	4,801	−5,173	237
1932	−2,309	385	2,800	−5,109	−129
1933	956	521	3,789	−2,833	1,230

[a]Millions of dollars.

gation bias (as opposed to everything being accounted for by individual firms actually smoothing dividends).

To gain some sense of the bias, I used the implied average corporate income-tax rate from the Fabricant data to construct estimates of earnings by corporations with positive profits.[20] Table 4 reports these estimates along with the difference between the after-tax earnings of these corporations and aggregate dividends. Note that throughout the Depression, (estimated) aggregate earnings by these corporations are sufficient to cover dividends, the one exception being a slight shortfall in 1932.[21] I don't mean to suggest that only firms with positive profits paid dividends, but rather that the bulk of dividend payments came from this group and not, as the authors imply, firms with highly negative earnings.

Indeed, according to Fabricant, it was mainly large firms with positive earnings that continued to pay dividends throughout the Depression.[22]

20. To construct the average tax rates I divided Fabricant's (1934) estimates of total corporate taxes (see his Table 1) by profits of corporations with positive earnings (see his Table 2). Since his data only go through 1932, I used for 1933 the same implied average tax rate as for 1932. The average tax rates I used accordingly for 1929–1933 are 9.89, 10.54, 10.37, 13.75, and 13.75. To then get the estimate of total profits for corporations with positive earnings I divided the national income and product accounts (NIPA) measure of corporate income taxes by the estimated average tax rates. Note that Fabricant's measures of total corporate income, dividends, and taxes differ a bit from the NIPA data, since the former do not eliminate double counting from cross-holdings of stock. Finally, my calculations do not adjust for inventory valuation adjustment, which implies that profits are understated somewhat for 1929–1932 and overstated somewhat for 1933.
21. Fabricant (1935) estimates that net saving of firms with positive profits in 1932 was $132 million, suggesting that a small portion of aggregate dividends was paid by firms making losses, but that on the whole firms with positive profits accounted for the bulk of dividend payments.
22. Examples of industries in which large firms were in a position to maintain a relatively steady flow of dividend payments include: food, tobacco, chemicals, public utilities, and communications.

The small and medium-sized firms that experienced heavy losses largely suspended dividend payments. A look at the disaggregated evidence, accordingly, suggests that firms in financial distress were indeed adjusting dividend behavior as one would expect.

Why didn't large companies reduce dividends to zero? First, the fact that these companies on average maintained positive profits throughout the Depression suggests that they were at least capable of making payouts without dipping into capital. Second, cutting dividends is not costless, especially during a period where shareholders have already experienced significant financial distress. Pressure to smooth consumption of liquidity-constrained shareholders may have affected dividend policy.

In sum, one cannot conclude, from the simple aggregate evidence on dividends and profits that the authors report, that financial constraints were unimportant.

5.3 JAPAN

The authors present some Japanese data from the time of the collapse of the Nikkei index to suggest that theories which emphasize asset prices as a source of variation in financial conditions were not likely at work during the Depression. Here I argue that scratching just a bit below the surface leads one to exactly the opposite conclusion. Again, the issue boils down to taking account of all the relevant heterogeneity.

The authors argue at the time of the decline in stock prices—from early 1990 to mid 1992—Japanese output did not drop significantly; and they conclude accordingly that the asset price collapse did not make a large impact on the economy. However, extending the sample period just a few years and disaggregating the data yields a quite different scenario. Figure 5 plots the behavior of four Japanese series over the period 1989:1 to 1995:4: real output, residential investment, nonresidential investment, and the sum of government purchases and net exports. Each series is detrended using the authors' procedure. Each variable is normalized to be 100 at the beginning of the stock-market downturn. Finally, the two vertical lines denote the beginning and end of the Nikkei collapse: 1990:1 and 1992:2, respectively.

Note first that in the midst of the crash residential investment drops precipitously. By late 1992 it is down 25% relative to trend and remains in this rough vicinity for the next three years. By late 1991, nonresidential investment also begins a sharp decline. It is 15% below trend by early 1993 and bottoms out at 25% below trend by 1994:1, remaining at this level for the next two years. The behavior of investment overall is entirely consistent with financial theories.

Figure 5 JAPANESE GDP AND ITS COMPONENTS: 1989:1–1995:4

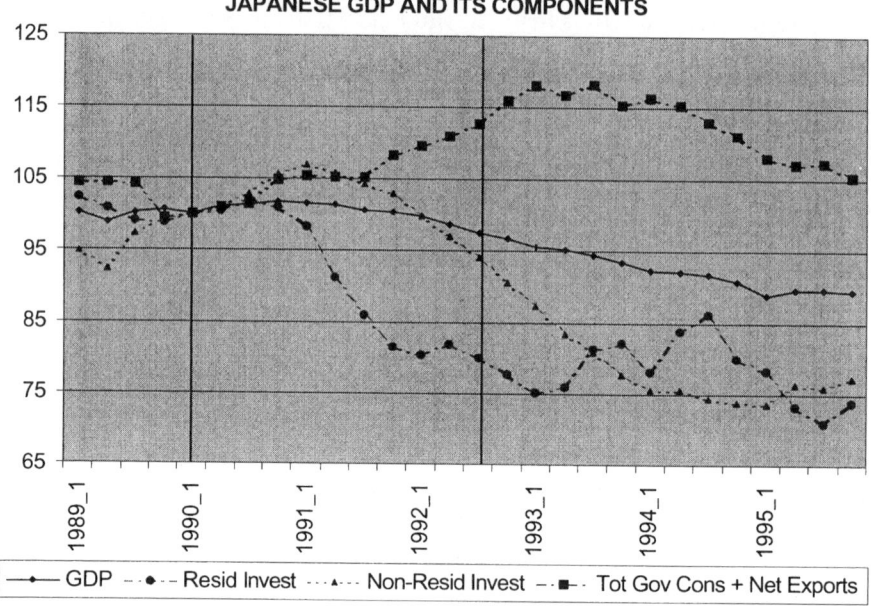

Given the investment collapse, why did Japanese output not fall more precipitously early on? Here it is important to account for a number of key differences from the Great Depression. First, in contrast to the United States during the 1930s, Japanese government spending rose significantly over the early 1990s, particularly public investment expenditures. Second, while U.S. monetary policy was constrained by the gold standard, depreciation of the yen over this time helped induce a rise in Japanese net exports. Figure 5 shows that the sum of government spending and net exports rose steadily from early 1990 to early 1993, reaching more than 15% above trend at this time. This additional source of stimulus—which did not arise in the Depression—helped moderate the overall impact of the contraction in domestic investment.

Finally, unlike the laissez-faire banking system in the United States during the 1930s, the Japanese banking system was heavily protected by public guarantees, which permitted lending to continue through the early 1990s, even though the collapse of both stock and land prices directly weakened bank balance sheets. By 1993, however, the severe problems in Japanese banking surfaced (see, e.g., Hoshi and Kashyap, 1999). Only at this point do significant constraints on banking activities begin. In contrast, U.S. banks during the Depression did not enjoy this period of protection from the initial financial crisis.

Once the banking problems were no longer contained, Japanese output began a steady contraction. By early 1993 output was 5% below trend, dropping to 10% below trend by the end of 1995. The stagnation continues, and many observers cite the weak financial system as a key factor.

The descriptive evidence I have just cited, of course, does not prove that financial factors were at work in Japan. But nor does the authors' simple evidence suggest otherwise. More systematic empirical work is required to resolve the issue.

6. Concluding Remarks

Elsewhere the authors have done interesting work on the Depression. Cole and Ohanian (2000) propose an interesting explanation of why the slump persisted for nearly six years after 1933, based on reduced competition induced by New Deal regulatory policies. The purpose of the current paper, however, is simply to try to dismiss monetary and financial theories of the 1929–1933 downturn, without offering a clear alternative to judge. In my opinion, the authors do not succeed.

It is critical, however, to develop a quantitative model to show that monetary and financial factors can indeed account for the key features of the Depression. I would guess that such a framework would likely have to incorporate all of the following features: (1) some form of nominal rigidity, and possibly also a real labor-market rigidity, to permit a significant contraction in aggregate demand in conjunction with a relatively small movement in real wages; (2) a central bank constrained by a gold standard; and (3) frictions in the credit market that can disrupt spending by households and small and medium-sized firms. Perhaps one new lesson from this discussion for modern business-cycle theories that feature monetary and financial factors is that more emphasis should be placed on how credit-market frictions may constrain household spending, given the key role of the collapse of consumer demand in the early stages of the Depression.

REFERENCES

Bernanke, B. (1983). Non-monetary effects of the financial crisis in the propagation of the Great Depression. *American Economic Review* 73(3):257–276.
———, and H. James. (1991). The gold standard, deflation and financial crises: An international comparison. In *Financial Markets and Financial Crises*, R. G. Hubbard (ed.). Chicago: University of Chicago Press, pp. 33–68.

———, and C. S. Lown. (1991). The credit crunch. *Brookings Papers on Economic Activity*, 2, 205–39.

Bordo, M., C. Erceg, and C. Evans. (2000). *American Economic Review*, forthcoming.

Calomiris, C. W., and B. Wilson. (1998). Bank capital and portfolio management: The 1930s capital crunch and scramble to shed risk. Cambridge, MA: National Bureau of Economic Research. NBER Working Paper 6649.

Campa, J. M. (1990). Exchange rates and economic recovery in the 1930s: An extension to Latin America. *Journal of Economic History* 50(September):677–682.

Choudri, E. U., and L. A. Kochin. (1980). The exchange rate and the international transmission of business cycle disturbances. *Journal of Money, Credit and Banking* 12(November):565–574.

Cole, H., and L. Ohanian. (2000). New Deal policies and the persistence of the Great Depression: A general equilibrium analysis. Federal Reserve Bank of Minneapolis. Mimeo.

Eichengreen, B. (1992). *Golden Fetters: The Gold Standard and the Great Depression, 1919–39*. New York: Oxford University Press.

Elton, E., M. Gruber, D. Agrawal, and C. Mann. (2001). Explaining the rate spread on corporate bonds. *Journal of Finance*, February.

Fabricant, S. (1934). Recent Corporate Profits in the United States. National Bureau of Economic Research. Bulletin 50.

———. (1935). Profits, losses and business assets, 1929–34. National Bureau of Economic Research. Bulletin 55.

Friedman, M., and A. J. Schwartz. (1963). *A Monetary History of the United States, 1867–1960*. Princeton: Princeton University Press.

Hamilton, J. (1987). Monetary factors in the Great Depression. *Journal of Monetary Economics*, 19(2):145–170.

Hoshi, T., and A. Kashyap. (1999). The Japanese banking crisis. In *NBER Macroeconomics Annual*, B. Bernanke and J. Rotemberg (eds.). Cambridge, MA: The MIT Press, pp. 129–201.

Kindelberger, C. (1986). *The World in Depression: 1929–39*. Berkeley: University of California Press.

Mishkin, F. S. (1978). The household balance sheet and the Great Depression. *Journal of Economic History* 38(4):918–937.

Olney, M. (1999). Avoiding default: The role of credit in the consumption collapse of 1930. *Quarterly Journal of Economics* 114(1):319–335.

Romer, C. (1993). The nation in depression. *Journal of Economic Perspectives* 7(2):19–39.

Temin, P. (1989). *Lessons from the Great Depression*. Cambridge, MA: The MIT Press.

Discussion

Hal Cole and Lee Ohanian began by replying to the discussants. There was agreement about the need for general equilibrium modeling of the Depression. In response to Mark Gertler, Cole agreed that small firms faced severe financial distress; but if many large firms were solvent, why didn't they take over the small firms, their markets, or both? In response to Michael Bordo, Ohanian noted that the small effects found by their wage-rigidity model were not due to a lack of intrinsic persistence in the model, but rather resulted from partial-equilibrium employment effects being partially undone by general equilibrium effects. Ohanian also re-emphasized the problems with 1930s wage data, citing Stanley Lebergott on the potential importance of compositional effects. Specifically, if low-paid workers (or employees of small firms, which paid lower wages) were more likely to lose their jobs, then aggregate wage data overstate the increase in the real wage of the typical worker.

Beginning the general discussion, Rick Mishkin argued for a broader interpretation of financial shocks, which would take into account the deterioration of balance sheets as well as banking problems. To the extent that households and firms were in financial distress in the 1930s, increased moral hazard in credit relationships would have reduced their access to credit. Cole argued that the Japanese experience of the 1990s, following the boom and bust in Japanese asset prices, suggests that a sustained slowdown in growth, rather than a collapse of output, is the likely result of balance-sheet problems. Ben Friedman criticized the assumption of the paper that the importance of bank credit to the economy could be measured by the share of banking in value added; he argued that credit may play an essential role that is not well captured by a smooth neoclassical production function. Diego Comin noted that total factor productivity declined sharply during the Depression, a fact that might be construed in support of a real-side interpretation of the collapse.

Robert Gordon emphasized the difficulty of disentangling cause and effect in an environment when all sectors of the economy are contracting simultaneously; he argued for more use of cross-national comparisons to identify causal factors. He also pointed out that, even though inventories are a small part of the economy, changes in inventory investment play a large role in fluctuations. The fact that banks finance a large portion of inventories suggests another possible channel of influence from banks to the real economy. On the cross-state evidence on bank failures, Gordon noted that "this is one economy"; that is, we would not necessarily expect the severity of the Depression to differ greatly across states even if the incidence of bank failures differed geographically.

Susanto Basu suggested an alternative banking model in which firms have access to two technologies, one that uses financial intermediation and is relatively efficient and one that does not use intermediation and is less efficient. If a firm is unable to get a loan, it uses the second technology. In this model, some part of the observed TFP decline reflects the loss of financial services; further, firms forced to use the less efficient technology will want less capital and may choose to liquidate part of the firm. Pierre Gourinchas cautioned that general equilibrium models of the Depression might not be able to employ the usual technique of approximating around the steady state, as the deviations from the steady state in the 1930s were presumably large and nonlinearities might be quite important. Ohanian noted that the relatively simple models used in their paper permitted exact solution and did not require approximations around the steady state.

Michael Woodford pointed out that the paper's sticky-wage model has the highly counterfactual implication that unemployment is zero, as workers displaced in the sticky-wage sector find work in the flexible-wage sector. He also noted that the effects of higher real wages on employment depend critically on the elasticity of marginal product with respect to employment. It may be that elasticity is low in the short run (that is, the labor demand curve is flat) due to factors such as variable capital utilization; if so, relatively small changes in real wages could have large employment effects.

Ben Bernanke criticized the paper for ignoring cross-country evidence. According to studies encompassing 20–30 countries, those countries that left gold earlier (and thus were able to reflate their money supplies and price levels) did better than those that remained on gold. There is also some cross-country evidence in favor of the banking hypothesis, e.g., in his work with Harold James. Bernanke also objected to the modeling of the effects of banking crises; instead of putting financial services in the production function, he prefers an approach that allows for increased agency costs of lending when financial conditions deteriorate. Commenting further on the model of banking, he pointed out that intermediation services affect spending as well as production; for example, if buffer-stock consumers face increased unemployment risk while simultaneously losing access to credit, they are likely to sharply reduce their spending. If financial distress affects spending more than production, the lack of correlation between bank failures and production at the state level is not surprising, as already suggested by Bob Gordon; for example, if financial distress reduces the demand for automobiles in Alabama, output in Michigan rather than in Alabama will be most affected. Finally, Bernanke noted several differences between the experiences of 1920–1921 and 1929–1933; these included (1) the fact that the 1920–1921 deflation, unlike the later deflation, followed a sharp inflation that was widely expected to be temporary and (2) institutional changes in labor markets that reduced wage flexibility and increased labor hoarding in the latter episode.

Francisco Rodríguez and Dani Rodrik
UNIVERSITY OF MARYLAND AND HARVARD UNIVERSITY

Trade Policy and Economic Growth: A Skeptic's Guide to the Cross-National Evidence

It isn't what we don't know that kills us. It's what we know that ain't so.
—Mark Twain

1. Introduction

Do countries with lower barriers to international trade experience faster economic progress? Few questions have been more vigorously debated in the history of economic thought, and none is more central to the vast literature on trade and development.

The prevailing view in policy circles in North America and Europe is that recent economic history provides a conclusive answer in the affirmative. Multilateral institutions such as the World Bank, the IMF, and the OECD regularly promulgate advice predicated on the belief that openness generates predictable and positive consequences for growth. A recent report by the OECD (1998, p. 36) states: "More open and outward-oriented economies consistently outperform countries with restrictive trade and [foreign] investment regimes." According to the IMF (1997, p.

We thank Dan Ben-David, Sebastian Edwards, Jeffrey Frankel, David Romer, Jeffrey Sachs, and Andrew Warner for generously sharing their data with us. We are particularly grateful to Ben-David, Frankel, Romer, Sachs, Warner, and Romain Wacziarg for helpful email exchanges. We have benefited greatly from discussions in seminars at the University of California at Berkeley, University of Maryland, University of Miami, University of Michigan, MIT, the Inter-American Development Bank, Princeton, Yale, IMF, IESA, and the NBER. We also thank Ben Bernanke, Roger Betancourt, Allan Drazen, Gene Grossman, Ann Harrison, Chang-Tai Hsieh, Doug Irwin, Chad Jones, Frank Levy, Douglas Irwin, Rick Mishkin, Arvind Panagariya, Ken Rogoff, James Tybout, and Eduardo Zambrano for helpful comments, Vladimir Kliouev for excellent research assistance, and the Weatherhead Center for International Affairs at Harvard for partial financial support.

84): "Policies toward foreign trade are among the more important factors promoting economic growth and convergence in developing countries."

This view is widespread in the economics profession as well. Krueger (1998, p. 1513), for example, judges that it is straightforward to demonstrate empirically the superior growth performance of countries with "outer-oriented" trade strategies. According to Stiglitz (1998, p. 36), "[m]ost specifications of empirical growth regressions find that some indicator of external openness—whether trade ratios or indices or price distortions or average tariff level—is strongly associated with per-capita income growth." According to Fischer (2000), "[i]ntegration into the world economy is the best way for countries to grow."

Such statements notwithstanding, if there is an inverse relationship between trade barriers and economic growth, it is not one that immediately stands out in the data. See for example Figure 1. The figure displays the (partial) associations over 1975–1994 between the growth rate of per capita GDP and two measures of trade restrictions. The first measure is an average tariff rate, calculated by dividing total import duties by the volume of imports. The second is a coverage ratio for nontariff barriers to trade.[1] The figures show the relationship between these measures and growth after controlling for levels of initial income and secondary education. In both cases, the slope of the relationship is only slightly negative and nowhere near statistical significance. This finding is not atypical. Simple measures of trade barriers tend not to enter significantly in well-specified growth regressions, regardless of time periods, subsamples, or the conditioning variables employed.

Of course, neither of the two measures used above is a perfect indicator of trade restrictions. Simple tariff averages underweight high tariff rates because the corresponding import levels tend to be low. Such averages are also poor proxies for overall trade restrictions when tariff and nontariff barriers are substitutes. As for the nontariff coverage ratios, they do not do a good job of discriminating between barriers that are highly restrictive and barriers with little effect. And conceptual flaws aside, both indicators are clearly measured with some error (due to smuggling, weaknesses in the underlying data, coding problems, etc.).

In part because of concerns related to data quality, the recent literature on openness and growth has resorted to more creative empirical strategies. These strategies include: (1) constructing alternative indicators of openness (Dollar, 1992; Sachs and Warner, 1995); (2) testing robustness by using a wide range of measures of openness, including subjective indica-

---

1. Data for the first measure come from World Bank (1998). The second is taken from Barro and Lee (1994), and is based on UNCTAD compilations.

Figure 1 PARTIAL ASSOCIATION BETWEEN GROWTH AND DIRECT MEASURES OF TRADE RESTRICTIONS

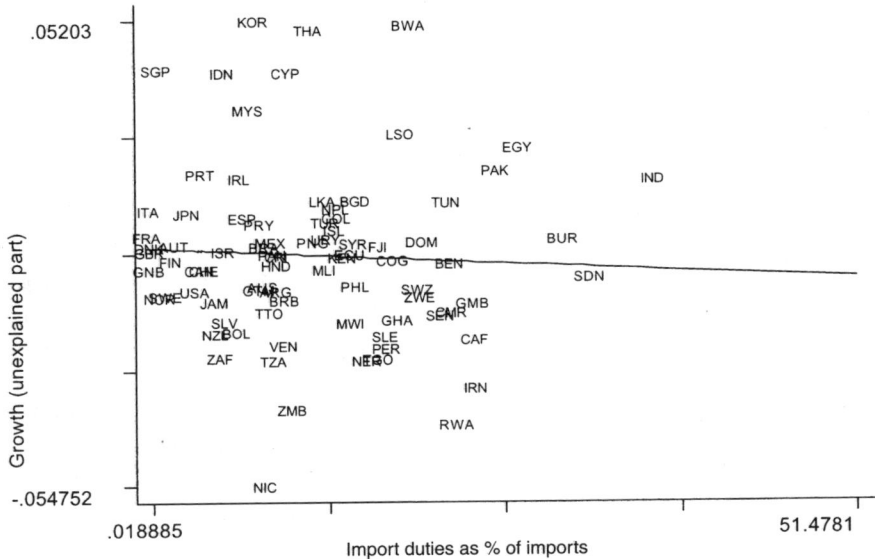

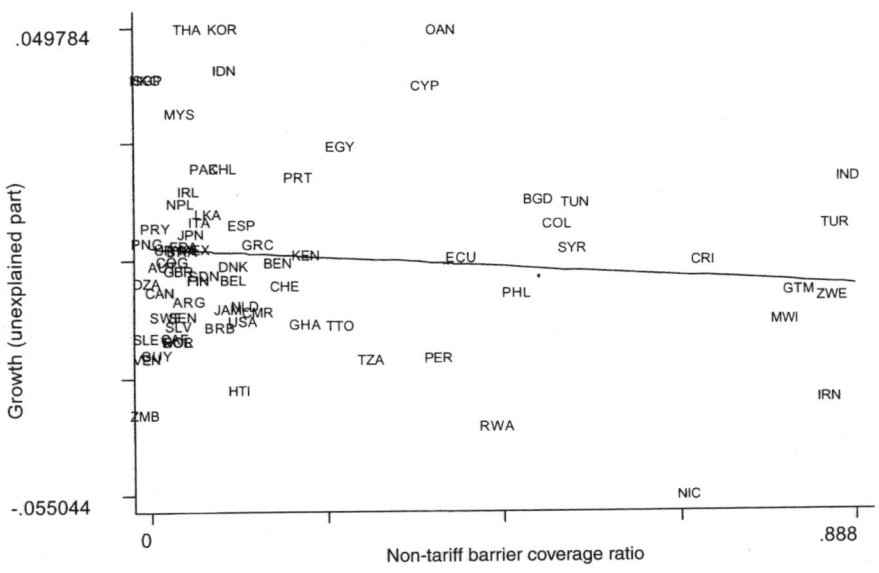

tors (Edwards, 1992, 1998); and (3) comparing convergence experience among groups of liberalizing and nonliberalizing countries (Ben-David, 1993). This recent round of empirical research is generally credited with having yielded stronger and more convincing results on the beneficial consequences of openness than the previous, largely case-based literature. Indeed, the cumulative evidence that has emerged from such studies provides the foundation for the previously noted consensus on the growth-promoting effects of trade openness. The frequency with which these studies are cited in international economics textbooks and in policy discussions is one indicator of the influence that they have exerted.

Our goal in this paper is to scrutinize this new generation of research. We do so by focusing on what the existing literature has to say on the following question: *Do countries with lower policy-induced barriers to international trade grow faster, once other relevant country characteristics are controlled for?* We take this to be the central question of policy relevance in this area. To the extent that the empirical literature demonstrates a positive causal link from openness to growth, the main operational implication is that governments should dismantle their barriers to trade. Therefore, it is critical to ask how well the evidence supports the presumption that doing so would raise growth rates.

Note that this question differs from an alternative one we could have asked: *Does international trade raise growth rates of income?* This is a related, but conceptually distinct question. Trade policies do affect the volume of trade, of course. But there is no strong reason to expect their effect on growth to be quantitatively (or even qualitatively) similar to the consequences of changes in trade volumes that arise from, say, reductions in transport costs or increases in world demand. To the extent that trade restrictions represent policy responses to real or perceived market imperfections or, at the other extreme, are mechanisms for rent extraction, they will work differently from natural or geographical barriers to trade and other exogenous determinants. Frankel and Romer (1999) recognize this point in their recent paper on the relationship between trade volumes and income levels. These authors use the geographical component of trade volumes as an instrument to identify the effects of trade on income levels. They appropriately caution that their results cannot be directly applied to the effects of trade policies.

From an operational standpoint, it is clear that the relevant question is the one having to do with the consequences of trade *policies* rather than trade *volumes*. Hence we focus on the recent empirical literature that attempts to measure the effect of trade policies. Our main finding is that this literature is largely uninformative regarding the question we posed above. There is a significant gap between the message that the consumers of this literature have derived and the facts that the literature has actually demonstrated. The gap emerges from a number of factors. In many cases, the indicators of openness used by researchers are problematic as measures of trade barriers or are highly correlated with other sources of poor economic performance. In other cases, the empirical strategies used to ascertain the link between trade policy and growth have serious shortcomings, the removal of which results in significantly weaker findings.

The literature on openness and growth through the late 1980s was usefully surveyed in a paper by Edwards (1993). This survey covered detailed multicountry analyses (such as Little, Scitovsky, and Scott, 1970, and Balassa, 1971) as well as cross-country econometric studies (such as Feder, 1983, Balassa, 1985, and Esfahani, 1991). Most of the cross-national econometric research that was available up to that point focused on the relationship between exports and growth, and not on trade policy and growth. Edwards's evaluation of this literature was largely negative (1993, p. 1389):

> [M]uch of the cross-country regression-based studies have been plagued by empirical and conceptual shortcomings. The theoretical frameworks used have been increasingly simplistic, failing to address important questions such as the exact mechanism through which export expansion affects GDP growth, and ignoring potential determinants of growth such as educational attainment. Also, many papers have been characterized by a lack of care in dealing with issues related to endogeneity and measurement errors. All of this has resulted, in many cases, in unconvincing results whose fragility has been exposed by subsequent work.

Edwards argued that such weaknesses had reduced the policy impact of the cross-national econometric research covered in his review.

Our paper picks up where Edwards's survey left off. We focus on a number of empirical papers that either were not included in or have appeared since that survey. Judging by the number of citations in publications by governmental and multilateral institutions and in textbooks, this recent round of empirical research has been considerably more influential in policy and academic circles.[2] Our detailed analysis covers the

2. We gave examples of citations from international institutions above. Here are some examples from recent textbooks. Yarbrough and Yarbrough (2000, p. 19) write "[o]n the trade-growth connection, the empirical evidence is clear that countries with open markets experience faster growth," citing Edwards (1998). Caves, Frankel, and Jones (1999, pp. 256–257) warn that "[r]esearch testing this proposition is not unanimous" but then continue to say "productivity growth does seem to increase with openness to the international economy and freedom from price and allocative distortions in the domestic econ-

four papers that are probably the best known in the field: Dollar (1992), Sachs and Warner (1995), Ben-David (1993), and Edwards (1998). We also include an analysis of Frankel and Romer (1999), and shorter discussions of Lee (1993), Harrison (1996), and Wacziarg (1998).

A few words about the selection of papers. The paper by Dollar (1992) was not reviewed in Edwards's survey, perhaps because it had only recently been published. We include it here because it is, by our count, the most heavily cited empirical paper on the link between openness and growth. Sachs and Warner (1995) is a close second, and the index of openness constructed therein has now been widely used in the cross-national research on growth.[3] The other two papers are also well known, but in these cases our decision was based less on citation counts than on the fact that they are representative of different types of methodologies. Ben-David (1993) considers income convergence in countries that have integrated with each other (such as the European Community countries). Edwards (1998) undertakes a robustness analysis using a wide range of trade-policy indicators, including some subjective indicators. Some of the other recent studies on the relationship between trade policy and growth will be discussed in the penultimate section of the paper.

Our bottom line is that the nature of the relationship between trade policy and economic growth remains very much an open question. The issue is far from having been settled on empirical grounds. We are in fact skeptical that there is a general, unambiguous relationship between trade openness and growth waiting to be discovered. We suspect that the relationship is a contingent one, dependent on a host of country and external characteristics. Research aimed at ascertaining the circumstances under which open trade policies are conducive to growth (as well as those under which they may not be) and at scrutinizing the channels through which trade policies influence economic performance is likely to prove more productive.

---

omy," citing Sachs and Warner (1995) and Dollar (1992). Husted and Melvin (1997) cite Ben-David (1993) in support of the FPE theorem (p. 111), and Sachs and Warner (1995) in support of the statement that "[o]nly a few countries have followed outward-oriented development strategies for extensive periods of time, but those that have done so have been very successful" (p. 287). Krugman and Obstfeld (1997, 260) write that by the late 1980s "[s]tatistical evidence appeared to suggest that developing countries that followed relatively free trade policies had on average grown more rapidly than those that followed protectionist policies (although this statistical evidence has been challenged by some economists)."

3. From its date of publication, Dollar's paper has been cited at least 92 times, according to the *Social Science Citations Index*. Sachs and Warner (1995) is a close second, with 81 citations. Edwards (1992), Ben-David (1993), and Lee (1993) round off the list, with 57, 38, and 17 citations, respectively.

Finally, it is worthwhile reminding the reader that growth and welfare are not the same thing. Trade policies can have positive effects on welfare without affecting the rate of economic growth. Conversely, even if policies that restrict international trade were to reduce economic growth, it does not follow that they would necessarily reduce the level of welfare. Negative coefficients on policy variables in growth regressions are commonly interpreted as indicating that the policies in question are normatively undesirable. Strictly speaking, such inferences are invalid.[4] Our paper centers on the relationship between trade policy and growth because this is the issue that has received the most attention in the existing literature. We caution the reader that the welfare implications of empirical results regarding this link (be they positive or negative) must be treated with caution.

The outline of this paper is as follows. We begin with a conceptual overview of the issues relating to openness and growth. We then turn to an in-depth examination of each of the four papers mentioned previously (Dollar, 1992; Sachs and Warner, 1995; Edwards, 1998; and Ben-David 1993), followed by a section on Frankel and Romer (1999). The penultimate section discusses briefly three other papers (Lee, 1993; Harrison, 1996; and Wacziarg 1998). We offer some final thoughts in the concluding section.

2. Conceptual Issues

Think of a small economy that takes world prices of tradable goods as given. What is the relationship between trade restrictions and real GDP in such an economy? The modern theory of trade policy as it applies to such a country can be summarized in the following three propositions:

1. In static models with no market imperfections and other pre-existing distortions, the effect of a trade restriction is to reduce the level of real GDP at world prices. In the presence of market failures such as externalities, trade restrictions *may* increase real GDP (although they are hardly ever the first-best means of doing so).
2. In standard models with exogenous technological change and diminishing returns to reproducible factors of production (e.g., the neo-

---

4. Some of the main problems with economic growth as a measure of welfare are that: (1) the empirically identifiable effect of policies on rates of growth—especially over short intervals—could be different from their effect on levels of income; (2) levels of per capita income may not be good indicators of welfare because they do not capture the distribution of income or the level of access to primary goods and basic capabilities; and (3) high growth rates could be associated with suboptimally low levels of present consumption.

classical model of growth), a trade restriction has no effect on the long-run (steady-state) rate of growth of output.[5] This is true regardless of the existence of market imperfections. However, there may be growth effects during the transition to the steady state. (These transitional effects may be positive or negative, depending on how the long-run level of output is affected by the trade restriction.)

3. In models of endogenous growth generated by nondiminishing returns to reproducible factors of production or by learning-by-doing and other forms of endogenous technological change, the presumption is that lower trade restrictions boost output growth in the world economy as a whole. But a subset of countries may experience diminished growth, depending on their initial factor endowments and levels of technological development.

Taken together, these points imply that there should be no theoretical presumption in favor of finding an unambiguous, negative relationship between trade barriers and growth rates in the types of cross-national data sets typically analyzed.[6] The main complications are twofold. First, in the presence of certain market failures, such as positive production externalities in import-competing sectors, the long-run levels of GDP (measured at world prices) can be higher with trade restrictions than without. In such cases, data sets covering relatively short time spans will reveal a positive (partial) association between trade restrictions and the growth of output along the path of convergence to the new steady state. Second, under conditions of endogenous growth, trade restrictions may also be associated with higher growth rates of output whenever the restrictions promote technologically more dynamic sectors over others. In dynamic models, moreover, an increase in the growth rate of output is neither a necessary nor a sufficient condition for an improvement in *welfare*.

Since endogenous-growth models are often thought to have provided the missing theoretical link between trade openness and long-run growth, it is useful to spend a moment on why such models in fact provide an ambiguous answer. As emphasized by Grossman and Helpman (1991), the general answer to the question "Does trade promote

5. Strictly speaking, this statement is true only when the marginal product of the reproducible factors ("capital") tends to zero in the limit. If this marginal product is bounded below by a sufficiently large positive constant, trade policies can have an effect on long-run growth rates, similar to their effect in the more recent endogenous growth models (point 3 below). See the discussion in Srinivasan (1997).

6. See Buffie (1998) for an extensive theoretical discussion of the issues from the perspective of developing countries.

innovation in a small open economy?" is "It depends."[7] In particular, the answer depends on whether the forces of comparative advantage push the economy's resources in the direction of activities that generate long-run growth (via externalities in research and development, expanding product variety, upgrading product quality, and so on) or divert them from such activities. Grossman and Helpman (1991), Feenstra (1990), Matsuyama (1992), and others have worked out examples where a country that is behind in technological development can be driven by trade to specialize in traditional goods and experience a reduction in its long-run rate of growth. Such models are in fact formalizations of some very old arguments about infant industries and about the need for temporary protection to catch up with more advanced countries.

The issues can be clarified with the help of a simple model of a small open economy with learning-by-doing. The model is a simplified version of that in Matsuyama (1992), except that we analyze the growth implications of varying the import tariff, rather than simply comparing free trade with autarky. The economy is assumed to have two sectors, agriculture (a) and manufacturing (m), with the latter subject to learning-by-doing that is external to individual firms in the sector but internal to manufacturing as a whole. Let labor be the only mobile factor between the two sectors, and normalize the economy's labor endowment to unity. We can then write the production functions of the manufacturing and agricultural sectors, respectively, as

$$X_t^m = M_t n_t^\alpha,$$
$$X_t^a = A(1 - n_t)^\alpha,$$

where n_t stands for the labor force in manufacturing, α is the share of labor in value added in the two sectors (assumed to be identical for simplicity), and t is a time subscript. The productivity coefficient in manufacturing, M_t, is a state variable evolving according to

$$\dot{M}_t = \delta X_t^m,$$

where an overdot represents a time derivative and δ captures the strength of the learning effect.

We assume the economy has an initial comparative disadvantage in manufacturing, and normalize the relative price of manufactures on world markets to unity. If the ad valorem import tariff on manufactures is τ, the domestic relative price of manufactured goods becomes $1 + \tau$.

---

7. This is a slight paraphrase of Grossman and Helpman (1991, p. 152).

Instantaneous equilibrium in the labor market requires the equality of value marginal products of labor in the two sectors:

$$A(1 - n_t)^{\alpha-1} = (1 + \tau)M_t n_t^{\alpha-1}.$$

It can be checked that an increase in the import tariff has the effect of allocating more of the economy's labor to the manufacturing sector:

$$\frac{dn_t}{d\tau} > 0.$$

Further, for a constant level of τ, n_t evolves according to

$$\hat{n}_t = \frac{\delta}{1 - \alpha}(1 - n_t)n_t^\alpha,$$

where ^ denotes proportional changes.

Let Y_t denote the value of output in the economy evaluated at world prices:

$$Y_t = M_t n_t^\alpha + A(1 - n_t)^\alpha.$$

Then the instantaneous rate of growth of output at world prices can be expressed as follows:

$$\hat{Y}_t = \delta\left(\lambda_t + \frac{\alpha}{1 - \alpha}(\lambda_t - n_t)\right)n_t^\alpha,$$

where λ_t is the share of manufacturing output in total output when both are expressed at world prices (i.e., $\lambda_t = X_t^m/Y_t$).

Consider first the case when $\tau = 0$. In this case, it can be checked that $\lambda_t = n_t$ and the expression for the instantaneous growth rate of output simplifies to $\hat{Y}_t = \delta\lambda_t n_t^\alpha$, which is strictly positive whenever $n_t > 0$. Growth arises from the dynamic effects of learning, and is faster the larger the manufacturing base n_t. A small tariff would have a positive effect on growth on account of this channel because it would enlarge the manufacturing sector (raise n_t).

When $\tau > 0$, the manufacturing share of output at world prices is less than the labor share in manufacturing, and $\lambda_t < n_t$. Now the second term in the expression for $\hat{Y}_t$ is negative. The intuition is as follows. The tariff imposes a production-side distortion in the allocation of the economy's resources. For any given gap between λ_t and n_t, the productive efficiency cost of this distortion rises as manufacturing output (the base of the distortion) gets larger.

Figure 2 GROWTH RATES OF GDP AT WORLD PRICES

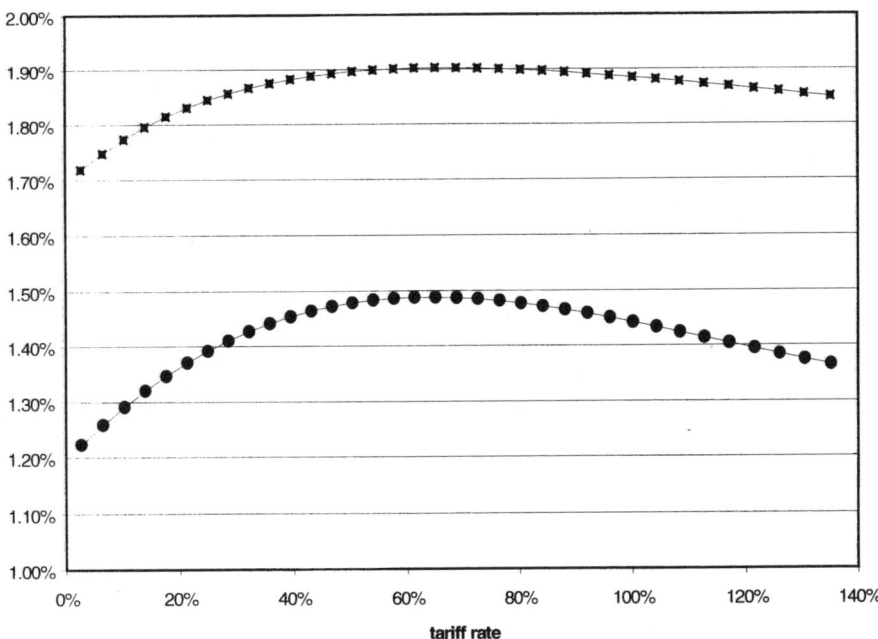

Hence the tariff exerts two contradictory effects on growth. By pulling resources into the manufacturing sector, it enlarges the scope for dynamic scale benefits, thereby increasing growth. But it also imposes a static efficiency loss, the cost of which rises over time as the manufacturing sector becomes larger.[8] Figure 2 shows the relationship between the tariff and the rate of growth of output (at world prices) for a particular parameterization of this model. Two curves are shown, one for the instantaneous rate of growth (based on the expression above), and the other for the average growth rate over a twenty-year horizon [calculated as $\frac{1}{20}(\ln Y_{20} - \ln Y_0)$]. In both cases, growth increases in τ until a critical level, and then diminishes in τ. This pattern is, however, by no means

8. We emphasize once again that these results on the growth of *output* do not translate directly into welfare consequences. In this particular model, the *level* effect of a tariff distortion also has to be taken into account before a judgment on welfare can be passed. Hence it is possible for welfare to be reduced (raised) even though the growth rate of output is permanently higher (lower).

general, and other types of results can be obtained under different parameterizations.

The model clarifies a number of issues. First, it shows that it is relatively straightforward to write a well-specified model that generates the conclusions that many opponents of trade openness have espoused—namely, that free trade can be detrimental to some countries' economic prospects, especially when these countries are lagging in technological development and have an initial comparative advantage in "nondynamic" sectors. More broadly, the model illustrates that there is no determinate theoretical link between trade protection and growth once real-world phenomena such as learning, technological change, and market imperfections (here captured by a learning-by-doing externality) are taken into account. Third, it highlights the exact sense in which trade restrictions distort market outcomes. A trade barrier has resource-allocation effects because it alters a *domestic* price ratio: it raises the domestic price of import-competing activities relative to the domestic price of exportables, and hence introduces a wedge between the domestic relative-price ratio and the opportunity costs reflected in relative border prices.[9] While this point is obvious, it bears repeating, as some of the empirical work reviewed below interprets openness in a very different manner.

3. David Dollar (1992)

As mentioned previously, the paper by Dollar (1992) is one of the most heavily cited studies on the relationship between openness and growth. The principal contribution of Dollar's paper lies in the construction of two separate indices, which Dollar demonstrates are each negatively correlated with growth over the 1976–1985 period in a sample of 95 developing countries. The two indices are an "index of real exchange-rate distortion" and an "index of real exchange-rate variability" (henceforth DISTORTION and VARIABILITY). These indices relate to "outward orientation," as understood by Dollar (1992, p. 524), in the following way:

> Outward orientation generally means a combination of two factors: first, the level of protection, especially for inputs into the production process, is

---

9. Some authors have stressed the effects that the high levels of discretion associated with trade policies can have on rent seeking and thus on economic performance (Krueger, 1974; Bhagwati, 1982). These effects go beyond the direct impact on resource allocation that we discuss. They are however related more directly to the discretionary nature of policies than to their effect on the economy's openness. Discretionary export promotion policies—which will make an economy more open—should in principle be just as conducive to rent seeking as protectionist policies.

relatively low (resulting in a sustainable level of the real exchange rate that is favorable to exporters); and second, there is relatively little variability in the real exchange rate, so that incentives are consistent over time.

We shall argue that DISTORTION has serious conceptual flaws as a measure of trade restrictions, and is in any case not a robust correlate of growth, while VARIABILITY, which appears to be robust, is a measure of instability more than anything else.

In order to implement his approach, Dollar uses data from Summers and Heston (1988, Mark 4.0) on comparative price levels. Their work compares prices of an identical basket of consumption goods across countries. Hence, letting the United States be the benchmark country, these data provide estimates of each country i's price level (RPL_i) relative to the United States: $RPL_i = 100 \times P_i/(e_i P_{US})$, where P_i and P_{US} are the respective consumption price indices, and e_i is the nominal exchange rate of country i against the U.S. dollar (in units of home currency per dollar).[10] Since Dollar is interested in the prices of tradable goods only, he attempts to purge the effect of systematic differences arising from the presence of nontradables. To do this, he regresses RPL_i on the level and square of GDP per capita and on regional dummies for Latin America and Africa, as well as year dummies. Let the predicted value from this regression be denoted $\widehat{RPL}_i$. Dollar's index DISTORTION is $RPL_i/\widehat{RPL}_i$, averaged over the ten-year period 1976–1985. VARIABILITY is in turn calculated by taking the coefficient of variation of the annual observations of $RPL_i/\widehat{RPL}_i$ for each country over the same period.

Dollar interprets the variation in the values of DISTORTION across countries as capturing cross-national differences in the restrictiveness of trade policy. He states: "the index derived here measures the extent to which the real exchange rate is distorted away from its free-trade level by the trade regime" and "a country sustaining a high price level over many years would clearly have to be a country with a relatively large amount of protection" (Dollar 1992, p. 524). Since this type of claim is often made in other work as well,[11] we shall spend some time on it before reviewing Dollar's empirical results. We will show that a comparison of price indices for tradables is informative about levels of trade protection only under very restrictive conditions that are unlikely to hold in practice.

---

10. Our notation differs from Dollar's (1992). In particular, the exchange rate is defined differently.
11. For example, in Bhalla and Lau (1992), whose index is also used in Harrison (1996). We will discuss Harrison's paper in the penultimate section.

3.1 TRADE POLICIES AND PRICE LEVELS

We will not discuss further Dollar's method for purging the component of nontradable-goods prices that is systematically related to income and other characteristics.[12] Assuming the method is successful, the DISTORTION measure approximates (up to a random error term) the price of a country's tradables relative to the United States. Letting P^T stand for the price index for tradables and neglecting the error, the DISTORTION index for country i can then be expressed as $P_i^T/(e_i P_{US}^T)$.

Let us, without loss of generality, fix the price level of tradables in the United States, P_{US}^T, and assume that free trade prevails there. The question is under what conditions trade restrictions will be associated with higher levels of $P_i^T/(e_i P_{US}^T)$. Obviously, the answer depends on the effect of the restrictions on P_i^T (and possibly on e_i).

Note that P_i^T is an aggregate price index derived from the domestic prices of two types of tradables: import-competing goods and exportables. Hence P_i^T can be expressed as a linearly homogenous function of the form

$$P_i^T = \pi(p_i^m, p_i^x),$$

where p_i^m and p_i^x are the domestic prices of import-competing goods and exportables, respectively. Since Summers–Heston price levels are estimated for an identical basket of goods, the price-index function $\pi(\cdot)$ applies equally to the United States:

$$P_{US}^T = \pi(p_{US}^m, p_{US}^x).$$

Next, define t_i^m and t_i^x as the ad valorem equivalent of import restrictions and export restrictions, respectively. Assume that the law of one price holds (we shall relax this below). Then, $p_i^m = e_i p_{US}^m (1 + t_i^m)$ and $p_i^x = e_i p_{US}^x/(1 + t_i^x)$. Consequently, the domestic price of tradables relative to U.S. prices can be expressed as

$$\frac{P_i^T}{e_i P_{US}^T} = \frac{\pi(P_{US}^m(1+t_i^m;), p_{US}^x/1+t_i^x)}{\pi(p_{US}^m, p_{US}^x)} = \frac{(1 + t_i^m)\pi\left(p_{US}^m, \dfrac{p_{US}^x}{(1+t_i^x)(1+t_i^m)}\right)}{\pi(p_{US}^m, p_{US}^x)},$$

---

12. For a good recent discussion of the problems that may arise on this account see Falvey and Gemell (1999).

where we have made use of the linear homogeneity of $\pi(\cdot)$. Note that the nominal exchange rate has dropped out thanks to the assumption of the law of one price.

Consider first the case where there are binding import restrictions, but no export restrictions ($t_i^m > 0$ and $t_i^x = 0$). In this instance, it is apparent that $P_i^T > e_i P_{US}^T$, and trade restrictions do indeed raise the domestic price of tradables (relative to the benchmark country). Judging from the quotations above, this is the case that Dollar seems to have in mind.

On the other hand, consider what happens when the country in question rescinds all import restrictions and imposes instead export restrictions at an ad valorem level that equals that of the import restrictions just lifted ($t_i^m = 0$ and $t_i^x > 0$). From the Lerner (1936) symmetry theorem, it is evident that the switch from import protection to export taxation has no resource-allocation and distributional effects for the economy whatsoever. The relative price between tradables, p_i^m/p_i^x, remains unaffected by the switch. Yet, because export restrictions reduce the domestic price of exportables *relative to world prices*, it is now the case that $P_i^T < e_i P_{US}^T$. The country will now appear, by Dollar's measure, to be outward-oriented.

One practical implication is that economies that combine import barriers with export taxes (such as many countries in sub-Saharan Africa) will be judged less protected than those that rely on import restrictions alone. Conversely, countries that dilute the protective effect of import restrictions by using export subsidies ($t_i^x < 0$) will appear more protected than countries that do not do so.

Hence the DISTORTION index is sensitive to the form in which trade restrictions are applied. This follows from the fact that trade policies work by altering relative price *within* an economy; they do not have unambiguous implications for the level of prices in a country relative to another. A necessary condition for Dollar's index to do a good job of ranking trade regimes according to restrictiveness is that export policies (whether they tax or promote exports) play a comparatively minor role. Moreover, as we show in the next section, this is not a sufficient condition.

3.2 HOW RELEVANT IS THE LAW OF ONE PRICE IN PRACTICE?

The discussion above was framed in terms that are the most favorable to Dollar's measure, in that we assumed the law of one price (LOP) holds. Under this maintained hypothesis, the prices of tradable goods produced in different countries can diverge from each other, when expressed in a common currency, only when there exist trade restrictions (or transport costs).

However, there is a vast array of evidence suggesting that LOP does not accurately describe the world we live in. In a recent review article,

Rogoff (1996, p. 648) writes of the "startling empirical failure of the law of one price." Rogoff concludes: "commodities where the deviations from the law of one price damp out very quickly are the exception rather than the rule" (Rogoff, 1996, p. 650). Further, the evidence suggests that deviations from LOP are systematically related to movements in nominal exchange rates (see references in Rogoff, 1996). Indeed, it is well known that (nominal) exchange-rate policies in many developing countries are responsible for producing large and sustained swings in *real* exchange rates. Trade barriers or transport costs typically play a much smaller role.

Dollar (1992, p. 525) acknowledges that "there might be short-term fluctuations [unrelated to trade barriers] if purchasing-power parity did not hold continuously," but considers that these fluctuations would average out over time. Rogoff (1996, p. 647) concludes in his survey that the speed of convergence to purchasing-power parity (PPP) is extremely slow, of the order of roughly 15% per year. At this speed of convergence, averages constructed over a time horizon of 10 years (the horizon used in Dollar's paper) would exhibit substantial divergence from PPP in the presence of nominal shocks.

Under this interpretation, a significant portion of the cross-national variation in price levels exhibited in DISTORTION would be due not to trade policies, but to monetary and exchange-rate policies. Unlike trade policies, nominal exchange-rate movements have an unambiguous effect on the domestic price level of traded goods relative to foreign prices when LOP fails: an appreciation raises the price of both import-competing and exportable goods relative to foreign prices, and a depreciation has the reverse effect. Countries where the nominal exchange rate was not allowed to depreciate in line with domestic inflation would exhibit an appreciation of the real exchange rate (a rise in domestic prices relative to foreign levels), and correspondingly would be rated high on the DISTORTION index. Countries with aggressive policies of devaluation (or low inflation relative to the trend depreciation of their nominal exchange rate) would receive low DISTORTION ratings.

Transport costs provide another reason why DISTORTION may be unrelated to trade policies, especially in a large cross-section of countries. Dollar's index would be influenced by geographic variables such as access to sea routes and distance to world markets, even when LOP—appropriately modified to allow for transport costs—holds. Hence in practice DISTORTION is likely to capture the effects of geography as well as of exchange-rate policies. Indeed, when we regress Dollar's DISTORTION index on the black-market premium (a measure of exchange-rate policy), a set of continent dummies, and two trade-related geo-

Table 1 EFFECT OF GEOGRAPHICAL AND EXCHANGE-RATE POLICY VARIABLES ON DOLLAR'S DISTORTION INDEX

Variable	(1)	(2)
bmpav	0.07*** (1.971)	0.083** (2.47)
rcoast	−0.045* (−3.321)	−0.053* (−3.032)
tropics	0.209*** (1.829)	0.145 (1.004)
Latin America	0.012 (0.097)	−0.037 (−0.257)
SSA	0.451* (3.319)	0.46** (2.43)
East Asia	−0.12 (−0.921)	−0.145 (−0.889)
TAR		−0.017 (−0.08)
NTB		−0.276*** (−1.851)
R^2	0.52	0.58
N	89	71

Heteroskedasticity-corrected t-statistics in parentheses. See appendix for variable definitions. Regressions include a constant term and cover only developing countries. Levels of statistical significance indicated by asterisks: * 99%; ** 95%, *** 90%.

graphic variables (the coastal length over total land area and a dummy for tropical countries), we find that these explain more than 50% of the variation in Dollar's distortion index. Furthermore, two trade-policy variables (tariffs and quotas) enter with the wrong sign (Table 1)!

To summarize, DISTORTION is theoretically appropriate as a measure of trade restrictions when three conditions hold: (1) there are no export taxes or subsidies in use, (2) LOP holds continuously, and (3) there are no systematic differences in national price levels due to transport costs and other geographic factors. Obviously, all of these requirements are counterfactual. Whether one believes that DISTORTION still provides useful empirical information on trade regimes depends on one's priors regarding the practical significance of the three limitations expressed above.[13] Our view is that the second and third of these—the departure from LOP and the effect of geography—are particularly important in practice. We regard it as likely that it is the variation in nominal exchange-rate policies and geography, and not the variation in trade restrictions, that drives the cross-sectional variation of DISTORTION.

3.3 WHY VARIABILITY?

As mentioned previously, Dollar (1992) uses his measure of distortion in conjunction with a measure of variability, the latter being the coefficient of variation of DISTORTION measured on an annual basis. He is driven to do this because the country rankings using DISTORTION produce some "anomalies." For example, "Korea and Taiwan have the highest distortion measures of the Asian developing economies" and "the rankings within the developed country groups are not very plausible" (Dollar, 1992, pp. 530–531). The ten least-distorted countries by this measure include not only Hong Kong, Thailand, and Malta, but also Sri Lanka, Bangladesh, Mexico, South Africa, Nepal, Pakistan, and Syria! Burma's rating (90) equals that of the United States. Taiwan (116) is judged more distorted than Argentina (113). Our discussion above indicated that DISTORTION is highly sensitive to the form in which trade policies are applied and to exchange-rate policies as well as omitted geographic characteristics. So such results are not entirely surprising.

Dollar states that the "number of anomalies declines substantially if the real exchange rate distortion measure is combined with real exchange rate variability to produce an outward orientation index" (Dollar, 1992, p. 531). He thus produces a country ranking based on a weighted average of the DISTORTION and VARIABILITY indices. Since these two indices are entered separately in his growth regressions, we shall not discuss this combined index of "outward orientation" further.

However, we do wish to emphasize the obvious point that the VARIABILITY index has little to do with trade restrictions, as commonly understood, or with inward or outward orientation per se. What does VARIABILITY really measure? The ten countries with the highest VARIABILITY scores are Iraq, Uganda, Bolivia, El Salvador, Nicaragua, Guyana, Somalia, Nigeria, Ghana, and Guatemala. For the most part, these are countries that have experienced very high inflation rates and/or se-

---

13. The sensitivity of Dollar's index to these assumptions highlights a generic difficulty with regression-based indices which use the residual from a regression to proxy for an excluded variable: such indices capture variations in the excluded variable accurately only as long as the model is correctly and fully specified. If some variables are excluded from the estimated equation, they will form part of the index.

vere political disturbances during 1976–1985. It is plausible that VARIABILITY measures economic instability at large. In any case, it is unclear to us why we should think of it as an indicator of trade orientation.

3.4 EMPIRICAL RESULTS

The first column of Table 2 shows our replication of the core Dollar (1992) result for 95 developing countries. Dollar's benchmark specification includes on the right-hand side the investment rate (as a share of GDP, averaged over 1976–1985) in addition to DISTORTION and VARIABILITY. As shown in column (1), DISTORTION and VARIABILITY both enter with negative and highly significant coefficients using this specification. [Our results are virtually identical to those in Dollar (1992), with the

Table 2 REPLICATION AND EXTENSION OF DOLLAR'S (1992) RESULTS

	(1)	(2)	(3)	(4)	(5)
DISTORTION	−0.018*	−0.008	−0.003	−0.004	−0.008
	(−3.128)	(−1.009)	(−0.406)	(−0.514)	(−0.899)
VARIABILITY	−0.080*	−0.080**	−0.103*	−0.107*	−0.099*
	(−2.64)	(−2.084)	(−3.3)	(−3.51)	(−3.212)
Investment/GDP	0.137*	0.100**			
	(3.515)	(2.278)			
Latin America		−0.015**	−0.016*	−0.014**	−0.019*
		(−2.34)	(−2.65)	(−2.362)	(−3.337)
East Asia		0.007	0.010	0.011	0.004
		(0.747)	(0.937)	(0.976)	(0.382)
SSA		−0.018**	−0.026*	−0.029*	−0.028*
		(−2.419)	(−3.824)	(−4.129)	(−3.411)
Log initial income				−0.004	−0.011**
				(−1.097)	(−2.182)
Schooling, 1975					0.005**
					(2.531)
N	95	95	95	95	80
R^2	0.38	0.45	0.40	0.41	0.49

Dependent variable: growth of real GDP per capita, 1976–1985. Heteroskedasticity-corrected t statistics in parentheses. Regressions include a constant term and cover only developing countries. Levels of statistical significance indicated by asterisks: * 99%; ** 95%; *** 90%.

difference that our *t*-statistics are based on heteroskedasticity-corrected standard errors.]

None of Dollar's runs include standard regressors such as initial income, education, and regional dummies. The other columns of Table 2 show the results as we alter Dollar's specification to make it more compatible with recent cross-national work on growth (e.g., Barro, 1997). First, we add regional dummies for Latin America, East Asia, and sub-Saharan Africa to ensure that the results are not due to omitted factors correlated with geographical location (column 2). Next we drop the investment rate (column 3), and add in succession initial income (column 4) and initial schooling (column 5).[14] The dummies for Latin America and sub-Saharan Africa are negative and statistically significant. Initial income and education also enter significantly, with the expected signs (negative and positive, respectively).

We find that the VARIABILITY index is robust to these changes, but that DISTORTION is not. In fact, as soon as we introduce regional dummies in the regression, the estimated coefficient on DISTORTION comes down sizably and becomes insignificant. Whatever DISTORTION may be measuring, this raises the possibility that the results with this index are spurious, arising from the index's correlation with (omitted) regional effects.

Dollar's original results were based on data from Mark 4.0 of the Summers–Heston database (Summers and Heston, 1988). We have recalculated Dollar's DISTORTION and VARIABILITY indices using the more recent version (Mark 5.6) of the Summers–Heston data, confining ourselves to the same period examined by Dollar (1976–1985). The revised data allow us to generate these indices for 112 developing countries. We have also rerun the regressions for cross sections over different periods, as well as in panel form with fixed effects. We do not report these results here, for reasons of space (see the working-paper version of this paper, Rodríguez and Rodrik, 1999). The bottom line that emerges is similar to the conclusion just stated: the estimated coefficient on VARIABILITY is generally robust to alterations in specifications; the coefficient on DISTORTION is not.

4. *Jeffrey Sachs and Andrew Warner (1995)*

We turn next to the paper "Economic reform and the process of global integration" by Jeffrey Sachs and Andrew Warner (1995). This extremely

---

14. The income variable comes from the Summers–Heston (Mark 4.0) data set used in Dollar (1992). Schooling is from Barro and Lee (1994).

influential paper[15] is an ambitious attempt to solve the measurement-error problem in the literature by constructing an index of openness that combines information about several aspects of trade policy. The Sachs–Warner (SW) openness indicator (OPEN) is a zero–one dummy, which takes the value 0 if the economy was closed according to *any* one of the following criteria:

1. it had average tariff rates higher than 40% (TAR);
2. its nontariff barriers covered on average more than 40% of imports (NTB);
3. it had a socialist economic system (SOC);
4. it had a state monopoly of major exports (MON);
5. its black-market premium exceeded 20% during either the decade of the 1970s or the decade of the 1980s (BMP).[16]

The rationale for combining these indicators into a single dichotomous variable is that they represent different ways in which policymakers can close their economy to international trade. Tariffs set at 50% have exactly the same resource-allocation implications as quotas at a level that raised domestic market prices for importables by 50%. To gauge the effect of openness on growth, it is necessary to use a variable that classifies as closed those countries that were able to effectively restrict their economies' integration into world markets through the use of different combinations of policies that would achieve that result. Furthermore, if these openness indicators are correlated among themselves, introducing them separately in a regression may not yield reliable estimates, due to their possibly high level of collinearity.

The SW dummy has a high and robust coefficient when inserted in growth regressions. The point estimate of its effect on growth (in the original benchmark specification) is 2.44 percentage points[17]: economies that pass all five requirements experience on average economic growth two and a half percentage points higher than those that do not. The *t*-statistic is 5.50 (5.83 if estimated using robust standard errors). This coefficient appears to be highly robust to changes in the list of controls: in a recent paper which subjects 58 potential determinants of growth to

---

15. A partial listing of papers that have made use of the Sachs–Warner index includes Hall and Jones (1998), Wacziarg (1998), Sala-i-Martin (1997), Burnside and Dollar (1997), and Collins and Bosworth (1996).
16. Sachs and Warner use data from the following sources: Lee (1993) for nontariff barriers, Barro and Lee (1993) for tariffs, World Bank (1994) for state monopoly of exports, Kornai (1992) for the classification of socialist and nonsocial countries, and International Currency Analysis (various years) for black-market premia.
17. In the long run, such an economy would converge to a level of per capita GDP 2.97 times as high as if it had remained closed.

an exhaustive sensitivity analysis, the average p-value for the SW index is less than 0.1%.[18]

In this section we ask several questions about Sachs and Warner's results. First, we ask which, if any, of the individual components of the index are responsible for the strength of the SW dummy. We find that the SW dummy's strength derives mainly from the combination of the black-market premium (BMP) and the state-monopoly-of-exports (MON) variables. Very little of the dummy's statistical power would be lost if it were constructed using only these two indicators. In particular, there is little action in the two variables that are the most direct measures of trade policy: tariff and nontariff barriers (TAR and NTB).

We then ask to what extent the black-market premium and state-monopoly variables are measures of trade policy. We suggest that their significance in explaining growth can be traced to their correlation with other determinants of growth: macroeconomic problems in the case of the black-market premium, and location in sub-Saharan Africa in the case of the state-monopoly variable. We conclude that the SW indicator serves as a proxy for a wide range of policy and institutional differences, and that it yields an upward-biased estimate of the effects of trade restrictions proper.

4.1 WHICH INDIVIDUAL VARIABLES ACCOUNT FOR THE SIGNIFICANCE OF THE SW DUMMY?

We start by contrasting Sachs and Warner's result with the results of controlling separately for individual components of their index. Column 1 of Table 3 reproduces their baseline regression, and column 2 shows what happens when each of the components of the SW index is inserted separately into the same specification.[19] The variables BMP and MON are highly significant, whereas the rest are not. An F-test for the joint significance of the other three components (SOC, TAR, and NTB) yields a p-value of 0.25.

---

18. Sala-i-Martin (1997). The variable used by Sala-i-Martin is the number of years an economy was open according to the SW criteria, whereas here we follow Sachs and Warner's (1995) original article and use a dummy which captures whether or not the economy was open during 1970–1989.
19. We use the same set of controls used by Sachs and Warner. These are log of GDP n 1970, secondary schooling in 1970, primary schooling in 1970, government consumption as a percentage of GDP, number of revolutions and coups per year, number of assassinations per million population, relative price of investment goods, and ratio of investment to GDP. However, our results are highly robust to changes in the list of controls. For example, the simple correlations of TAR, NTB, and SOC with growth are, respectively, $-.048$, $-.083$ and $-.148$. Our result is also not due to multicollinearity: the R^2's from regressions of any one of SOC, NTB, and TAR on the other two are, respectively, 0.02, 0.05, and 0.05.

Table 3 EFFECT OF DIFFERENT OPENNESS INDICATORS ON GROWTH

	(1)	(2)	(3)	(4)	(5)	(6)	(7)
OPEN	2.44*						
	(5.83)						
BMP		−1.701*					
		(−3.65)					
MON		−2.020*					
		(−2.84)					
SOC		−1.272					
		(−1.39)					
NTB		−0.453					
		(−0.81)					
TAR		−0.134					
		(−0.18)					
BM			2.086*		2.119*	2.519*	2.063*
			(4.82)		(5.09)	(5.94)	(4.64)
SQT				0.877***	0.735	0.663	
				(1.82)	(1.59)	(1.30)	
SOC							.389
							(.56)
QT							.657
							(1.28)
R^2	0.593	0.637	0.522	0.455	0.617	0.522	0.619
N	79	71	78	75	74	74	74

Dependent variable: growth of GDP per capita, 1970–1989. All equations except that for column 6 include the following controls: log of GDP in 1970, investment rate in 1970, government consumption/GDP, assassinations per capita, deviation from world investment prices, secondary-schooling ratio, primary-schooling ratio, revolutions and coups, and a constant term. Column 6 drops the investment rate and deviation from world investment prices. Numbers in parentheses are t-statistics based on Huber–White heteroskedasticity-consistent standard errors.

To check whether it is mainly the combination of BMP and MON that drives the Sachs and Warner's result, we ask the following question: suppose that we had built a dummy variable, in the spirit of Sachs and Warner, which classified an economy as closed only if it was closed according to BMP and MON. That is, suppose we ignored the information the other three variables give us as to the economy's openness.

How significant would the coefficient of our variable be in a growth regression? How different would the partition between open and closed economies that it generates be from that generated by the SW dummy? Suppose alternatively that we also constructed an openness dummy based only on the information contained in SOC, NTB, and TAR. How significant would that variable be in a growth regression? And how correlated would it be with the SW index?

Columns (3)–(6) of Table 3 address the question of significance. We denote by BM a variable that takes the value 1 when the economy is open according to criteria 4 and 5 above, whereas SQT equals 1 when the economy passes criteria 1, 2, and 3. We substitute these variables for the SW openness index in the regression Sachs and Warner present in their paper. Entered on its own, BM is highly significant, with an estimated coefficient that is very close to that on OPEN (2.09 vs. 2.44; see column 3). When SQT is substituted for BM, the estimated coefficient on SQT is much smaller (0.88) and significant only at the 90% level (column 4). We next enter BM and SQT simultaneously: the coefficient of SQT now has a t-statistic of 1.59, whereas the coefficient on BM retains a t-statistic of 5.09 and a point estimate (2.12) close to that on the openness variable in the original equation (column 5). Once the investment rate and investment prices, which are likely to be endogenous, are taken out of the equation, the t-statistic on SQT drops to 1.30 and that on BM rises to 5.94 (column 6).

The comparability of the results in Table 3 is hampered by the fact that the sample size changes as we move from one column to the next. This is because not all of the 79 countries in the sample have data for each of the individual SW components. To check whether this introduces any difficulties for our interpretation, we have also run these regressions holding the sample size fixed. We restricted the sample to those countries which have the requisite data for all the components, using both the original specification ($n = 71$) and a specification where we drop two of the SW regressors with t-statistics below unity (primary schooling, and revolutions and coups) to gain additional observations ($n = 74$). In both cases, our results were similar to those reported above: Regardless of whether BM and SQT are entered separately or jointly, the coefficient on BM is highly significant (with a point estimate that is statistically indistinguishable from that on OPEN) while the coefficient on SQT is insignificant.[20]

Hence, once BM is included, there is little additional predictive power

---

20. The largest t-statistic we obtained for SQT in these runs is 1.4. These results are not shown, to save space, but are available on request.

coming from regime type (socialist or not), level of tariffs, or coverage of nontariff barriers.[21] The strength of the SW index derives from the low growth performance of countries with either high black-market premia or state export monopolies (as classified by Sachs and Warner).[22]

The reason why BM performs so much better than SQT is that BM generates a partition between closed and open economies that is much closer to that generated by OPEN than the partition generated by SQT. Only six economies are classified differently by BM and by OPEN, while OPEN and SQT disagree in 31 cases. The disagreement between OPEN and SQT is concentrated in 15 African and 12 Latin American economies which SQT fails to qualify as closed but BM (and therefore OPEN) does: the African economies are found to be closed because of their state monopolies of exports, and those of Latin America because of their high black-market premia. The average rate of growth of these economies is 0.24, much lower than the sample average of 1.44.[23]

In view of the overwhelming contribution of the black-market premium and the dummy for state monopoly of exports to the statistical performance of the SW openness index, it is logical to ask what exactly it is that these two variables are capturing. To what extent are they indicators of trade policy? Could they be correlated with other variables that have a detrimental effect on growth, therefore not giving us much useful information on trade openness per se? We turn now to these questions, first with an analysis of the state-monopoly-of-exports variable, and then with a discussion of the black-market premium variable.

21. A different form in which the "horse race" can be run, suggested to us by Jeffrey Sachs, is to introduce OPEN and BM together in the regression, to see if OPEN clearly "wins." When we do this, we find that the point estimate of the coefficient on OPEN is generally larger than that on BM, but that the two coefficients are statistically indistinguishable from each other, because OPEN and BM are highly collinear with each other (as we discuss further below). On the other hand, when OPEN and SQT are entered together, SQT has the wrong (negative) sign and the equality of coefficients can easily be rejected.
22. Harrison and Hanson (1999) have studied the SW dummy and reach a similar conclusion, namely that the effect of trade-policy indicators (tariffs and quotas) on the strength of the SW dummy is small and not significant. The key difference between our work and Harrison and Hanson's is that they introduce the subcomponents of the SW index separately in their regression whereas we construct the subindexes described in the text.
23. Our result is not due to an arbitrary distinction between BM and SQT. SQT performs more poorly than any other openness index constructed on the basis of three of the five indicators used by Sachs and Warner, and BM performs more strongly than any index constructed with two of these five indicators. A similar result applies to partitions along other dimensions: those constructed using four indicators which exclude either BMP or MON do more poorly than any of those which include them; and either BMP or MON individually does better than any of the other indicators. Details of these exercises can be found in the working-paper version of our paper (Rodríguez and Rodrik, 1999).

4.2 WHAT DOES THE STATE-MONOPOLY-OF-EXPORTS VARIABLE REPRESENT?

Sachs and Warner's rationale for using an indicator of the existence of a state monopoly on major exports is the well-known equivalence between import and export taxes (Lerner, 1936). The variable MON is meant to capture cases in which governments taxed major exports and therefore reduced the level of trade (exports *and* imports). Sachs and Warner use an index of the degree of distortion caused by export marketing boards, taken from the World Bank study *Adjustment in Africa: Reforms, Results, and the Road Ahead* (World Bank, 1994).[24]

We note that the World bank study covers only 29 African economies that were under structural adjustment programs from 1987 to 1991. This results in a double selection bias. First, non-African economies with restrictive policies towards exports automatically escape scrutiny. Second, African economies with restrictive export policies but not undergoing adjustment programs in the late 1980s are also overlooked. Since Africa was the slowest-growing region during the period covered, and since economies that need to carry out structural adjustment programs are likely to be doing worse than those that do not, the effect is to bias the coefficient on openness upwards on both accounts.

How this selection bias affects the country classification can be illustrated by two examples: Indonesia and Mauritius. Both of these economies are rated as open in Sachs and Warner's sample. Both are excluded from the sample used to construct the state-monopoly-on-exports variable: Indonesia because it is not in Africa, and Mauritius because it was doing well and was not undergoing a World Bank adjustment program during the period covered by the World Bank study. Yet both of these economies would seem to satisfy the conditions necessary to be rated as closed according to the export-monopoly criterion: Indonesian law restricts oil and gas production to the state oil company, Pertamina; and Mauritius sells all of its export sugar production through the Mauritius Sugar Syndicate.[25] Indonesia and Mauritius are also among the ten fastest-growing economies in Sachs and Warner's sample.

---

24. Sachs and Warner (1995) cite a different source in their paper, but World Bank (1994) appears to be the correct source.
25. See Pertamina (1998) for Indonesia, and Gulhati and Nallari (1990, p. 22) as well as World Bank (1989, p. 6) for Mauritius. Oil represented 61.2% of Indonesian exports and sugar represented between 60–80% of Mauritius exports during the period covered by Sachs and Warner's study (see World Bank, 1983, Table E, and 1998). Although manufactures have recently outstripped sugar as Mauritius's main export, this is a recent development: in 1980 sugar represented 65% of Mauritius's total exports, and agriculture was surpassed by manufacturing as the main source of exports only in 1986 (World Bank, 1998).

One of the problems that this selection bias causes in Sachs and Warner's estimation is that it makes the variable MON virtually indistinguishable from a sub-Saharan Africa dummy.[26] There are 13 African countries (out of 47) in Sachs and Warner's study that are not rated as closed according to MON. (Twelve of these were not included in World Bank study.) But for all but one of these observations MON adds no additional information, either because they are dropped from the sample due to unavailability of other data or because they are rated as closed by other trade-policy indicators used to construct the index. The result is that the only difference between having used an export-marketing-board variable to construct the SW index and having used a sub-Saharan Africa dummy is a single observation. That observation is Mauritius, the fastest-growing African economy in the sample.[27]

We conclude that the export-marketing-board variable, as implemented, is not a good measure of trade policy and creates a serious bias in the estimation. Except for Mauritius, whose classification as open seems to us to be due exclusively to selection bias, the inclusion of MON in the SW dummy is indistinguishable from the use of a sub-Saharan Africa dummy. In that respect, the only information that we can extract from it is that African economies grew more slowly than the rest of the world during the seventies and eighties.

4.3 WHAT DOES THE BLACK-MARKET PREMIUM VARIABLE MEASURE?

The second source of strength in the SW openness variable is the black-market premium. Indeed, the simple correlation between the openness dummy and BMP is 0.63. A regression of growth on the black-market premium dummy and all the other controls gives a coefficient of -1.05 with a t-statistic of nearly 2.5 in absolute value. How good an indicator of openness is the black-market premium?

The black-market premium measures the extent of rationing in the market for foreign currency. The theoretical argument for using the black-market premium in this context is that, under certain conditions, foreign exchange restrictions act as a trade barrier. Using our notation from the previous section (but omitting country subscripts), the domes-

26. This is true despite the fact that the SW dummy's coefficient is still significant after the estimation is carried out controlling for a sub-Saharan Africa dummy. The reason is that the SW dummy still has substantial explanatory power left due to its use of the black-market premium variable.
27. Both Lesotho and Botswana had higher growth rates than Mauritius, but Lesotho was not rated due to insufficient data (Sachs and Warner 1995, p. 85), and Botswana is dropped from their sample because of unavailability of government-consumption data.

tic price of import-competing goods relative to exportables can be expressed as follows:

$$\frac{p^m}{p^x} = \frac{e^m p^{m*}(1+t^m)(1+t^x)}{e^x p^{x*}},$$

where an asterisk refers to border prices. We now allow for the possibility that the exchange rates applicable to import and export transactions (e^m and e^x, respectively) can differ. Foreign-currency rationing can drive a wedge between these two exchange rates.

Suppose the form that rationing takes is as follows: all imports are financed at the margin by buying foreign currency in the black market, while all export receipts are handed to the central bank at the official exchange rate. In this case, $e^m/e^x = 1 + \text{BMP}$, and the presence of a black-market premium has the same resource-allocation consequences as a trade restriction. On the other hand, if at the margin exporters can sell their foreign-currency receipts on the black market as well, then the wedge between e^m and e^x disappears. In this case, the black-market premium does not work like a trade restriction.[28] Neither does it do so when the premium for foreign currency is generated by restrictions on capital-account (as opposed to current-account) transactions.

But there is a deeper problem with interpreting the black-market premium as an indicator of trade policy. Sachs and Warner rate an economy closed according to BMP if it maintains black-market premia in excess of 20% for a whole decade (the 1970s or the 1980s). Such levels of the black-market premium are indicative of sustained macroeconomic imbalances. Overvaluation of this magnitude is likely to emerge (1) when there is a deep inconsistency between domestic aggregate-demand policies and exchange-rate policy, or (2) when the government tries to maintain a low exchange rate in order to counteract transitory confidence or balance-of-payments crises. Such imbalances may be sparked by political conflicts, external shocks, or sheer mismanagement, and would typically manifest themselves in inflationary pressures, high and growing levels of external debt, and a stop–go pattern of policymaking. In addition, since black-market premia tend to favor government officials who can trade exchange-rate allocations for bribes, we would expect them to be high wherever there are high levels of corruption. Therefore, countries with greater corruption, a less reliable

---

28. In one respect, Sachs and Warner (1995) treat BMP differently from a trade restriction: the cutoff for tariffs (TAR) is set at 40%, while that for BMP is set at 20%.

bureaucracy, and lower capacity for enforcement of the rule of law are also likely have higher black-market premia.

Hence it is reasonable to suppose that the existence of sizable black-market premia over long periods of time reflects a wide range of policy failures. It is also reasonable to think that these failures will be responsible for low growth. What is more debatable, in our view, is the attribution of the adverse growth consequences exclusively to the trade-restrictive effects of black-market premia.

Many of the relationships just discussed are present in the data. The simple correlations of black-market premia with the level of inflation, the debt/exports ratio, wars, and institutional quality are all sufficiently high to warrant preoccupation. Indeed, of the 48 economies ranked as closed according to the BMP criteria, 40 had one or more of the following characteristics: average inflation over 1975–1990 higher than 10%, debt-to-GNP ratio in 1985 greater than 125%, a terms-of-trade decline of more than 20%, an institutional-quality index less than 5 (on a scale of 1 to 10), or involvement in a war.

We also view the fact that there exist important threshold effects in the black-market premium as indicative that this variable may simply be capturing the effect of widespread macroeconomic and political crises. If we insert the values of the black-market premium in the 1970s and 1980s as continuous variables in the regression, the estimated coefficients are extremely weak, and they fail to pass an F-test for joint significance at 10%. The strength of Sachs and Warner's result comes in great part from the dichotomous nature of the variable BMP and from the fact that the 20% threshold allows more weight to be placed on the observations for which the black-market premia—and probably also the underlying macroeconomic imbalances—are sufficiently high.

That the effect of the black-market premium is highly sensitive to the macroeconomic and political variables that one controls for is shown in Table 4, where we present the results of controlling for each of the indicators of macroeconomic and political distress that we have mentioned. In three out of five cases, each of these variables individually is enough to drive the coefficient on BMP below conventional levels of significance. If we insert all our controls together, the estimated coefficient on BMP goes down by more than half and the t-statistic drops below 1.

This kind of evidence does not by itself prove that higher black-market premia are unrelated to growth performance. The results in Table 4 might be due to high multicollinearity between the black-market premium and the indicators of macroeconomic and political distress that we have chosen. But what they do show is that there is very little in the data

Table 4 EFFECT OF BLACK-MARKET PREMIUM ON GROWTH BEFORE AND AFTER CONTROLLING FOR MEASURES OF MACROECONOMIC AND POLITICAL DISEQUILIBRIUM;

	(1)	(2)	(3)	(4)	(5)	(6)	(7)
Black-market premium	−1.044** (−2.47)	−0.727 (−1.57)	−0.768 (−1.62)	−1.200* (−2.84)	−0.945** (−2.31)	−0.551 (−1.66)	−0.438 (−.98)
Inflation, 1975–1990		−3.201*** (−1.78)					−1.024 (−.58)
Debt/GDP ratio in 1985			−0.015* (−5.75)				−0.011* (−3.21)
Terms-of-trade shock				1.038 (0.42)			3.894 (1.48)
War					−1.378** (−2.32)		−0.135 (−0.15)
Quality of institutions						0.441* (2.86)	0.433*** (2.00)
Summary statistics							
R^2	0.476	0.382	0.589	0.496	0.507	0.567	0.703
N	80	76	54	77	80	75	46

Dependent variable: growth of GDP per capita, 1970–1989. All equations include the following controls: log of GDP in 1970, investment rate in 1970, government consumption/GDP, assassinations per capita, deviation from world investment prices, secondary-schooling ratio, primary-schooling ratio, revolutions and coups, and a constant term. Numbers in parentheses are t-statistics based on Huber–White heteroskedasticity-consistent standard errors.

to help us distinguish the effect of high black-market premia from those of other plausible right-hand-side variables relating to macroeconomic distress. In other words, they show that the black-market premium is not a good measure of trade policy, because it is also a proxy for many other variables unrelated to trade policy.

4.4 SENSITIVITY AND GENERAL IMPLICATIONS

The interpretational problems with the state-monopoly-of-exports and black-market premium variables would not be so important if these two variables were responsible for only part of the effect of the SW index on growth. But the fact that they seem to be its overwhelming determinant makes us worry about the extent to which the results speak meaningfully about the role of trade policies.

The arguments in the previous two sections have shown that the individual coefficients on MON and BMP are not very robust to controlling for variables such as an Africa dummy or indicators of macroeconomic and political distress. However, much of the force of the SW variable comes from its combination of the effects of MON and BMP. The reason is that the SW dummy uses MON to classify as closed all but one of the economies in sub-Saharan Africa and then uses BMP to classify as closed a set of economies with macroeconomic and political difficulties. It thus builds a "supervariable" which is 1 for all non-African economies without macroeconomic or political difficulties. This variable will be statistically stronger than either an African dummy or macroeconomic controls, because it jointly groups information from both.[29]

In the working-paper version of this paper (Rodríguez and Rodrik, 1999) we show that the coefficient on the SW variable, although generally robust to changes in the list of controls, is particularly sensitive to the inclusion of other summary indicators of macroeconomic and political crises. In particular, both the summary indicator of institutional quality developed by Knack and Keefer (1995) and a dummy variable that captures the effect of being in Africa and high macroeconomic disequilibria can easily drive the coefficient of the SW dummy below conventional significance levels. This sensitivity is important not because it shows the existence of a specification in which the SW dummy's significance is not robust, but because this lack of robustness shows up precisely when it is other indicators of political and macroeconomic imbalances that are introduced in the regression. This appears to suggest that

---

29. If MON and BMP are inserted separately, together with an Africa dummy and a measure of institutional quality, then neither MON nor BMP is individually significant, and the p-value for a joint significance test is 0.09 (0.31 after controlling for NTB, TAR, and SOC), but OPEN gets a t-statistic of 3.06 and BM one of 2.93 (SQT gets 1.46).

the SW variable may be acting as a proxy for these imbalances rather than as an indicator of trade policy.

We do not pretend to have a good answer to the question of whether it is macroeconomic and political distress that drive trade policy or the other way around.[30] Nor do we give an answer to the question of whether all of these are determined in turn by some other underlying variables such as poor institutions or antimarket ideology. What we believe we have established is that the statistical power of the SW indicator derives not from the direct indicators of trade policy it incorporates, but from two components that we have reasons to believe will yield upward-biased estimates of the effects of trade restrictions. The SW measure is so correlated with plausible groupings of alternative explanatory variables—macroeconomic instability, poor institutions, location in Africa—that it is risky to draw strong inferences about the effect of openness on growth based on its coefficient in a growth regression.

5. Sebastian Edwards (1998)

The third paper that we discuss is Sebastian Edwards's recent *Economic Journal* paper "Openness, productivity and growth: What do we really know?" (Edwards, 1998). The papers by Dollar and by Sachs and Warner deal with data problems by constructing new openness indicators. Edwards takes the alternative approach of analyzing the robustness of the openness–growth relationship to the use of different existing indicators. Edwards writes: "the difficulties in defining satisfactory summary indexes suggest that researchers should move away from this area, and should instead concentrate on determining whether econometric results are robust to alternative indexes" (1998, p. 386). The presumption is that the imperfections in specific indicators would not seem quite as relevant if the estimated positive coefficient on openness were found to be robust to differences in the way openness is measured.

To carry out this robustness analysis, Edwards runs regressions of total factor productivity growth on nine alternative indicators of openness. (Initial income and a measure of schooling are used as controls.[31])

---

30. Sachs and Warner's view is that causality goes from restrictive trade policies to macroeconomic instability (personal communication with Sachs). For the purposes of the present paper, we are agnostic about the existence or direction of any causality. An argument that macroeconomic imbalances are largely unrelated to trade policies is not difficult to make, and receives considerable support from cross-national evidence (see Rodrik, 1999, Chap. 4).
31. In an earlier and heavily cited paper, Edwards (1992) carried out a similar analysis for growth rates of real GDP per capita using a somewhat different set of nine alternative indicators of trade-policy distortions. We focus here on Edwards (1998) because it is more recent and the data set used in the earlier paper was not available.

His estimates of total factor productivity growth are the Solow residuals from panel regressions of growth on changes of capital and labor inputs. The nine indicators of openness he uses are: (1) the SW openness index; (2) the World Bank's subjective classification of trade strategies in *World Development Report 1987*; (3) Leamer's (1988) openness index, built on the basis of the average residuals from regressions of trade flows; (4) the average black-market premium; (5) the average import tariffs from UNCTAD via Barro and Lee (1994); (6) the average coverage of nontariff barriers, also from UNCTAD via Barro and Lee (1994); (7) the subjective Heritage Foundation index of distortions in international trade; (8) the ratio of total revenues on trade taxes (exports + imports) to total trade; and (9) Holger Wolf's (1993) regression-based index of import distortions for 1985.

The results Edwards presents are weighted least squares (WLS) regressions of TFP growth on indicators (1)–(9), where the weighting variable is GDP per capita in 1985. They are shown in column 1, rows 1–9, of Table 5: six of the nine indicators are significant, and all but one have the "expected" sign. He repeats the analysis using instrumental weighted least squares (column 2), and finds five of nine indicators significant at 10% (three at 5%) and all having the "correct" sign.[32] He also builds an additional indicator as the first principal component of indicators (1), (4), (5), (6), and (9), which he finds to be significant in WLS estimation (row 10). He concludes that "these results are quite remarkable, suggesting with tremendous consistency that there is a significantly positive relationship between openness and productivity growth."

We will argue that Edwards's evidence does not warrant such strong claims. The robustness of the regression results, we will show, is largely an artifact of weighting and identification assumptions that seem to us to be inappropriate. Of the 19 different specifications reported in Edwards (1998), only three produce results that are statistically significant at conventional levels once we qualify these assumptions. Furthermore, the specifications that pass econometric scrutiny are based on data that suffer from serious anomalies and subjectivity bias.

5.1 THE PROBLEM WITH WEIGHTING

The justification for the resort to WLS estimation is not provided in the paper, but it is presumably to correct for possible heteroskedasticity in the residuals. If disturbances are not homoskedastic, ordinary least-squares estimates will be inefficient. If the form of the skedastic function

---

32. In his paper, Edwards erroneously claims that two additional variables are significant in the IV–2SLS estimation: Leamer's index and tariffs. This mistake was apparently due to two typographical errors in his Table 4, p. 393.

Table 5 ALTERNATIVE WEIGHTING ASSUMPTIONS

Openness indicator	(1) Weighted least squares (weight=GDP)	(2) Weighted 2SLS (weight=GDP)	(3) Weighted least squares (weight=ln GDP)	(4) Weighted 2SLS (weight=ln GDP)	(5) Robust standard errors	(6) 2SLS, Robust Standard Errors
1. Sachs–Warner	0.0094** (2.12)	0.0089*** (1.84)	0.0101*** (1.81)	0.0080 (1.28)	0.0102 (1.54)	0.0078 (1.06)
2. World Development Report	0.0075* (3.57)	0.0131* (3.36)	0.0070** (2.45)	0.0126** (2.64)	0.0068* (3.67)	0.0126** (2.13)
3. Leamer	0.0010 (1.03)	0.0123 (1.40)	0.0041 (0.82)	−0.0013 (−0.20)	0.0041 (0.82)	−0.0033 (−0.32)
4. Black-market premium	−0.0217* (−3.59)	−0.0192*** (−1.95)	−0.0108** (−2.57)	−0.0035 (−0.56)	−0.0098*** (−1.79)	−0.0027 (−0.54)
5. Tariffs	−0.0450* (−2.77)	−0.1001 (−1.52)	0.0065 (0.51)	0.0013 (0.03)	0.0114 (0.88)	0.0079 (0.28)

6. Quotas	−0.0047 (−0.45)	−0.0398 (−0.42)	0.0029 (0.35)	0.0461 (0.68)	0.0036 (0.43)	0.0401 (0.79)
7. Heritage Foundation	−0.0074* (−4.50)	−0.0133* (−3.75)	−0.0066** (−3.02)	−0.0195* (−3.30)	−0.0064* (−2.87)	−0.0202* (−3.24)
8. Collected-trade-taxes ratio	−0.4849* (3.04)	−1.6668** (−2.15)	−0.2808** (−2.15)	−1.8256 (−1.23)	−0.2676** (−2.25)	−1.8368 (−1.06)
9. Wolf's index of import distortions	3.5E−05 (0.27)	−2.6E−04 (−0.72)	4.8E−05 (0.41)	−3.7E−04 (−0.99)	4.1E−05 (0.36)	−3.3E−04 (−1.21)
10. Principal-components factor	−0.0070** (−2.38)		−0.0047 (−1.61)		−0.0043 (−1.37)	

Dependent variable: TFP growth, 1980–1990. These are the estimated coefficients from regressions where each of the trade-policy indicators is entered separately. Each equation also includes log GDP per capita in 1965 and schooling in 1965 as regressors [as in the original Edwards (1998) specification]. t-statistics are in parentheses (based on heteroskedasticity-consistent standard errors in column 3).

is known, then it is appropriate to use WLS. This is indeed what Edwards implicitly assumes when he uses GDP per capita as his weighting variable. If it is unknown, White's (1980) covariance-matrix estimator allows for the calculation of heteroskedasticity-robust standard errors that are invariant to the form of the skedastic function.

When there is heteroskedasticity, the standard deviation of the disturbance in the growth equation varies systematically across countries. Edwards's decision to weight his observations by the level of GDP per capita implies an assumption that the standard deviation of the disturbances in the growth equation is inversely proportional to the square root of the level of GDP per capita in 1985. In other words, if the United States is—as it in effect was in 1985 according to the Summers–Heston data—59 times wealthier than Ethiopia, the standard deviation of the growth rate conditional on having the United States's income is 7.7 ($59^{1/2}$) times lower than conditional on having Ethiopia's income. Using the estimates of the residuals' standard deviation from one of Edwards's equations, we can calculate the implied root-mean-square error of the growth rate conditional on having the incomes of the United States and of Ethiopia. The former is 0.8 percentage points, whereas the latter is 6 percentage points. It may be reasonable to suppose that growth data for poor countries are less reliable than those for rich countries, but the errors implied by Edwards's weighting assumption for poor countries' growth data seem to us to be unreasonably high. As a matter of fact, it is hard to think of a reason to be doing regression analysis on a broad cross section of primarily poor countries if we believe that underdeveloped nations' economic data are this uninformative.

Columns 3 and 4 of Table 5 repeat Edwards's regressions using the natural log of 1985 per capita GDP as the weighting variable. In terms of our calculations above, the ratio between the U.S. and Ethiopian standard deviations would now be a more reasonable 1.31. This set of regressions results in six of the eighteen coefficients having the "wrong" sign. Five out of nine coefficients are significant among the least-squares regressions (four at 5%), and two out of nine in the instrumental variables (IV) regressions. The coefficient on the principal-components variable now becomes insignificant.[33]

---

33. Why does weighting by GDP give such different results? The reason seems to be that there is a relationship between the openness indices used by Edwards and TFP growth at high levels of income. This relationship in itself is apparently driven by the fact that the great majority of economies with restrictive trade practices and high levels of GDP per capita in 1985 were oil exporters. Because of their high incomes, these economies are weighted very heavily in the WLS regressions. It is well known that oil-exporting economies had very low rates of growth during the 1980s (see for example the studies in Gelb, 1988). If one redoes regressions 1–19 using GDP per capita weights but includ-

One way to put aside doubts about the appropriateness of alternative assumptions regarding the nature of the skedastic function is to use White's (1980) heteroskedasticity-consistent standard errors, which are robust to the form of heteroskedasticity. We show these estimates in column 5 and 6 of Table 5. Four out of nine coefficients are now significant among the least-squares regressions (three at 5%), and two out of nine among the IV regressions. Only twelve of the eighteen coefficients have the correct sign. The principal components variable is also insignificant.

5.2 THE PROBLEM WITH IDENTIFICATION

The two significant IV coefficients in Table 5 are moreover quite sensitive to the specification of the instrument lists. In particular, the IV versions of equations 2 and 7 in Table 5 are two of the only three equations in which the Heritage Foundation Index of Property Rights Protection is used as an instrument by Edwards.[34] If this instrument is not excludable from the second-stage regression, Edwards's IV estimation will give biased estimates of the coefficient of openness on growth. Theoretically, it seems to us unreasonable to assert that the protection of property rights can effectively be assumed not to be an important determinant of growth, given the extensive literature concerned precisely with such an effect.[35] In Table 6, columns 1–4, we show that, if property rights are included in the second-stage regression for these two equations, this term gets a significant coefficient in indicator 2 (World Development Report index) and a positive albeit insignificant coefficient in indicator 7 (Heritage Foundation index). Chi-squared tests of the overidentifying restrictions also reject the null hypothesis that these restrictions hold for indicator 2. Furthermore, in both indicators the t-statistic on the openness proxy falls to well below 0.5 in absolute value.

If we take seriously the fact that property rights are not excludable from the productivity growth regressions, we are left with the conclusion that, among 17 different specifications in Tables 5 and 6, we find

---

ing a dummy for oil exporters, one gets very similar results to those in column 3 of Tables 5 and 6. Only the coefficients for the World Development Report index, the Heritage Foundation index, and the least-squares estimate of the collected-taxes ratio remain significant, and the least-squares coefficient on quotas changes sign.

34. His other instruments include TFP growth in the 1970s and the black-market premium, export/GDP, import/GDP and terms-of-trade changes for 1975–1979.
35. Barro (1997) names "the importance of institutions that ensure property rights and free markets" for economic growth as one of the "dominant themes" of his recent research (p. xiv). For examples of the literature emphasizing the importance of property rights for economic growth, see Clague et al. (1996), Acheson and McFetridge (1996), Jodha (1996), Tornell (1997), Park and Ginarte (1997), Grossman and Kim (1996), and Thompson and Rushing (1996).

Table 6 SENSITIVITY TO IDENTIFICATION ASSUMPTIONS AND CHOICE OF TRADE TAX INDICATOR

	(1)	(2)	(3)	(4)	(5)	(6)	(7)	(8)
World Development Report index	0.0126** (2.13)	0.0023 (0.40)						
Heritage Foundation index			−0.0202* (−3.24)	−0.003 (−0.24)				
Property rights		−0.0107* (−2.91)		−0.010 (−1.43)				
Collected-taxes ratio (Edwards)					−0.2676 (−2.25)**			
Average duty (World Bank)						0.0225 (1.01)		
Average import duty (World Bank)							0.0007 (2.30)**	0.0003 (0.884)
Average export duty (World Bank)							−0.0003 (−1.09)	
Test of overidentifying restrictions	29.3244		5.4072					
p-value	6.72E-06		0.2480					
N	30	30	56	56	45	43	43	66

Dependent variable: TFP Growth, 1980–1990. Each equation also includes log GDP per capita in 1965 and schooling in 1965 as regressors. t-statistics based on heteroskedasticity-consistent standard errors in parentheses.

evidence of a negative and statistically significant correlation between trade-restricting policies and productivity growth in only three cases. Those are the ones that use the collected-taxes ratio, the World Development Report index, or the Heritage Foundation index. We take up some problems with these indexes in the next subsection.

5.3 DATA ISSUES

Edwards reports that the collected-taxes ratio (which measures trade tax revenue as a proportion of total trade) is calculated from raw data provided by the IMF. We are puzzled by these data, because many of the numbers for developing countries are implausible. India, a country with one of the world's highest tariff rates, is listed as having an average ratio of 2.4% lower than the sample average and barely above the value for Chile (2.3%). The mean value of the collected-taxes ratio in the sample is 2.8%, which strikes us as very low.

We have attempted to replicate Edwards's results using data from the World Bank's World Development Indicators (1998). This source, which was not available at the time Edwards's analysis was first conducted, provides collected trade tax ratios for imports and exports separately, which we have combined to derive an index in the spirit of Edwards's variable.[36] According to this index, India's average trade tax is 37.3% (a more plausible figure than Edwards's 2.4%). We replicate equation 8 of Table 5 with these data, and the results are shown in columns 6–8 of Table 6. The coefficient on average duties is now insignificant and has the "wrong" sign (column 6). If we introduce import and export duties separately (column 7), then import duties in fact get a positive and *significant* coefficient (contrary to the expected negative coefficient), and export duties are insignificant.

One shortcoming of these specifications (including Edwards's) is the small sample size (between 43 and 45). Since export duties are not reported for many countries, one way of increasing the sample size is to introduce *only* the import-duty variable from the World Development Indicators database. This increases the sample size to 66 countries. The estimated coefficient on import duties is once again positive and insignificant (column 8).

These results are in line with others we have reported earlier: there is

36. As our earlier discussion showed, when imports and exports are both taxed, their distortionary effect is multiplicative rather than additive. So instead of summing import and export taxes, we use the formula $(1 + mdut)(1 + xdut) - 1$, where $mdut$ ($xdut$) is import (export) duties as a percentage of imports (exports). We take the average of observations for 1980–1985. Our results (on the sign and insignificance of the coefficient on trade taxes) are unchanged, however, when we take the simple sum $mdut + xdut$.

little evidence that simple averages of trade taxes are significantly and negatively correlated with growth.

The other two variables that are significant are the subjective indexes constructed by the World Bank and the Heritage Foundation. It is striking that two subjective indexes are the only variables that are robust to our econometric analysis, since subjective indexes are well known to suffer from judgment biases. Indeed, a look at the two indexes reveals some striking contrasts. In the Heritage Foundation Index, for example, Chile and Uganda are in the same category (4 on a scale of 1 to 5, where 5 is most protected). Perhaps even more problematic is the fact that the Heritage Foundation index rates policies in 1996, well after the end of Edwards's sample period (1980–1990). Similar problems are present in the World Bank index, where high-growth Korea is rated as more open than moderate-growth Malaysia despite having higher tariff rates and nontariff-barrier coverage as well as a lower export/GDP ratio, and moderate-growth Tunisia—which had average tariffs of 21% and average nontariff coverage of 54%—is classified in the same group as Chile, Malaysia, and Thailand. In fact, in his 1993 literature review, Edwards (1993, pp. 1386–1387) himself drew attention to serious problems with this index. As he noted, Chile, which in other studies is rated as the most open economy in the developing world, was grouped in the second category (moderately outward-oriented); Korea was classified in the group of most open economies for both 1963–1973 and 1973–1985 despite the fact that in the former period the Korean trade regime was considerably more restrictive than in the latter.

In the working-paper version of this paper we report the results of recomputing these subjective indexes using the quantitative information on which they are purportedly based. Given that these underlying data are no different from those used in some of the other empirical work that we have discussed in this and other sections of the paper, it should come as no surprise that these attempts generally yielded insignificant coefficients. The natural conclusion from these results appears to be that either the mismatch in time periods or subjectivity biases or both are the fundamental causes for the significance of the Heritage Foundation and World Bank indexes.

In sum, we do not concur with Edwards's assertion that the cross-country data reveal the existence of a robust relationship between openness and productivity or GDP growth.[37] In our view, there is little evi-

---

37. Our results are basically unaltered if we use growth of GDP per capita from 1980 to 1990 instead of TFP growth as the dependent variable. In this case the World Bank and Heritage Foundation indexes remain significant, but the collected-trade-taxes ratio is now only significant at a 10% level and the black-market premium is insignificant. Similar results emerge for IV estimation.

dence to support such an assertion. The results reviewed in this section are for the most part highly dependent on questionable weighting and identification assumptions. The trade-policy indicators whose significance is not affected by these assumptions either are subjective indexes apparently highly contaminated by judgement biases or lack robustness to the use of more credible information from alternative data sources.

6. Dan Ben-David (1993)

Ben-David's (1993) *QJE* paper "Equalizing exchange: Trade liberalization and income convergence" takes an altogether different approach to studying the effect of openness on economic growth. Ben-David analyzes the effect of trade policies on income by asking whether trade liberalization leads to a reduction in the dispersion of income levels among liberalizing countries (i.e., whether it contributes to what has been called σ-convergence). We pick Ben-David as an example of a strand of the literature which has centered on studying the effect of trade on convergence. Another distinctive aspect of Ben-David's work is that it is nonparametric and not regression-based.

The expectation that trade liberalization might lead to income convergence is grounded in the factor price equalization (FPE) theorem. According to trade theory, free trade in goods leads to the equalization of factor prices under certain conditions (including an equal number of goods and factors, identical technologies, and absence of transport costs). As barriers to trade are relaxed (and assuming in addition that differences in capital–labor ratios and labor-force participation ratios do not countervail), a tendency towards FPE can be set into motion, resulting in convergence in per capita incomes.

There is no necessary relationship between the level of dispersion in incomes and the growth rate. Countries could in principle be converging to lower levels of GDP per capita. But in the case of the European Community, on which Ben-David concentrates, the convergence experienced was indeed to higher incomes. Overall growth from 1945 to 1994 of the EC5 (Belgium, France, the Netherlands, Italy, and Germany) was 3.45% compared to 1.21% percent from 1900 to 1939 and 1.16% from 1870 to 1899. Therefore, if Ben-David's claim is right, convergence in the EEC was achieved by raising the income of poor countries rather than by lowering that of rich countries.

Ben-David's argument goes beyond simply ascertaining that a decrease in dispersion occurred during the postwar era. He tries to show that trade liberalization caused this decrease by discarding other plausible alternatives. Thus he argues (1) that the observed convergence was

Figure 3 EFFECT OF EXCLUDING GERMANY IN DISPERSION CALCULATIONS

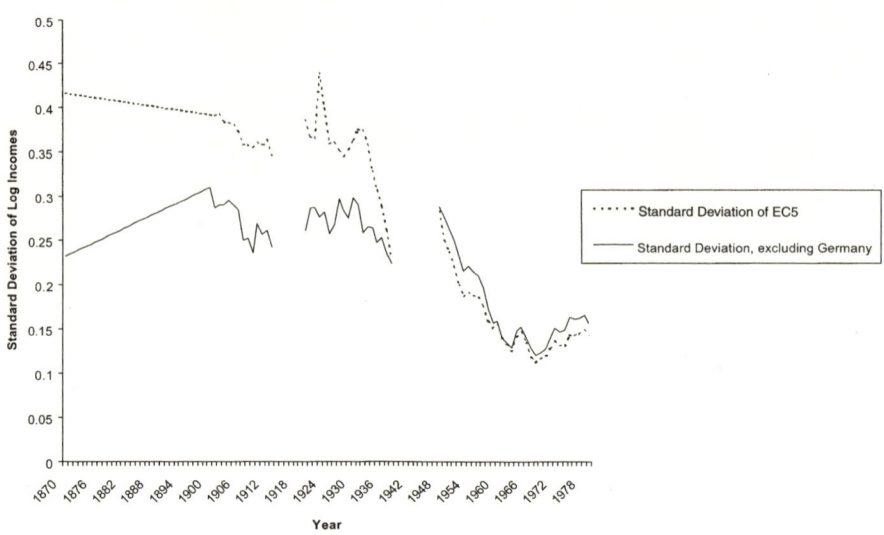

not simply a continuation of a long-term convergence trend unrelated to postwar economic integration; (2) that the European countries that chose not to enter a free-trade agreement did not experience the same extent of convergence as the EEC; and (3) that other subsets of economies in the world that were not economically integrated did not experience convergence. We examine each of his arguments in turn.

6.1 WAS EUROPEAN CONVERGENCE A CONTINUATION OF A LONG-TERM TREND?

In support of the argument that the reduction in dispersion was not simply the continuation of a long-run trend, Ben-David argues that the series of per capita income dispersion (solid line in Figure 3) does not show any visible downward tendency before the postwar era. When presenting this series, Ben-David excludes Germany from the calculations,[38] arguing that not doing so would bias the conclusion in favor of convergence:

> Germany was always among the poorest, in per capita terms, of the six countries. Today, it is one of the wealthiest countries in Europe. As a result of its heightened prosperity, it might be claimed that all of the convergence that

---

38. Luxembourg is also excluded, because Maddison (1982) does not provide data for it.

has been witnessed within the EEC is due to the behavior of Germany. Thus, its exclusion should bias the results away from convergence. (Ben-David, 1993, p. 662)

Note however that the purpose of Figure 3 (Figure VII in Ben-David's paper) is not only to establish the existence of convergence following postwar liberalization, but also to establish the *absence* of a long-term trend in convergence predating it. Thus the exclusion of Germany from the series, which biases the results against convergence, would also bias the results in favor of the hypothesis that there was no prewar convergence trend, had Germany's convergence occurred before the postwar period.

That is indeed what happened. Between 1870 and the eve of World War II, Germany's income went from less than 50% to 75% of the average for the remaining members of the EEC. And by 1958, one year after the EEC was formed, Germany had surpassed Belgium as the leader of the five. The exclusion of Germany therefore has the effect of understating the fall in dispersion before the creation of the EEC. The dashed line in Figure 7, which displays the dispersion of log per capita incomes including Germany, shows this. Once Germany is included in the sample, it appears that dispersion has been on a downward trend since 1870. The hypothesis that postwar convergence was simply a continuation of a long-term trend can no longer be rejected easily, raising doubts about the conclusion that convergence was caused by postwar trade policies.[39]

Figure 4 plots the standard deviation of log incomes for the original members of the EEC, now using Maddison's more recent (1995) estimates and including Germany. We reach the same conclusion as in Figure 3: dispersion has followed a downward trend since the beginning of the twentieth century. From a peak of 0.36 in 1897, dispersion had fallen to 0.25 in 1930, and 0.19 in 1939. By the time the EEC was created, it had fallen to 0.16. It appears therefore that the further reduction in disper-

39. Ben-David (in personal communication) has pointed out to us that much of the prewar convergence is due to the fact that "while the other countries were in the Depression, Germany surged ahead as Hitler built his war machine." Indeed, dispersion appears trendless from 1900 to 1932, and starts falling only as Germany's income rises during the National Socialist period. But we are not sure of what to make of that fact. Germany's income remained high after the war—compared to other European countries—suggesting that not all of the convergence was due to the policies of the Nazi period or to the buildup of the war machine. In any case, Nazi Germany pursued highly protectionist policies, so that its experience sheds doubt on the argument that poor countries that close their economies experience slower growth. Finally, the observation for 1870 in Figure 7 suggests that dispersion was much higher in the late nineteenth century than in 1930. The last point is confirmed when we examine Maddison's (1995) more recent estimates (see Figure 8), which provide a fuller picture of trends in dispersion since 1820. These estimates were not available to Ben-David at the time his paper was written.

Figure 4 DISPERSION OF PER CAPITA INCOMES AND TRADE POLICY EVENTS

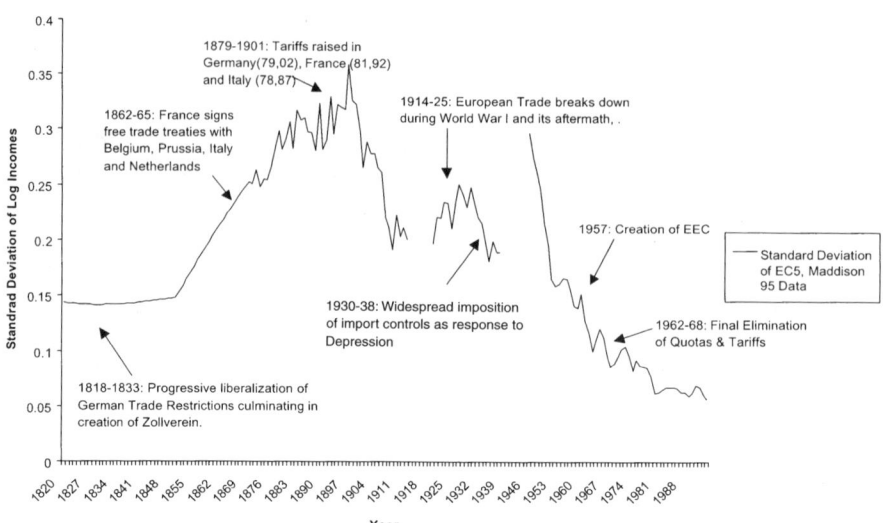

sion that followed the creation of the EEC (to 0.06 by 1994) was a continuation of a long-term trend that predated European integration. Moreover, this conclusion is not sensitive to whether Germany is included in the sample: that is because Maddison's (1995) revised estimates suggest that there was a uniform pattern of convergence during the pre-World War I period, with Italy, France, and Germany *all* catching up with Belgium and the Netherlands.

A closer look at Figure 4 suggests that there is in fact very little association between episodes of economic integration and σ-convergence over time. The period leading up to 1878 was an era of continuous trade liberalization, at the level of both national markets and international ones. This period witnessed the creation of the German *Zollverein* (1833) and the unification of Italy (1860), as well as the signing of free-trade agreements between Prussia and Belgium (1844), France and Belgium (1842), France and Prussia (1862), France and Italy (1863), and France and the Netherlands (1865).[40] Most of these bilateral agreements had

40. The discussion in this and the following two paragraphs borrows heavily from Chapter V of Pollard (1974). Above we list treaties between countries included in Figure 4, but the extent of trade liberalization from 1820 to 1878 in Europe was impressive. Prussia signed free-trade treaties with Britain (1841 and 1860), Turkey (1839), Greece (1840), Austria (1868), Spain (1868), Switzerland (1869), Mexico (1869), and Japan (1869); France with Britain (1860), Switzerland (1864), Sweden, Norway, the Hanse Towns,

most-favored-nation clauses, extending the benefits of bilateral liberalization to third countries. Yet, despite increasing economic integration, dispersion more than doubled from 1820 to 1880 (from 0.14 to 0.29).[41]

The retreat from free trade started during the 1880s, with Germany's Tariff Act of 1879. Italy raised tariffs in 1878 and 1887, France in 1881 and 1892.[42] This rise in protection followed the depression of the 1870s and was motivated by the desire to protect European farmers from the influx of cheap American grain imports (which began to undersell German grain in 1875) while at the same time compensating industry for the increased wages of workers.[43] Nevertheless, as Figure 4 shows, the period from the 1880s to World War I was, if anything, one of convergence.[44]

The breakdown in world trade that followed World War I and the spread of beggar-thy-neighbor protectionist policies adopted during the Great Depression seem also to have had very little effect on dispersion. Even though fascist governments in Italy and Germany raised agricultural tariffs and other protectionist barriers, and in France the power of agricultural groups was large enough to drive the French price of wheat in 1939 to three times its price in London (Cobban, 1965, p. 156), on the eve of World War II dispersion stood at its lowest level since the 1860s.

In sum, Figure 4 shows no long-run tendency for trade liberalization to be associated with greater convergence in per capita incomes. If anything, it shows increasing dispersion during the nineteenth century and falling dispersion during the twentieth century. While one can interpret this evidence in different ways, we find the most straightforward read-

---

and Spain (1865), Austria (1866), and Portugal (1867); Belgium with Britain (1862); Italy with Britain (1862) and Turkey and Greece (1839–1940). Aside from the MFN clause, measures were taken to ease international trade such as the inclusion in the Treaties of Berlin of clauses extending commercial freedoms to foreign citizens (1878, 1885). There were even attempts to create customs unions between France and Germany and between France and its neighbors.

41. A caveat applies here: for 1820–1850 we rely on just two observations: one for 1820, and another one for 1850. Since the 1850 observation for Italy was not available, we constructed it as the result of a linear interpolation between the 1820 and the 1870 observation. Even if we disregard the evidence before 1870, the yearly data from 1870–1880 indicate that the increase in dispersion predated the first protectionist measures.

42. Again, tariff adoption was widespread, with only Holland and the United Kingdom resisting the reversion towards protectionism.

43. In effect, high tariffs worked to the detriment of labor in what came to be known in Germany as the "compact of rye and iron." See Gerschenkron (1943) and Rogowski (1989) for detailed discussions of this era. As Rogowski points out, the reversion towards protectionism was more accentuated in capital-poor countries such as Germany, Italy, and France than in capital-rich countries such as Belgium and the Netherlands.

44. O'Rourke's (1997) econometric study of this period (1975–1914), covering a panel of 10 countries, finds that higher tariffs were correlated with *faster* economic growth, and that the estimated effects are quantitatively large.

ing to be that post-World War II convergence was in fact a continuation of a long-run trend that got started around the turn of the twentieth century.

6.2 DID NON-EEC EUROPEAN COUNTRIES EXPERIENCE CONVERGENCE?

Ben-David also claims that countries in Europe that did not undertake trade liberalization failed to experience convergence. He supports his argument by showing that (a) there was no convergence among the United Kingdom, Denmark, and Ireland until they began to relax their trade restrictions vis-à-vis Europe, and that (b) EFTA countries experienced significant convergence with the EEC as trade barriers among them were liberalized.

To demonstrate (a), Ben-David plots the standard deviation among the United Kingdom, Denmark, and Ireland, all of which started liberalizing trade with the EEC in the mid-1960s. He shows that their dispersion *among themselves* started falling only after 1965. It is not clear to us why this is the relevant test, since the trade liberalization in question took place between these countries and Europe as well as amongst themselves. In Figure 5, we show that even if there is an indication of convergence among these three countries after 1965, it is not caused by conver-

Figure 5 GDP OF UNITED KINGDOM, DENMARK, AND IRELAND, RELATIVE TO EEC MEAN

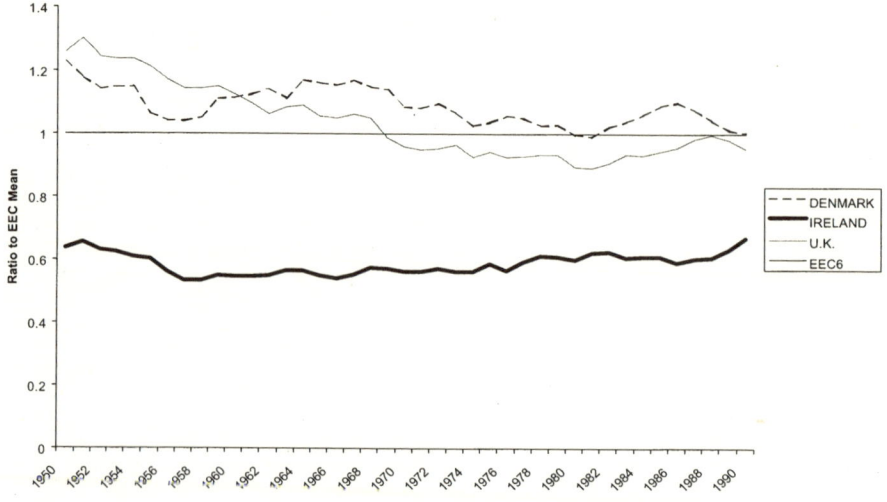

Figure 6 CONTRIBUTION TO VARIANCE AROUND EUROPEAN MEAN

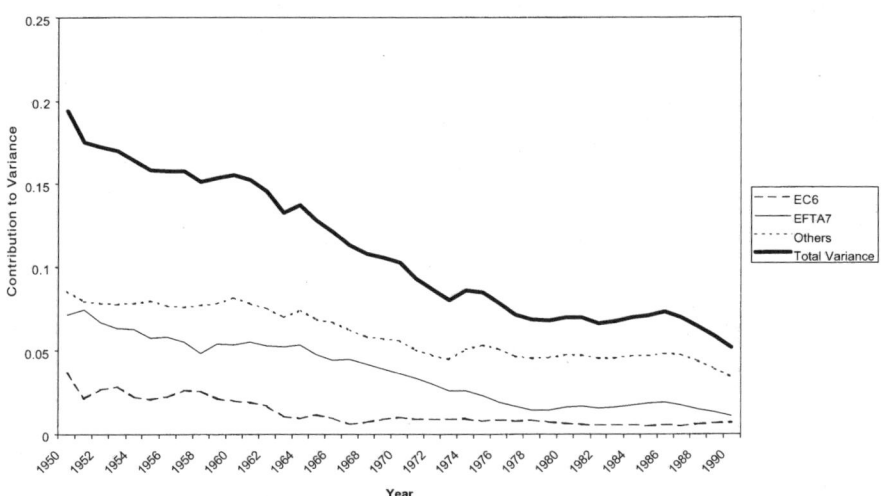

gence to the mean income of EEC members. Ireland has shown very little convergence to the EEC until recent years, and Denmark has oscillated close to the EEC average since the 1950s. The United Kingdom has been converging—downward—to the EEC level steadily (at least) since the 1950s. None of the three countries seem to experience different patterns of convergence after they relaxed trade restrictions with the EEC in 1965.

As regards (b), there has indeed been substantial convergence by EEC and EFTA member countries to the European mean since the 1950s. But we are skeptical whether such convergence can be attributed to trade liberalization. In Figure 6, we plot the contribution to the variance around the European mean[45] of three subsets of European countries: the six members of the European Economic Community, the seven members of the European Free Trade Association,[46] and six remaining European countries which did not join either EFTA or the EEC.[47] It is evident from

45. This is defined as $(1/N_{\text{EUROPE}}) \Sigma_{i \in J} [(y_i - \bar{y}_{\text{EUROPE}})/\bar{y}_{\text{EUROPE}}]^2$ for J = {EEC6, EFTA6, others}. Normalization by the mean achieves the same purpose as calculating the variance of log incomes (and is more appropriate for large income differences), and putting the expression in terms of the variance (not the standard deviation) ensures that the three components sum to the total.
46. Austria, Switzerland, Sweden, Denmark, Norway, Finland, and the United Kingdom. Even though Portugal was officially a member of EFTA, it was allowed to implement tariffs and to deviate from EFTA policies, so we follow Ben-David in treating it as a non-EFTA country.
47. Cyprus, Greece, Iceland, Ireland, Portugal, and Spain.

Figure 6 that all subgroups have experienced substantial convergence. The non-EFTA and non-EEC countries have seen their contribution to the variance around the European mean fall from 0.085 to 0.034 from 1950 to 1992.[48] European convergence seems to be the result of factors largely unrelated to trade liberalization.

6.3 DID OTHER AREAS OF THE WORLD EXPERIENCE CONVERGENCE?

To add plausibility to the story that trade liberalization was behind the European trend towards convergence in the postwar era, Ben-David shows that subsets of countries that have not become integrated have experienced no tendency to converge. He points to the well-known fact that the dispersion of world incomes has not decreased in the postwar era (it has actually increased). He also shows that the dispersion of incomes among the world's 25 richest countries (excluding the EEC6) has not decreased either. He compares these experiences with those of economically integrated Europe and U.S. states to show that convergence seems to occur only when there is substantial trade liberalization.

There is an asymmetry in his selection of diverging and converging areas, however. Whereas the regions he shows to be converging are all close to each other geographically, those which are diverging are not. To have a fair standard of comparison, one must ask whether trade liberalization—or its absence—among geographically adjacent economies would lead towards convergence or divergence.

Did subsets of geographically adjacent economies that liberalized trade tend to observe convergence? There are at least two important cases in which the trends in convergence go counter to what we would expect on the basis of Ben-David's argument. Consider the experiences of East Asia and Latin America, two regions with radically different trade policies and which constitute the canonical examples of open and closed economies. If the liberalizatoin–convergence view is right, the relatively open East Asian economies should have converged, whereas the relatively closed Latin American economies should have diverged. In fact, countries in East Asia have steadily diverged since the 1960s, with the standard deviation of their log incomes going from 0.47 in 1960 to 0.81 in 1989.[49] As for

---

48. If one includes Turkey as a seventh country in this group, the contribution to dispersion goes from 0.103 in 1950 to 0.053 in 1992. An alternative measure of dispersion around the European mean is the standard deviation of log incomes around the mean log income. The latter measure for the non-EEC, non-EFTA countries falls from 0.15 in 1950 to 0.05 in 1990 (0.20 to 0.10 if Turkey is included).

49. The East Asian countries are Hong Kong, Indonesia, Japan, South Korea, Malaysia, Philippines, Singapore, Taiwan, and Thailand. Data are from Summers and Heston (1994). If the Philippines is excluded, the rise in dispersion is from 0.50 to 0.73.

Latin America, there has been a steady *decrease* in dispersion during the period of import substitution, from 0.55 before the Great Depression to 0.20 in the late 1980s.[50] More striking, dispersion has sharply risen since the late 1980s, just as Latin American countries liberalized their trade. (See Rodríguez and Rodrik, 1999, for more details.)

Another important counterexample comes from the historical experience of the United States. Figure 7 plots the ratio of GDP per capita for the United States to the average GDP per capita for its three main European trading partners (the United Kingdom, France, and Germany) up to 1938.[51] Trade with Europe was approximately two-thirds of total U.S. trade during the nineteenth century,[52] and the bulk of that was with those three countries. It is however evident from Figure 7 that despite declining levels of import duties, the United States and Europe steadily diverged between 1820 and 1938. Again, there seems to be no evident relationship between trade liberalization and income convergence.[53]

We close by drawing attention to Slaughter's (2000) recent examination of the same issue. Slaughter undertakes a systematic analysis by compar-

---

50. The Latin American countries are Argentina, Brazil, Chile, Colombia, Mexico, and Peru. Data are from Maddison (1995), Summers and Heston (1994), and World Bank (1998). Latin American import substitution policies started rather spontaneously as a response to the collapse of world-wide demand for raw materials in 1929 and the adoption of protectionist measures by the United States and Britain in 1930 and 1931. Most countries abandoned convertibility and imposed trade barriers during this period and did not liberalize until recent years (see Díaz-Alejandro, 1981).
51. The cutoff date of 1938 is chosen because during World War II the Americas overtook Europe as the main destination for U.S. exports. The Americas overtook Europe as the main source of imports much earlier, during World War I. Including observations after 1940 would not change our results: the GDP per capita in 1994 for the United States was still 27% higher than that of its three main European trading partners, despite the fact that after 1944 tariff rates stayed well into the single digits (Bureau of the Census, 1989). Choosing the Americas instead of Europe as a standard of comparison would strengthen our results, as the divergence between U.S. and Latin American incomes during the nineteenth and twentieth centuries has been extremely high (see Haber, 1997), and Canada represents only about half of U.S. trade with the Americas.
52. Before World War II, exports to Europe were 43% of total exports and imports from Europe were 29% of total imports (Bureau of the Census, 1989).
53. Our broader conclusion is not necessarily inconsistent with Ben-David's own reading of the evidence. Ben-David (in personal communication) writes that the main conclusions that can be drawn from his research are that "trade liberalization is associated with income convergence only when (a) the liberalization is comprehensive and (b) the liberalization occurs between countries that trade extensively with each other," and that "there is no evidence that these outcomes hold for poor countries." In fact, Ben-David (1999) has argued that trade flows will be of little use in transferring knowledge to countries with low levels of human capital. This contrasts strongly with much of the discussion in the literature, which has interpreted Ben-David as making the much stronger claim that liberalization leads developing countries to converge with their richer trading partners. A few examples are IMF (1997, p. 84), World Bank (1996, p. 32), Vamvakidis (1996, p. 251), and Richardson et al. (1997, p. 100), all of which refer to Ben-David in discussions about developing economies.

Figure 7 RATIO OF U.S. TO EUROPEAN GDP AND IMPORT DUTIES, 1820–1938

ing convergence patterns among liberalizing countries before and after liberalization with the convergence pattern among randomly chosen control countries before and after liberalization. As he emphasizes, this difference-in-differences approach avoids the pitfalls of before-and-after comparisons (nonliberalizing countries too may exhibit the same pattern before and after) or of comparing liberalizing countries with non-liberalizing ones (the liberalizing countries may have been converging prior to the liberalization as well). Hence Slaughter's approach amounts to a more systematic version of the kind of exercise we have carried out above by way of specific illustrations (but using only post-World War II data). Slaughter focuses specifically on four instances of trade liberalization: formation of the EEC, formation of EFTA, liberalization between EEC and EFTA, and Kennedy Round tariff cuts under GATT. His conclusion is that there is no systematic link between trade liberalization and convergence. In fact, he reports that much of the evidence suggests trade liberalization diverges incomes among liberalizers. This parallels our results above.

7. *Jeffrey Frankel and David Romer (1999)*

Frankel and Romer's (1999) very recent *AER* paper on trade and incomes has received considerable attention since its publication. This paper analyzes the relationship between trade and income by estimating cross-country regressions of income per capita on the trade–GDP ratio and two measures of country size (population and land area). The authors' aim is to address the problem of the likely endogeneity of trade with respect to income. So the trade share is instrumented by first estimating a gravity equation, where bilateral trade flows are regressed on geographic characteristics (countries' size, their distance from each other, whether they share a common border, and whether they are landlocked). The fitted trade values are then aggregated across partners to create an instrument for the actual trade share. An earlier version of Frankel and Romer's paper included initial income among the regressors in the second-stage equation, so that the results could also be given a growth interpretation. The main finding of the paper is that the IV estimate of the effect of trade on income is if anything greater than the OLS estimate.

As we mentioned in the introduction, this paper is concerned with the relationship between incomes and the *volume* of trade, and does not have immediate implications for trade *policy*. The reason is that the implications of geography-induced differences in trade, on the one hand, and policy-induced variations in trade, on the other, can be in principle quite different. Selective trade policies work as much by altering the structure of trade as they do by reducing its volume. To the extent that policy is targeted on market failures, trade restrictions can augment incomes (or growth rates) even when indiscriminate barriers in the form of geographical constraints would be harmful. Of course, to the extent that selective trade policies are subject to rent seeking, it is also possible that geography-induced variations in trade *under*estimate the real costs of trade restrictions. Ultimately, whether on balance trade policies are used towards benign ends or malign ends is an empirical question, on which Frankel and Romer's paper is silent.

With regard to the role of trade flows proper, we are concerned that Frankel and Romer's geographically constructed trade share may not be a valid instrument. The reason is that geography is likely to be a determinant of income through a multitude of channels, of which trade is (possibly) only one. Geography affects public health (and hence the quality of human capital) through exposure to various diseases. It influences the quality of institutions through the historical experience of colonialism, migrations, and wars. It determines the quantity and quality of natural endowments, including soil fertility, plant variety, and the abundance of minerals. The geographically determined component of trade may be correlated with all these other factors, imparting an upward bias to the IV estimate unless these additional channels are explicitly controlled for in the income equation.

As there is a single instrument used in Frankel and Romer's regressions, conventional exclusion–restriction tests performed conditional on a subset of the instruments being excludable from the second-stage regression cannot be carried out. To check whether Frankel and Romer's result can be attributed to nontrade effects of geography, we simply test whether some summary statistics of the geographical factors influencing trade can be excluded from the second-stage regression. We rerun Frankel and Romer's income regressions, adding three summary indicators of geography: (1) distance from the equator (used in Hall and Jones, 1998); (2) the percentage of a country's land area that is in the tropics (from Radelet, Sachs, and Lee, 1997); and (3) a set of regional dummies.

Table 7 shows the results. Columns 1 and 5 replicate Frankel and Romer's (1999) results in their Table 3, for the OLS and IV versions of the income equation, respectively. The other columns show the consequences of introducing the geography variables. The results are highly

Table 7 FRANKEL–ROMER REGRESSIONS WITH ADDITIONAL GEOGRAPHICAL VARIABLES

Variable	1	2	3	4	5	6	7	8
Trade share	0.85 (3.47)	0.57 (3.00)	0.46 (2.36)	0.61 (3.88)	1.97 (1.99)	0.34 (0.41)	0.21 (0.26)	0.25 (0.41)
Disteq		3.58 (9.26)				3.65 (7.98)		
Tropics			−1.42 (−9.84)				−1.46 (−8.03)	
East Asia				−1.21 (−7.71)				−1.21 (−7.59)
Latin America				−0.67 (−4.48)				−0.74 (−3.83)
Sub-Saharan Africa				−1.94 (−14.72)				−1.99 (−12.82)
Method	OLS	OLS	OLS	OLS	IV	IV	IV	IV
n	150	150	145	150	150	150	145	150
R^2	0.0949	0.4312	0.4628	0.66	0.43	0.44	0.4563	0.65

The dependent variable is log of income per person in 1985. IV standard errors include adjustment for generated regressors. All equations include the logs of population and land area. Disteq is distance from equator, as measured by Hall and Jones (1998). Tropics is fraction of country's area in tropics, as measured by Radelet, Sachs, and Lee (1997).

suggestive. The new variables enter with highly significant coefficients, indicating that they belong in the income equation. Moreover, once the additional geography variables are included, (1) the IV coefficient estimates on trade become statistically insignificant (with t-statistics around 0.4 or below), and (2) the IV point estimates on trade are reduced below their OLS counterparts. These findings are consistent with the hypothesis that nontrade effects of geography are the main driving force behind the findings of Frankel and Romer.[54]

8. Other Recent Work

Before we close, we mention briefly some other recent papers that have examined the connection between openness and economic growth. We focus on three papers in particular: Lee (1993), Harrison (1996), and Wacziarg (1998). These papers are of interest because they contain some methodological innovations.

Lee (1993) reasons, on the basis of an analytical model, that the distortionary effects of trade restrictions should be larger in economies that, in the absence of trade restrictions, would be more exposed to trade. Hence he interacts an indicator of trade policy with a measure of what he calls "free trade openness" (FREEOP).[55] The latter is constructed by regressing observed import shares on land area, distance from major trading partners, import tariffs, and black-market premia, and then calculating the predicted value of imports when the actual values of tariffs black-market premia are replaced by zeros. He finds that this composite measure (FREETAR) enters a growth regression with an estimated coefficient that is negative and statistically significant.

Lee uses two indicators of trade policy: an import-weighted tariff average and the black-market premium. We have discussed above the shortcomings of the latter as a measure of trade policy (when reviewing Sachs and Warner, 1995). The problem with Lee's tariff variable, as Lee (1993, p. 320) acknowledges, is that the underlying tariff data are from "various years in the 1980s"—the tail end of the 1960–1985 period over which his growth regressions are run. This raises the possibility of reverse causation: countries that perform well tend to liberalize their trade regime eventually. To check for this possibility, we have repeated Lee's regression, using the same specification and tariff variable, but over the subse-

---

54. We have carried out this exercise for various other samples [e.g., the higher-quality 98-country sample used by Frankel and Romer (1999), and samples excluding possible outliers such as Luxembourg and Hong Kong] and reach identical conclusions.
55. Specifically, the composite measure is constructed as FREETAR = FREEOP log(1 + tariff).

quent time period 1980–1994.[56] While the estimated coefficient on FREETAR is negative for this later period, it is nowhere near significant (t-statistic -0.80).

Harrison's (1996) main methodological contribution is to examine the relationship between trade policy and growth in a *panel* setting, using fixed effects for countries. This approach has the advantage that it enables the analyst to look for evidence of the effects of trade liberalization *within* countries.[57] But it has the disadvantage that the available time series are necessarily short, requiring the use of annual data or (at most) five-year averages. It may be a lot to ask of such data to reveal much about the relationship between trade policy and growth, because of the likely lags involved and the contamination from business-cycle effects.[58]

Harrison uses seven indicators of trade policy, and finds that three of these "exhibit a robust relationship with GDP growth" (1996, p. 443). These three are the following: (1) the black-market premium, (2) a measure based on the price level of a country's tradables (relative to international prices), and (3) a subjective measure of trade liberalization constructed at the World Bank. We have already discussed at length the problems involved in interpreting measures of each of these types as indicators of trade policy.

Finally, the paper by Wacziarg (1998) is an ambitious attempt to uncover the channels through which openness affects economic growth. Wacziarg's index of trade policy is a linear combination of three indicators: (1) the average import duty rate, (2) the NTB coverage ratio, and (3) the SW indicator.[59] The weights used to construct the combined index come from a regression of trade volumes (as a share of GDP) on these three indicators plus some other determinants. Using a panel made up of five-year averages for 57 countries during 1970–1989, Wacziarg finds that investment is the most important channel through which openness increases growth, accounting for more than 60% of the total effect.

We have two worries about this paper. First, we are not sure that the

---

56. Since Summers–Heston data are not available for the 1990s, we used World Bank data on GDP per capita (at constant prices).
57. Harrison (1996) cites disappointing results with cross-section regressions as a motivation for going the panel route.
58. Indeed, when Harrison (1996) controls for some business-cycle conditions, about half of her significant coefficients (on openness-related variables) disappear. The empirical evidence on the *short-run* relationship between trade liberalization and economic growth is judiciously reviewed in Greenaway, Morgan, and Wright (1998), who point to both positive and negative findings. These authors attempt to trace out the dynamics of the output response using three different indicators of policy (including the SW index), and report finding a J-curve effect: output first falls and then increases.
59. More specifically, Wacziarg uses the timing of trade liberalization in Sachs and Warner (1995) to assign a value to each country for any given five-year period.

regularities revealed by the data over time horizons of five years or less are particularly informative about the relationship between trade policy and long-run economic performance. It would be interesting to see if the results hold up with averages constructed over a decade or more. Second, as discussed previously, we are skeptical that the SW measure, on which the Wacziarg indicator is partly based, is a meaningful indicator of trade policy. Wacziarg remarks in a footnote (1998, footnote 9) that the "exclusion of [the SW indicator] from the trade policy index reduced the precision of the estimates . . . but did not change the qualitative nature of the results." We would have preferred to see estimates based only on tariff and NTB indicators.

9. Concluding Remarks

We have scrutinized in this paper the most prominent recent empirical studies on the relationship between trade barriers and economic growth. While we do not pretend to have undertaken an exhaustive survey, we believe that the weaknesses we have identified are endemic to this literature.

We emphasize that our difficulty with this literature is *not* a variant of the standard robustness criticism often leveled at cross-country growth empirics. Going back at least to Levine and Renelt (1992), a number of authors have pointed to the sensitivity of growth regressions to changes in the list of controls, and to the failure of these coefficients to pass the test of "extreme-bounds analysis." Whatever position one takes on this debate, the general point that we wish to make about the empirical literature on openness and growth is much simpler. For the most part, the strong results in this literature arise either from obvious misspecification or from the use of measures of openness that are proxies for other policy or institutional variables that have an independent detrimental effect on growth. When we do point to the fragility of the coefficients, it is to make the point that the coefficients on the openness indicators are particularly sensitive to controls for these other policy and institutional variables. To the extent that these objections can be conceptualized as variants of the robustness criticism, it is robustness at a much more basic level than that typically discussed in the Bayesian literature.

Still, in view of the voluminous research on the subject, a natural question that arises is whether we shouldn't take comfort from the fact that so many authors, using varying methods, have all arrived at the same conclusion. Don't we learn something from the cumulative evidence, even if individual papers have shortcomings?

We take a different message from this large literature. Had the negative relationship between trade restrictions and economic growth been convincingly demonstrated, we doubt that this issue would continue to generate so much empirical research. We interpret the persistent interest in this area as reflecting the worry that the existing approaches haven't gotten it quite right. One indication of this is that the newer papers are habitually motivated by exegeses on the methodological shortcomings of prior work.

We are especially struck and puzzled by the proliferation of indexes of trade restrictions. It is common to assert in this literature that simple trade-weighted tariff averages or nontariff coverage ratios—which we believe to be the most direct indicators of trade restrictions—are misleading as indicators of the stance of trade policy. Yet we know of no papers that document the existence of serious biases in these direct indicators, much less establish that an alternative indicator performs better (in the relevant sense of calibrating the restrictiveness of trade regimes).[60] An examination of simple averages of taxes on imports and exports and NTB coverage ratios leaves us with the impression that these measures in fact do a decent job of rank-ordering countries according to the restrictiveness of their trade regimes. In the working-paper version of this paper, we provide a simple measure of import duties for a large sample of countries and three different periods, so that the reader can form his/her judgement on this (Rodríguez and Rodrik, 1999, Table VIII.1).[61]

As we mentioned in the introduction, we are skeptical that there is a strong negative relationship in the data between trade barriers and economic growth, at least for levels of trade restrictions observed in practice.[62] We view the search for such a relationship as futile. We think there are two other fruitful avenues for future research.

60. Pritchett (1996) comes closest. The point of his paper, however, is to document the weak correlation between commonly used indicators of trade restrictions, and not to argue for the superiority of one indicator over the others.
61. This is the measure of import tariffs we used in Figure 1 (top panel).
62. In his comment on this paper, Chad Jones acknowledges the fragility of many of the results in the literature, but reports a range of exercises that leads him to conclude, as a best estimate, that trade restrictions are harmful to long-run incomes and that the effects are potentially large. We caution the reader about regressions where the *level* of per capita income is regressed on measures of trade restrictions. It is well known that countries reduce their trade barriers as they get richer, so levels regressions are subject to problems of reverse causality. It is difficult to overcome this problem via instrumentation, since adequate instruments (exogenous variables that are correlated with trade restrictions, but are otherwise uncorrelated with incomes) are particularly difficult to find in this context (as our discussion in Section 7 highlights). When regressions are run in growth form, we find that none of the available continuous measures of trade restrictions (simple tariff averages or nontariff coverage ratios) enter significantly in the vast majority of reasonable specifications. Some dichotomous measures based on the continuous variables do somewhat "better," but only if the break point is set at a sufficiently high level (e.g., a tariff rate or nontariff coverage ratio in excess of 40%).

First, in cross-national work, it might be productive to look for *contingent* relationships between trade policy and growth. Do trade restrictions operate differently in low- vs. high-income countries? In small vs. large countries? In countries with a comparative advantage in primary products vs. those with comparative advantage in manufactured goods? In periods of rapid expansion of world trade vs. periods of stagnant trade? Further, it would help to disaggregate policies and to distinguish the possibly dissimilar effects of different types of trade policies (or of combinations thereof). Are tariff and nontariff barriers to imports of capital goods more harmful to growth than other types of trade restrictions? Does the provision of duty-free access to imported inputs for exporters stimulate growth? Are export-processing zones good for growth? Does the variation in tariff rates (or NTBs) across sectors matter? The cross-national work has yet to provide answers to such questions.

Second, we think there is much to be learned from microeconometric analysis of plant-level datasets. These datasets constitute a rich source for uncovering the ways in which trade policy influences the production, employment, and technological performance of firms (see Roberts and Tybout, 1996). Recent research by Bernard and Jensen (1995, 1998), Aw, Chung, and Roberts (1998), and Clerides, Lach and Tybout (2000) has already shed new light on the relationship between trade and firm performance. For example, these papers (based on the experiences of countries as diverse as the United States, Taiwan, and Mexico) find little evidence that firms derive technological or other benefits from exporting per se; the more common pattern is that efficient producers tend to self-select into export markets. In other words, causality seems to go from productivity to exports, not vice versa. Relating these analyses to trade *policies* is the obvious next step in this line of research.

Let us close by restating our objective in this paper. We do not want to leave the reader with the impression that we think trade protection is good for economic growth. We know of no credible evidence—at least for the post-1945 period—that suggests that trade restrictions are systematically associated with higher growth rates. What we would like the reader to take away from this paper is some caution and humility in interpreting the existing cross-national evidence on the relationship between trade policy and economic growth.

The tendency to greatly overstate the systematic evidence in favor of trade openness has had a substantial influence on policy around the world. Our concern is that the priority afforded to trade policy has generated expectations that are unlikely to be met, and it may have crowded out other institutional reforms with potentially greater payoffs. In the real world, where administrative capacity and political capital are scarce, having a clear sense of policy priorities is of utmost importance. The effects of trade liberalization may be on balance beneficial on standard comparative-advantage grounds; the evidence provides no strong reason to dispute this. What we dispute is the view, increasingly common, that integration into the world economy is such a potent force for economic growth that it can effectively substitute for a development strategy.

Data Appendix

SECTION 1

1. Import duties as a percentage of imports. Source: World Bank (1998).
2. Nontariff barriers. Source: Barro and Lee (1994).

SECTION 3

3. bmpav: average black-market premium. Source: Sachs and Warner (1995).
4. rcoast: coastal length over total land area. Source: Radelet, Sachs, and Lee (1997).
5. tropics: dummy for tropical countries. Source: Radelet, Sachs, and Lee (1997).
6. Latin America: dummy for countries in Latin America and the Caribbean.
7. SSA: dummy for countries in sub-Saharan Africa.
8. East Asia: dummy for countries in East Asia.
9. TAR: own-import-weighted ratio of tariff revenues to trade. Source: Barro and Lee (1994).
10. NTB: own-import-weighted nontariff frequency on capital goods and intermediates. Source: Barro and Lee (1994).
11. DISTORTION: ratio of consumption price level to U.S. price level, measured in identical currencies, divided by the fitted value of a regression on GDP, GDP squared, year dummies, and continent dummies. Source: Dollar (1992).
12. VARIABILITY: Coefficient of variation of DISTORTION. Source: Dollar (1992).
13. Investment/GDP: Source: Summers and Heston (1988) for Table 2.
14. Log initial income: Source: Summers and Heston (1988) for Table 2.
15. Schooling, 1975: Barro and Lee (1994).

SECTION 4

16. BMP: Dummy variable equal to 1 if black-market premium exceeds 20% during either the 1970s or the 1980s. Source: Sachs and Warner (1995).
17. BMP70, BMP80: Black-market premium during (respectively) 1970s and 1980s. Source: Sachs and Warner (1995).
18. MON: Dummy variable equal to 1 if the country had a score of 4 (highest score) on the Export Marketing Index in World Bank (1994). Source: Sachs and Warner (1995).
19. SOC: Dummy variable equal to 1 if the country was classified as socialist in Kornai (1992). Source: Sachs and Warner (1995).
20. TAR: own-import-weighted ratio of tariff revenues to trade. Source: Barro and Lee (1994).
21. NTB: own-import-weighted nontariff frequency on capital goods and intermediates. Source: Barro and Lee (1994).
22. OPEN: Variable equal to 0 if the country had BMP = 1, MON = 1, SOC = 1, TAR > 0.4, or NTB > 0.4. Source: Sachs and Warner (1995).
23. BM, SQT, QT, etc.: Openness indexes constructed using subsets of the Sachs and Warner's information. The label for each index denotes the openness indicators used to construct that index: M = state monopoly of main export, S = socialist economic system, Q = nontariff barriers, T = tariffs, B = black-market premium. For example, SMQT is set to 0 if it is closed according to either of the criteria for S, M, Q, or T, and to 1 otherwise.
24. Inflation, 1975–1990. Source: World Bank (1998).
25. Debt/exports, 1985. Source: World Bank (1998).
26. Change in terms of trade. Source: Barro and Lee (1994).
27. War: dummy for countries that participated in at least one external war over the period 1960–1985. Source: Barro and Lee (1994).
28. Quality of institutions: Institutional quality index from Knack and Keefer (1995).
29. Government budget surplus, 1970–1990. Source: World Bank (1998).
30. Population growth. Source: World Bank (1998).

SECTION 5

31. Sachs–Warner: Same as OPEN in Section 4.
32. World Development Report: World Development Report outward-orientation index, 1973–1985. Source: Edwards (1998).

33. Leamer: Openness index estimated by Leamer (1988) using residuals from disaggregated trade-flow regressions. Source: Edwards (1998).
34. Black-market premium: same as BMP80 in Section 4.
35. Tariffs: Same as TAR in Section 4.
36. Quotas: Same as NTB in Section 4.
37. Heritage Foundation: Subjective index of the extent to which government policies distort trade, from Johnson and Sheehy (1996). Source: Edwards (1998).
38. Collected-trade-taxes ratio: Average for 1980–1985 of ratio of total revenues on international trade taxes to total trade. Source: Edwards (1998).
39. Wolf's index of import distortions: A regression-based index from Wolf (1993). Source: Edwards (1998).
40. Principal-components factor: First principal component of OPEN, black-market premium, tariffs, quotas, and Wolf's index. The equation used to calculate it is
    COM = $-0.469 \times$ OPEN $+ 0.320 \times$ BLACK $+ 0.494 \times$ TARIFF $+ 0.553 \times$ QR $+ 0.354 \times$ WOLF.
41. Log of GDP per capita, 1985. From Summers and Heston (1994). Source: Edwards (1998).
42. Property rights: Heritage Foundation index of property-rights protection, from Johnson and Sheehy (1996). Source: Edwards (1998).
43. Average import and export duties (World Bank): From World Bank (1998). Average duty is calculated as $(1 + \text{export duty}) \times (1 + \text{import duty}) - 1$.
44. Merged duty index: Simple average of average duty (43) and (38).
45. Trade distortion index based on Lee's data. Analog of Heritage index using data from Lee (1993) in Barro and Lee (1994). Countries are rated on a score of 1 to 5 according to the maximum of tariff rate and nontariff-barrier coverage ratio: higher than 20%: "very high" (a rating of 5); between 15 and 20%: "high" (4); between 10% and 15%: "moderate" (3); between 5% and 10%: "low" (2); and between 0 and 5%: "very low" (1).

SECTION 6

46. Contributions to variance around EC mean, from Summers and Heston (1994).
47. GDP per capita (Figure 3): Maddison (1982). Source: Ben-David (1993).
48. GDP per capita (Figure 4, Table 7): Maddison (1995).

49. GDP per capita (Figures 5–7): Summers and Heston (1994).
50. Ratio of import duties to imports, United States, from Bureau of the Census (1989, Series U211).

REFERENCES

Acheson, A. L. K. and D. McFetridge. (1996). Intellectual property and endogenous growth. In *The Implications of Knowledge-Based Growth for Microeconomic Policies*. P. Howitt (ed.). Calgary: University of Calgary Press.

Aw, B. Y., S. Chung, and M. J. Roberts. (1998). Productivity and turnover in the export market: Micro evidence from Taiwan and South Korea. Pennsylvania State University.

Balassa, B. (1971). *The Structure of Protection in Developing Countries*. Baltimore: Johns Hopkins University Press, 1971.

———. (1985). Exports, policy choices, and economic growth in developing countries after the 1973 oil shock. *Journal of Development Economics* 18(2): 23–35.

Barro, R. J. (1997). *Determinants of Economic Growth: A Cross-Country Empirical Study*. Cambridge, MA: The MIT Press.

———, and J.-W. Lee. (1993). International comparisons of educational attainment. *Journal of Monetary Economics* 32(3):363–394.

———, and ———. (1994). Data set for a panel of 138 countries. Harvard University.

Ben-David, D. (1993). Equalizing exchange: Trade liberalization and income convergence. *Quarterly Journal of Economics* 108(3).

———. (1999). Teach your children well: Planting the seeds of education and harvesting the benefits of trade. Tel Aviv University.

Bernard, A. B., and J. B. Jensen. (1995). Exporters, jobs, and wages in U.S. manufacturing, 1975–1987. In *Brookings Papers on Economic Activity: Microeconomics 1995*, pp. 67–112.

———, and ———. (1998). Exporting and productivity. Presented at 1998 Summer Institute, NBER, Cambridge, MA.

Bhagwati, J. N. (1982). Directly unproductive, rent-seeking (DUP) Activities. *Journal of Political Economy* 90(5):988–1002.

Bhalla, S., and L. J. Lau. (1992). Openness, technological progress, and economic growth in developing countries. World Bank.

Buffie, E. (1998). *Trade Policy in Developing Countries*. Unpublished manuscript.

Bureau of the Census. (1989). *Historical Statistics of the United States, Colonial Times to 1970*. White Plains, NY: Kraus International Publications.

Burnside, C., and D. Dollar. (1997). Aid, policies, and growth. World Bank. Policy Research Working Paper 1777.

Caves, R. E., J. A. Frankel, and R. W. Jones. (1999). *World Trade and Payments: An Introduction*. 8th ed. Reading, MA: Addison-Wesley, 1999.

Clague, C., P. Knack, S. Keefer, and M. Olson. (1996). Property and contract rights in autocracies and democracies. *Journal of Economic Growth* 1(2):243–276.

Clerides, S., S. Lach, and J. Tybout. (2000). Is "Learning-by-exporting" important? Micro-dynamic evidence from Colombia, Mexico, and Morocco. *Quarterly Journal of Economics*, forthcoming.

Cobban, A. (1965). *A History of Modern France*. New York: Braziller.

Collins, S. M. and B. P. Bosworth. (1996). Economic growth in East Asia:

Accumulation versus assimilation. *Brookings Papers on Economic Activity* 1996 (2):135–191.

Díaz-Alejandro, C. (1981). Southern Cone stabilization plans. In *Economic Stabilization in Developing Countries*, W. Cline and S. Weintraub (eds.). Washington: The Brookings Institution.

Dollar, D. (1992). Outward-oriented developing economies really do grow more rapidly: Evidence from 95 LDCs, 1976–85. *Economic Development and Cultural Change* 1992:523–544.

Edwards, S. (1992). Trade orientation, distortions, and growth in developing countries. *Journal of Development Economics* 39(1):31–57.

———. (1993). Openness, trade liberalization, and growth in developing countries. *Journal of Economic Literature* XXXI(3):1358–1393.

———. (1998). Openness, productivity and growth: What do we really know? *Economic Journal* 108(March):383–398.

Esfahani, H. S. (1991). Exports, imports, and growth in semi-industrialized countries. *Journal of Development Economics* 35(1):93–116.

Falvey, R., and N. Gemell. (1999). Factor endowments, nontradables prices and measures of "openness." *Journal of Development Economics* 58(February):101–122.

Feder, G. (1983). On exports and economic growth. *Journal of Development Economics* 12(1/2):59–73.

Feenstra, R. (1990). Trade and uneven growth. Cambridge, MA: National Bureau of Economic Research. NBER Working Paper 3276.

Fischer, S. (2000). Lunch address given at the conference on "Promoting Dialogue: Global Challenges and Global Institutions," Washington: American University.

Frankel, J., and D. Romer. (1999). Does trade cause growth? *American Economic Review* 89(3):379–399.

Gelb, A. H., and Associates. (1988). *Oil Windfalls: Blessing or Curse?* New York: Oxford University Press.

Gerschenkron, A. (1943). *Bread and Democracy in Germany*, Berkeley and Los Angeles: University of California Press.

Greenaway, D., W. Morgan, and P. Wright. (1998). Trade reform, adjustment and growth: What does the evidence tell us? *The Economic Journal* 108 (September):1547–1561.

Grossman, G., and E. Helpman. (1991). *Innovation and Growth in the Global Economy.* Cambridge, MA: The MIT Press.

Grossman, H., and M. Kim. (1996). Predation and accumulation. *Journal of Economic Growth* 1(3):333–350.

Gulhati, R. and R. Nallari. (1990). *Successful Stabilization and Recovery in Mauritius.* Washington: The World Bank.

Haber, S. (1997). *How Latin America Fell Behind: Essays on the Economic Histories of Brazil and Mexico, 1800–1914.* Stanford, CA: Stanford University Press.

Hall, R. E., and C. I. Jones. (1998). Why do some countries produce so much more output per worker than others? Cambridge, MA: National Bureau of Economic Research. NBER Working Paper W6564.

Harrison, A. (1996). Openness and growth: A time-series, cross-country analysis for developing countries. *Journal of Development Economics* 48:419–447.

———, and G. Hanson. (1999). Who gains from trade reform? Some remaining puzzles. *Journal of Development Economics* 50:125–154.

Husted, S., and M. Melvin. (1997). *International Economics,* 4th ed. Reading, MA: Addison-Wesley.
IMF. (1997). *World Economic Outlook,* Washington.
International Currency Analysis. (1995). *World Currency Yearbook.* Brooklyn, NY: International Currency Analysis, Inc.
Jodha, N. (1996). Property rights and development. In *Rights to nature: Ecological, economic, cultural and political principles of institutions for the environment,* S. Hanna (ed.). Washington: Island Press.
Johnson, B. T., and T. P. Sheehy. (1996). *1996 Index of Economic Freedom.* Washington: The Heritage Foundation.
Knack, S., and P. Keefer. (1995). Institutions and economic performance: Cross-country tests using alternative institutional measures. *Economics & Politics,* November, pp. 207–228.
Kornai, J. (1992). *The Socialist System: The Political Economy of Communism.* Princeton, NJ: Princeton University Press.
Krueger, A. O. (1974). The political economy of the rent-seeking society. *American Economic Review* 64(June):291–303.
———. (1998). Why trade liberalisation is good for growth. *The Economic Journal* 108(September):1513–1522.
Krugman, P. R., and M. Obstfeld. (1997). *International Economics: Theory and Policy,* 4th ed. Reading, MA: Addison-Wesley, 1997.
Leamer, E. (1988). Measures of openness. In *Trade Policy and Empirical Analysis,* R. Baldwin (ed.). Chicago: University of Chicago Press.
Lee, J.-W. (1993). International trade, distortions, and long-run economic growth. *International Monetary Fund Staff Papers* 40(2):299–328.
Lerner, A. P. (1936). The symmetry between import and export taxes. *Economica* 11:306–313.
Levine, R., and D. Renelt. (1992). A sensitivity analysis of cross-country growth regressions. *American Economic Review* 82(4):942–963.
Little, I., T. Scitovsky, and M. Scott. (1970). *Industry and Trade in Some Developing Countries.* London and New York: Oxford University Press.
Maddison, A. (1982). *Phases of Capitalist Development.* Oxford and New York: Oxford University Press.
———. (1995). *Monitoring the World Economy: 1820–1992.* Development Centre Studies. Paris and Washington: Organisation for Economic Co-operation and Development, 1995.
Matsuyama, K. (1992). Agricultural productivity, comparative advantage, and economic growth. *Journal of Economic Theory* 58(2):317–334.
OECD. (1998). *Open Markets Matter: The Benefits of Trade and Investment Liberalisation.* Paris: OECD. 1998.
O'Rourke, K. H. (1997). Tariffs and growth in the late nineteenth century. Center for Economic Policy Research. Discussion Paper 1700.
Park, W. and J. C. Ginarte. (1997). Intellectual property rights and economic growth. *Contemporary Economic Policy* 15(3):51–61.
Pertamina. (1998). http://www.pertamina.co.id/ptmhp.htm.
Pollard, S. (1974). *European Economic Integration, 1815–1970.* London: Thames and Hudson.
Pritchett, L. (1996). Measuring outward orientation: Can it be done? *Journal of Development Economics* 49(2).

Radelet, S., J. D. Sachs, and J.-W. Lee. (1997). Economic growth in Asia. Harvard Institute for International Development. Development Discussion Paper.

Richardson, P., et al. (1997). Globalization and linkages: Macro-structural challenges and opportunities. OECD Economic Surveys 28.

Roberts, M. J., and J. R. Tybout, eds. (1996). *Industrial Evolution in Developing Countries*. New York: Oxford University Press for the World Bank.

Rodríguez, F., and D. Rodrik. (1999). Trade policy and economic growth: A skeptic's guide to the cross-national literature. Cambridge, MA: National Bureau of Economic Research. NBER Working Paper 7081.

Rodrik, D. (1999). *The New Global Economy and Developing Countries: Making Openness Work*. Washington: Overseas Development Council.

Rogoff, K. (1996). The purchasing power parity puzzle. *Journal of Economic Literature* XXXIV (June):647–668.

Rogowski, R. (1989). *Commerce and Coalitions: How Trade Affects Domestic Political Alignments*. Princeton: Princeton University Press.

Sachs, J., and A. Warner. (1995). Economic reform and the process of global integration. *Brookings Papers on Economic Activity* 1995(1):1–118.

Sala-i-Martin, X. (1997). I just ran two million regressions. *American Economic Review* 87(2):178–183.

Slaughter, M. J. (2000). Trade liberalization and per capita income convergence: A difference-in-differences analysis. *Journal of International Economics*, forthcoming.

Srinivasan, T. N. (1997). As the century turns: Analytics, empirics, and politics of development. Economic Growth Center, Yale University.

Stiglitz, J. E. (1998). Towards a new paradigm for development: Strategies, policies, and processes. 1998 Prebisch Lecture, UNCTAD, Geneva.

Summers, R., and A. Heston. (1988). A new set of international comparisons of real product and price levels: Estimates for 130 countries, 1950–1985. *Review of Income and Wealth* 34(March):1–25.

———, and ———. (1994). *Penn World Tables Mark 5.6*. http://www.nber.org.

Thompson, M., and F. Rushing. (1996). An empirical analysis of the impact of patent protection on economic growth. *Journal of Economic Development* 21(2): 61–79.

Tornell, A. (1997). Economic growth and decline with endogenous property rights. *Journal of Economic Growth* 2(3):219–250.

Vamvakidis, A. (1996). Regional integration and economic growth. *The World Bank Economic Review* 12(2):251–270.

Wacziarg, R. (1998). Measuring the dynamic gains from trade. World Bank Working Paper 2001.

White, H. L. (1980). A heteroskedasticity-consistent covariance matrix estimator and a direct test for heteroskedasticity. *Econometrica* 48:817–838.

Wolf, H. (1993). Trade orientation: Measurement and consequences. *Estudios de Economia* 20(20):52–72.

World Bank. (1983). *Mauritius Economic Memorandum: Recent Developments and Prospects*. Washington: The World Bank.

———. (1989). *Mauritius: Managing Success*. Washington: The World Bank.

———. (1994). *Adjustment in Africa: Reforms, Results, and the Road Ahead*. Washington: The World Bank.

———. (1996). *Global Economic Prospects and the Developing Countries*. Washington: The World Bank.

———. (1998). *World Development Indicators CD-ROM*. Washington: The World Bank.

Yarbrough, B. M., and R. M. Yarbrough. (2000). *The World Economy: Trade and Finance*, 5th ed. Fort Worth, TX: Harcourt College Publishers.

Comment

CHANG-TAI HSIEH
Princeton University

Francisco Rodríguez and Dani Rodrik argue that the conventional wisdom among multilateral institutions in Washington (and many economists) that lower trade barriers results in significantly faster growth is based on weak empirical evidence. Their main point is that the empirical evidence that purportedly shows a negative correlation between trade barriers and growth typically relies on measures that are either measures of macroeconomic imbalances or bad institutions, and are not actually measures of trade barriers. For example, they argue that a widely used measure of trade restrictions—deviation of domestic prices of tradables from world prices—reflects deviations from PPP due to overvalued exchange rates, and is not a measure of trade barriers. To take another example, Rodríguez and Rodrik argue that the widely used Sachs–Warner openness index is largely a dummy variable for sub-Saharan Africa and countries with large macroeconomic imbalances, which again is not a measure of trade barriers.

However, the fact that trade barriers are not robustly correlated with growth once controls for macroeconomic imbalances and bad institutions are introduced does not imply that trade barriers do not have deleterious effects of growth. There is a fundamental identification problem in separating the effects of trade restrictions from those of macroeconomic imbalances and bad institutions, since countries with bad macroeconomic policies and weak institutions also have severe trade restrictions. And when countries liberalize their trade regimes, it typically takes place along with a macroeconomic stabilization program. Therefore, there may not be enough cross-country variation in trade restrictions orthogonal to macroeconomic imbalances to identify the effect of trade on growth, even if trade restrictions do have significant negative effects on growth. For example, even if the Sachs–Warner index is a dummy for sub-Saharan Africa, it is still the case that most sub-Saharan countries have in fact imposed significant trade restrictions.

Nonetheless, I find their main point—that there is a large standard error around precisely how much trade barriers matter for growth—

largely convincing. But we shouldn't find the results surprising. Starting from Levine and Renelt (1992), there is overwhelming evidence that very little—not even factors such as increases in human capital that *a priori* would seem to be important in explaining growth—is robust in the empirical growth literature. Therefore, there is no reason to expect measures of trade barriers to be robustly correlated with growth, even if we were to obtain accurate measures of trade restrictions. Furthermore, given the diversity of countries around the world and the different forms which trade barriers take, it is silly to think that one can find a consistent cross-country relationship between trade restrictions and growth. First of all, trade barriers take many different forms. We do not expect there to be significant deleterious growth effects from a well-administered uniform 20–30% tariff. In contrast, a country in which trade barriers are set in a discretionary manner with rampant rent seeking will probably have poor growth performance. Second of all, countries are very different. Small countries probably benefit more from trade than large countries. Countries that are more specialized benefit more from trade than countries that are already well diversified. Finally, we know that trade barriers introduce distortions, but so does every form of government intervention, and there is no reason to believe that the costs of trade distortions are significantly different from the costs of other government interventions. So there is a sense in which the empirical studies that attempt to find a robust cross-country correlation between trade restrictions and growth are as sensible as a cross-country regression of growth on, say, sales taxes or income taxes.

One way to make progress in understanding how trade restrictions affect growth is to differentiate between the effects of different types of trade barriers. Here, the empirical growth literature gives us some guidance on what to look for. Specifically, starting from De Long and Summers (1991), many authors have found that investment in machinery and equipment is the only variable (other than a dummy for sub-Saharan Africa) that is robustly correlated with growth. This is sensible. After all, countries that have grown rapidly are ones that have invested resources in using the machines that embody the technologies of the industrial revolution. Trade policy—specifically, restrictions on imports of capital goods—can affect machinery and equipment investment by increasing the price of imported machinery and equipment. Restrictions on capital-good imports are even more harmful in a developing country that has little domestic production of capital goods and would thus benefit the most from purchasing capital goods embodying the most advanced technologies.

As far as I am aware, there is no study that specifically studies the growth effects of restrictions on capital-good imports. There is, however, suggestive evidence that such restrictions have important effects. It is well known, for example, that Taiwan and Korea have had highly distorted trade regimes, but which nonetheless always kept domestic prices of capital goods close to world prices. Consequently, despite their distorted trade regimes, the share of imports and investment in machinery and investment in these two countries were among the highest in the world. Another piece of evidence is from Charles Jones's (1994) intriguing paper—the dual of De Long and Summers's paper—that shows that the relative price of capital differs enormously between rich and poor countries (by a factor of four). Further, this relative price is significantly correlated with growth even after controlling for initial income, so we know the correlation is not driven by reverse causation due to a Balassa–Samuelson effect. Clearly, the way in which the relative price of capital affects growth is by lowering the amount of capital equipment; if a country increases the relative price of capital and thus of growth, there is going to be less of both.

The main problem is that we do not know whether the large differences in relative price of capital (orthogonal to GDP/worker) are due to differences between trade barriers for capital goods and barriers for consumption goods, or due to domestic distortions that affect the relative price of all capital goods. Clearly, if capital goods are mostly imports, the distinction is moot. However, a simple way to test this is to see whether the share of imports in total machinery and equipment investment is correlated with the relative price of capital. The idea is that if differences in the relative price of capital are due entirely to domestic distortions, then they should affect the aggregate quantity of investment in machinery and equipment but should have no effect on the *composition* of investment between imports and domestically produced capital goods. Table 1 shows that, controlling for initial income and the manufacturing share of GDP, a doubling in the relative price of capital (about the difference between Korea and India) lowers the import share of investment by almost 6 percentage points in the full sample. The effect is even stronger in developing countries, where a similar increase in the relative price of capital lowers the import share by almost 10 percentage points.[1] It would obviously be better to get direct measures of restrictions on imports of capital goods. In addition, the sample, particularly that for the non-OECD countries, is small, since we are restricted to the countries that

---

1. The data on initial income and manufacturing share are from the *Penn World Tables* (Mark 5.6). The relative price of capital is from Charles Jones's Web site (http://www.stanford.edu/~chadj/RelPrice.asc), and imports of machinery and equipment relative to total investment in machinery and equipment were graciously provided by Lee Jong-Wha (who compiled them from the OECD's trade-statistics datatapes).

Table 1 CROSS-COUNTRY DIFFERENCES IN RELATIVE PRICE OF CAPITAL AFFECT IMPORTS OF CAPITAL GOODS

Variable	Full sample	Non-OECD countries
log(relative price of capital)	−0.0574 (0.0359)	−0.0986 (0.0453)
Manufacturing share of GDP	0.3881 (0.2639)	0.7954 (0.3049)
log(initial income per capita)	−0.1040 (0.1085)	−0.0738 (0.1685)
N	52	35
SEE	0.1498	0.1490
R^2	0.12	0.26

Dependent variable is imports of capital goods from OECD countries/total investment in machinery and equipment.

have participated in the benchmark surveys of the United Nations International Comparisons Project. Nonetheless, these results provide suggestive evidence that part of the cross-country difference in the relative price of capital is due to trade barriers.

One can also turn to narrative histories of particular countries for evidence of the impact of capital-good restrictions. For example, I have always found Carlos Diaz-Alejandro's (1970) story of Argentina's economic decline particularly compelling and disturbing. Starting with the Great Depression, Argentina sought to redistribute wealth from rural landowners and exporting elites to the urban working class by making imports of consumer goods freely available but severely restricting imports of capital goods. This policy of redistribution doubled the relative price of capital in Argentina from the late 1930s to the late 1940s (see Figure 1), which led to anemic rates of investment in machinery and equipment in Argentina since the end of World War II. Consequently, a country that was among the wealthiest nations in the world in the early twentieth century is now decidedly a Third World nation.

In the other direction, the experience of India in the 1990s provides evidence that the removal of restrictions on capital-good imports can have significant positive effects on growth. Specifically, India liberalized imports of capital goods in the early 1990s without lowering barriers on imports of consumer goods (which it has done only recently). Due to the

Figure 1 CHANGE IN RELATIVE PRICE OF MACHINERY AND EQUIPMENT: ARGENTINA, 1935–1964

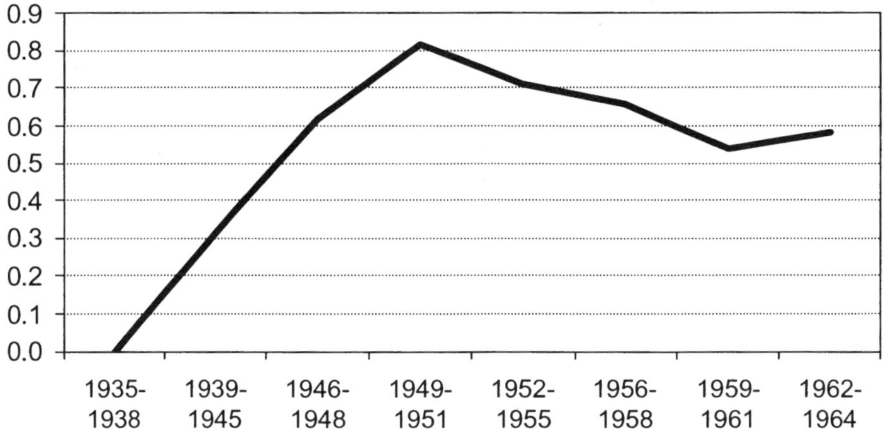

[Chart showing values rising from near 0.0 in 1935-1938 to about 0.82 in 1949-1951, then declining to around 0.55-0.58 by 1962-1964, with x-axis periods: 1935-1938, 1939-1945, 1946-1948, 1949-1951, 1952-1955, 1956-1958, 1959-1961, 1962-1964]

Source: Diaz-Alejandro (1970).

removal of trade barriers on capital goods, there has been a surge of capital-good imports in India over the last decade. Although it is difficult to disentangle the effect of this policy change from that of other policy reforms introduced by the Indian Government at the same time, the fact is that India has experienced high growth rates over the last decade.

Ultimately then, this paper should not change one's prior idea that trade restrictions are bad for growth, but it is useful to point out that there is a large standard error surrounding the point estimate of its negative effect. If we want to narrow this error band, it is important to differentiate between the very different types of trade restrictions that countries have put into place. For example, I have provided some suggestive evidence that restrictions on capital-good imports have important adverse effects on growth. To the extent that this paper prompts us to ask (and attempt to answer) more refined questions about how trade restrictions affect growth, it serves a useful purpose. Nonetheless, I worry about the potential misuse of the authors' fine work by opponents of free trade in the political arena. After all, there are many vested interests that benefit from trade restrictions and much fewer interest groups that actively support free trade. It would be a shame if opponents of free trade (wrongly) interpret this paper as claiming that trade restrictions do not have adverse effects on growth, rather than as saying we don't precisely know how much trade barriers affect growth.

REFERENCES

De Long, J. B., and L. Summers. (1991). Equipment investment and economic growth. *Quarterly Journal of Economics* 106(2):445–502.
Diaz-Alejandro, C. (1970). *Essays on the Economic History of the Argentina Republic.* New Haven, CT: Yale University Press.
Jones, C. (1994). Economic growth and the relative price of capital. *Journal of Monetary Economics* 34(3):359–382.
Levine, R., and Renelt, D. (1992). A sensitivity analysis of cross-country growth regressions. *American Economic Review* 82(4):942–963.

Comment

CHARLES I. JONES
Stanford University and NBER

1. Introduction

Rodríguez and Rodrik replicate and check for robustness the results of several of the most influential papers in the cross-country growth literature on trade policy and economic growth. These studies suggest that policies that distort trade are associated with reduced growth rates over some period of time, and that the effects are fairly important in magnitude and relatively robust in terms of statistical significance.

Interpreted narrowly, the findings of Rodríguez and Rodrik suggest that the results of these existing studies are not as strong as the papers indicate. First, Rodríguez and Rodrik remind us that theory provides no clear indication of the net effect: trade restrictions could reduce income levels or growth rates through the usual channels such as specialization, but the common infant-industry argument, for example, suggests that trade restrictions could in some circumstances promote long-run performance. Second, we do not know exactly how we should measure trade restrictions, which leads to a large number of different approaches in the literature. However, it is not obvious that the variables used in these studies truly capture policy restrictions on trade, making the evidence difficult to interpret. Finally, Rodríguez and Rodrik argue that the results of these studies are not particularly robust. Including additional variables that plausibly belong in the specification, especially some measure of macroeconomic distortions (such as the black-market premium) or some measure of institutional quality or property rights [such as the Knack–Keefer (1995) measure], typically reduces the magnitude of the effect and enlarges the confidence interval substantially so that the trade-policy variable is not statistically significant at traditional levels.

Interpreted broadly, the paper seems to suggest that trade-policy restrictions may not be particularly harmful to long-run economic performance, and that other factors could be much more important.

In preparing my discussion, I contacted several of the authors of four of the papers discussed by Rodríguez and Rodrik to get their general reactions. Because the issues are complicated and it would constitute a paper in itself, I have decided not to report and discuss their comments point by point. Suffice it to say that there are disagreements about a number of the criticisms among the parties involved.[1] Related to the "broad" interpretation of the paper, these authors reminded me that the belief among some economists that trade restrictions are harmful in the long run is based on many kinds of evidence, including case studies and micro studies. However, because this broader discussion is not my area of expertise, and because surely cross-country regressions are one piece of evidence upon which these beliefs are based, I will limit the scope of my discussion in the way the paper is limited.

My comment on Rodríguez and Rodrik's paper will focus on the magnitude of the effect of trade restrictions on economic performance, providing a slightly different emphasis from that presented in the paper. First, I would like to review a useful way that cross-country growth regressions can be interpreted, focusing especially on the magnitude of the estimated effects in the long run. Second, I will attempt to interpret in this framework some specifications that Rodríguez and Rodrik seem to approve of most. In particular, I'd like to look at two questions: "What is our best estimate of the effect of trade restrictions on long-term eco-

---

1. I will report my interpretation of a few of the most interesting ones, though I surely will not do the authors justice. Andrew Warner pointed out to me that the "monopolizes exports" component of the Sachs–Warner index is *not* a dummy for sub-Saharan Africa. It is based on a careful analysis of the subject by the World Bank. It may closely resemble an Africa dummy, but maybe that is a good thing! One could include an Africa dummy with the Sachs–Warner openness measure to check for robustness; in my tests, the openness measure survives. Also, the spirit of their index is that a country can close itself off in a number of different ways that may differ across countries, and Sachs and Warner try to provide an index to capture this phenomenon. This nonlinearity means that running a horse race among the components of the index will not capture the same forces. Dan Ben-David reminded me of Figures XII and XIII in his paper, which provide an additional piece of evidence supporting his view: the reduction in tariffs between the United States and Canada in the late 1960s associated with the Kennedy round, and the associated behavior of incomes. He also noted that the breakdown of European trade in the interwar period is associated with a cessation of convergence, and the resumption of convergence occurs with the reduction of tariffs and quotas after the war. Sebastian Edwards noted that he has tried in earlier work to address measurement-error concerns by running "reverse" regressions. With respect to heteroskedasticity, he also commented that there are conceptual concerns about White-robust errors and that different weightings give different results (for example, weighting by exports per capita gives results like those he obtained). David Dollar provided a broader perspective that is incorporated throughout my comment.

nomic performance?" and "How confident are we about the magnitude of this effect?"

2. Interpreting Cross-Country Growth Regressions

The interpretation of cross-country growth regressions that I find most useful is provided by Mankiw, Romer, and Weil (1992) and Barro and Sala-i-Martin (1992). These papers derive a basic cross-country growth specification from a neoclassical growth model. The derived specification suggests that the growth rate of a particular country over some time period, like thirty years, is a function (often linearized) of the gap between where the country starts out and the country's steady state. To be more accurate, the simplest neoclassical growth model has one state variable, such as the ratio of per capita income to the technology index ($\tilde{y} \equiv y/A$), and the model predicts that the growth rate of this state variable is approximately proportional to the gap between its current value and its steady-state value:

$$\frac{\dot{\tilde{y}}_{it}}{\tilde{y}_{it}} = -\lambda(\log \tilde{y}_{it} - \log \tilde{y}_i^*),$$

where λ is commonly called the speed of convergence. The technology index is often assumed to follow some simple process, such as

$$\log A_{it} = \log A_i + \log Z_t + \epsilon_{it}.$$

That is, we assume that a country's technology index is the product of a parameter A_i indexing a country's long-run productivity level, the world technology index (which is assumed to grow at a constant rate g), and an idiosyncratic disturbance around this trend.

The first equation can be integrated and combined with the second to yield a cross-country growth specification:

$$\bar{g}_{iT} = \text{constant} - \beta \log y_{i0} + \beta \log (\tilde{y}_i^* A_i) + \beta \epsilon_{i0} + \frac{1}{T}(\epsilon_{it} - \epsilon_{i0}), \tag{1}$$

where $\bar{g}_{iT} \equiv (1/T)(\log y_{iT} - \log y_{i0})$ and $\beta \equiv (1/T)(1 - e^{-\lambda T})$.

A difficulty with this approach is that one does not observe directly the steady state to which countries are converging, nor the total factor productivity parameter. Variables such as investment rates in physical or human capital can be connected to $\tilde{y}^*$ theoretically, but of course these variables are typically endogenous as well. This leads to the difficult situation in which the econometrician does not know the correct specification but has a large number of candidate regressors at hand. An additional problem with this approach is the possible correlation of the candidate regressors with the error term(s), including the possibility of omitted-variable bias and endogeneity.

What I'd like to point out about this specification, however, is that the reason variables like trade policy or the quality of institutions are thought to enter these regressions is that they are potential determinants of the steady-state income level (detrended by the world technology index) toward which an economy is converging. This suggests an alternative specification of the regression that Mankiw, Romer, and Weil (1992) explore and that Hall and Jones (1999) have emphasized recently, a specification in levels rather than growth rates:

$$\log y_{it} = \text{constant} + \log(\tilde{y}_i^* A_i) + \epsilon_{it} - \frac{1}{\beta} \bar{g}_{\tilde{y}i}. \tag{2}$$

If levels of output per worker at time t are randomly distributed around their steady-state values, then this specification has the potential to work well. Notice that it uses different variation in the data, in that the estimation does not first condition on an earlier level of output per worker. One advantage is that more precise estimates may be obtained as a result. Of course, there are still endogeneity and omitted-variable problems, but these issues are also relevant for the specification in terms of growth rates; in some ways, they are simply made more explicit by the levels specification.

In terms of interpretation, the coefficients from the cross-country growth specification are really the product of two factors: a speed-of-convergence factor (β) and the coefficient that relates the particular variable to the steady-state level of income. One can interpret this product of coefficients as the effect on average growth rates over a particular period, but when the length of the time period is changing, as it is across these studies, the size of the coefficient will change for this reason (note that β depends on T), making comparisons across specifications difficult.

An alternative useful interpretation is obtained by calculating the long-run effect on the steady state, either by dividing by the coefficient on initial income or simply by running the levels regression directly.[2] One may of course also care about the rate at which the economy con-

---

2. These two methods will generally yield different results, since different variation in the data is used to estimate the effects; both are useful in practice.

verges to its steady state, and this rate, λ, can be calculated from the estimate of β.

3. A Closer Look at Some Results

Rodríguez and Rodrik examine a large number of measures of trade restrictions in their evaluation of the literature. Many are criticized for reasons discussed briefly above, but a few are put forward as being reasonable measures. These are typically the most direct measures of tariff rates or nontariff barriers. I will focus on three particular measures: (1) the QT component of the Sachs–Warner openness measure, which takes a value of 1 unless the country had average tariff rates higher than 40% or nontariff barriers covered more than 40% of imports, in which case it takes a value of 0; (2) an average tariff rate measure from Barro and Lee (1993) (owti); and (3) the simple average of the available statistics on import duties as a percentage of imports, which are reported in Table VIII of the conference version of their paper and which Rodríguez and Rodrik refer to in their conclusion. For some reason that I do not understand, they do not use this import-duties variable in any of their robustness checks in the paper.

I should make clear from the beginning that a narrow version of Rodríguez and Rodrik's conclusion survives my analysis of these data: estimates using these variables are not completely robust, in the sense that confidence intervals are large in some specifications. However, I'd like to go further and examine the magnitude of the effects and the confidence interval itself. What is our best guess about the effect of trade restrictions on long-run economic performance, and what is our range of uncertainty?

Table 1 summarizes my findings from estimating approximately 100 specifications; from among these, I've selected the 13 that strike me as most appropriate, and I've further summarized these 13 specifications by averaging the coefficients and p-values and reporting some statistics. A few of the specifications are growth regressions, replicating results in Rodríguez and Rodrik's paper; most are levels regressions of the same basic specifications, which generally improved the precision of the estimates.[3] One possible problem with these levels regressions is reverse causality: poor countries may resort to tariffs to raise revenue more than rich countries, e.g., because their tax systems are not well developed. In results not reported, I made some attempt to address issues of endogeneity by instrumenting with the variables used in Hall and Jones

---

3. The growth-regression specifications produced estimates of the long-run effect of 0.535 for QT and −1.80 for owti, roughly in line with the results from the levels regressions.

Table 1 SOME ADDITIONAL RESULTS

	Sachs–Warner QT	Tariff rate, owti	Avg. import duties
Results for All Specifications but Worst			
Average long-run effect	0.485	−1.714	−2.758
S.d. of variable	{0,1}	0.17	0.079
Average *p*-value	0.064	0.055	0.005
Number of specifications	4	4	2
Fraction with $p < .10$	3/4	3/4	2/2
Results from Worst Specification			
Long-run effect	0.158	−0.411	−0.447
p-value	0.275	0.509	0.375
95% conf. interval	(−0.13, 0.45)	(−1.6, 0.83)	(−3.17, 2.27)
Proportional Reduction of SS Output per Worker from a Large Increase in Trade Restrictions			
All but "worst"	39%	69%	58%
"Worst"	15%	24%	13%

The worst specification for the Sachs–Warner QT variable occurs when Knack and Keefer's (1995) quality-of-institutions variable (icrge) is added to the specification. The worst specification for the tariff rate (owti) occurs when both icrge is added and simultaneously the outlier India is dropped. The worst specification for the average-import-duties variable occurs when an indicator variable for the African continent is added to the specification. The calculations of long-run effects report the proportionality factor by which incomes would be reduced in the long run if a hypothetical country increased trade restrictions by 4 standard deviations (or went from a 1 to a 0 in the Sachs–Warner case). It is calculated as, e.g., $1 - \exp(\beta \times 4 \times \text{stdev})$. All but two of the regression results are from levels regressions; a growth regression is run for each of these first two variables (and is the specification with the largest *p*-value in the first part of the table). The first two columns use the Rodríguez–Rodrik dataset Sw.dat and include gvxdxe, assassp, revcoup, and be as additional regressors, sometimes adding africa and icrge. Results for the last column include variables from Hall and Jones (1999) as additional regressors.

(1999); in general, the point estimates were actually a little larger in magnitude, perhaps because of measurement error, but the estimates were less precise. A similar result is found by Frankel and Romer (1999).

The table is divided into three parts. In the first, I report the average effect on steady-state incomes from two to four specifications that exclude the specification that is *worst* in the sense of having the least-significant (and, it turns out, smallest) estimate. In the second, I report this worst specification.

In general, there are a number of reasonable specifications that lead to precisely estimated effects, as summarized in the first part of the table. In my brief experience, however, there were typically one or two key things that could be added to these specifications that led to problems (see the notes to the table). For example, adding the quality-of-institutions variable from Knack and Keefer (1995) often led the trade-policy variable to be estimated imprecisely. This could mean that the trade-policy variable is in part proxying for other kinds of distortions that are omitted from the specification. On the other hand, the Knack–Keefer variable is itself not without problems, as it is a subjective measure constructed by a consulting firm.

The third section of the table examines the magnitude of the effects estimated in the previous two parts. Specifically, I calculate the change in steady-state income associated with a large change in trade policy, viz. a movement of 4 standard deviations, or a movement from 1 to 0 for the Sachs–Warner variable. For all but the worst specifications, our best estimate of the size of the effect is substantial—a decline in income by 40% to 70%. For the worst specification, the effects are smaller: income declines by between 13% and 24% in the long run.

Overall, these numbers are similar to results calculated from some of the specifications reported by Rodríguez and Rodrik, such as in Table 3. However, at least in the conference version of their paper, they do not provide enough detail for the reader to make these calculations.

4. Final Thoughts

There are two other recent papers that I think should be mentioned in this context. The first is an omission from the conference version of the paper that has to some extent been addressed in the published version: the study of openness and income levels by Frankel and Romer (1999). Frankel and Romer's measure of openness is the trade share of GDP rather than a policy variable, and their general finding is a relatively robust relationship between openness and income levels: a change that increases the trade share by one percentage point raises income levels by 1% to 2%. A key contribution of the paper is to show that this finding is robust to endogeneity concerns by using the geographical determinants of trade as an instrument. Another finding, however, is that the magnitude of the effect is somewhat imprecisely estimated, and 95% confidence intervals include zero in a number of specifications.

Another paper that I've found helpful is Sala-i-Martin (1997). People sometimes conclude from the cross-country growth regression literature that virtually none of the relationships are robust, a statement that would seem to receive support from Rodríguez and Rodrik. Sala-i-Martin builds on the robustness work by Levine and Renelt (1992) by examining the entire distribution of coefficient estimates on particular variables from running more than 32,000 permutations of growth regressions. As a general matter, Sala-i-Martin highlights a number of variables that are robust across specifications, including the Sachs–Warner openness measure. On the other hand, consistent with the present paper—and with the original results of Levine and Renelt (1992)—Sala-i-Martin finds that the other measures of trade policy he examines are among the least robust variables in his study, being statistically significant at the 95% level less than 4% of the time. He does find that the coefficients have the "right" sign in 60% to 80% of the specifications he considers, depending on the measure.

In conclusion, it seems to me that the cross-country growth regression evidence leads to the following results. Our best estimate is that trade restrictions are harmful to long-run incomes, and that the effects are potentially large. For this reason, I worry a little about the "broad" interpretation of the paper that I provided at the beginning of my remarks. In addition, however, there is a large amount of uncertainty regarding the magnitude of the effect; it could be small, and there are some specifications that allow for the possibility that the effect works in the opposite direction. Cross-country growth regressions appear to be a coarse tool for this particular question, and, at least so far, are unable to provide a more precise answer.

REFERENCES

Barro, R. J., and J. Lee. (1993). International comparisons of educational attainment. *Journal of Monetary Economics* 32(December):363–394.
———, and X. Sala-i-Martin. (1992). Convergence. *Journal of Political Economy* 100(2):223–251.
Frankel, J. A., and D. Romer. (1999). Does trade cause growth? *American Economic Review* 89(3):379–399.
Hall, R. E., and C. I. Jones. (1999). Why do some countries produce so much more output per worker than others? *Quarterly Journal of Economics* 114(1):83–116.
Knack, S., and P. Keefer. (1995). Institutions and economic performance: Cross-country tests using alternative institutional measures. *Economics and Politics* 7(November):207–227.
Levine, R., and D. Renelt. (1992). A sensitivity analysis of cross-country growth regressions. *American Economic Review* 82(4):942–963.
Mankiw, N. G., D. Romer, and D. Weil. (1992). A contribution of the empirics of economic growth. *Quarterly Journal of Economics* 107(2):407–438.
Sala-i-Martin, X. (1997). I just ran four million regressions. *American Economic Review* 87(2):178–183.

Discussion

Andrew Warner disputed the authors' conclusion that there are no strong results in the literature linking trade openness to growth. He asserted that the simplest possible measure of protectionism, average tariff rates, is significantly and negatively correlated with growth, controlling for initial income and growth and even excluding Africa from the sample. With respect to his own work with Jeff Sachs, Warner argued that there are many ways to close an economy to trade—hence the strategy of constructing a composite variable which treats a country as being closed to trade if any of a number of criteria are met. Dani Rodrik said that it is difficult to interpret the bivariate relationship of tariff rates and growth, as rich countries tend to lower tariff rates, which leads to the possibility of reverse causality; he also questioned whether the estimated relationship between tariff rates and growth holds up in more recent data. Rodrik agreed in general with Sachs and Warner's strategy of combining indicators. However, given the paper's finding that much of the statistical effect of the Sachs–Warner indicator is due to only two of the variables that make it up, he argued that one must be careful to determine whether these key variables truly measure trade policies or instead reflect other country characteristics.

Alberto Alesina argued that growth rates may be an especially poor measure of the benefits of trade; for example, trade permits people to enjoy a wide variety of products not produced at home. On the other hand, Alesina and Allan Drazen both emphasized the point that trade policy is not made by social planners but by lobbies and interest groups. It may be that interest groups fight harder to protect their income shares through trade protection when income is growing slowly overall; this is yet another possible source of reverse causation. Pursuing the political-economy issue, Daron Acemoglu pointed out that the correlation between restrictive trade policies and corrupt, rent-seeking governments may not be an accident; the two may be mutually supporting. Thus, one benefit of more open trade is that it may reduce the scope for governmental corruption.

Marvin Goodfriend differentiated between the classical static efficiency benefits of trade and the dynamic gains associated with the diffusion of knowledge and technology. Possibly, he suggested, improving communications (including developments such as the Internet) will reduce the importance of trade policy for information flows.

Greg Mankiw was not surprised by the lack of robustness in the cross-country results, given the large number of candidate variables relative to the number of country observations. He conjectured that economists support free trade because they believe Ricardo, not because they have been convinced by regressions. Rodrik agreed that there is a strong presumption that trade restrictions are distortionary, but that magnitudes are important. For example, if the growth effects of trade liberalization are small, economic advisors may do better by giving a higher priority to other types of reforms.

Maurice Obstfeld and Kenneth Rogoff
UNIVERSITY OF CALIFORNIA, BERKELEY AND NBER;
AND HARVARD UNIVERSITY AND NBER

The Six Major Puzzles in International Macroeconomics: Is There a Common Cause?

1. Introduction

International macroeconomics is a field replete with truly perplexing puzzles, and we generally have five to ten (or more) alternative answers to each of them. These answers are typically very clever but far from thoroughly convincing, and so the puzzles remain. Why do people seem to have such a strong preference for consumption of their home goods (the home-bias-in-trade puzzle)? Why do observed OECD current-account imbalances tend to be so small relative to saving and investment when measured over any sustained period (the Feldstein–Horioka puzzle)? Why do home investors overwhelmingly prefer to hold home equity assets (the home-bias portfolio puzzle)? Why isn't consumption more highly correlated across OECD countries (the consumption correlations puzzle)? How is it possible that the half-life of real exchange-rate innovations can be three to four years (the purchasing-power-parity puzzle)? Why are exchange rates so volatile and so apparently disconnected from fundamentals [the exchange-rate disconnect puzzle, of which the Meese–Rogoff (1983) forecasting puzzle and the Baxter–Stockman (1989) neutrality-of-exchange-rate-regime puzzle are manifestations]?

What we attempt to do in this paper is to offer a unified basis for

We thank Jay Shambaugh and Juan Carlos Hallak for excellent research assistance, and the National Science Foundation for support. We gratefully acknowledge Charles Engel for sharing data and Robert Feenstra for helpful advice. We have benefited from comments by Owen Kosling, Michael Kremer, Richard Portes, Assaf Razin, Hélène Rey, Alan Taylor, Jeffrey Williamson, and our discussants, Charles Engel and Olivier Jeanne, on an earlier conference draft version.

understanding *all* of these puzzles, in which the key friction is a (significant but plausible) level of international trade costs in *goods* markets. These trade costs may include transport costs but also tariffs, nontariff barriers, and possibly other broader factors that impede trade.

We do not pretend to be the first to make this connection. In a fundamental contribution to the literature on international trade and finance, Samuelson (1954) argued that the existence of an international transfer problem depends critically on whether there is a home bias in consumption, and he showed explicitly how a home bias could be derived from transport costs.[1] In subsequent research, however, Samuelson's straightforward approach has generally been abandoned in favor of a more stylized paradigm based on breaking up a country's products into two dichotomous categories, traded and nontraded goods.[2] The analysis of the present paper suggests that for many purposes, this dichotomous grouping is far less helpful than the natural alternative of simply introducing trade costs.

Especially in our treatment of capital-market anomalies, the approach in this paper differs from the one that is conventionally taken in the literature. Typically, an author chooses from a menu of plausible capital-market imperfections the one best suited to explain a particular puzzle. We do not deny the importance of a variety of imperfections peculiar to international asset markets. Our goal here, however, is to show how far one can go in elucidating major empirical riddles without appealing to intrinsically international capital-market imperfections. Remarkably, we find that once one allows for trade costs in *goods* markets, many of the main empirical objections to the canonical models of international macroeconomics disappear. Our approach, which is based on a very simple stylized model, seems to be particularly successful in resolving the real-side quantity puzzles. To explain adequately the various pricing puzzles, we would need to develop a much richer framework featuring imperfect

---

1. Obstfeld and Rogoff (1996, Chapter 4) embed trade costs in a version of the Dornbusch–Fischer–Samuelson (1977) Ricardian model and show that Samuelson's transfer-problem analysis can be extended to a modern dynamic setting. See Krugman (1991) on the relevance of the transfer problem to contemporary debates in international macroeconomics.
2. A notable exception is Backus, Kehoe, and Kydland (1992), who find that their approximate method for incorporating small trade costs does not resolve the consumption correlations puzzle in a calibrated one-good global real-business-cycle model. Another is Dumas (1992), who looks at a dynamic, stochastic, one-good open economy model with transport costs and explores a number of issues, including the forward exchange-rate premium. His work is theoretical and qualitative, however, and he does not calibrate his model's empirical implications for the various puzzles we look at here. Also, our main points in this paper really require an extension to the multigood case. In a more recent contribution, Ravn and Mazzenga (1999) examine further the business-cycle implications of transport costs in a variant of the Backus–Kehoe–Kydland model.

competition plus sticky prices and/or wages, as in the extensive recent literature on the "new open-economy macroeconomics." Although we do not present such a model here, we do demonstrate why trade costs must constitute an essential element, implicitly if not explicitly.

The first puzzle we address is the home-bias-in-trade puzzle (McCallum, 1995), which, as we have already noted, is closely related to the classic transfer problem. Following Wei (1998) and Evans (1999), we discuss how empirically plausible trade costs, combined with fairly standard estimates of elasticities of substitution across imports and exports, can explain much of the puzzle.

Having established the trade friction at the core of our analysis, we next turn to one of the most robust and intractable puzzles in international finance, the Feldstein–Horioka puzzle. We show that trade costs can create a wedge between the effective real interest rates faced by borrowers and lenders. In our model, the effect is highly nonlinear, manifesting itself strongly only when current-account imbalances become very large. We argue that it is precisely such incipient real-interest-rate effects that keep observed current-account imbalances within a modest range. Though we rely primarily on the theoretical force of the argument, we do demonstrate empirically that current-account-deficit countries tend to have higher real interest rates, as our model predicts.

Next, we show that the same approach can simply and elegantly explain the widely discussed home bias in equity holdings (or, more generally, in overall asset positions). The following section covers the consumption correlations puzzle, which is closely related to the preceding three, so it is not surprising our same approach again applies. We also briefly address other related puzzles.

We largely ignore nominal rigidities in our discussion of the first four puzzles, because our main argument does not depend upon having them. But as we turn to our last two puzzles—the purchasing-power-parity puzzle and the exchange-rate disconnect puzzle—we obviously must think about adding other ingredients, in the form of imperfect competition and some degree of price or wage rigidity. We nevertheless argue that trade costs in output markets must be an essential ingredient in resolving these puzzles as well. The final section concludes and also evaluates our results in the light of long-term trends in world transport costs.

2. The Puzzle of Home Bias in Trade (Puzzle 1)

The starting point for all the puzzles we examine is the growing evidence that international *goods* markets appear to be far more segmented than is commonly supposed. Perhaps the most dramatic suggestion of segmentation stems from the work of McCallum (1995). Using a simple Tinbergen (1962) gravity model of trade that controls for distance, trading-partner sizes, and a small number of other factors, McCallum found that trade among individual Canadian provinces was *twenty* times greater than trade between individual Canadian provinces and individual U.S. states, a surprisingly high differential. It is true that the subsequent literature has both tempered McCallum's estimates and challenged their interpretation. McCallum's calculations were based on the year 1988, still at the dawn of the U.S.–Canada free-trade agreement, and before trade patterns had time to adjust fully. Using data for 1993–1996, Helliwell (1998) found that the unexplained home bias had fallen to a factor of 12, which remains a surprisingly large number. Though intracountry trade data are available only for Canada and the United States, Wei (1998) and Evans (1999) use indirect methods to test home bias for other OECD country pairs. Wei suggests that the average bias may be as low as 2.5, while Evans finds values intermediate between Wei's and Helliwell's.[3] Van Wincoop (2000) argues that even though McCallum controls for state and province size in his gravity equation, his trade-diversion measure gives an exaggerated impression of home bias in global trade because it calculates the bias from the perspective of the small country, Canada, rather than from the perspective of the large country, the United States.[4] Overall, a balanced interpretation of the literature is that countries do exhibit a considerable degree of home bias in trade, but the bias is not as extreme as McCallum's original estimates suggested.

But if there is still a significant degree of home bias in international trade, how can we explain it? Clearly, international trade does involve added border costs such as tariffs, nontariff barriers, and exchange-rate risk (and it is also possible that domestic transportation costs are lower due to greater coordination problems in constructing international transportation networks). Do these border costs need to be implausibly large to generate observed home bias, even in the more modest range of Wei's

---

3. Wei (1998) tries to estimate home bias indirectly by assuming that the amount a country imports from itself is the difference between total production and total exports. However, Wei's 2.5 home bias estimate could be downward biased due to his exclusion of the service sector. Evans (1999) uses data on selected industries for a number of OECD countries.

4. Van Wincoop (2000) shows that McCallum's measure of trade bias must be carefully interpreted to ascertain the negative border effect on U.S.–Canada trade. Because Canada's economy is so small relative to that of the United States, a moderate percentage diversion of U.S.–Canada trade into intra-Canada trade amounts to a spectacular percentage increase in intra-Canada trade. Using U.S. interstate trade data, van Wincoop estimates that the U.S.–Canada border reduces trade between the two countries by at most 30%.

and Evans' estimates? Not necessarily, since what really matters is the interaction between border costs and the elasticity of substitution between home and foreign goods. As this is a recurring theme in our discussion of the various quantity puzzles, it is helpful to take up a simple illustrative example.

2.1 A MODEL OF THE INTERACTION BETWEEN TRADE COSTS AND THE PRICE ELASTICITY OF DEMAND

Here, we show how costs of international trade can dramatically skew domestic consumption in favor of home-produced goods.

Consider an extremely simple two-country endowment economy, in which the utility function of the representative home consumer is given by

$$C = \left(C_H^{(\theta-1)/\theta} + C_F^{(\theta-1)/\theta} \right)^{\theta/(\theta-1)}, \tag{1}$$

where C_H is home consumption of the home-produced good and C_F is home consumption of the foreign-produced good. Foreign agents are assumed to have identical utility functions in C_H^* and C_F^*. Home agents are endowed with Y_H per capita of the home good, and foreign agents are endowed with Y_F. We assume *iceberg* shipping costs τ, so that for every unit of home (foreign) good shipped abroad, only a fraction $1 - \tau$ arrives at the foreign (home) shore. Let P_H (P_F) be the home price of the home (foreign) good, and P_H^* (P_F^*) the corresponding foreign prices, with all prices measured in terms of a common world monetary unit. (Since we are in a flexible-price world here, it is not important whether the two countries share a common currency.) Then, if markets are competitive, arbitrage implies that

$$P_F = P_F^*/(1 - \tau), \tag{2}$$

$$P_H = (1 - \tau)P_H^*. \tag{3}$$

Thus, if $p \equiv P_F/P_H$, and $p^* \equiv P_F^*/P_H^*$,

$$p^* = p(1 - \tau)^2. \tag{4}$$

(We will maintain the assumption of competitive markets through the first four sections, though our main points would still apply in an imperfectly competitive setting, as in our discussion of puzzles 5 and 6.)

From the first-order conditions for utility maximization by home and foreign agents, we have

$$\frac{C_H}{C_F}=p^\theta, \qquad \frac{C_H^*}{C_F^*}=(p^*)^\theta. \tag{5}$$

Combining (4) and (5) implies

$$\frac{C_H}{C_F}=(1-\tau)^{-2\theta}\frac{C_H^*}{C_F^*}. \tag{6}$$

For illustrative purposes, consider the easy symmetric case in which $Y_H = Y_F$. Under that assumption, $C_H/C_F = C_F^*/C_H^*$ and equation (6) reduces to

$$\frac{C_H}{C_F}=\frac{C_F^*}{C_H^*}=(1-\tau)^{-\theta}=p^\theta.$$

This equation shows that the ratio of home (foreign) expenditure on imports relative to home (foreign) goods is

$$\frac{C_H}{pC_F}=\frac{p^*C_F^*}{C_H^*}=(1-\tau)^{1-\theta}.$$

Thus, for example, if there were no trade costs ($\tau = 0$), then $pC_F/C_H = 1$. If $\tau = 0.25$ (a large number just for goods actually traded but conservative when applied to all of GNP) and $\theta = 6$, then $C_H/pC_F = 4.2$. This ratio is consistent with those we observe for many OECD countries, and the degree of home bias can easily be made larger by raising τ, raising θ, or assuming that the home country is a small one trading with many like-sized foreign partners.

2.2 THE NONLINEAR RELATIONSHIP BETWEEN TRADE COSTS AND HOME BIAS IN TRADE

The higher trade costs (the closer τ is to 1), the greater the impact of a 1% reduction in τ on home bias:

$$\frac{d \log(C_H/pC_F)}{d \log \tau}=\frac{\tau}{1-\tau}(\theta-1).$$

For our baseline case of $\tau = 0.25$ and $\theta = 6$, the elasticity of home bias with respect to trade costs is $\tau(\theta-1)/(1-\tau) = 1.67$.

Obviously, this example is wildly oversimplified. It implicitly assumes a common substitution elasticity across any individual pair of home and foreign goods, and similarly lumps all goods together as having common trade costs. It ignores the potential importance of substitution between domestic and foreign inputs in production. Nevertheless, it neatly illustrates how a high elasticity of substitution can explain a large observed home trade bias even with low trade costs. What then are plausible values for the parameters τ and θ?

2.3 EMPIRICAL ESTIMATES OF θ

Though there is a range of estimates for θ, recent trade studies typically find values for the elasticity of import demand with respect to price (relative to the overall domestic consumption basket) in the neighborhood of 5 to 6. Examples include Trefler and Lai (1999), who present panel estimates over 1972–1992 for a panel of 28 industries in 36 countries; their preferred estimate is 5.3. That average number reflects estimated disaggregated substitution elasticities as high as 21.4 (for industrial chemicals) and 18.9 (for electrical machinery and electronics) but as low as 1.2 (for printing and publishing). Harrigan (1993) looks at three-digit 1983 SITC data for 13 OECD countries representing 90% of OECD output and finds elasticities in the range of 5 to 12.

Recognizing that much of trade involves imperfectly competitive industries, one can attempt to infer the value of θ by looking at markups of price over marginal cost. Using that approach, Cheung, Chinn, and Fujii (1999) look at two-digit industry level data for a range of OECD countries, and impute elasticities typically in the range of 3.5 to 4. Hummels (1999a) tries to disentangle the effects of trade elasticities from those of substitution elasticities within a cross-section framework. Using linear least squares, he comes up with an average markup of 22%, translating into a θ of 5.6, although other of his estimates of θ are higher. Finally, in their classic article on the demand for automobiles—including both domestic and foreign makes—Berry, Levinsohn, and Pakes (1995) find price elasticities of demand between 3.1 and 6.4.[5]

Of course, these studies refer to goods actually traded. As Hummels emphasizes, one would expect that elasticities of substitution would be higher on average for goods that are not traded. In this case, an estimate

---

5. Studies of monopoly markups in domestic sales, while not necessarily directly applicable here, also yield similar estimates for θ. For example, Rotemberg and Woodford (1992) find a markup for the United States of around 20%, corresponding to $\theta = 6$. In subsequent discussion, Rotemberg and Woodford (1995) argue that there is great uncertainty about actual markups in U.S. industry, but favor estimates in the range of 20% to 40%, that is, θ between about 3.5 and 6.

of $\theta = 20$, as Wei proposes, does not seem so wild-eyed. Brown and Stern (1989) use $\theta = 15$ for their policy experiments.

2.4 EMPIRICAL ESTIMATES OF TRADE COSTS τ

There is far less consensus about the size of trade costs, which include (among other things), tariffs, nontariff barriers, and transport costs. For 1993, average tariffs, on a domestic-production-weighted basis, were 4.9% for the United States, 7.7% for the European Union, 3.5% for Japan, and 8.9% for Canada.[6] As for nontariff barriers, official statistics only give information on their existence, not their effectiveness, which must be estimated using an economic model. Anderson and Neary (1998) use a simple computable general equilibrium model to estimate uniform tariff equivalents for nontariff barriers for a broad range of countries, and typically find estimates on the same order of magnitude as for tariffs, larger of course for some countries (such as Japan) than for others (such as the United States). This result is also consistent with the trade-equation estimates of Lee and Swagel (1997).[7]

Differential international transportation costs are also an important potential element of τ.[8] If one looks across all commodities on a value-weighted basis, freight and insurance charges for U.S. imports averaged 3.6% in 1995, and 3.3% in 1996 and 1997.[9] But these numbers considerably understate average costs in international shipping. First, As Hummels (1999a) shows, average costs are much higher for many other countries (the United States has a vast coastline, and sea shipping tends to be much cheaper than shipping by land). Second, these numbers do not include other considerable costs of international shipping, including preparing the paperwork (bills of lading) needed to clear international customs, and the costs of delays either in transit or at port of entry.

Just as empirical measures of the elasticity of substitution between home and foreign goods may be biased downwards, it is also likely that simple estimates of average transport costs grossly understate average τ across all goods in the economy (due to substitution effects). Table 1 is drawn from Hummels (1999a), who based his estimates on highly disag-

---

6. See OECD (1996, Table 1.1, row 9).
7. Harrigan (1993), however, finds nontariff barriers insignificant compared to tariffs and transportation costs.
8. Recall that Helliwell's and McCallum's estimates use distance in an attempt to control for transport costs. Geographical distance is an imperfect measure of these, however.
9. The authors are grateful to Robert Feenstra for compiling these numbers based on *U.S. Imports of Merchandise*, U.S. Census Bureau. The estimates give shipping and freight charges as a percentage of total value of imports excluding these charges. Importantly, these numbers do not include any inland shipping at point of departure or port of arrival.

Table 1 COMMODITY DISTRIBUTION OF FREIGHT RATES (UNITED STATES, 1994)[a]

	Average freight rate	
Commodity	Trade-weighted	unweighted
All goods	3.8	
Food and live animals	8.2	14.1
Beverages and tobacco	6.9	14.4
Crude materials	8.2	15.1
Mineral fuels, lubricants	6.6	15.7
Animal and veg. oils, fats	7.1	10.6
Chemicals and related products	4.5	9.0
Manuf. goods (by material)	5.3	10.3
Machinery and transp. equip.	2.0	5.7
Misc. manufactures	4.7	8.3
All other goods, NES	1.0	2.5

[a]Source: Hummels (1999a), compiled from U.S. Census Bureau, *U.S. Imports of Merchandise*. Freight costs include shipping and insurance as a percentage of total FAS value. Calculations are based on 10-digit Harmonized System level data (over 15,000 categories of goods). Unweighted shipping costs are based on all individual goods imported.

gregated 10-digit data. We see from the table that shipping costs for many categories of goods are quite a bit larger than the average (trade-weighted) shipping costs—and this table excludes goods that are not traded at all.

What other factors might be included in τ? In a provocative paper, Rose (2000) uses a gravity model to argue that countries with currency unions trade two to three times as much with each other as countries with separate currencies. Certainly, currency conversion costs and exchange-rate uncertainty can add to trade costs. While exchange-rate variability can have direct negative effects on capital flows, any direct negative effect on trade flows will result in an additional, indirect source of capital-market imperfection according to our analysis. A similar point can be made for various informational costs of international trade; see Rauch (1999) and Portes and Rey (1999) for discussion and some empirical evidence.[10] Differences in legal and payments systems may also add to τ.

Last, but not least, it is important to emphasize that our analysis has assumed no home bias in preferences. Suppose we replace the representative home agent's utility function (1) with

---

10. Anderson and Marcouiller (1999) argue that corruption and imperfect contract enforcement are major factors in disrupting trade, especially in developing countries. Since our main focus is on industrialized countries, we will not consider these categories of trade cost further here.

$$U = (C_H^{(\theta-1)/\theta} + \omega C_F^{(\theta-1)/\theta})^{\theta/(\theta-1)} \tag{7}$$

and the representative foreign agent's utility function with

$$U^* = (\omega C_H^{*(\theta-1)/\theta} + C_F^{*(\theta-1)/\theta})^{\theta/(\theta-1)}.$$

One can easily show that the effects of home bias in preferences ($\omega < 1$) can be isomorphic to the effects of trade costs τ. Helpman (1999) argues that once one controls for income, there is no clear evidence of home bias in preferences. Indeed, it is more illuminating to derive trade biases from other frictions. Nevertheless, it is important to recognize that a home bias in demand for goods can work similarly to trade costs, at least for the trade and portfolio-bias puzzles.

2.5 OTHER REAL-TRADE PUZZLES

Though international-finance puzzles are our main focus, we note that trade costs can explain a number of real-trade puzzles as well. For example, Trefler's (1995) favored explanation of the "missing trade" puzzle combines Hicks-neutral productivity differences across countries with a home bias in consumption (which, per our discussion above, may be induced by transport costs).[11] Deardorff (1998) points out that with transport costs, the standard conditions for factor-price equalization in a Heckscher–Ohlin world break down, also implying greater specialization. Since factor-price equalization fails miserably empirically, this implies another important puzzle that can be at least partially resolved by transport costs. Anderson (1979), Deardorff (1998), and others have shown that transport costs can help explain the surprising empirical robustness of the gravity equation of trade flows. Not only do trade costs help to resolve a number of puzzles in the data, they also seem to be important in determining economic performance. Radelet and Sachs (1998) argue that countries that have high shipping costs due to adverse geography (for example, high mountains or limited port access) grow much more slowly than countries with natural transport advantages. Finally, we note that evidence on international price differentials seems quite consistent with the high degree of market segmentation evinced on the quantities side; we shall refer to this work later in discussing puzzles 5 and 6.

Armed with a simple understanding of how plausible trade costs together with high elasticities of substitution in consumption can explain

---

11. "Missing trade" is how Trefler describes the puzzle that the imputed factor content of trade does not seem to reflect comparative advantage.

substantial home biases in trade, we are ready to explore the linkages to other macro puzzles.

3. The Feldstein–Horioka Puzzle (Puzzle 2)

There has been no shortage of explanations for the famous saving–investment puzzle of Feldstein and Horioka (1980), with numerous articles on the topic having been published in most of the leading journals. The problem is that none of the explanations advanced to date (including our own attempts) has been terribly convincing. Most explanations tend to be clever but empirically inadequate and, more troublesome still, tend to fix one puzzle at the expense of creating others. The fact that the Feldstein–Horioka regularity does not seem to characterize intranational regional data suggests that factors intrinsic to trade between different nations are at work.[12]

3.1 STILL A PUZZLE

What Feldstein and Horioka actually demonstrated, of course, is that across OECD countries, long-period averages of national saving rates are highly correlated with similar averages of domestic investment rates. Indeed, in the original data sample examined by Feldstein and Horioka, covering 1960 through the mid-1970s, cross-section regressions of investment on saving yielded slope coefficients near unity. True, this Feldstein–Horioka coefficient—which the original work interpreted as measuring the effect of the saving rate on the investment rate, or a "savings retention" measure—has fallen over time. As Table 2 illustrates, however, it still remains large and significant. The table gives simple cross-country regressions of investment (relative to GDP) against national saving (relative to GDP), taking eight-year averages for the most recent period, 1990–1997. For the OECD countries, the coefficient (0.60) is a good deal smaller than the 0.89 found in Feldstein and Horioka's original work, but it is still larger than one might expect in a world of fully integrated capital markets where global savings should flow to the regions with the highest rates of return. The coefficient falls further once one includes countries outside the OECD (particularly poor countries), although the extended results must be viewed with extreme caution given the poor quality of national income and product data for most non-OECD countries. (The data underlying the regressions in Table 2 are reported in Table 7 in the appendix, which also describes how the countries in the sample were chosen.)

---

12. See Obstfeld (1995), Obstfeld and Rogoff (1996), and Coakley, Kulasi, and Smith (1998) for recent surveys.

Table 2 FELDSTEIN–HORIOKA REGRESSIONS, $I/Y = \alpha + \beta\, NS/Y + \epsilon$, 1990–1997[a]

	No. of obs.	α	β	R^2
All countries[b]	56	0.15 (0.02)	0.41 (0.08)	0.33
Countries with GNP/cap. > 1000	48	0.13 (0.02)	0.48 (0.09)	0.39
Countries with GNP/cap. > 2000	41	0.07 (0.02)	0.70 (0.09)	0.62
OECD countries[c]	24	0.08 (0.02)	0.60 (0.09)	0.68

[a]OLS regressions. Standard errors in parentheses.
[b]Israel is excluded from all regressions in this table. If Israel is added to the samples of size (56, 48, 41), the estimates of β are (0.39, 0.45, 0.63).
[c]If one adds Korea to the OECD sample, the estimate for β rises to 0.76. Korea is included in the larger samples.

The Feldstein–Horioka puzzle is durable because the core regression simply summarizes in a compact way the fact that OECD current accounts tend to be surprisingly small relative to total saving and investment, especially when one averages over any sustained period. For developing countries, notably the many that have repeatedly had trouble servicing debts, it is perhaps not so surprising that creditors prevent them from running up large sustained deficits. But it is hard to appeal to sovereign-default risk for OECD countries, especially when one considers that gross international flows of financial assets are much bigger than *net* international flows. Indeed, for OECD countries, asset price comparisons suggest a high degree of integration; arbitrage in similar nominally risk-free assets appears to be nearly perfect. We leave it to the reader to look at other sources (for example, Obstfeld and Rogoff, 1996, Chapter 3) for assessments of previous attempts to explain the Feldstein–Horioka conundrum.

A fair summary of the literature is that there are at least five or six leading explanations (and ten or so close seconds). All are unconvincing empirically—some because they are based on very special assumptions about the nature of the exogenous shocks (e.g., Obstfeld, 1986, or Mendoza, 1991), others because they raise collateral empirical contradictions. For example, in the asymmetric information model of Gordon and Bovenberg (1996), a "lemons" problem is invoked to explain why foreigners finance so little domestic investment, yet departures from covered interest parity must also be assumed if there is to be any foreign equity inflow at all. Explanations that try to maintain the assumption of perfect capital mobility often have the strong implication that one should also observe high saving–investment correlations across states or regions within a given country. But the partial evidence available on saving and investment by subnational regions simply does not produce the Feldstein–Horioka regularity; see, for example, Helliwell (1998, Chapter 4). We are going to propose here an entirely new explanation, based on transaction costs for international trade in goods. An especially attractive feature of our approach is that it seems to help resolve other puzzles rather than exacerbating them.

It is important to emphasize that whereas our model includes trade costs for goods, it is consistent with free and costless trade in securities. Thus, it is perfectly consistent with the observation that gross international flows of securities are substantial even though net flows are small. Our account is also notable both for endogenizing the price and interest effects of trade impediments, and for showing how moderate transport costs could generate empirically significant international differences in real interest rates despite full asset-market integration.

3.2 TRANSPORT COSTS CAN INDUCE A NONLINEAR RELATIONSHIP BETWEEN THE CURRENT ACCOUNT AND THE REAL INTEREST RATE

The basic intuition of why transport costs can temper current-account imbalances can be illustrated in a standard two-period, two-good, small-country endowment model. It would not be difficult to endogenize the world real interest rate, or to incorporate uncertainty (as in the next section), but neither generalization is essential here. We will later discuss investment to confirm that the basic argument we make still goes through.

The model below is entirely standard except that we will again allow for Samuelsonian "iceberg" costs in trade, so that τ percent of any good is lost in transit. The utility function of a representative home resident is

$$u(C_1) + \delta u(C_2),$$

where total real consumption C depends on consumption of the home and foreign goods, C_H and C_F, with constant elasticity of substitution θ as in equation (1). The small country is endowed only with good H, with $Y_{H,1}$ in period 1, and $Y_{H,2}$ in period 2. Good F must always be imported. (Endowing the country with both goods would not overturn our argument.) The home country is small in the sense that its actions have no effect on the world prices P_H^* and P_F^*, which are constant across the two periods in terms of a world unit of account (money). Nor can it affect the foreign real interest rate r^* (which equals the foreign nominal interest rate assuming there is zero foreign inflation). Because of iceberg transit costs τ in shipping either good, however, home consumption patterns can affect home relative prices and the home real interest rate.

Though we shall give a formal analysis below, the basic argument is simple. Suppose, for example, that the country's endowment pattern and rate of time preference δ are such that in the first period, net exports of good H are negative (in which case intertemporal solvency dictates they must be positive in period 2). Then, as we shall shortly confirm, the relative price of good H will be higher in period 1 than in period 2. There will be expected deflation, and the home real interest rate will be above r^*. The situation is reversed when the country is initially running a sufficiently large current-account surplus, so that its real consumption-based lending rate must lie below r^*. As we demonstrate formally below, this effect can be quite dramatic, assuming realistic values for trade costs τ and the elasticity of substitution θ (values similar to those needed to resolve the home-bias-in-trade puzzle).[13]

3.3 BUDGET CONSTRAINTS AND TRANSPORT COSTS

A formal analysis requires one to think carefully about the budget constraints facing the representative agent. In general, the first-period budget constraint can be written as

$$P_{H,1}Y_{H,1} + D = P_{H,1}C_{H,1} + P_{F,1}C_{F,1} = P_1C_1,$$

where P_H (P_F) is the home-soil price of good H (F) in terms of the world currency unit, and D is borrowing from abroad in world currency units. The overall home price level, in terms of world currency units, is

$$P = (P_H^{1-\theta} + P_F^{1-\theta})^{1/(1-\theta)}. \tag{8}$$

Therefore, given a total real consumption level C in any period, the consumptions of the two individual home and foreign goods are

$$C_H = \left(\frac{P_H}{P}\right)^{-\theta} C, \quad C_F = \left(\frac{P_F}{P}\right)^{-\theta} C. \tag{9}$$

---

13. Dumas (1992) likewise shows how international real interest-rate differentials can arise in a model with transport costs, though, as we have already noted, his one-good model is very different and he does not explore the implications for the Feldstein–Horioka puzzle.

Similarly, the second-period budget constraint, measured in world currency units, is

$$P_{H,2}Y_{H,2} - (1 + r^*)D = P_{H,2}C_{H,2} + P_{F,2}C_{F,2} = P_2C_2.$$

Combining the period budget constraints gives the consolidated intertemporal budget constraint as

$$P_1C_1 + \frac{P_2C_2}{1 + r^*} = P_{H,1}Y_{H,1} + \frac{P_{H,2}Y_{H,2}}{1 + r^*},$$

or, in terms of the domestic real interest rate $1 + r = (1 + r^*)P_1/P_2$, as

$$C_1 + \frac{C_2}{1 + r} = \frac{P_{H,1}Y_{H,1}}{P_1} + \left(\frac{1}{1 + r}\right)\frac{P_{H,2}Y_{H,2}}{P_2}. \tag{10}$$

3.4 INFLATION

Since good F is always imported, its home price, $P_F = P_F^*/(1 - \tau)$, must be higher than the foreign price in both periods, per equation (2). By the same logic, when good H is exported— as it must be in at least one of the two periods—its home price $P_H = P_H^*(1 - \tau)$ must be lower than the foreign price, per equation (3). However, if total domestic spending is high enough relative to income in any given period, it is possible that good H is *imported* rather than exported ($C_H > Y_H$), in which case its home price $P_H = P_H^*/(1 - \tau)$ must be *higher* than the foreign price. As we shall see, there are also important intermediate cases where $C_H = Y_H$ in one period, in which case P_H will turn out to lie between $P_H^*(1 - \tau)$ and $P_H^*/(1 - \tau)$, despite the fact that no goods roundtrip.

3.5 A GRAPHICAL ANALYSIS OF THE LINK BETWEEN REAL INTEREST RATES AND CURRENT ACCOUNTS

The link between the effective real interest rate faced by the home country and its first-period borrowing decision is illustrated in Figure 1, which plots total real consumption in period 1, C_1, against the domestic real interest rate, $1 + r$. (Note that the period 1 current account deficit is simply $Y_1 - C_1$). The resulting graph is a step function that can be divided up into five segments; it shows the schedule of effective real interest rates faced by the country as a function of its borrowing–lending decision.

In the first segment C_1 is so low, and the period 1 current-account surplus so high, that in period 2 the country will consume an amount

Figure 1 DOMESTIC SPENDING AND THE DOMESTIC REAL INTEREST RATE IN A TWO-GOOD MODEL WITH TRADE COSTS

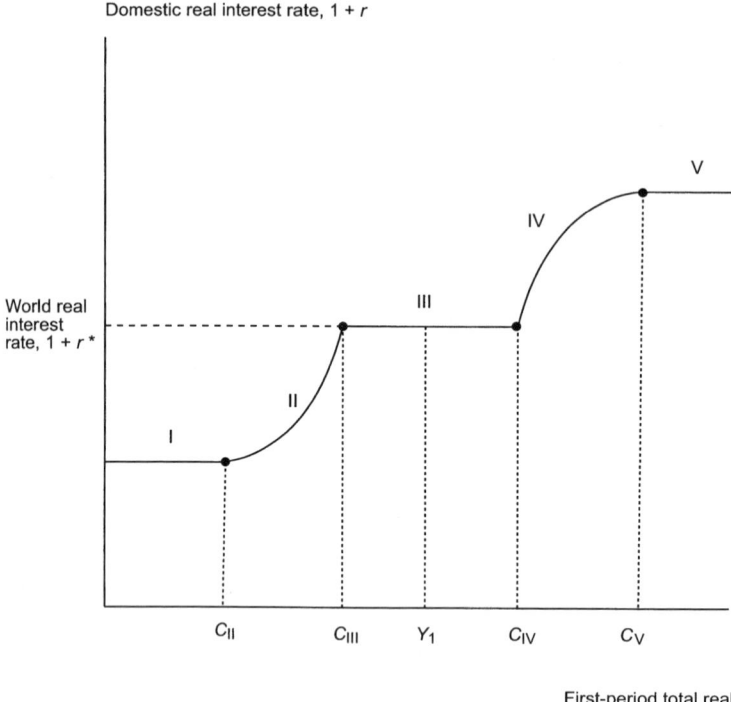

$C_{H,2} > Y_{H,2}$. Since in period 2 the home good must be imported, while in period 1 it is exported, we have

$$1 + r = \frac{(1 + r^*)\,(P_{H,1}^{1-\theta} + P_F^{1-\theta})^{1/(1-\theta)}}{(P_{H,2}^{1-\theta} + P_F^{1-\theta})^{1/(1-\theta)}}$$

$$= \frac{(1 + r^*)\,\{[P_H^*(1 - \tau)]^{1-\theta} + P_F^{1-\theta}\}^{1/(1-\theta)}}{\{[P_H^*/(1 - \tau)]^{1-\theta} + P_F^{1-\theta}\}^{1/(1-\theta)}} < 1 + r^*$$

in segment I. If the country contemplates being a big lender, it will face an effective real interest rate significantly *below* the world real interest rate.

Segment II starts when period 1 consumption first reaches the level C_{II} such that $C_{H,2} = Y_{H,2}$. In this region, $P_{H,2}$ is determined by equation (8) and the first relation in equation (9), with $C_{H,2} = Y_{H,2}$ (so there is no round-tripping). Period 2 consumption of the home good remains constant at $Y_{H,2}$ as long as $P_{H,2}$ remains strictly between $P_H^*(1-\tau)$ and $P_H^*/(1-\tau)$, but equation (9) implies that $P_{H,2}$ falls as C_1 rises and C_2 falls, until $P_{H,2}$ reaches $P_H^*(1-\tau)$. Accordingly, the real interest rate *rises* over segment II.[14] At the point $C_1 = C_{III}$, Segment III begins as the home country becomes a period 2 exporter of its endowment good. On this stretch, $1 + r = 1 + r^*$. Because here, $C_H < Y_H$ in both periods, the overall price level is constant over time. In region III, the country is running a sufficiently small current-account surplus or deficit that there is never any reversal of the pattern of trade in either good. It is precisely in this region that trade costs have no effect on the real interest rate.

At $C_1 = C_{IV}$, however, $C_{H,1}$ reaches $Y_{H,1}$, and the real interest rate begins to rise once more. In segment IV, $C_{H,1}$ remains stuck at $Y_{H,1}$ as C_1 rises, pushing $P_{H,1}$ up with it until $P_{H,1}$ reaches $P_H^*/(1-\tau)$. As $P_{H,1}$ rises along segment IV, with $P_{H,2}$ constant at $P_H^*(1-\tau)$, the real interest rate rises. At C_V, however, where $P_{H,1}$ first reaches $P_H^*/(1-\tau)$, the country becomes a period 1 importer of its own endowment good, and the real interest rate stabilizes (along segment V) at the level

$$1 + r = \frac{(1 + r^*) \{[P_H^*/(1-\tau)]^{1-\theta} + P_F^{1-\theta}\}^{1/(1-\theta)}}{\{[P_H^*(1-\tau)]^{1-\theta} + P_F^{1-\theta}\}^{1/(1-\theta)}} > 1 + r^*.$$

The range of possible real interest rates produced by this simple example can encompass a wide distribution. For example, with $r^* = 0.05$, $\tau = 0.1$, $\theta = 6$, and $P_H^* = P_F^* = 1$, we find that the highest possible real interest rate is 20% (15% above the world level) while the lowest is -8% (13% below the world level). The interplay between the commodity transport costs τ and the substitution elasticity θ is similar to what we saw in the preceding section. As θ rises, the maximum and minimum real domestic interest rates move apart—with higher substitutability, the price-level impacts of changes in P_H are more pronounced. In the limiting case as $\theta \to \infty$ the two goods are asymptotically perfect substitutes, in which case the country's effective real borrowing rate will be 30%, and its lending rate, -15%!

Of course, the range of real domestic interest rates encompassed by Figure 1 is far greater than what we usually observe in practice, especially for OECD countries. But this simply reflects the fact that incipient

---

14. The increasing portions of the schedule have the shapes we show for θ-values that are plausibly high.

real interest differentials put a sharp check on a country's incentives to run large current-account deficits or surpluses.[15]

3.6 EXTENSIONS AND ALTERNATIVE FORMULATIONS

The preceding account of the effect of domestic spending on real interest rates is overly stylized, but a number of obvious extensions can add to realism without diluting the main message.

3.6.1 A Continuum of Goods and Transport Costs Assume, for example, that countries are endowed with multiple goods in various proportions and that these goods display a distribution of transport costs. Then, as domestic spending rises, progressively more types of goods are imported from abroad, leading to a steadily rising real domestic interest rate. In this more realistic setup, the relationship between expenditure and the home real interest rate will still resemble a version of Figure 1, but with very many small steps—to the naked eye, a smoothly upward-sloping curve. With a rich enough range of goods, transport costs, and elasticities of substitution, even small current-account deficits may produce trade reversals in a small number of goods, thereby resulting in an interest-rate effect. We conjecture, though it remains to be proved, that one would obtain a similar nonlinearity to that depicted in Figure 1, with small current-account imbalances having relatively little effect on interest differentials.

3.6.2 Long-Term Borrowing and Lending An obvious question is how the results here might be tempered in a model with many periods so that there are opportunities for long-term borrowing and lending. For example, if a country ran a big current-account deficit in the initial periods, it could repay slowly over many periods. Though a more careful analysis is required than we can provide here, it seems unlikely that this consideration would overturn our basic point; there would still be a big price swing between the big deficit periods and surplus periods—which is precisely why a country would seek to avoid such swings. We note also that in a richer model with a continuum of goods, the current account would not necessarily have to swing between deficit and surplus to induce real-interest-rate effects. In general, the range and type of goods

---

15. The suggestion that idiosyncratic real-interest-rate developments might help explain the Feldstein-Horioka puzzle can be found in earlier work, for example, Frankel (1986). However, to the extent that real-interest-rate effects have been touched upon in the literature, no one has taken the idea very seriously, since earlier models could not give any reason why the real interest rate might be so important quantitatively. Nor could they really explain the durability of the Feldstein-Horioka relationship across different time periods and regimes.

being imported and/or exported will vary more or less continuously in the level of trade-balance deficit (or surplus). Thus, the real-interest-rate effect will arise along any path where there are big trade-balance swings, either over any short period, or cumulatively over any long period. This would be true even in a setting with growth in which countries could, in principle, run perpetual deficits and surpluses.

3.6.3 Investment How is the preceding analysis affected by introducing investment? In the case where the country desires to be a large net borrower (segments IV and V), the real-interest-rate effect will be tempered to the extent the country can cut back on investment instead of borrowing from abroad. But that very mechanism dictates that reductions in national saving will be accompanied by reductions in domestic investment. In segments I and II, the country could channel some of its higher savings into higher investment, again tempering the fall in the effective real interest rate but creating the positive Feldstein–Horioka correlation between increases in saving and increases in investment.[16]

3.6.4 Deriving Similar Results in a More Conventional Setup with Traded and Nontraded Goods The reader may well ask whether we needed such an extravagant formulation to make the basic point that the consumption-based real interest rate can be linked to the current account. Couldn't we have made the same point in the context of a standard Salter–Swan model having two classes of goods, one with infinite trade costs and the other with zero trade costs (as discussed, for example, in Chapter 4 of Obstfeld and Rogoff, 1996)? Indeed, for a pure endowment case, the standard traded–nontraded model does produce a graph very much like Figure 1. Holding endowments of both goods flat, if the country chooses to run a large deficit in period 1, the price of nontraded goods will be high in that period, and low in the following period. This implies a consumption-based real interest rate above the world interest rate, just as in segments IV and V of Figure 1, and the effect can similarly be nonlinear. We prefer our formulation largely because it is much easier to think concretely about trade costs than about the arbitrary dividing line between traded and nontraded goods. Perhaps the ideal model would be a richer one incorporating a range of transport costs in which the degree of tradability is endogenous and some goods are consistently produced exclusively for the home market.

16. Though their focus is on the short-run time-series properties of the data rather than on the Feldstein–Horioka regularity, Backus, Kehoe, and Kydland (1992) do note that a small trade cost can sharply reduce the variability of net exports in their simulations.

3.6.5 Monopoly Pricing and Sticky Prices Our analysis assumes that prices are flexible and set in competitive markets. Introducing realistic features such as price rigidity and monopoly pricing, as in our discussion of puzzles 5 and 6, would enrich the model without overturning the main points. Also, the most troubling manifestations of the Feldstein–Horioka puzzle are at medium-term horizons of five to fifteen years, when price flexibility is much greater and firms' ability to preserve monopoly power is less.

3.7 EMPIRICS

The model does contain one simple prediction that can easily be checked. Countries running current-account surpluses should have lower real interest rates than countries running deficits.

This connection is illustrated in the panel regression results reported in Table 3. Specification 1 regresses the domestic real interest rate, defined as the average three-month nominal interest rate in a given year less lagged annual inflation, on the ratio of the current-account surplus to GDP. Specification 2 forms real interest rates by using December average nominal interest rates in year t less year t inflation, in an attempt to

Table 3 REAL INTEREST RATES AND THE CURRENT ACCOUNT, 1975–1998

	Coefficient on CA/GDP	Significance	ρ	R^2
Specification 1				
OLS	−36.9	0.00	0.65	0.05
Country fixed effects	−46.3	0.00	0.65	0.08
Country fixed effects, time dummies	−32.3	0.00	0.55	0.50
Specification 2				
OLS	−17.9	0.00	0.58	0.02
Country fixed effects	−19.4	0.00	0.58	0.05
Country fixed effects, time dummies	−18.9	0.01	0.54	0.32

The dependent variable is the annualized three-month nominal interest rate less lagged annual inflation CPI rate (specification 1) or less the contemporaneous inflation rate (specification 2). The sample uses annual data and covers the years 1975–1998 and all OECD countries except Iceland, Korea, Mexico, and Turkey. Current accounts (as a percentage of GDP) are reported by the OECD. We use three-month interest rates, usually a Treasury bill rate, but an interbank rate if no government rate is available. These data come from *International Financial Statistics* and the OECD. CPI inflation rates are based on IFS data. For the specification 2 regressions, four countries did not report monthly interest-rate data until after the start of our sample. The countries, with their starting dates in parentheses, are Spain (1977), Greece (1980), Portugal (1985), and Finland (1987).

capture that agents can incorporate contemporaneous information into forming inflation expectations. In both specifications we employ an autoregressive correction. We report estimates for simple ordinary least squares (OLS), a model with country fixed effects, and a model with fixed effects and time dummies (the latter to capture global influences on national real interest rates).

The results show highly significant negative correlations between the current-account surplus and the real domestic interest rate, as our model suggests. However, the two specifications differ somewhat in their numerical predictions, with specification 1 giving an effect that is substantially larger than that given by specification 2. Taking the regressions with country fixed effects and time dummies as likely to be most reliable, we see that a 1% of GDP rise in an OECD country's current-account surplus is associated with roughly a 20- to 30-basis-point decline in its real interest rate.[17]

4. The Puzzle of Home Bias in Equity Portfolios (Puzzle 3)

Despite the rapid growth of international capital markets toward the close of the twentieth century and a much expanded world market for equities, stock-market investors maintain a puzzling preference for home assets. When they first highlighted the extent of the home-bias portfolio puzzle at the end of the 1980s, French and Poterba (1991) observed that Americans held roughly 94% of their equity wealth in the U.S. stock market whereas the Japanese held roughly 98% of their equity wealth at home.[18] Figure 2, drawn from Tesar and Werner (1998), suggests that the home equity bias is muted for smaller countries and has shown some tendency to decline over time—by the mid-1990s about 10% of U.S. equity wealth was invested abroad. Standard models of optimal international portfolio diversification imply, however, that equity investors still have not diversified internationally nearly as much as they should, and so the puzzle remains.[19]

17. We experimented with a number of other specifications, expected inflation proxies, and time periods, almost always finding results similar to those reported in Table 3. Gordon and Bovenberg (1996) also establish a relationship between current accounts and real interest rates for OECD countries, but their test and their specification are motivated by a model that is very different than ours.
18. See also Golub (1990), who compared gross international asset flows with gross domestic asset creation for OECD countries.
19. University of California investment policies illustrate the extent and persistence of home bias even for large, sophisticated investors. On April 20, 2000, the U.C. regents announced a revision in investment guidelines for the university's retirement and endowment funds. The overall target portfolio share for equities remained at 65%, but the recommended target share for non-U.S. equities, previously *zero*, was raised

Figure 2 HOME BIAS IN EQUITY PORTFOLIOS: 1987–1996

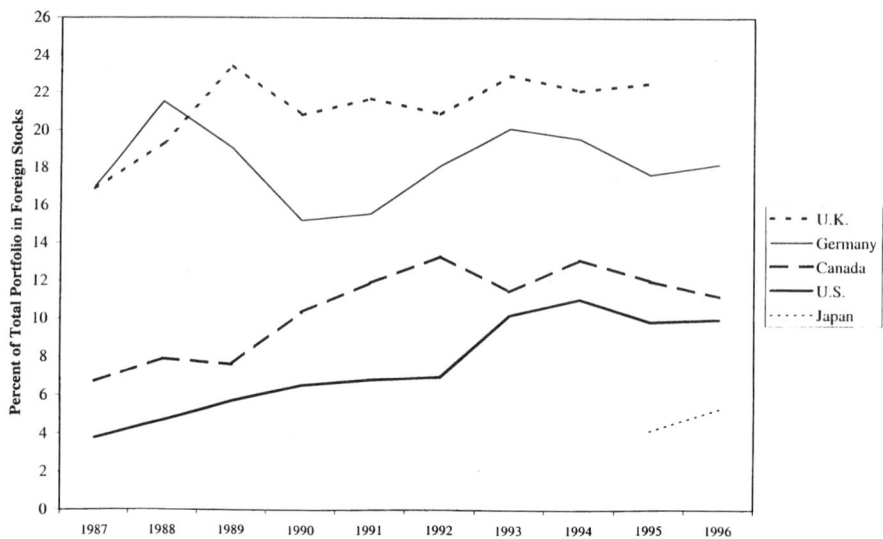

From Tesar and Werner (1998)

Potential explanations range from nontraded factors such as human capital (which may worsen or reduce the puzzle; see Baxter and Jermann, 1997) to nontraded consumption goods to asymmetries of information to data inadequacy. Yet it is fair to say that none of the available stories alone has provided a quantitatively satisfactory account of the observed home bias; see Lewis (1999) for an up-to-date and thorough survey.

To set the stage for our discussion of trade costs, it is worthwhile briefly reviewing what is perhaps the leading explanation, which is based on the classic Salter–Swan traded–nontraded-goods dichotomy we have already mentioned. While these two types of goods lie at polar extremes in terms of their tradability, equity claims on *either* type of industry can be frictionlessly traded. Thus, even though cement is prohibitively costly to transport, there is nothing to stop foreign investors from buying shares in the domestic cement industry. Earnings, of course, must be redeemed in traded goods, since nontradables cannot be shipped to foreign equity holders by assumption. The key result one gets out of this framework is that, for the baseline case of separable

---

to 7%. The positive target position in foreign equities, meant to "reduce risk and broaden portfolio diversification while maintaining or improving investment performance," represents a substantial advance. It still falls far short, however, of the optimal foreign equity share that simple models of international diversification would predict.

preferences (across the two types of good), investors hold a globally diversified portfolio of traded-goods industries. But nontraded-goods industries are held entirely domestically. The intuition is that, since payments can only be made in traded goods and utility is separable, there is no way to enhance risk sharing in tradables by linking the allocation of tradables consumption to returns in nontraded-goods industries. (That intuition has to be modified for the case of nonseparable preferences, but it is still a useful reference point.[20]) Thus, if nontraded goods constitute, say, 50% of total output (a popular rule of thumb based on the fact that for many OECD countries, services, construction, and transport constitute roughly 50% of GDP; see Stockman and Tesar, 1995), then agents will (loosely speaking) hold more than half their equity in home assets.

While elegant, this explanation still is not entirely satisfactory. First, although it goes some way toward explaining home bias, it falls short of explaining the 80% to 90% domestic equity shares we actually observe (Figure 2). Second, the sharp dichotomy between traded and nontraded goods is a contrived one, since in reality transport costs differ across goods, and a particular good may or may not enter trade under different market conditions. For most goods, tradability is not absolute and tradedness is endogenous.[21]

Here we will take an approach based on intuition similar to that in the preceding discussion. We explore just how far can one get in explaining the home portfolio bias by explicitly introducing trade costs, rather than splitting goods into two arbitrary and dichotomous categories. What we will show is that, with a plausible elasticity of substitution across goods and reasonable-sized costs for trading them, our model can produce a very high and realistic level of home portfolio bias.

4.1 A SIMPLE MODEL

We now add uncertainty to the two-country general equilibrium version of our model, with each country having a random endowment of its distinct perishable consumption good, along the lines of Lucas (1982) or Cole and Obstfeld (1991). To keep notation simple, we again abstract from dynamics and consider a one-period portfolio problem. We assume a completely symmetric joint distribution for the national outputs (Y_H, Y_F).

A home or foreign individual chooses state-contingent consumptions C_H and C_F of the home and foreign goods in order to maximize

---

20. Baxter, Jermann, and King (1998) develop some results for the case of nonseparable preferences.
21. For a more thorough discussion, see Obstfeld and Rogoff (1996, Chapter 5).

$$EU = E\left\{\frac{1}{1-\rho}\left[\left(C_H^{(\theta-1)/\theta} + C_F^{(\theta-1)/\theta}\right)^{\theta/(\theta-1)}\right]^{1-\rho}\right\} = E\frac{C^{1-\rho}}{1-\rho}. \quad (11)$$

Above, C is the index of total real consumption [per equation (1)], θ is consumers' elasticity of substitution between the two goods, and ρ is the coefficient of relative risk aversion.

There is free and costless international trade in a complete set of state-contingent Arrow–Debreu securities. (Imagine again that the securities' payoffs are made in a costlessly tradable international monetary unit of account.) We continue to assume that there are iceberg costs of trade, such that only a fraction $1 - \tau$ of a unit of good shipped abroad reaches its destination, so that under competitive markets $P_F = P_F^*/(1 - \tau)$ and $P_H = (1 - \tau)P_H^*$, per equations (2) and (3).[22]

Because, in addition, the countries are symmetric, free trade in Arrow–Debreu securities yields an allocation in which

$$\frac{1}{P_H}\frac{\partial U}{\partial C_H} = \frac{1}{P_H^*}\frac{\partial U^*}{\partial C_H^*}$$

and

$$\frac{1}{P_F}\frac{\partial U}{\partial C_F} = \frac{1}{P_F^*}\frac{\partial U^*}{\partial C_F^*},$$

for every state of nature, or

$$C_H^{-1/\theta} C^{1/\theta-\rho} = (1 - \tau)C_H^{*-1/\theta} C^{*1/\theta-\rho} \quad (12)$$

and

$$(1 - \tau)C_F^{-1/\theta} C^{1/\theta-\rho} = C_F^{*-1/\theta} C^{*1/\theta-\rho}. \quad (13)$$

Together these conditions imply the ex post consumption efficiency condition

$$\left(\frac{P_F}{P_H}\right)^\theta = \frac{C_H}{C_F} = (1-\tau)^{-2\theta}\frac{C_H^*}{C_F^*} = (1-\tau)^{-2\theta}\left(\frac{P_F^*}{P_H^*}\right)^\theta.$$

The model is closed by the output-market clearing conditions:

---

22. Just as in our discussion of the trade-bias puzzle, one could obtain similar results on home bias in equity holdings if trade costs were zero but there existed a home bias in preferences along the lines of equation (7).

$$C_H^* = (1 - \tau)(Y_H - C_H),$$
$$C_F = (1 - \tau)(Y_F - C_F^*).$$

Four of the preceding five equations are independent and yield solutions for the consumption levels C_H, C_F, C_H^*, and C_F^*.

4.2 INTERPRETING THE MODEL

It may puzzle some readers that we focus on the Arrow–Debreu allocation when in fact we are interested in relating our analysis to observed trade in the narrower class of equity-type assets that one observes in the real world. One rationale, perhaps, is that we do not want our theoretical home bias results to be driven by ad hoc assumptions about the kinds of securities that can be traded, especially since many assets like debt and direct foreign investment have complex optionlike qualities that may be difficult to summarize in a simple model. A second, more pragmatic, rationale is that the equilibrium for the complete-markets case is relatively simple to compute. A final rationale, as we shall see, is that for realistic parameters, trade in equities alone can come quite close to attaining the complete-markets consumption allocation, so that the home bias evident under complete markets is a good guide to the home bias in an equities-only model.

4.3 EVALUATING THE HOME BIAS

It is helpful to begin by analyzing the special case $\rho = 1/\theta$, in which the Arrow–Debreu conditions (12) and (13) simplify enormously. One can also show that the Arrow–Debreu allocation is then identical to the one in which people can trade only straight equity shares. Given our assumption of symmetry, the equilibrium portfolio shares are

$$\chi_H = \frac{1}{1 + (1 - \tau)^{\theta-1}} Y_H,$$

$$\chi_H^* = \frac{(1 - \tau)^{\theta-1}}{1 + (1 - \tau)^{\theta-1}} Y_H,$$

$$\chi_F = \frac{(1 - \tau)^{\theta-1}}{1 + (1 - \tau)^{\theta-1}} Y_F^*,$$

$$\chi_F^* = \frac{1}{1 + (1 - \tau)^{\theta-1}} Y_F^*,$$

where χ_H (χ_F) denotes the home agent's share of total equity in the home (foreign) industry, and χ_H^* (χ_F^*) denotes the foreigner's optimal equity shares. Note that if we were to translate these equity positions into *consumption* shares, we would find c_F and c_H^* lower than χ_F and χ_H^* by a factor of $1 - \tau$, reflecting the trade costs. Of course, in the absence of trade costs all the portfolio (and consumption) shares would equal 0.5, reflecting full diversification (under symmetry).

For $\theta = 6$ and trade costs of $\tau = 0.25$ (again, a seemingly reasonable number when applied to all of output, especially compared to the usual assumption that fully half of output is nontraded), one obtains $\chi_H = 0.81$, $\chi_H^* = 0.19$. Since share prices will be equal due to symmetry, this implies a home equity share of 81%. If $\theta = 10$, then the home portfolio share of home equities is 72% even with trade costs of just 10%. (As in the case of home bias in trade, there is significant nonlinearity: the elasticity of foreign shareholdings with respect to trade costs is very high when τ is near 1, but falls as trade costs fall.) The preceding calculations constrain the value of ρ to equal $1/\theta$, but, as we shall now demonstrate numerically, the results turn out to be remarkably insensitive to this assumption, given realistic levels of output uncertainty.

If we relax our restriction $\rho = 1/\theta$, the exact conditions needed to implement the Arrow–Debreu allocation through equity trade alone are broken. Trade costs create an international wedge between marginal rates of substitution such that standard stock-market spanning theorems no longer apply.[23] Nevertheless, one can still gain a good deal of insight into home bias by computing the *state-contingent* consumptions of the two goods in the Arrow–Debreu efficient allocation.

We can reduce the dimensionality of our numerical simulations by noting that, in equilibrium, the ratios of consumption to output, $c_H \equiv C_H/Y_H$, $c_F \equiv C_F/Y_F$, $c_H^* \equiv C_H^*/Y_H$, and $c_F^* \equiv C_F^*/Y_F$, depend only on the output ratio $y_H \equiv Y_H/Y_F$. Table 4 illustrates how the consumption ratios c_H and c_F differ both across states of nature and across a number of settings of the parameters τ, θ, and ρ.[24] (The values of c_H^* and c_F^* are apparent from the assumed symmetry of the model.) Notice that the home country's output shares decline across states of nature as its relative endowment rises. That pattern compensates the foreign country for the greater share of transport costs it must pay in states of nature such that home output is relatively high, and it is naturally more pronounced the higher the risk aversion parameter ρ.

For the cases in which $\theta = 6$ and τ is 10% or 20%, the table documents

---

23. See Obstfeld and Rogoff (1996, Section 5.3).
24. In a "baseline" model with trade frictions in which individuals nonetheless consume the proceeds from fully diversified portfolios, we would have $c_H = \frac{1}{2}$ and $c_F = (1 - \tau)/2$.

Table 4 PORTFOLIO POSITIONS IN HOME AND FOREIGN GOODS FOR STATE OF NATURE $y_H \equiv Y_H/Y_F$

Parameter settings			Portfolio shares c_H, c_F				
τ	θ	ρ	$y_H = 0.8$	0.9	1.0	1.1	1.2
0.1	2	2	0.53, 0.43	0.53, 0.43	0.53, 0.43	0.53, 0.43	0.52, 0.42
0.1	3	2	0.56, 0.41	0.55, 0.40	0.55, 0.40	0.55, 0.40	0.55, 0.40
0.1	5	2	0.61, 0.37	0.61, 0.36	0.60, 0.36	0.60, 0.35	0.60, 0.35
0.1	6	$1/\theta$	0.63, 0.33	0.63, 0.33	0.63, 0.33	0.63, 0.33	0.63, 0.33
0.1	6	2	0.64, 0.35	0.63, 0.34	0.63, 0.33	0.62, 0.33	0.62, 0.32
0.1	6	5	0.64, 0.35	0.64, 0.34	0.63, 0.33	0.62, 0.33	0.62, 0.32
0.2	2	2	0.56, 0.36	0.56, 0.36	0.56, 0.36	0.55, 0.35	0.55, 0.35
0.2	6	$1/\theta$	0.75, 0.20	0.75, 0.20	0.75, 0.20	0.75, 0.20	0.75, 0.20
0.2	6	2	0.78, 0.22	0.76, 0.21	0.75, 0.20	0.74, 0.19	0.73, 0.18
0.2	6	5	0.78, 0.22	0.77, 0.21	0.75, 0.20	0.74, 0.18	0.73, 0.18
0.3	6	2	0.89, 0.13	0.87, 0.11	0.86, 0.10	0.84, 0.09	0.83, 0.08
0.3	8	2	0.95, 0.08	0.94, 0.07	0.92, 0.05	0.91, 0.04	0.89, 0.04

how insensitive the portfolio shares are even to large changes in ρ. Because the results turn out to be fairly insensitive to ρ, we find that our earlier calculations are indeed little affected by relaxing the assumption $\rho\theta = 1$. The low sensitivity to ρ over the range of relative output outcomes in Table 4 is consistent with the conjecture by Cole and Obstfeld (1991) that, for moderate uncertainty, the gains from global risk sharing may be so low as to be mostly offset by costs of trade. Here, the equilibrium with a rich variety of assets is not so different from the one in which individuals can hold only equity. Another conclusion we can draw from these numbers is that trade costs have to be quite large before there is a substantial discrepancy between the Arrow–Debreu consumption allocation and the one that trade in equities alone would produce. Even for trade costs of 30%, an equity allocation that gave each country the same consumption share in *every* state of nature as it would have in the Arrow–Debreu equilibrium only when the realization was $y_H = 1$ would not entail a large departure from efficiency. As a result, even when $\rho\theta \neq 1$, the home bias evident in the complete-markets example is quite close to what a model of pure equity trade would imply.[25]

25. Backus, Kehoe, and Kydland (1992) report some relevant experiments with their calibrated two-country, complete-markets version of the Brock–Mirman stochastic growth model. It is true that they do not focus on the equity home-bias puzzle and that they allow for only a single consumption good, effectively making the elasticity of substitution between national outputs infinite. However, the fact that they find that moderate transportation costs produce an allocation close to that with full autarky is quite in accord with our results here.

4.4 CAVEATS

We do not believe that trade costs in goods markets are necessarily the whole story in explaining observed portfolio biases, and we certainly expect that the kinds of information asymmetries and legal restrictions emphasized in earlier work also play a role. These frictions can be viewed as trade costs in a broader sense, as we have noted, and they can affect portfolios through the trade-cost channel that we have emphasized in this paper. Nevertheless, it is remarkable that our simple model based on the trade-cost channel alone matches up so well to the data. As we have noted, our explanation not only has the merit of (extreme) simplicity, but is also more convincing because the same basic approach seems to help explain such a diverse range of puzzles. Finally, we note that our results are consistent with recent empirical work by Portes and Rey (1999). They find that international trade in both equities and goods is surprisingly well explained by an enhanced gravity model in which informational distance proxies supplement the standard set of geographical explanatory variables.[26] These results are certainly in accord with our model's prediction that equity biases in large measure reflect goods-market biases.[27]

A caveat to our findings is that transaction costs, and the resulting home bias, would be reduced somewhat in a fully dynamic model. Investors could then reinvest dividends abroad rather than repatriating them immediately. As is true for a tax-deferred asset, they could earn dividends on wealth that would otherwise be burned up as shipping costs. The question deserves further research. Dumas and Uppal (2000) develop a dynamic two-country growth model with shipping costs, but their focus is on welfare rather than on the home-bias puzzle. (They also assume $\theta = \infty$ throughout by positing a single consumption good.) Our guess is that trade costs will remain an important determinant of home bias even in a realistic dynamic setting.

We have used a complete-markets model to illustrate how trade costs can generate a home equity bias. By taking that modeling approach, however, we certainly do not intend to endorse an empirical view that

---

26. Portes and Rey (1999) report that their information variables are quite significant in explaining goods-market trade, even after controlling for geographical distance.
27. One consideration that dovetails nicely with our explanation is illustrated in the model of Martin and Rey (1999), which provides the closest antecedent to our approach. In Martin and Rey's (endogenously) incomplete-markets setup, the main driving force behind home bias is that owners of home firms retain a disproportionate share of their equity in order to extract a higher monopoly price for remaining shares from other agents. Martin and Rey focus on transaction costs in asset rather than in goods markets, in the tradition of Aiyagari and Gertler (1991). They posit an asymmetry between transaction costs for home and foreign agents, and this cost also affects share values. It does not interact with θ, however, so the effects are much smaller than here.

real-world asset markets are complete or nearly complete, either domestically or internationally. The complete-markets assumption is not essential, and our arguments would go through in a fully articulated incomplete-markets model, for example, one in which households have unequal access to equity markets, so that only some hold equity (Mankiw and Zeldes, 1991). The home-equity-bias puzzle has a strong empirical basis that is independent of any narrow theoretical framework. The consumption correlations puzzle, which we turn to next, encompasses a broader notion of market completeness, but its exact formulation is also more model-specific.

5. *The International Consumption Correlations Puzzle (Puzzle 4)*

If one believes that both domestic and international capital markets are well approximated by an Arrow–Debreu complete-markets framework, then it is a puzzle that international consumption growth correlations are not much higher than they appear to be. In an Arrow–Debreu world, country-specific output risks should be significantly pooled, and therefore domestic per capita consumption growth should not depend too heavily on country-specific income shocks. Of course, in some sense, the consumption correlations puzzle is almost a corollary of the Feldstein–Horioka and home-equity-bias puzzles. Given that the most transparent market means of consumption smoothing—debt and equity trade—are far less operative across borders than within them, it should not come as any great surprise that international consumption correlations are low. However, there are many reasons for thinking about consumption correlations independently. One is that we have only very imperfect measures of international trade in equity and debt, and another is that there may be other market channels, such as direct investment, for pooling risk.

The international consumption correlations puzzle has spawned a variety of subpuzzles. Backus, Kehoe, and Kydland (1992) highlight the fact that international output growth rates are actually more highly correlated than consumption growth rates. Backus and Smith (1993) note that in a world with traded and nontraded goods, efficient risk sharing calls for giving higher rates of consumption growth to countries that experience relative drops in the real price of consumption. (Very loosely speaking, the United States and Canada should write contracts that imply big transfers to Canada in states of nature where the Canadian dollar is very weak so that Canadians can exploit bargain Canadian prices, and vice versa when the Canadian dollar is high.)

As we shall see, most consumption correlations puzzles tend to be quite model-specific (depending on factors like the completeness of markets and the exact form of the utility function), so they are not quite as obviously puzzles about the real world in the same way that, say, the equity-home-bias puzzle is. One does not have to believe that the world is Arrow–Debreu to think it a puzzle that agents do not take more advantage of international diversification opportunities. Nevertheless, consumption correlation puzzles play a very important role in assessing alternative general equilibrium models, and, at a more fundamental level, we can ask why consumption risk pooling tends to be higher across regions within a country's boundaries than across national boundaries.

5.1 THE PUZZLE OF LOW INTERNATIONAL CONSUMPTION CORRELATIONS

Consider a single-good world with time-separable preferences in which all agents have identical period utility functions of the form $u(C) = C^{1-\rho}/(1-\rho)$. Then, if there are no trade costs, trade in a complete set of Arrow–Debreu securities would imply that home and foreign consumption growth rates are equalized:

$$\frac{C_{t+1}}{C_t} = \frac{C^*_{t+1}}{C^*_t}, \tag{14}$$

regardless of relative shocks to home and foreign outputs. (See Obstfeld and Rogoff, 1996, Chapter 5.) This is hardly what one observes in practice, as Table 5, which gives consumption growth-rate correlations based on Penn World Table data from the Group of Seven industrial countries, illustrates. The strong prediction of equation (14) is relaxed somewhat in models where utility depends nonseparably on both consumption and leisure. However, in this case, the benchmark frictionless world economy model of Backus, Kehoe, and Kydland (1992) still predicts a cross-country consumption correlation of almost 0.9, far above the correlations we see in the table.

Since, as we have already noted, the low-consumption-correlation puzzle is virtually a corollary of the previous two puzzles we have studied, the reader will hardly be surprised when we note that introducing trade costs works just as well in explaining it. Indeed, our model of the equity-home-bias puzzle can easily generate correlations of the sort seen in Table 5.[28]

---

28. Lewis (1999) points out that when a significant share of output is absolutely nontradable, international consumption correlations will be sharply reduced. However,

Table 5 CORRELATIONS IN PER CAPITA PRIVATE CONSUMPTION GROWTH, 1973–1992

	France	Germany	Italy	Japan	U.K.	U.S.
Canada	0.25	0.31	0.44	0.05	0.40	0.64
France		0.52	0.27	0.68	0.43	0.51
Germany			0.27	0.40	0.33	0.51
Italy				0.21	0.30	0.13
Japan					0.59	0.50
U.K.						0.65

Source: Penn World Table. Correlations of log differences in per capita real consumption. Simple average of correlation coefficients is 0.40.

5.2 THE BACKUS–SMITH PUZZLE

Backus and Smith (1993) derive a generalization of equation (14) that holds when trade is costly and, as a consequence, national price levels for the consumption baskets entering $u(C)$ generally differ. Let P denote the home price level and P^* the foreign price level, with both price levels measured in the same numeraire currency. As in the last section, currency and securities can be traded without transport costs even though goods are costly to trade. Then complete markets in state contingent assets ensure that growth rates in the marginal utility of *currency*—the medium in which state-contingent insurance payments are made—are equalized across countries. If the utility-of-consumption function exhibits constant relative risk aversion and is independent of leisure, as in equation (11), that equality implies

$$\frac{C_{t+1}^{-\rho}/P_{t+1}}{C_t^{-\rho}/P_t} = \frac{C_{t+1}^{*-\rho}/P_{t+1}^*}{C_t^{*-\rho}/P_t^*}. \tag{15}$$

This generalizes equation (14) in that $P = P^*$ absent international trade frictions.

Given the high volatility of real exchange rates under floating together with the low volatility of consumption, it is perhaps not surprising that Backus and Smith's empirical work forcefully rejects the optimal risk-sharing condition (15). In fact, the empirical rejection of condition (15) is

---

Stockman and Tesar (1995) observe that, insofar as the data can be trusted, international consumption correlations for apparently tradable goods are not appreciably higher than those for goods generally classified as nontradable. Their finding supports the view that the dichotomous distinction between tradables and nontradables is overdrawn, and simultaneously suggests that there are substantial impediments to international risk sharing in traded goods.

even more devastating, since even very high values of ρ cannot reconcile that condition with the data. One possible explanation is that their assumption that preferences are separable in consumption and leisure is too strong, so that one needs to look instead at a generalized version of (15). In our view, however, incompleteness of asset markets is the major reason why condition (15) fails so miserably in practice. Indeed, given the volatility of exchange rates, the size of transfers required for (15) to hold would require a level of risk sharing even greater than we observe in domestic markets.

The alert reader will note that a version of the Backus–Smith condition will hold in a dynamic extension of our earlier model of the home-equity-bias puzzle. That model implicitly assumed flexible nominal prices, and would not produce nearly the level of real-exchange-rate volatility one sees in the data. We do not take this as damning, since for us the complete-markets assumption was only a useful device for calibration, and not a conviction. Trade costs would play essentially the same role in a world with, say, trade in debt and equities but not a complete set of Arrow–Debreu securities. Indeed, in the context of this paper, the really interesting issue is not why international consumption correlations are difficult to replicate in a complete-markets model, but the extent to which consumption risk sharing is less prevalent across distinct countries than within countries.

5.3 INCOMPLETENESS OF DOMESTIC VS. INTERNATIONAL MARKETS

Certainly, empirical studies based on domestic micro data reject resoundingly the proposition that markets are complete. For example, Attanasio and Davis (1996) find that consumption risk sharing is strikingly incomplete within the United States, and for reasons that apparently are unrelated to asymmetric information. The question the present paper raises is whether risk sharing is even more impaired internationally than domestically due to costs of specifically international trade. Our discussion of home equity bias, which does not rely fundamentally on a complete-markets assumption, suggests that this should be the case, since regional equity bias seems to be far less than the strong national home bias that we see in international data. Backus and Smith's theoretical proposition points in the same direction.

A growing body of empirical evidence supports the prediction that financial markets are less effective in promoting risk sharing among countries than among regions within a country. A full review of this literature would take us too far afield, but we can mention briefly a few relevant papers. Atkeson and Bayoumi (1993), in one of the first empirical studies in this area, find that regional financial transfers within the United States are much larger than those among the major industrial countries. A comparison of the variance-decomposition results of Asdrubali, Sørensen, and Yosha (1996) on the United States with those of Sørensen and Yosha (1998) on the OECD suggests that financial markets play a much bigger role in consumption smoothing among U.S. states than is the case among industrial countries. Crucini (1999), using an alternative method, concludes that Canadian provinces pool risks more effectively than U.S. regions, and that either country shows more internal risk pooling than does the sample of industrial countries. Bayoumi and Klein (1997) find that Canadian provinces display more financial integration with each other than with the outside world.[29]

So there indeed is a puzzle as to why *intra*national consumption risk sharing is more efficient than *inter*national risk sharing, but it can be resolved in the same manner as we have resolved the home-bias and Feldstein–Horioka puzzles.

5.4 THE RELATIVE CORRELATIONS OF INTERNATIONAL CONSUMPTION AND OUTPUT GROWTH RATES

Backus, Kehoe and Kydland (1992) emphasize the puzzle that empirical consumption correlations are actually lower than output correlations. That pattern holds in the Penn World Table data analyzed here: the average international correlation in per capita real GDP growth rates is 0.53 over 1973–1992, while the corresponding average consumption correlation is only 0.40.

Our model, on its own, does not offer a new rationalization of their finding. However, we do not consider this to be a fundamental problem, since the existence of international risk sharing need not generate higher correlation among consumptions than outputs across countries. The reason is that only the output remaining after investment and government consumption can be shared by private consumers. Thus, a more appropriate comparison to assess the degree of global risk sharing is that between international consumption correlations and correlations in growth rates of output *net* of investment and government consumption ($Y - I - G$). Table 6 reports these correlations for the same sample period and data set used to construct Table 5. The average international correlation in the growth of $Y - I - G$ is 0.17, far below the average correlation 0.40 of international consumption growth rates. For six of the 21 country pairs that ranking is reversed, but in most of these cases the discrepancy is not significant.

So in fact, the puzzle concerning the relative variability of output and

---

29. Obstfeld (1995) adds a number of caveats to some of this literature.

Table 6 CORRELATIONS IN PER CAPITA $Y - I - G$ GROWTH, 1973–1992

	France	Germany	Italy	Japan	U.K.	U.S.
Canada	0.17	0.19	0.36	−0.18	0.50	0.66
France		0.13	0.34	0.20	0.02	0.11
Germany			0.19	−0.19	0.13	0.18
Italy				−0.31	0.33	0.46
Japan					−0.25	−0.22
U.K.						0.73

Source: Penn World Table. Correlations of log differences in per capita real GDP net of investment and government consumption. Simple average of correlation coefficients is 0.17.

consumption is not necessarily incompatible with a high level of international asset market integration. Indeed, using a dynamic new open-economy macroeconomic model, Chari, Kehoe, and McGrattan (1998) are able to produce realistic cross-country correlations of output as well as of consumption.[30] The main additional assumptions that lie behind their results include sticky nominal prices and, implicitly, transport costs high enough to result in segmented national output markets. Both transport costs and nominal rigidities are central to the resolution of the fifth and sixth puzzles, to which we now turn.

6. *The Purchasing-Power-Parity Puzzle (Puzzle 5) and the Exchange-Rate Disconnect Puzzle (Puzzle 6)*

Our last two puzzles differ from the preceding ones in being fundamentally about the real effects of a nominal variable—the exchange rate, which is the relative price of currencies. Here, also in contrast to the preceding four puzzles, the difficulty seems to lie primarily in explaining short- to medium-term phenomena rather than phenomena that persist over very long periods. (The Feldstein–Horioka puzzle, for example, is typically framed using decade-average data). Finally, the last two puzzles can be viewed as pricing puzzles, because they refer to price behavior, including the dynamic covariation between prices and other macroeconomic variables.

Any realistic attempt to address these pricing puzzles formally would require a much more elaborate framework than the one we have used thus far, incorporating, among other things, elements of monopoly and sticky

---

30. In the Chari–Kehoe–McGrattan sticky-price model, highly correlated national monetary shocks can make national outputs covary more closely than national consumptions. Highly correlated monetary shocks, however, also tend to reduce real-exchange-rate variability counterfactually in the model. We suspect that an extended version of the model could handle the latter problem.

nominal prices for goods and/or labor. In fact, there is already a great deal of exciting research along these lines now taking place [see, for example, the recent survey by Lane (2001) on the new open-economy macroeconomics]. Unfortunately, we do not have nearly enough space remaining here to present a fully articulated model. Nevertheless, we will try to make clear why trade costs are as essential to resolving the pricing puzzles as they are to resolving puzzles 1 through 4, which are quantity puzzles.

The first pricing puzzle we take up is the purchasing-power-parity (PPP) puzzle (Rogoff, 1996), which highlights just how weak the connection is between exchange rates and national price levels. It is based on the observation that in hundreds of studies, using widely varying techniques and data sets, researchers have repeatedly found very long half-lives—on the order of 3 to 4 years—for shocks to real (CPI) exchange rates. As we shall explain, half-lives of this magnitude are hard to understand if financial-market disturbances with only transitory real effects are very important in explaining short-run volatility.

Our term for the second pricing puzzle is the *exchange-rate disconnect puzzle*, a name that alludes broadly to the exceedingly weak relationship (except, perhaps, in the longer run) between the exchange rate and virtually *any* macroeconomic aggregates. It manifests itself in a variety of ways. For example, Meese and Rogoff (1983) showed that standard macroeconomic exchange-rate models, even with the aid of ex post data on the fundamentals, forecast exchange rates at short to medium horizons no better than a naive random walk. Baxter and Stockman (1989) argued that transitions to floating-exchange-rate regimes lead to sharp increases in nominal- and real-exchange-rate variability with no corresponding changes in the distributions of fundamental macroeconomic variables.[31] (The PPP puzzle is really just an example, albeit a very important one, of the broader exchange-rate disconnect puzzle.)

A critical difference between the (relatively short-term) pricing puzzles and the (longer-term) quantity puzzles is that we can no longer appeal to high elasticities of substitution to lever up the effects of modest-sized trade costs. (At the very least, the connection is no longer as simple and direct.) If there are only modest obstacles to short-term price arbitrage across borders, there can be only modest short-term price differentials. In fact, at the consumer level, arbitrage costs *are* likely to be rather large, and, after all, most goods embody very large nontraded content once they reach consumers at the retail level. But one cannot make this argument for wholesale importers who trade in bulk, so here

---

31. Flood and Rose (1995) extend Baxter and Stockman's results and arrive at similar conclusions.

we need a more nuanced discussion. As we shall see, importer-level prices do appear to exhibit somewhat less anomalous behavior than do consumer-level prices.

6.1 THE PPP PUZZLE

Let Q be the real exchange rate between two countries, and consider the regression equation

$$\log Q_t = \alpha + \eta t + \gamma \log Q_{t-1} + \epsilon_t,$$

where ϵ_t is a random disturbance. The real exchange rate, Q, is defined as $\mathscr{E} P^*/P$ using overall CPI data for price levels, where the nominal exchange rate $\mathscr{E}$ is the price of foreign currency in terms of home currency. (In deference to conventional usage, we now switch notation and use P to denote the domestic price level measured in home currency and P^* the foreign price level measured in foreign currency.)

Using monthly 1973–1995 data for Canada, France, Germany, Japan, and the United States, and constructing all 10 possible real exchange rates in this sample, we find values of γ ranging from 0.99 (U.S.–Canada, implying a half-life of 69 months) to 0.97 (Germany–Japan, implying a half-life of 21 months). The mean half-life across these real exchange rates is around 39 months, or $3\frac{1}{4}$ years.[32]

Such long half-lives would not necessarily be a puzzle but for the remarkable volatility of real and nominal exchange rates, volatility that seems hard to explain without assigning a major role to monetary and financial shocks. If monetary and financial shocks are the predominant source of volatility, however, it is hard to imagine what source of nominal rigidity could be so persistent as to explain the prolongation of real-exchange-rate deviations. This is the PPP puzzle.

6.2 THE PPP PUZZLE FOR TRADABLES VERSUS NONTRADABLES

One might think that the slow mean reversion just documented applies primarily to goods with extremely high international trade costs, whereas, at least for goods that are heavily traded, mean reversion in relative international consumer prices might be more rapid. That is not the case, however, as documented most strikingly by Engel (1999).

If we are willing to set our qualms aside temporarily and adopt a conventional dichotomy of traded versus nontraded consumer goods, we can use Figure 3 to illustrate the empirical significance of the distinc-

---

32. Data on end-of-month nominal exchange rates and on consumer price indexes come from *International Financial Statistics*.

tion for real-exchange-rate dynamics. The figure is based on monthly 1962–1995 data from Engel (1999, Section I) for the United States, France, Germany, and Japan. The overall real exchange rate $Q = \mathcal{E}P^*/P$ is compared with relative price indexes for tradables and nontradables, $\mathcal{E}P_T^*/P_T$ and $\mathcal{E}P_N^*/P_N$, where we adopt Engel's disaggregation of OECD sectoral CPI data into tradable and nontradable subindexes.[33] Each panel of the figure plots the correlations of percentage changes between pairs of relative prices, where the number of months over which the data are differenced is measured on the horizontal axis.

Consistent with Engel's results, the data reveal no significant difference between short-term and long-term correlations, indicating extremely slow mean reversion in shocks to the relative prices of tradables. Interestingly, it seems to make rather little difference whether we use tradables or nontradables prices to compute real exchange rates: all the price ratios are highly correlated with each other even out to horizons of five years. Engel's results focused on the U.S. real exchange rate against various trading partners, but as one can see from the figure, the results are (almost) as striking for a pairing of Germany and Japan. Other non-U.S. pairings that we have examined look similar.

We have argued that the traded–nontraded-goods distinction is much too finely drawn—at the retail level, many "traded" goods already embody very large nontraded components, and the dividing line is arbitrary and likely endogenous. It is nevertheless surprising just how little difference there is between the measures of real exchange rates in Figure 3. These findings probably cannot be ascribed merely to price aggregation problems, since many researchers report similar sluggish responses even for relatively disaggregated data on consumer goods that are commonly perceived as highly tradable. (See, for example, Isard, 1977; Giovannini, 1988; and Engel and Rogers, 1996.) The results certainly seem to suggest that even over the medium term, the consumer prices of supposedly tradable goods are nearly as insulated from the forces of international arbitrage as are the consumer prices of nontradables.

6.3 ADJUSTMENT IS FASTER AT THE PRODUCER LEVEL

It is important to emphasize that there seems to be considerably more adjustment of prices to exchange-rate changes at the importer level than at the consumer level. In their excellent survey of the empirical literature on exchange rates and international prices, Goldberg and Knetter (1997) conclude that the passthrough of exchange rates to relative international prices is about 50% after one year, much faster than what we have just

---

33. See Appendix A of Engel (1999). Figure 3 looks much the same if attention is restricted to data from the floating-exchange-rate period, 1973–1995.

Figure 3

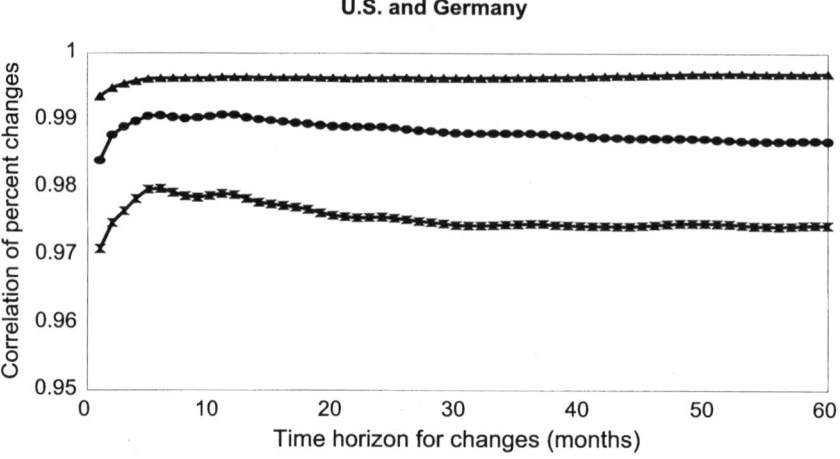

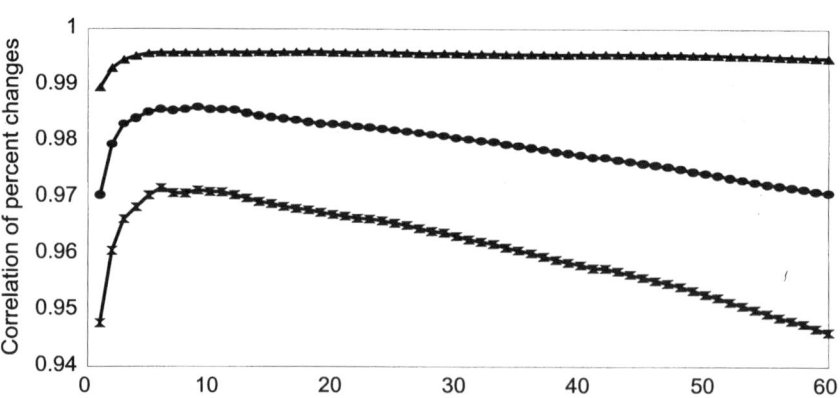

seen in the consumer-price data. Thus, relatively large elasticities in international trade between exporters and importers can be consistent with exceedingly sluggish adjustment in the relative *consumer* prices of tradables.

Obstfeld and Rogoff (2000) observe that if this were not the case—if prices paid by importers moved as sluggishly as prices paid by con-

Figure 3 continued

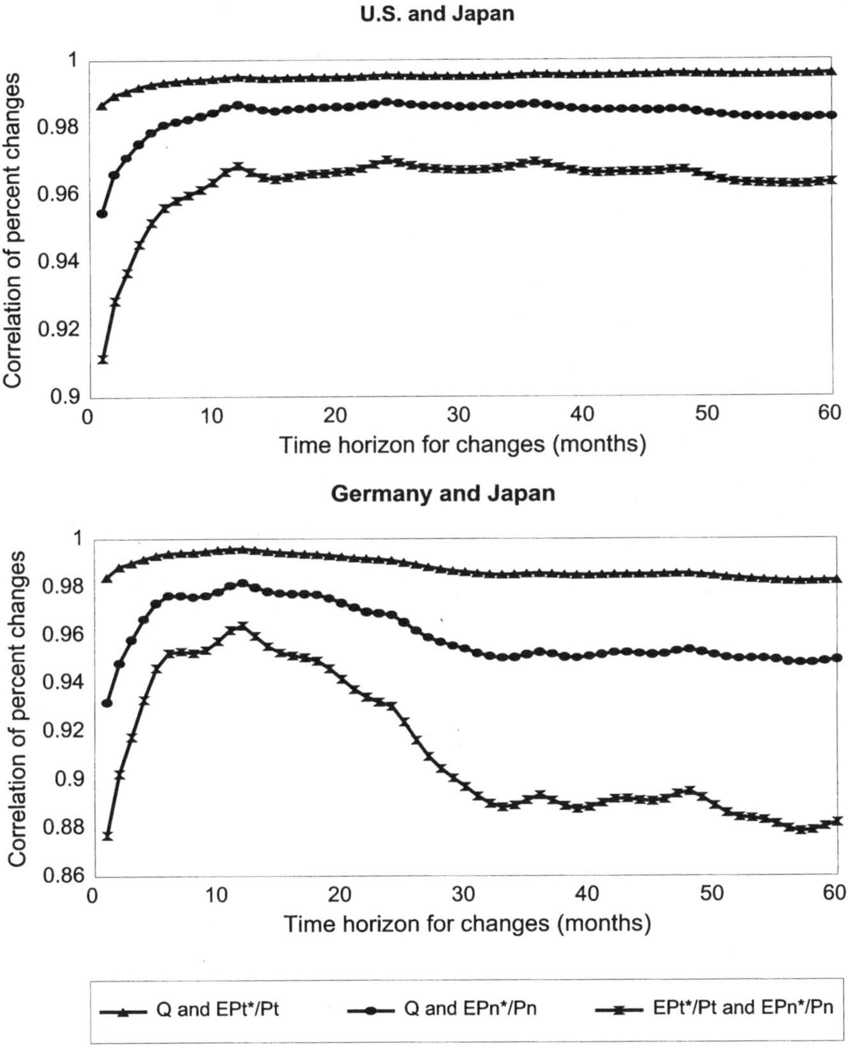

sumers—a country's terms of trade would actually improve, rather than worsen, after a depreciation of the exchange rate. For example, if the dollar depreciates against the pound and all prices are sticky, the dollar price paid by Americans for British goods remains fixed whereas the price paid by British citizens for American goods *rises* when translated into dollars. They find that this does not seem to be the case empirically, and instead find significant support for the conventional view—that exchange-rate depreciation worsens the term of trade of the depreciating country.

6.4 TRADE COSTS AND PRICING TO MARKET

Whereas the home bias in trade could, in principle, be explained simply by a home bias in preferences, the failure of markets to arbitrage international price differentials for seemingly identical goods cannot. The most popular explanation of persistent international price differentials argues that most goods are supplied monopolistically, and that (by assumption) monopoly producers have very broad scope to *price to market* by charging different prices in home and foreign markets (see, for example, Dornbusch, 1987; Krugman, 1987; Betts and Devereux, 1996; Bergin and Feenstra, 2000; or Devereux and Engel, 2000). Goldberg and Knetter (1997) survey a large body of supportive empirical evidence.

This explanation of international price differences for very similar or identical goods is appealing, but incomplete. What is to prevent consumers from arbitraging between home and foreign prices? Any explanation—and the pricing-to-market literature offers many; see Dornbusch (1987)—has to be consistent with the tenuous connection between exchange rates and the relative prices for virtually any type of consumer good. Rationales for pricing to market that might make sense for big-ticket items such as cars (the steering wheels on American and Japanese cars are on opposite sides, dealers can refuse warranty service for vehicles purchased abroad, etc.) are not very appealing when applied to, say, basic clothing items.

In our view, trade costs simply must play a central role in any explanation of international price differentials. However, to make sense of the price data, we must refine our earlier discussion of trade costs to distinguish between bulk wholesale and individual consumer trade costs. We must also think carefully about the ability of producers to control international distribution chains at the wholesale level. Otherwise—if the only wedge between home and foreign markets were moderate trade costs—one would only observe moderate price differentials.

6.5 WHOLESALE BULK VS. RETAIL INDIVIDUAL TRANSSHIPPING COSTS

At the consumer level, it is likely that for many goods, trading costs are in fact quite large, and far, far larger than trading costs faced by bulk wholesale shippers. (Individual consumers cannot profitably arbitrage even large differences in Coca-Cola prices across countries, but bulk wholesalers can.) The real question is what prevents international price arbitrage at the wholesale level. One answer is that in many cases, a firm can establish legal rights to control distribution of its product in different countries. Exclusive national marketing licenses are extremely common. For example, to protect its ability to price-discriminate across home and foreign markets, the Coca-Cola company sued a couple of small American wholesalers who, during the late 1990s, were trying to arbitrage the difference between Coca-Cola's $11.50-per-case wholesale price in Japan (as of January 2000) and its wholesale $5.50-per-case price in the United States—a differential far in excess of bulk shipping costs.[34] True, for small firms, the costs of establishing sole country distribution rights, and even more the legal costs of enforcing such rights, are likely to be prohibitive. Such firms also are likely to deal only with a very small number of bulk wholesalers, however, so it is still quite possible that they can price-discriminate, either by exploiting long-term relationships with their downstream wholesalers or even by taking over more portions of their wholesale distribution network.

6.6 PRICING TO MARKET AND THE PPP PUZZLE

To explain the data adequately, one must flesh out many details that we are omitting here. Very simple models of the kind we used in the first four sections are simply not adequate. For example, it is well known that with constant elasticities of demand, a monopolist may charge different prices in different countries, but exchange-rate changes will not cause fluctuations in relative prices charged [see Dornbusch (1987) and Marston (1990) for partial equilibrium models, and Betts and Devereux (1996), Obstfeld and Rogoff (1996, Chapter 10), and Hau (2000a) for general equilibrium models]. The nature of price rigidities is also quite important; Devereux and Engel (2000) emphasize that to make sense of the consumer-price data, one must think of final consumer goods prices as being sticky largely in domestic-currency terms for both domestically produced goods and importables.

Once one allows for pricing to market, however, it does become possible to develop models that can generate large price differentials exhibiting considerable persistence. Leading examples of such models are in Bergin and Feenstra (2001) and Chari, Kehoe, and McGrattan (1998), both of which develop new open-economy macroeconomic models with rich price dynamics. These authors do not explicitly base their models on trade costs—they do not try to rationalize the existence of pricing to market, but just assume it—so trade costs are only implicit. An example of a model with explicit trade costs is given by Dumas (1992), who observes that moderate trade costs can generate real-exchange-rate per-

---

34. See Constance L. Hays, "In Japan, What Price Coca-Cola?" *New York Times,* January 26, 2000, p. C1.

sistence even in a competitive world of fully flexible prices. However, the Dumas model cannot simultaneously generate anywhere near the volatility and persistence needed to match the data. Monopoly and nominal rigidities appear to be essential elements of any resolution of the PPP puzzle.[35]

Finally, one should note that in the presence of trade costs, econometric estimates of the half-life of real-exchange-rate movements may be exaggerated. Price differentials dissipate very slowly within transaction-cost bands, but more quickly outside them, and proper econometric estimation should take these nonlinearities into account (see Michael, Nobay, and Peel, 1997; Obstfeld and Taylor, 1997; and Taylor, 2001).[36]

6.7 THE EXCHANGE-RATE DISCONNECT PUZZLE

The same reasoning we have applied to thinking about the PPP puzzle can be applied to a much broader range of puzzles, all relating to the remarkably weak short-term feedback links between the exchange rate and the rest of the economy. We term this broader class of puzzles the *exchange-rate disconnect puzzle*. In a sense, the PPP puzzle is simply a very important special example of this broader class of phenomena. Of course, one may well ask why the exchange-rate disconnect puzzle should be any different from the *stock-price disconnect puzzle*, that is, the fact that stock markets seem to gyrate wildly without having any sizable contemporaneous effects on the real economy. We ourselves (Obstfeld and Rogoff, 1996, Chapter 9) have argued that to understand exchange-rate volatility, one ultimately needs a broader model that explains the high volatility we seem to observe in all asset markets. While we still maintain that view, it is also true that the links between the exchange rate and the real economy are much more direct than for stock prices. In most economies, the exchange rate is the single most important relative price, one that potentially feeds back immediately into a large range of transactions. Because the potential links are so direct, it is surprising indeed that they are not stronger.

Though much work remains to be done, it appears to us that a framework such as the one we have outlined earlier in this section (under puzzle 5) holds great potential for explaining the other disconnect puzzles as well. For example, exchange rates are remarkably volatile relative to any model we have of underlying fundamentals such as interest rates,

35. Working in a competitive flexible-price model with transport costs, Ravn and Mazzenga (1999) are also unable to rationalize both the real-exchange-rate volatility and the real-exchange-rate persistence in the data. Ohanian and Stockman (1997) develop an exploratory theoretical model of trade costs in a flexible-price monetary model.
36. Rogoff (1996) posits trading-cost bands as an essential element of any explanation of the PPP puzzle.

outputs, and money supplies, and no model seems to be very good at explaining exchange rates even ex post. The traditional thinking is that even though a broad range of goods is nontraded, there is always a broad range of goods that *are* traded, and these tie down the exchange rate. But a recurring theme here is that markets for most "traded" goods are not fully integrated, and segmentation due to various trade costs can be quite pervasive. In fact, the spectrum of goods subject to low trade costs may be very narrow.

In the type of model we described earlier in this section, a financial-market shock that moves the exchange rate may have little economic effect even over a fairly long horizon. With pervasive pricing to market at the retail level, consumers will be largely insulated from exchange-rate effects until these have had the time to feed through to wholesale import prices and, from there, to retailers. The magnitude of the PPP puzzle suggests how long that process might take.

Thus, interacting with the segmentation caused by trade costs, nominal price rigidities can produce a disconnect in which the exchange rate responds wildly to shocks. With the prices of most goods preset in local currency and real variables such as aggregate consumption largely insulated from exchange rates in the short run, exchange-rate adjustments have minimal short-run economic effects and therefore must be huge to clear financial markets. Only gradually will the responses of importers and exporters feed through to the retail level—and the adjustments might well be too slow to be picked up in the kinds of tests performed by Baxter and Stockman (1989). High volatility and the exchange-rate disconnect therefore both result from a combination of trade costs (costs that are especially high for consumers), monopoly, and pricing to market in local currency. A full model would incorporate those factors, while also modeling fully the dynamics of price adjustment through retail distribution networks, as well as other channels through which exchange rates might affect the real economy.[37]

We do not have space to explore the many implications that this intriguing class of models suggests. Can heightened exchange-rate volatility due to transport costs act to further segment markets internationally, with a resulting multiplier effect on volatility?[38] What are the welfare

37. Engel (1996) proposes that if all consumer prices are preset in local currency and firms fully hedge currency risks, exchange-rate changes will have no real effects and therefore exchange rates will be indeterminate. Hau (2000b) develops a new open-economy macroeconomic model in which exchange-rate volatility is decreasing in the degree of openness to international trade.

38. The theoretical work of Bacchetta and van Wincoop (1998) and Obstfeld and Rogoff (1998, 2000) and the empirical work of Obstfeld and Taylor (1997) and Rose (2000) suggest that currency volatility may itself act as a barrier to international trade.

costs of the exchange-rate disconnect? But the general approach strikes us as a very promising and realistic way to think about a host of exchange-rate volatility puzzles.

7. Conclusions

The need for research on the effects of trade costs in standard models of international finance seems compelling to us. We find that introducing plausible proportional (iceberg) trade costs into the most standard international macroeconomics models substantially resolves many of the core empirical puzzles in the field, including especially the (seemingly intractable) Feldstein–Horioka puzzle, the home-bias-in-equities puzzle, the home-bias-in-trade puzzle, and the low-consumption-correlations puzzle. We cannot claim the same degree of success in elucidating pricing puzzles as in the case of quantity puzzles, at least not with the kind of very simple models we have featured here. To tackle the PPP puzzle and the exchange-rate disconnect puzzle properly, a much richer framework featuring imperfect competition and wage-price rigidities is needed (therefore one in which, at a very fundamental level, neither domestic nor international markets are perfect). It is also necessary to build in a distinction between retail and wholesale pricing to account for the sharply different behavior of terms-of-trade indexes vs. consumer price indexes in response to exchange-rate changes (see Obstfeld and Rogoff, 2000, and Tille, 2000). We have argued, however, that introducing trade costs (implicitly or explicitly) must be an essential ingredient in resolving the international pricing puzzles as well. Richer models might consider fixed costs of trade as well as the proportional costs on which we have focused here.[39]

Although we take an eclectic perspective on the degree of completeness of international capital markets, our analysis does not rely on the assumption that their performance is intrinsically inferior to that of domestic capital markets (at least not in analyzing data for OECD countries). Our focus, instead, is on the distinctive ramifications for asset-market performance of the imperfect integration of *goods* markets. One attractive feature of our approach is that it is entirely consistent with the observation that gross flows in international capital markets are much larger than the small net flows.

An obvious potential criticism of our central theme is that transport technology has been steadily improving over the past half century, and tariffs have fallen dramatically, especially among the OECD countries. Has the home bias in trade and equities lessened, and are the consump-

---

39. O'Connell and Wei (1997) give an example of a theoretical model of price arbitrage involving fixed as well as variable costs.

tion-correlations and Feldstein–Horioka puzzles less acute than they were half a century ago? The short answer is that trade, capital movements, and equity flows all *have* expanded sharply since 1950, so the major quantity puzzles *are* less acute. For example, the ratio of total trade (the sum of imports and exports) to GDP has roughly doubled across the OECD between 1950 and 1995; for the United States, it has risen from 9% in 1950 to 24% in 1995.[40] (This calculation may significantly understate the true growth rate, since a large fraction of trade is in manufactures, the relative price of which has been falling over time.) And, as we have already seen, OECD savings–investment correlations have fallen significantly (from 0.89 for 1960–1974 to 0.60 for 1990–1997), while holdings of foreign equity have risen sharply (for the United States, from a 4% share in 1987 to a 10% share in 1996). At the same time, while transport technology has steadily improved, labor costs have risen sharply, so there is actually some debate about whether net transport costs have fallen. Hummels (1999b) argues that, until recently, the overall effect has been relatively small, with shipping costs falling sharply for bulk commodities but actually rising for manufactures, which account for over 70% of OECD trade. Greenspan (1989), on the other hand, emphasizes that trade is getting lighter, as many of the goods and services being traded today are highly knowledge-intensive. Overall, the data for the past half century certainly do not provide any prima facie case against our approach.

It would be interesting to look at time spans beyond just the past fifty years, so that trend declines in trade costs become more pronounced. Williamson (2000) calculates that transport costs for internationally traded goods fell by 1.5% per annum in real terms from 1850 to 1913, with the rate slowing down substantially over 1913–1950. Although prewar data are much thinner than postwar, and although there are many other factors to control for (large fluctuations in tariff rates, decolonization, wars, changes in the international monetary regime, etc.), this would nevertheless be a useful exercise. Cross-sectional empirical work is also needed.

Finally, a small apology to readers who were expected us also to address the forward-premium puzzle. We simply have not yet tackled this particular pricing puzzle, which we regard as much more of a pure finance question than a macroeconomic puzzle (and hence this paper's title). We note, however, that Dumas (1992) has produced a model of the forward premium in which trade costs do pull in the right direction, so getting a trade-cost model with the right quantitative effects may indeed be possible.

40. The only outliers are Australia and Japan, with trade ratios that remained roughly constant between 1950 and 1995 at 40% and 19%, respectively. See Baldwin and Martin (1999) or World Bank, *World Development Report, 1995*.

Appendix

Table 7 presents saving and investment rates by country for 1990–1997.

Table 7 SAVING AND INVESTMENT RATES, 1990–1997

Country	NS/Y^a	I/Y^b	$OECD^c$
Switzerland	0.29	0.23	1
Japan	0.33	0.30	1
Norway	0.27	0.23	1
Singapore	0.50	0.36	
Denmark	0.17	0.15	1
Iceland	0.16	0.17	1
United States	0.15	0.17	1
Germany	0.21	0.22	1
Austria	0.23	0.24	1
Belgium	0.22	0.18	1
Sweden	0.15	0.16	1
France	0.20	0.19	1
Netherlands	0.25	0.21	1
Finland	0.18	0.18	1
United Kingdom	0.14	0.15	1
Australia	0.17	0.22	1
Italy	0.19	0.19	1
Canada	0.16	0.18	1
Ireland	0.21	0.19	1
Countries with GNP/cap.^{d} > 18,000 (ave.)	0.22	0.21	
New Zealand	0.16	0.19	1
Israel	0.07	0.24	
Spain	0.20	0.22	1
Greece	0.15	0.17	1
Korea	0.35	0.37	
Portugal	0.22	0.22	1
Countries with GNP/cap. 5000–18,000 (ave.)	0.19	0.24	
Saudi Arabia	0.28^e	0.21	
Uruguay	0.12	0.13	
Chile	0.21	0.25	
Malaysia	0.33	0.39	
Trinidad and Tobago	0.18^f	0.16	
Mauritius	0.24	0.29	
Mexico	0.19	0.23	1
Venezuela	0.22	0.17	
Turkey	0.20	0.21	1
Panama	0.23	0.25	

Table 7 continued

Country	NS/Y[a]	I/Y[b]	OECD[c]
Thailand	0.34[f]	0.41	
Costa Rica	0.21	0.27	
Iran, I.R. of	0.26	0.27	
Colombia	0.18	0.21	
Namibia	0.15	0.21	
Tunisia	0.17	0.27	
Paraguay	0.12	0.23	
Countries with GNP/cap. 2000–5000 (ave.)	0.21	0.24	
El Salvador	0.01	0.17	
Dominican Republic	0.13	0.23	
Ecuador	0.16	0.20	
Jordan	0.01	0.32	
Guatemala	0.07[g]	0.15	
Morocco	0.18	0.22	
Philippines	0.17	0.23	
Sri Lanka	0.14	0.25	
Zimbabwe	0.14[f]	0.21	
Honduras	0.17	0.30	
Pakistan	0.16	0.19	
Zambia	0.10	0.24	
Kenya	0.13	0.20	
Burkina Faso	0.07	0.24	
Malawi	0.01	0.18	
Countries with GNP/cap. < 2000 (ave.)	0.11	0.22	
All countries (average)	0.19	0.22	

[a]NS/Y: gross national saving/gross domestic product, averaged over 1990–1997. For OECD countries, data on NS and Y are from the OECD database. For non-OECD countries, NS was constructed, from *International Financial Statistics* (IMF), as follows: NS = GNP − private consumption − government consumption. Our measure of NS for non-OECD countries does not exactly match the theoretical definition. The main difference is that it does not take account of the balance-of-payments component "net current transfers from abroad." Most of the countries that report data to the IMF and are not in the sample were excluded for one of four reasons: (1) IFS has data only for GDP and not GNP; (2) there are no IFS data on inventory investment; (3) there is a significant statistical discrepancy either between GDP and its components (more than 3%), or between GNP and the sum of GDP and net factor income/payments from abroad (more than 2%); (4) population is under 1 million.
[b]I/Y: investment/GDP, average over 1990–1997. Investment is the sum of gross fixed capital formation and increase (decrease) in inventory stocks. Sources are as in note a.
[c]The OECD sample of countries includes those that were members in 1995.
[d]GNP per capita measured in U.S. dollars, for 1997.
[e]No data for 1996 and 1997.
[f]No data for 1997.
[g]No data for 1991.

REFERENCES

Aiyagari, R., and M. Gertler. (1991). Asset returns with transactions costs and uninsured individual risk. *Journal of Monetary Economics* 27:311–331.

Anderson, J. (1979). Theoretical foundations of the gravity equation. *American Economic Review* 69(March):106–116.

———, and D. Marcouiller. (1999). Trade, insecurity, and home bias: An empirical investigation. Cambridge, MA: National Bureau of Economic Research. NBER Working Paper 7000.

———, and P. Neary. (1998). The mercantilist index of trade policy. Boston College. Mimeo.

Asdrubali, P., B. Sørensen, and O. Yosha. (1996). Channels of interstate risk sharing: United States 1963–90. *Quarterly Journal of Economics* 111(November):1081–1110.

Atkeson, A., and T. Bayoumi. (1993). Do private capital markets insure regional risk? Evidence from the United States and Europe. *Open Economies Review* 4:303–324.

Attanasio, O., and S. Davis. (1996). Relative wage movements and the distribution of consumption. *Journal of Political Economy* 104(December):1227–1262.

Backus, D., P. Kehoe, and F. Kydland. (1992). International real business cycles. *Journal of Political Economy* 100(August):745–775.

———, and G. Smith. (1993). Consumption and real exchange rates in dynamic economies with non-traded goods. *Journal of International Economics* 35(November):297–316.

Bacchetta, P., and E. van Wincoop. (1998). Does exchange rate stability increase trade and capital flows? Cambridge, MA: National Bureau of Economic Research. NBER Working Paper 6704.

Baldwin, R., and P. Martin. (1999). Two waves of globalization: Superficial similarities, fundamental differences. Cambridge, MA: National Bureau of Economic Research. NBER Working Paper 6904.

Baxter, M., and U. Jermann. (1997). The international diversification puzzle is worse than you think. *American Economic Review* 87(March):170–191.

———, ———, and R. King. (1998). Nontraded goods, nontraded factors, and international non-diversification. *Journal of International Economics* 46:211–229.

———, and A. Stockman. (1989). Business cycles and the exchange rate regime: Some international evidence. *Journal of Monetary Economics* 23(May):377–400.

Bayoumi, T., and M. Klein. (1997). A provincial view of economic integration. *International Monetary Fund Staff Papers* 44(December):534–556.

Bergin, P., and R. Feenstra. (2001). Pricing-to-market, staggered contracts, and real exchange rate persistence. *Journal of International Economics*, forthcoming.

Berry, S., J. Levinsohn, and A. Pakes. (1995). Automobile prices in market equilibrium. *Econometrica* 63(July):841–890.

Betts, C., and M. Devereux. (1996). The exchange rate in a model of pricing to market. *European Economic Review* 40(April):1007–1021.

Brown, D., and R. Stern. (1989). Computable general equilibrium estimates of the gains from U.S.–Canadian trade liberalization. In *Economic Aspects of Regional Trading Arrangements*, D. Greenaway, T. Hyclak, and R. Thornton (eds.). New York: New York University Press.

Chari, V., P. Kehoe, and E. McGrattan. (1998). Monetary shocks and real exchange rates in sticky price models of international business cycles. Federal Reserve Bank of Minneapolis. Research Department Staff Report No. 223.

Cheung, Y., M. Chinn, and E. Fujii (1999). Market structure and the persistence of sectoral real exchange rates. Cambridge, MA: National Bureau of Economic Research. NBER Working Paper 7408.

Coakley, J., F. Kulasi, and R. Smith. (1998). The Feldstein–Horioka puzzle and capital mobility: A review. *International Journal of Finance and Economics* 3:169–188.

Cole, H., and M. Obstfeld. (1991). Commodity trade and international risk sharing: How much do financial markets matter? *Journal of Monetary Economics* 28(August):3–24.

Crucini, M. (1999). On international and national dimensions of risk sharing. *Review of Economics and Statistics* 81(February):73–84.

Deardorff, A. (1998). Determinants of bilateral trade: Does gravity work in a neoclassical world? In *The Regionalization of the World Economy*, J. Frankel (ed.). Chicago: University of Chicago Press.

Devereux, M., and C. Engel. (2000). Monetary policy in the open economy revisited: Price setting and exchange rate flexibility. Cambridge, MA: National Bureau of Economic Research. NBER Working Paper 7665.

Dornbusch, R. (1987). Exchange rates and prices. *American Economic Review* 77(March):93–106.

———, S. Fischer, and P. Samuelson. (1977). Comparative advantage, trade, and payments in a Ricardian model with a continuum of goods. *American Economic Review* 67(December):823–839.

Dumas, B. (1992). Dynamic equilibrium and the real exchange rate in a spatially separated world. *Review of Financial Studies* 5:153–180.

———, and R. Uppal. (2000). Global diversification, growth and welfare with imperfectly integrated markets for goods. *Review of Financial Studies*, forthcoming.

Engel, C. (1996). A model of foreign exchange rate indetermination. Cambridge, MA: National Bureau of Economic Research. NBER Working Paper 5766.

———. (1999). Accounting for U.S. real exchange rate changes. *Journal of Political Economy* 107(June):507–538.

———, and J. Rogers. (1996). How wide is the border? *American Economic Review* 86(December):1112–1125.

Evans, C. (1999). *Do national borders matter?* Doctoral Dissertation, Harvard University.

Feldstein, M., and C. Horioka. (1980). Domestic savings and international capital flows. *Economic Journal* 90(June):314–329.

Flood, R., and A. Rose. (1995). Fixing the exchange rate regime: A virtual quest for fundamentals. *Journal of Monetary Economics* 36(August):3–37.

Frankel, J. (1986). International capital mobility and crowding-out in the U.S. economy: Imperfect integration of financial markets or of goods markets? In *How Open Is the U.S. Economy?* R. W. Hafer (ed.). Lexington, MA: Lexington Books.

French, K., and J. Poterba. (1991). Investor diversification and international equity markets. *American Economic Review* 81(May):222–226.

Giovannini, A. (1988). Exchange rates and traded goods prices. *Journal of International Economics* 24(February):45–68.

Goldberg, P., and M. Knetter. (1997). Goods prices and exchange rates: What have we learned? *Journal of Economic Literature* 35(September):1243–1272.

Golub, S. (1990). International capital mobility: Net versus gross stocks and flows. *Journal of International Money and Finance* 9:424–439.

Gordon, R., and L. Bovenberg. (1996). Why is capital so immobile internationally? Possible explanations and implications for capital income taxation. *American Economic Review* 86(December):1057–1075.

Greenspan, A. (1989). The economic value of ideas: Looking to the next century. *Japan Society of New York Newsletter* 36 (July).

Harrigan, J. (1993). OECD imports and trade barriers in 1983. *Journal of International Economics* 35:91–111.

Hau, H. (2000a). Real exchange rate volatility and economic openness: Theory and evidence. Centre for Economic Policy Research. Working Paper 2356.

———. (2000b). Exchange rate determination: The role of factor rigidities and nontradables. *Journal of International Economics* 50(April):421–427.

Helliwell, J. (1996). Do national borders matter for Quebec's trade? *Canadian Journal of Economics* 29(August):507–522.

———. (1998). *How Much Do National Borders Matter?* Washington: Brookings Institution.

Helpman, E. (1999). The structure of foreign trade. *Journal of Economic Perspectives* 13(Spring):121–144.

Hummels, D. (1999a). Toward a geography of trade costs. University of Chicago, Graduate School of Business. Mimeo.

———. (1999b). Have international transportation costs declined? University of Chicago, Graduate School of Business. Mimeo.

Isard, P. (1977). How far can we push the law of one price? *American Economic Review* 67(December):942–948.

Krugman, P. (1987). Pricing to market when the exchange rate changes. In *Real-Financial Linkages among Open Economies*, S. Arndt and J. Richardson (eds.). Cambridge, MA: The MIT Press.

———. (1991). *Has the Adjustment Process Worked?* Washington: Institute for International Economics.

Lane, P. (2001). The new open economy macroeconomics: A survey. *Journal of International Economics*, forthcoming.

Lee, J., and P. Swagel. (1997). Trade barriers and trade flows across countries and across industries. *Review of Economics and Statistics* 79:372–382.

Lewis, K. (1999). Trying to explain the home bias in equities and consumption. *Journal of Economic Literature* 37(June):571–608.

Lucas, R. E., Jr. (1982). Interest rates and currency prices in a two-country world. *Journal of Monetary Economics* 10(November):335–360.

Mankiw, N., and S. Zeldes. (1991). The consumption of stockholders and nonstockholders. *Journal of Financial Economics* 29(March):97–112.

Marston, R. (1990). Pricing to market in Japanese manufacturing. *Journal of International Economics* 29(December):217–236.

Martin, P., and H. Rey. (1999). Financial supermarkets: Size matters for asset trade. Centre for Economic Policy Research. Working Paper 2232.

McCallum, J. (1995). National borders matter: Canada–U.S. regional trade patterns. *American Economic Review* 85(June):615–623.

Meese, R., and K. Rogoff. (1983). Empirical exchange rate models of the seventies: Do they fit out of sample? *Journal of International Economics* 14(February):3–24.

Mendoza, E. (1991). Real business cycles in a small open economy. *American Economic Review* 81(September):797–818.
Michael, P., A. Nobay, and D. Peel. (1997). Transaction costs and nonlinear adjustments in real exchange rates: An empirical investigation. *Journal of Political Economy* 105(August):862–879.
Obstfeld, M. (1986). Capital mobility in the world economy: Theory and measurement. *Carnegie-Rochester Conference Series on Public Policy* 24(Spring):55–103.
———. (1995). International capital mobility in the 1990s. In *Understanding Interdependence: The Macroeconomics of the Open Economy*, P. B. Kenen (ed.). Princeton, NJ: Princeton University Press.
———, and K. Rogoff. (1996). *Foundations of International Macroeconomics*. Cambridge, MA: The MIT Press.
———, and ———. (1998). Risk and exchange rates. Cambridge, MA: National Bureau of Economic Research. NBER Working Paper 6694.
———, and ———. (2000). New directions for stochastic open economy models. *Journal of International Economics* 50(February):117–153.
———, and A. Taylor. (1997). Nonlinear aspects of goods-market arbitrage and adjustment: Heckscher's commodity points revisited. *Journal of the Japanese and International Economies* 11(December):441–479.
O'Connell, P., and S. Wei. (1997). "The bigger they are, the harder they fall": How price differences across U.S. cities are arbitraged. Cambridge, MA: National Bureau of Economic Research. NBER Working Paper 6089.
Ohanian, L., and A. Stockman. (1997). Arbitrage costs and exchange rates. University of Rochester, Mimeo.
Organization for Economic Cooperation and Development. (1996). *Indicators of Tariff and Nontariff Barriers*. Paris: Organization for Economic Cooperation and Development.
Portes, R., and H. Rey. (1999). The determinants of cross-border equity flows: The geography of information. Cambridge, MA: National Bureau of Economic Research. NBER Working Paper 7336.
Radelet, S., and J. Sachs. (1998). Shipping costs, manufactured exports, and economic growth. Harvard Institute for Economic Development. Mimeo.
Rauch, J. (1999). Networks versus markets in international trade. *Journal of International Economics* 48(June):7–35.
Ravn, M., and E. Mazzenga. (1999). Frictions in international trade and relative price movements. London Business School. Mimeo.
Rogoff, K. (1996). The purchasing power parity puzzle. *Journal of Economic Literature* 34(June):647–668.
Rose, A. (2000). One money, one market: Estimating the effect of common currencies on trade. *Economic Policy* 30(April):7–45.
Rotemberg, J., and M. Woodford. (1992). Oligopolistic pricing and the effects of aggregate demand on economic activity. *Journal of Political Economy* 100 (December):1153–1207.
———, and ———. (1995). Dynamic general equilibrium models with imperfectly competitive output markets. In *Frontiers of Business Cycle Research*, T. F. Cooley (ed.). Princeton, NJ: Princeton University Press.
Samuelson, P. (1954). The transfer problem and transport costs: Analysis of effects of trade impediments. *Economic Journal* 64(June):264–289.
Sørensen, B., and O. Yosha. (1998). International risk sharing and European monetary unification. *Journal of International Economics* 45:211–238.

Stockman, A., and L. Tesar. (1995). Tastes and technology in a two-country model of the business cycle: Explaining international comovements. *American Economic Review* 85(March):168–185.
Taylor, A. (2001). Potential pitfalls for the purchasing-power-parity puzzle? Sampling and specification biases in mean-reversion tests of the law of one price. *Econometrica*, forthcoming.
Tesar, L., and I. Werner. (1998). The internationalization of securities markets since the 1987 crash. In *Brookings-Wharton Papers on Financial Services*, R. Litan and A. Santomero (eds.). Washington: The Brookings Institution.
Tille, C. (2000). "Beggar-thy-neighbor" or "beggar-thyself"? The income effect of exchange rate fluctuations. Federal Reserve Bank of New York. Mimeo.
Tinbergen, J. (1962). An analysis of world trade flows. In *Shaping the World Economy*, J. Tinbergen (ed.). New York: Twentieth Century Fund.
Trefler, D. (1995). The case of the missing trade and other mysteries. *American Economic Review* 85(December):1029–1046.
———, and H. Lai (1999). The gains from trade: Standard errors with the CES monopolistic competition model. University of Toronto. Mimeo.
van Wincoop, E. (2000). Borders and trade. Federal Reserve Bank of New York. Mimeo.
Wei, S. (1998). How reluctant are nations in global integration? Harvard University. Mimeo.
Williamson, J. (2000). Land, labor, and globalization in the preindustrial third world. Cambridge, MA: National Bureau of Economic Research. NBER Working Paper 7784.

Comment

OLIVIER JEANNE
International Monetary Fund

1. Introduction

One of the pleasures in reading this paper is that it has the flavor of a conspiracy theory. It explains a set of apparently unconnected and unexplained phenomena in terms of a single cause, which, the authors argue, is not as implausible as it sounds. And they succeed at least in instilling doubts—this on the basis of careful theoretical reasoning and some empirical evidence. This is a thought-provoking paper, which I expect to be influential and inspire a number of theoretical and empirical papers: it raises a number of hypotheses that are both theoretically intriguing and potentially testable.

The thesis in this paper is that the main puzzles in international macroeconomics can be explained as the result of costs in the trade of goods and services. The paper nicely weaves together empirical evidence and theoretical arguments, some of which are explicitly modeled with the pedagogic elegance that is one of the authors' trademarks. Obstfeld and Rogoff (OR) start with the rather uncontroversial point that trade costs can generate a significant degree of segmentation in the goods market, before moving to the more provocative part of their thesis: the international segmentation of *asset* markets could result from the same trade costs. In other words, it might be unnecessary to invoke the many frictions specific to the asset markets that have been discussed in the literature.[1]

I shall focus my comments on the Feldstein–Horioka puzzle, the international-consumption-correlation puzzle, and the exchange-rate disconnect puzzle, since this is where OR are more innovative and provocative. It is rather uncontroversial in principle that trade costs can generate a significant degree of international segmentation in the goods market, especially if goods are sufficiently substitutable and if trade costs are defined in a sufficiently broad way. OR go beyond this theoretical remark, and convincingly argue, on the basis of estimates for transportation costs and the elasticity of substitution between goods, that trade costs can explain a large degree of international segmentation in trade. An important challenge, for the scholars who will pursue this line of reasoning, will be to refine the mapping between the various trade costs (distinguishing, in particular, between those that are border-related and those that are not) and the pattern of trade segmentation that we observe in the real world.

2. *Explaining Asset Market Segmentation by Trade Costs*

OR's discussion of the different channels by which frictions can spill over from goods markets to asset markets is truly impressive in its theoretical breadth and originality of insight. I shall restrict the scope of my comments to the two channels which OR have chosen to model explicitly. The first model is presented by OR in connection with the Feldstein–Horioka puzzle; it relies on an implicit wedge in the real-interest-rate parity condition. The second model attempts to explain the home bias in equity portfolios; it looks at the implication of nontraded goods for portfolio choice.

---

1. The home bias in equity portfolios has been attributed to informational asymmetries (Kang and Stulz, 1994; Portes and Rey, 1999), cultural and linguistic barriers, and differences in national tax systems and regulations (Tesar and Werner, 1995). Kraay and Ventura (1999) show that in a portfolio perspective the Feldstein–Horioka puzzle can be viewed as a direct consequence of the home bias in asset portfolios.

The link between nontraded goods and portfolio choice is the object of a growing literature, which is difficult to review in a short space. Let me simply note that this literature may seem a bit less optimistic, in its most recent developments, than OR in this paper. In her recent review, Lewis (1999) underlines several shortcomings of the approach; in particular, she argues that a key prediction of OR's Section 4 model—that investors hold a globally diversified portfolio of traded-good industries, but nontraded-good industries are held entirely domestically—is not supported by casual empiricism. Pesenti and Van Wincoop (1996) apply a model of optimal portfolio choice with nontraded goods to fourteen OECD countries, and find that it can explain only a small fraction of the home bias. The model presented here by OR differs from the previous literature by assuming a trade cost which applies to all domestic output, rather than drawing an arbitrary line between tradables and nontradables. It remains to be seen whether endogenizing the frontier between traded and nontraded goods significantly improves the model's ability to explain the home bias in equity portfolios.

I was more intrigued by the first channel, "an entirely new explanation, based on transaction costs for international trade in goods," (Section 3.1) and shall spend, accordingly, the rest of this section commenting on it.

2.1 TRADE COSTS AND INTERTEMPORAL PRICE WEDGES: A ONE-GOOD MODEL

In their explanation of the Feldstein–Horioka puzzle OR present a model of the consumption–saving choice in a small open economy with trade costs. First, let me rephrase OR's main point in the context of a one-good model (this is the limit of their two-good model where the two goods are perfectly substitutable). The one-good model is less general but makes the logic of OR's point more transparent.[2] I keep the same notation as OR except that the subscripts denoting the difference between home and foreign goods are dropped. For convenience, the representative agent's psychological discount rate is assumed to be equal to the world real interest rate.

The good can be exported to or imported from a global perfectly competitive market, where its price, P^*, is fixed in terms of the world currency unit. Because a fraction τ of the good "melts" in transit, the home price of the good (where home means net of trade costs) is given by

---

2. The one-good model was presented in the first version of OR's paper, although not in the same way as I am presenting it here.

$$P_t \begin{cases} = \dfrac{P^*}{1-\tau} & \text{if the country imports } (C_t > Y_t), \\ \in \left[(1-\tau)P^*, \dfrac{P^*}{1-\tau}\right] & \text{if the trade balance is equal to zero } (C_t = Y_t), \\ = (1-\tau)P^* & \text{if the country exports } (C_t < Y_t). \end{cases}$$

The home price of the good is a discontinuous function of domestic consumption. It jumps down when the trade balance switches from a deficit to a surplus.

The first-period and second-period budget constraints are respectively given by $P_1(C_1 - Y_1) = D$ and $P_2(Y_2 - C_2) = (1 + r^*)D$, where D is borrowing from abroad in world currency units. The domestic consumption–saving problem thus can be written

$$\max \quad u(C_1) + \beta u(C_2)$$

$$\text{s.t.} \quad C_1 + \frac{C_2}{(1+r^*)(P_1/P_2)} = Y_1 + \frac{Y_2}{(1+r^*)(P_1/P_2)}.$$

The representative consumer's intertemporal budget constraint is depicted in Figure 1. The budget constraint exhibits a kink at the point where the country consumes its endowment in each period, as it would do under autarky. The kink results from the iceberg cost which is paid on each way of the round trip when the country exports the good at one period and imports it at the other. Trade costs generate a wedge between the world real interest rate r^* and the rate at which domestic agents can substitute their consumption intertemporally, $r = (1 + r^*)(P_1/P_2) - 1$ (the "domestic real interest rate," in OR's words).

At the optimum the representative consumer's iso-utility curve must be tangent to the budget curve. If tangency is reached at the kink of the budget curve, as in Figure 1, there is no international trade in equilibrium.[3] This case arises if the difference between the period 1 and period 2 endowments, Y_1 and Y_2, is not too large. For example, if $u(c) = c^{1-\rho}/(1-$

---

3. Note that in order to solve the model one has to assume that the representative consumer is aware of the kink in the country's budget constraint, i.e., takes as given the world price of the good, P^*, and not the home price, P.

Figure 1

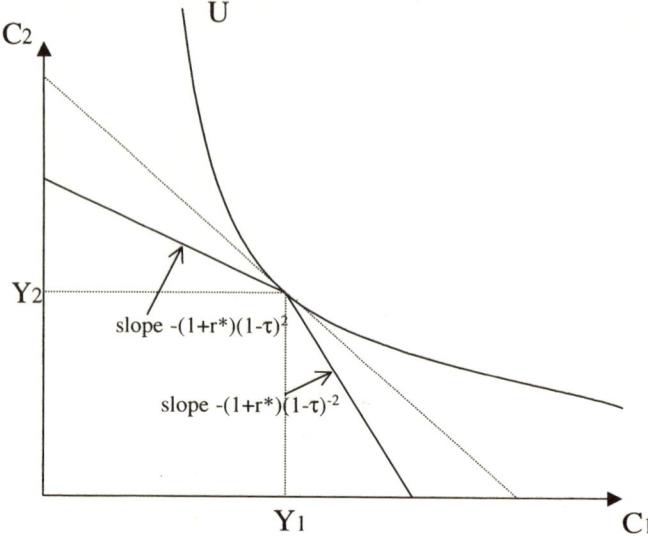

ρ) and the psychological discount rate is equal to the world interest rate $[\beta(1 + r^*) = 1]$, there is no trade provided that

$$(1 - \tau)^{2/\rho} < \frac{Y_2}{Y_1} < (1 - \tau)^{-2/\rho}. \tag{1}$$

The no-trade region can be pretty large for plausible values of the parameters. To illustrate, if utility is logarithmic and trade costs amount to 10% of trade volume (a very conservative estimate by OR's standards, who use a figure of 25% in their calibration), there is no trade as long as the difference between Y_1 and Y_2 does not exceed 20%.

It is interesting to note that these results do not hinge on particular assumptions on the time structure. The two periods could be separated by one month or one generation. If the model had more than two periods, or time were continuous, the no-trade region would still be characterized by a condition like (1). The model predicts that there is no international trade as long as domestic income does not deviate too much from its average level.

Figure 2 illustrates, in continuous time, how the model can explain the low international correlation of consumption (the Feldstein–Horioka puzzle). The figure shows domestic consumption and the trade balance

Figure 2

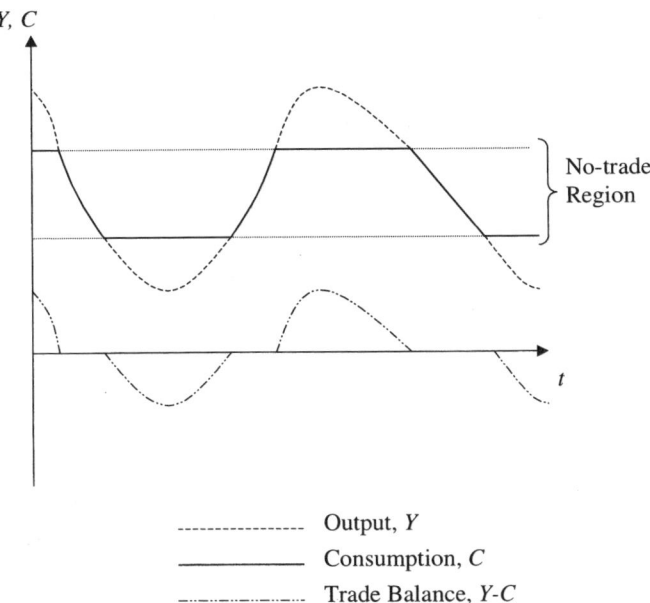

- - - - - - Output, Y
———— Consumption, C
- · - · - · - Trade Balance, Y-C

for an arbitrary continuous time path of domestic output. As long as domestic output remains in the no-trade region, the trade balance is equal to zero and the fluctuations in consumption mirror those of output. By contrast, consumption is completely smoothed when output takes extreme values outside the no-trade region. As a result, the correlation between domestic output and domestic consumption is equal to 1 in the no-trade region and equal to 0 outside. If output remains in the no-trade region most of the time, the observed average correlation will be close to 1. This might seem like a puzzle to the outside observer, who would expect consumption to be smoothed all the time, given that the capital market is perfectly integrated internationally (this is one way to define the international-consumption-correlation puzzle).

Explaining the Feldstein–Horioka puzzle by the same logic requires an explicit consideration of investment opportunities at home and abroad. Assume for example that residents have access to domestic investment opportunities with decreasing returns. If, in the two-period model, the return on the marginal domestic investment remains between $(1 - \tau)^2$ and $(1 - \tau)^{-2}$ times the return on investments abroad, then the representative domestic agent invests all his savings at home, and domestic saving and investment behave in the same way as under autarky. Domestic saving will be perfectly correlated with domestic investment, as in the Feldstein–Horioka puzzle.

2.2 THE MULTI-GOOD CASE

In order to explain the low correlation of international consumption (the Feldstein–Horioka puzzle), OR need trade costs to generate a wedge between the domestic real interest rate and the world real interest rate. In other words, they need the *instantaneous* price wedge generated by trade costs—which they use to explain the home bias in trade—to be augmented by an *intertemporal* wedge. As OR's two-good model shows, this intertemporal wedge can arise under more complex goods structures than the one-good model I have just presented, although in that case the analysis is more complicated.

Introducing a second good into the model allows us to focus on the composition of the country's imports and exports. In OR's two-good model the home and foreign goods are both exchanged in global competitive markets at given prices in terms of foreign currency units. While the foreign good is always imported, the home good may be exported or imported in equilibrium. Whether the home good is imported or exported, moreover, is crucial for the model's ability to produce a wedge between the domestic real interest rate and the world interest rate.

As OR show, if the trade balance involves a *round trip* in the home good—i.e., if this good is exported at one period and imported at the other—there is a wedge between the domestic real interest rate and the world interest rate.[4] In this case the consumption–saving behavior of domestic residents can be analyzed in the same terms as in the one-good model, the home good playing the same role as the single good in the one-good model. By contrast, if the domestic country exports the home good in both periods, there is no wedge in the real-interest-rate parity condition, and the intertemporal current account behaves in the same way, qualitatively, as in the absence of trade costs.[5] Although trade costs distort the relative price of the home and foreign goods in each period, they do not change the *intertemporal* rate of substitution of home consumption between period 1 and period 2.

This raises the question of the robustness of OR's explanation for the Felstein–Horioka puzzle to changes in the underlying assumptions on the goods structure. In particular, it would be interesting to explore how easily the logic of OR's argument can be transposed to a framework

---

4. The round-trip case corresponds to segments I and V of the curve in OR's Figure 1.
5. This case corresponds to segment III of the curve in OR's Figure 1.

where international trade involves differentiated goods. The transposition is not trivial, because trade in differentiated goods cannot exhibit the round trips which seem to play a role in OR's results. While a car-producing country may have a trade deficit or a trade surplus in cars at any given period, it is impossible *by construction* for this country's trade balance to exhibit a round trip in any of the differentiated goods, or brands, that compose the composite good "car." France, say, always exports Renaults and always imports Fords or Volkswagens.

Generalizing OR's model to differentiated goods would also enhance its empirical relevance. It is well known that most of the trade between industrial countries involves differentiated goods. This stylized fact has been widely documented in the literature on international trade under imperfect competition, for which it provided the founding motivation. It would be important to understand how the logic of OR's argument applies to this case, since it is precisely for developed economies that the Felstein–Horioka puzzle and the international-consumption-correlation puzzle are most puzzling (for less developed economies other factors, such as country risk, can be invoked, as OR note).

2.3 A LOOK AT THE DATA

Although it remains to be seen whether OR's analysis is robust to monopolistic competition, their assumptions seem plausible for international trade in raw commodities, which are generally exchanged in very competitive markets. Their model predicts that because of trade costs, we should observe few round trips in raw commodities. Is this prediction borne out by the data? Table 1 provides evidence on the occurrence of round trips for a sample of ten countries and five raw commodities. The table is constructed using the United Nations annual trade data set over the period 1988–1998. The $+$ $(-)$ sign indicates that the country has been an exporter (importer) of the commodity over the whole period, i.e., every single year from 1988 to 1998. The sign $\pm$ indicates that at least one round trip (change in the sign of the trade balance in the commodity) has been observed.

The results reported in Table 1 are consistent with the model's prediction. Of the 42 country–commodity pairs for which data are available, almost 90% do not show any round trip. This finding could be interpreted as evidence in favor of OR's hypothesis that round trips are discouraged by trade costs. However, it could also reflect the fact that trade in primary commodities is driven by comparative advantage, not by intertemporal consumption smoothing. In a world where comparative advantage is the driving force, we would observe very few round trips even in the absence of trade costs.

Table 1 ROUND TRIPS IN RAW COMMODITIES (1988–1998)

Country	Wheat	Natural rubber	Iron ore	Crude petroleum	Natural gas
Australia	+	−	+	±	±
France	+	−	−	−	−
Germany	+	−	−	−	−
Indonesia	NA	+	NA	+	+
Italy	−	−	−	−	±
Japan	NA	−	−	NA	−
New Zealand	−	NA	+	−	NA
Turkey	±	−	NA	−	NA
U.K.	±	−	−	+	−
U.S.	+	−	−	−	−

Source: United Nations; annual data 1988–1998. The SITC codes of the commodities are: 041 (wheat—including spelt—and meslin, unmilled); 231 (natural rubber and similar natural gums); 281 (iron ore and concentrates); 333 (petroleum oils and oils obtained from bituminous minerals, crude); 343 (natural gas, whether or not liquefied). The observation for a given country was treated as not available if three years or more of the corresponding annual data were not available in the UN data set. I initially considered a sample of 17 countries, and then excluded the 6 countries for which data were not available for at least three commodities.

3. *The Exchange-Rate Disconnect Puzzle*

OR present very stimulating developments on exchange-rate excess volatility and what they call the *exchange-rate disconnect*. Their point can be loosely summarized as follows: because of the combination of nominal stickiness and pricing to market at the level of the domestic consumers, the exchange rate matters very little for anything real in the domestic economy (at least in the short run), so that it can wander around under the impact of small shocks. OR's "disconnect" is between the exchange-rate and goods markets.

OR's point is related to an old question in exchange-rate economics: Should one view exchange rates primarily as asset prices or primarily as the determinants of relative prices in goods markets? Of course they are both to some extent, and one way to view the history of exchange-rate theory—from its early developments to the "new open macroeconomics"—is as a long struggle to integrate both aspects of exchange-rate determination in a coherent framework. The substance of the question, however, was in the adverb *primarily*. To rephrase the question: Is it practically more relevant to think of exchange rates as asset prices, or as determinants of relative prices in the markets for goods—if, leaving general equilibrium aside, one had to choose between the two views? I interpret OR's "exchange-rate disconnect" as the idea that exchange rates matter so little for relative prices that they can best be viewed as asset prices—at least to a first approximation.

3.1 A MODEL

A model can help us to better understand the link between the trade costs and exchange-rate volatility. I consider a monetary extension of the two-period one-good model discussed in the previous section. The log-linearized version of the model is given by the following set (S) of equations:

$$m_t - p_t = c_t, \quad t = 1,2, \quad \text{(LM)}$$
$$c_1 = -\frac{1}{\rho}[i_1 - (p_2^e - p_1)] + c_2^e, \quad \text{(IS)}$$
$$y_1 = \sigma p_1, \quad y_2^e = 0, \quad \text{(PC)}$$
$$c_1 + c_2 = y_1 + y_2, \quad \text{(BC)}$$
$$i_1 = s_2^e - s_1, \quad \text{(IP)}$$
$$p_t = s_t, \quad t = 1,2 \quad \text{(LOP)}$$

The model is written assuming no trade costs (introduced later). The domestic country issues its own currency, and nominal variables now refer to prices in terms of the domestic currency. The first equation is an interest-inelastic money demand equation of the type implied by a cash-in-advance constraint. The second equation is the Euler equation for consumption, sometimes called the "new Keynesian" IS curve. The following equations are Phillips curves where, viewed from period 1, the nominal wage is sticky in period 1 but flexible in period 2. The fourth equation is the country's intertemporal budget constraint (linearized under the assumption that Y_1 and Y_2 are very close and that the world real interest rate, r*, is equal to zero). The fifth equation is the interest parity condition (reflecting the perfect integration of the capital account). And the last equations correspond to the law of one price at periods 1 and 2, resulting from the assumption that there are no trade costs. The exogenous policy variables are the log deviations in domestic money supply, m_1 and m_2, which are both assumed to be stochastic. For convenience I assume that the values of m_1 and m_2 are revealed at period 1, so that there is no uncertainty about future money supply or any other variable when the first-period exchange rate is determined.[6]

Let us look at the following question: How does the variance of the exchange rate in period 1, $\text{Var}(s_1)$, depend on the level of trade costs, τ_1? To simplify the analysis I compare two extreme cases: perfect trade inte-

---

6. This explains why the risk premium can be ignored in the interest parity condition.

gration ($\tau_1 = 0$) and complete disintegration ($\tau_1 = +\infty$). In both cases trade costs are assumed to be zero in period 2 (I discuss below the case where τ_2 is non-zero).

First let us consider the case of perfect trade integration. Then the law of one price applies at period 1, i.e.,

$$s_1 = p_1. \tag{2}$$

It follows from interest parity and the Euler condition that expected consumption is equal to current consumption ($c_2^e = c_1$). Taking the expectation of the budget constraint then gives $c_1 = y_1/2$, i.e., half of the change in current disposable income is consumed in period 1, the other half being saved for consumption in period 2. The money-demand and Phillips-curve equations finally give an expression for the exchange rate:

$$s_1 = \frac{m_1}{1 + \sigma/2}. \tag{3}$$

If the nominal wage is flexible at period 1 ($\sigma = 0$), the exchange rate is proportional to the money supply. In the presence of nominal rigidity the impact of money supply on the exchange rate is damped by the accommodating response of output.

Let us now consider the case where the international exchange of good is prevented in period 1 by infinite trade costs ($\tau_1 = +\infty$). Then the law of one price no longer holds at period 1 and domestic consumption is equal to domestic output in both periods: $c_1 = y_1$ and $c_2^e = y_2^e = 0$. Taking the expectation of money demand at period 2 gives $s_2^e = m_2$, so that the nominal exchange rate at period 1 must satisfy

$$s_1 = m_2 - i_1. \tag{4}$$

Simple manipulations of the remaining equations then give the following reduced-form expression for the exchange rate:

$$s_1 = \frac{1 + \rho\sigma}{1 + \sigma} m_1. \tag{5}$$

Comparing equations (2) and (4) brings out the implication of trade costs for the determination of the exchange rate in this model. In the absence of trade costs the exchange rate is determined in the goods market: Equation (2) is an arbitrage condition between the domestic and the foreign price of the good. By contrast, in the presence of (high enough) trade costs, the exchange rate is determined in the asset market. Equation (4) is an arbitrage condition between domestic currency and foreign currency bonds. In this simple setup, infinite trade costs produce a complete exchange-rate disconnect at period 1 (in the sense that the exchange rate has no direct connection with domestic output or the domestic price level), and as a result, the equation for the exchange rate becomes a pure asset-pricing equation.[7]

3.2 CAN THE EXCHANGE-RATE DISCONNECT EXPLAIN EXCESSIVE EXCHANGE-RATE VOLATILITY?

Does the exchange rate become more volatile as a result of trade costs? Comparing equation (3) and equation (5) shows that the answer is yes if, and only if, $(1 + \rho\sigma)/(1 + \sigma) > 1/(1 + \sigma/2)$, i.e.,

$$\rho > \frac{1}{2 + \sigma}. \tag{6}$$

High trade costs increase exchange-rate volatility if the intertemporal substitutability of consumption, $1/\rho$, is low enough. This is because a lower intertemporal substitutability of consumption makes the interest rate—and so the exchange rate, when it is determined as an asset price—more volatile.

There is another sense in which trade costs can generate an exchange-rate disconnect in this model. If international trade involves a cost not only at period 1 but also at period 2 ($\tau_2 \neq 0$), then the nominal exchange may become *indeterminate* in both periods over some range of parameter values. This point is extremely easy to see in the extreme case where trade costs are infinite in both periods. Then the law of one price is removed from the set of equations (S) and there is nothing to pin down the exchange rate. Indeterminacy can be a significant cause of volatility if the exchange rate fluctuates widely in the range of indeterminacy, under the influence of market sentiments and other nonfundamental factors.[8]

---

7. The asset market is in equilibrium, and the interest parity condition holds, irrespective of trade costs. Under the exchange-rate disconnect, however, the interest parity condition endogenizes the exchange rate after the nominal interest rate has been solved for using the other equations. Under perfect trade integration it endogenizes the nominal interest rate after the exchange rate.
8. The intuition behind the exchange-rate indeterminacy can be conveyed by the following parable. Assume that humans come into contact with an extraterrestrial civilization with which telecommunications are easy, but the exchange of goods is ruled out forever because of the enormous distance between them and us. Assume that in a misconceived attempt to extend the reach of liberal capitalism to outer space, an electronic market for the exchange of extraterrestrial and terrestrial currencies and nominal bonds is estab-

The notion that exchange rates can be indeterminate, and that this indeterminacy could generate excess volatility, is not new.[9] From a theoretical point of view, moreover, indeterminacy is a rather brittle property of this model. It hinges on a complete and permanent absence of international trade. The certainty that countries will exchange at least one good, even in the distant future and in very small quantities, suffices to pin down the exchange rate—making indeterminacy an unconvincing explanation for excess exchange-rate volatility in a world where countries routinely trade with each other. Still the model may have some pedagogical value, if only to make the point that although their short-run dynamics may obey the rules of asset pricing, exchange rates are ultimately pinned down by international trade in goods.

Another question is the extent to which the exchange-rate disconnect makes the high volatility of exchange rates observed in the data less puzzling. This is not entirely clear to me. The only substantial implication of the exchange-rate disconnect for exchange-rate volatility, if I understand OR correctly, is that the volatility of exchange rates should be thought of in the same way as the price volatility of other assets.[10] The asset perspective, however, is precisely the one adopted by most of the empirical literature on the excess volatility of exchange rates.[11] The exchange-rate disconnect, then, just leaves us with the more general question: why are asset prices so volatile? Answering this question is likely to require departures from key assumptions (such as common knowledge or rational expectations) on which most exchange-rate models, including those in this paper, are based.

REFERENCES

Arifovic, J. (1996). The behavior of the exchange rate in the genetic algorithm and experimental economies. *Journal of Political Economy* 104:510–541.
Bartolini, L., and L. Giorgianni. (1999). Excess volatility and the asset-pricing exchange rate model with unobservable fundamentals. IMF. Working Paper 99/71.

---

lished. Then nominal exchange rates between terrestrial and extraterrestrial currencies can take completely arbitrary values when the new market is opened, since there is nothing in this universe to anchor their long-run values.

9. In a classical paper, Kareken and Wallace (1981) presented a model where exchange-rate indeterminacy resulted from currency substitution. The implications for exchange-rate volatility were explored in several papers, including King, Wallace, and Weber (1992) and Arifovic (1996).
10. This is indeed what they argue in their *Foundations*: "In trying to understand the difficulties in empirically modeling exchange rates, it is probably wrong to look for a special explanation of exchange rate volatility. Instead, one should seek a unifying explanation for the volatility that all major asset prices display, including those of stocks and bonds as well as currencies." (Obstfeld and Rogoff, 1996, p. 626)
11. See Bartolini and Giorgianni (1999) and the references therein.

Kang, J.-K., and R. M. Stulz. (1994). Why is there a home bias? An analysis of foreign portfolio equity ownership in Japan. *Journal of Financial Economics* 46:3–28.

Kareken, J. H., and N. Wallace. (1981). On the indeterminacy of equilibrium exchange rates. *Quarterly Journal of Economics* 96:207–222.

King, R. G., N. Wallace, and W. E. Weber. (1992). Nonfundamental uncertainty and exchange rates. *Journal of International Economics* 32:83–108.

Kraay, A., and J. Ventura. (1999). Current accounts in debtor and creditor countries. Department of Economics, MIT. Mimeo.

Lewis, K. K. (1999). Trying to explain home bias in equities and consumption. *Journal of Economic Literature* 37:571–608.

Obstfeld, M., and K. Rogoff. (1996). *Foundations of International Macroeconomics*. Cambridge, MA: The MIT Press.

Pesenti, P., and E. Van Wincoop. (1996). Do nontraded goods explain the home bias puzzle? Cambridge, MA: National Bureau of Economic Research. NBER Working Paper 5784.

Portes, R., and H. Rey. (1999). The determinants of cross-border equity flows. Center for Economic Policy Research. Discussion Paper 2225.

Tesar, L., and I. Werner. (1995). Home bias and high turnover. *Journal of International Money and Finance* 14:467–492.

Comment[1]

CHARLES ENGEL
University of Wisconsin and NBER

1. Introduction

Obstfeld and Rogoff have once again written an important paper that undoubtedly will be highly influential in developing our understanding of many of the major puzzles in international macroeconomics. They highlight the fact that goods markets for consumers appear to be very far from being perfectly integrated, and show how this imperfection can help provide a unified understanding of the puzzles that have eluded satisfactory explanation. These goods-market imperfections are a plausible direction to look toward because the empirical evidence suggests they are significant in magnitude. And Obstfeld and Rogoff (referred to as OR hereinafter) provide us with models that make sense at an intuitive level.

My comments primarily focus on three issues:

(a) How do we reconcile the numerical examples of OR, which show quantitatively plausible resolutions to the major puzzles arising

---

[1] I thank Andy Atkeson, Mick Devereux, and Fabrizio Perri for helpful input on these comments.

from costs of trade, with previous studies that have found that trade costs do not get us very far?

(b) Does the solution proposed by OR solve the puzzles at the expense of introducing new puzzles? That is, does their solution have counterfactual implications for other economic relationships? (The prime example of what I have in mind here is what OR call the "Backus–Smith puzzle.")

(c) Some of the problems connected with points (a) and (b) can be rectified by moving away from the assumption of complete asset markets. But, then, how do we assess how much of the solution to the puzzle is coming from trade costs vs. capital-market imperfections?

In reviewing some of the existing literature, it appears to me that trade frictions alone do not explain the puzzles. While they move things in the right direction, quantitatively goods frictions are insufficient. OR provide us with extraordinary intuition for why goods markets move things in the right direction, but we need more study to be able to reconcile their compelling but simplified examples with the results that emerge from simulation of more fully specified dynamic models. This very much reminds me of the literature on one puzzle that OR do not try to resolve—the forward-premium puzzle. There, the easy explanation that was proposed is that a foreign-exchange risk premium can lead to biased forecasts of the forward premium. But when researchers tried to embed risk premiums into calibrated equilibrium models and assess the size of that effect, they found that the risk premium was far too small to explain the magnitude of the deviations from uncovered interest parity. The parallel is that the literature so far has not found that goods-market imperfections alone can quantitatively explain the OR puzzles.

There is another parallel with the literature on the forward-premium puzzle. When researchers finally were able to construct models that got close to matching the magnitude and sign of the deviation from uncovered interest parity, they found that their models had a very unpleasant implication about the moments of another variable. In that case, the problem was that the models implied nominal-interest-rate volatility that was much greater than what is found in the data. The parallel here is that the models that OR propose imply a high correlation of real exchange rates with relative consumption levels across countries. OR call this the "Backus–Smith" problem. They appear to dismiss this issue, but in doing so leave me puzzled as to how we can reconcile the implications of their approach with the data.

My comments will focus on puzzles 2–4 of OR (which I call the *core puzzles*): the Feldstein–Horioka puzzle, the home-bias-in-equity-portfolios puzzle, and the international-consumption-correlations puzzle. These three puzzles are linked in that they can best be understood as pointing toward a surprising lack of risk sharing internationally. I comment only briefly on the other three puzzles.

To reiterate, I do think that costs of trade are fundamental in understanding these puzzles. Capital-market imperfections alone are not the answer. OR provide new insight into how trade costs can help resolve the puzzles, and should help to focus future research endeavors in this promising direction.

2. The Core Puzzles

To my tastes, the clearest way to demonstrate the claim that trade costs alone can explain the core puzzles would be to use the model of complete asset markets and no trade frictions as the benchmark, and show how far trade costs get us. For example, the home-bias-in-portfolios puzzle is no puzzle at all if the null model is one in which there are restrictions on asset trade or missing asset markets.

Let me briefly review the three core puzzles to help clarify. We find very low correlations of consumption internationally. That is puzzling because it seems to imply that there is very little sharing of idiosyncratic shocks to income. To me (and to OR) the puzzle is not that there is an absence of complete risk sharing. The puzzle is that there appears to be so little risk sharing—much less than we would expect given the wide array of assets that allow us to hedge risk. But how can we measure the ability of trade costs to explain the low correlation of consumption levels? The natural way to me (and apparently to OR) is to assess the effects of introducing trade costs into a model with complete asset markets. We know that the free-trade, complete-markets model implies perfect correlation—so how far does that correlation fall when there are plausible trade costs?

Home bias in portfolios is puzzling at an intuitive level. Investors could more effectively hedge risk by balancing their portfolios among assets from countries around the globe. Diversification is the fundamental principle of risk management. Again, however, it is helpful to have a benchmark to assess the effects of trade costs. In general, full diversification of equity holdings does not achieve complete risk sharing, but OR quite naturally focus on special models where that does occur. This special case is appealing because it gives us a simple benchmark to compare the effects of market imperfections against. Furthermore, as OR show in this paper (and in their 1996 textbook), "for realistic parameters, trade in equities alone can come quite close to attaining the complete-markets consumption allocation, so that the home bias evident under complete markets is a good guide to the home bias in an equities-only model."

The Feldstein–Horioka paradox has been a hard one to pin down. Why is the finding of low correlation of saving and investment a puzzle? OR's (1996) textbook has, for my tastes, the clearest explanation of the puzzle. In a Walrasian model with no trade barriers and complete asset markets, the amount of investment in a country's capital stock should be independent of the parameters that determine the country's consumption level. The simplest way to see this is to think of the special cases in which a diversified portfolio of equities mimics complete markets. In that case, the firm's decision to add to capital must be independent of the consumption choices of the individuals who live in the country where the firm produces. The firm is owned globally, so why would the consumption or saving decisions of the residents of the country where the firm is located have any special influence on its investment decision? So, again, a natural benchmark to compare the effects of trade costs alone is the free-trade, complete-markets Walrasian model.

3. The Literature

There are two reasons why I emphasize that the complete-asset-markets model is a natural benchmark. First, there actually exists a literature that looks into trade costs as an explanation for these puzzles. Using complete markets as the benchmark, introducing trade costs alone does not appear to get us very far in resolving the puzzles. The second reason I emphasize it is that while OR naturally gravitate toward the complete-markets model as a benchmark, in several instances they subsequently inveigh against that model on the grounds essentially that in the real world markets are not complete. True, but the complete-markets model is a useful benchmark. I address the literature in this section. In Section 5, I return to the benchmark issue.

The careful reader might have noticed footnote 2 in OR. It makes reference to Backus, Kehoe, and Kydland (1992), which is the piece that brought the consumption correlation puzzle to the attention of the profession. That paper actually devotes an entire section to whether the introduction of trade costs of precisely the type OR propose can explain the consumption correlation puzzle. Their model is a fairly detailed Walrasian, complete-markets model. They can assess directly the effect of trade costs on consumption correlations. And they find that the introduction of trade costs into their model actually makes the consumption correlation puzzle worse, not better. Further investigation by the same authors in a subsequent study using alternative specifications of trading costs (Backus, Kydland, and Kehoe 1995) confirms that the consumption correlation puzzle is not solved by trading costs.

In fact, however, the Feldstein–Horioka problem is partly explained by Backus, Kydland, and Kehoe when trading costs are introduced. And, as OR note in footnote 25, one can interpret some of their results as supporting the contention that moderate transportation costs help resolve the home-bias-in-equities puzzle. However, this illustrates where we need to go with the observations of OR. Does the solution to one puzzle make things worse for the others? When Backus, Kydland, and Kehoe build a benchmark complete-markets free-trade Walrasian model, they find that introducing trade costs helps in some dimensions but not others. And, as I shall discuss in the next section, there are some other dimensions along which the trade costs make things much worse.

I agree with OR that the dichotomy in many papers between traded goods and nontraded goods is not a useful one. As they say, we can probably think of all consumer goods as having a nontradable component. The problems they discuss in Sections 6.2–6.5 ought to be at the core of what we do research on in international macroeconomics. But, still, one wonders whether the literature in which nontraded goods are introduced as an explanation for these puzzles might be instructive as to how far trade costs will get us. By and large, the nontraded-goods models have not been particularly useful in resolving these puzzles. OR do provide a helpful description of the shortcomings of the nontraded-goods model with the portfolio diversification paradox, and show how trade costs might get us further. But what about the other core puzzles? And what about the Backus–Smith paradox?

4. Other Variables

As OR note in equation (15), the complete-markets models they introduce imply perfect correlation of the log of relative consumption levels internationally with real exchange rates. Backus and Smith (1993) were the first to derive this implication in a model with trade imperfections. (Theirs was a model with nontraded goods.) But the condition arises in a wide variety of contexts in which the law of one price fails.

The problem is that in the data there is virtually no correlation between relative consumption levels and real exchange rates. Backus and Smith document this in a fairly simple way for G7 countries. But Kollmann (1995) and Ravn (2000) thoroughly demolish the notion that these two variables are connected. Kollman shows that, generally for advanced countries, real exchange rates and relative consumption levels are not cointegrated and that there is no discernible short-run relationship.

Of course, models sometimes have ancillary implications that are not supported by the data but are not critical to the issue of interest. But here, the implication is central to the resolution of the puzzles. In the OR models of this paper, trade costs lead to deviations from the law of one price, and deviations from the law of one price are the sole reason for the failure of purchasing-power parity. The changes in the real exchange rate that are generated are, in turn, what break the link between consumption levels across countries. That is, it is precisely the nonconstancy of real exchange rates in their models that explains why there does not appear to be a great deal of risk sharing.

My sense is that it is knowledge of the empirical findings of Backus and Smith (1993) and Kollmann (1995) that has convinced researchers that trade costs per se, or more generally models with law-of-one-price deviations, are not the sole solution to these riddles. Perhaps researchers should not have been scared away from this avenue, but OR do little to help us out on this problem. They say that "Trade costs would play essentially the same role in a world with, say, trade in debt and equities but not a complete set of Arrow–Debreu securities." That may be true, but it needs to be demonstrated. Can trade costs play a quantitatively significant role in resolving the puzzles in such a model? At this stage, this seems not much more than a conjecture. The models that are presented in this paper all have the implication that relative consumption levels are perfectly correlated with real exchange rates. OR provide us with no evidence about models in which this link is broken.

It is also a bit disconcerting that OR focus exclusively on the implications of their models for the puzzles that the model is meant to address, and not on other implications of the model. The type of discipline that we rightly demand from the purveyors of general equilibrium Walrasian models (that is, the RBCers) is that they show us that the models can explain moments of some variables without generating unreasonable correlations among other variables. For example, would the OR models with trade costs imply negative correlation of inputs, such as arise in many of the RBC models (with and without trade frictions or nontraded goods)?

5. *The Benchmark*

OR seem to shrug off the Backus–Smith puzzle: "We do not take this as damning, since for us the complete-markets assumption was only a useful device for calibration, and not a conviction." Of course that is true for me too. But, where are we left? Apparently we need to concede that there is some deviation from complete markets to be able to accommodate the Backus–Smith problem. How far from completeness do they have to be? At what point have we stepped over the line and made capital-market imperfections part of the solution to the problem? In short, how can OR say that we can solve these riddles "without appealing to capital-market imperfections"?

6. The Other Puzzles

Let me briefly comment on some of the other issues raised by OR. First, I am not convinced that allowing for high elasticities of substitution goes that far in solving the home-bias-in-trade puzzle. There are small frictions in within-country trade as well, and one would suspect that goods produced within a country's borders are even closer substitutes than internationally traded goods. Yet, the small intranational trading costs do not seem to impose much of a barrier to intranational trade. Indeed, the revised version of Evans (2000) concludes that the story in which "high border effects arise almost entirely from high elasticities of substitution provides at best a partial explanation" of the home bias in trade.

The misleading thing about the OR examples in this regard is that there are no intranational frictions in trade. So they tell us that 0.25 is a modest value for proportional international trade costs, but implicitly assume that 0 is a modest value of intranational trade costs. It is easy to set up a model parallel to the one described in equations (1)–(6) of OR, but with two regions within each of two countries. Consider their calibration, allowing the elasticity of substitution intranationally and internationally to be equal to 6, but introduce within-country trade costs of 0.10. Then the ratio of intranational trade to international trade in the model falls to 2.5. If, in addition, one allows the intranational elasticity of substitution to be greater than the international elasticity (equal to 12 instead of 6), the trade-costs model goes only a small way toward explaining the home trade bias. The ratio of international to within-country trade explained by the model is merely 1.3.

I found OR's discussion of the final two puzzles engaging and stimulating. Let me make just two comments. First, I think even in trying to explain exchange-rate volatility it might turn out that we need more than just goods-market imperfections. Here is why I make this conjecture. Betts and Devereux (1996) consider exchange-rate volatility in which consumer goods markets are completely segmented and the law of one price fails. In their static model, indeed they find exchange-rate volatility is much larger (6 times larger) than a parallel model in which the law of one price and PPP hold. But when they move to a dynamic model with capital mobility (Betts and Devereux, 2000), the volatility effect is much smaller. The exchange-rate variance is only 1.7 times larger in the segmented-markets model than in the model with integrated goods market. OR's intuition is that the goods-market frictions modify the dampening effect that capital markets have on exchange-rate fluctuations. But, in a dynamic setting, Betts and Devereux's results suggest that the modification may not be large.

The second comment is that I think it is a mistake to link the exchange-rate disconnect puzzle with exchange-rate volatility. One way of putting it is that the exchange-rate disconnect puzzle is about why exchange rates are not correlated with fundamentals. It is a puzzle about correlations, not variances. In other words, I believe the case that OR are trying to make is that unobserved shocks might have a large effect on exchange rates if exchange rates are highly volatile. But observed shocks in the money supply and other fundamentals also should have large effects. It is not immediately clear that high volatility in the exchange rate implies a weak link between the exchange rate and fundamentals (which is what the exchange-rate disconnect puzzle is all about).

7. Concluding Comments

I think there may be a close link between the type of goods-market frictions OR describe and possible failures in the capital markets. Because the discipline imposed by goods markets on the equilibrium exchange rate is so weak, there may be more room (particularly in the short run) for noise in exchange rates. That is, "chartists" as in Frankel and Froot (1990), or noise traders as in Jeanne and Rose (1999), or order flow from foreign-exchange traders as in Evans and Lyons (1999), might influence the exchange rate in the short run because misalignments in the exchange rate do not provoke a large immediate response from the real side of the economy. OR may be hinting at this in their Section 6.7 (or they may not be). I think this is a promising avenue to explore to help understand exchange-rate volatility and the disconnect between exchange rates and fundamentals. But it will require formal modeling and testing.

While it may seem that I am very skeptical of the ideas OR have presented here, I am not. My hunch is that their view and mine on these issues are very close (at least compared to the huge lack of consensus in international macroeconomics). I am more cautious than OR about the degree to which trade costs alone have solved the puzzles. But this difference in tone probably mostly reflects the differing roles of paper writers and paper discussants.

One final thought: it may be that over the next 50 years or so, international goods markets will become much more integrated and efficient through cyberspace, making the types of goods-market frictions that OR discuss less important over time. By the time we have built the models that explain the puzzles, the models and the puzzles may be obsolete.

REFERENCES

Backus, D. K., P. J. Kehoe, and F. E. Kydland. (1992). International real business cycles. *Journal of Political Economy* 101:745–775.
———, ———, and ———. (1995). International business cycles: Theory and evidence. In *Frontiers of Business Cycle Research*, T. F. Cooley, (ed.). Princeton, NJ: Princeton University Press.
———, and G. Smith. (1993). Consumption and real exchange rates in dynamic exchange economies with nontraded goods. *Journal of International Economics* 35:297–316.
Betts, C., and M. B. Devereux. (1996). The exchange rate in a model of pricing to market. *European Economic Review* 40:1007–1021.
———, and ———. (2000). Exchange rate dynamics in a model of pricing-to-market. *Journal of International Economics* 50:215–244.
Evans, C. (2000). The economic significance of national border effects. Federal Reserve Bank of New York. Working Paper.
Evans, M. D. D., and R. K. Lyons. (1999). Order flow and exchange rate dynamics. Cambridge, MA: National Bureau of Economic Research. NBER Working Paper 7317.
Frankel, J. A., and K. A. Froot. (1990). Chartists, fundamentalists, and the demand for dollars. In *Private Behaviour and Government Policy in Interdependent Economies*, A. S. Courakis and M. P. Taylor (eds.). Oxford University Press.
Jeanne, O., and A. K. Rose. (1999). Noise trading and exchange rate regimes. Cambridge, MA: National Bureau of Economic Research. NBER Working Paper 7104.
Kollman, R. (1995). Consumption, real exchange rates and the structure of international asset markets. *Journal of International Money and Finance* 14:191–211.
Obstfeld, M., and K. Rogoff. (1996). *Foundations of International Macroeconomics*. Cambridge, MA: The MIT Press.
Ravn, M. O. (2000). Consumption dynamics and real exchange rates. London Business School. Working Paper.

Discussion

Responding to the discussants, Ken Rogoff noted that they had chosen simple examples to illustrate their main points but that the results would survive generalization. For example, it would not be difficult to add nominal rigidities or a sharp distinction between traded and nontraded goods to most of the examples—although, he noted, to get the same results as with moderate trade costs, it might be necessary to assume that a very large fraction of goods are nontraded.

Michael Klein observed that trading costs, broadly construed, seem to be declining over time, which should imply that some of the puzzles are becoming less pronounced. Maury Obstfeld agreed and cited results in the literature to the effect that home biases in asset holdings and consumption have become smaller recently. Valerie Ramey suggested that immigration patterns and policies may affect trading costs, as immigrants are often effective middlemen for trade between their country of origin and their current residence. Richard Portes agreed with discussant Charles Engel that a full explanation of asset-market puzzles would require asset-market as well as goods-market imperfections, such as asymmetric information.

Alberto Alesina asked how broadly trade costs should be defined. For example, do they include costs arising from different currencies, languages, and legal systems? Obstfeld said that they were comfortable with a quite broad interpretation of trade costs. Alesina also noted that the number of countries in the world is rising, which is a negative development if cross-border costs are high. Obstfeld replied that Alesina's own work suggests that countries are proliferating in part because national independence confers greater flexibility in establishing trading and other economic relationships; so perhaps this is not a concern.

Allan Drazen objected to the use of iceberg costs on the grounds that the most important effects empirically are not distance effects but border effects. Further, many trading costs are not exogenous but are endogenously chosen, e.g., trade barriers. He suggested that European economic integration provides an excellent test case to study the effects of falling trade costs. Obstfeld agreed that border-related trade costs are quite important; the decision to use iceberg costs was based primarily on considerations of tractability.

John Leahy expressed the concern that the effects identified in this paper might turn out to be quantitatively small in a realistically calibrated model. The authors agreed that more work needed to be done to flesh out their story but noted that their model differs in important ways from those previously studied in the literature.